The
RANDOM HOUSE
BOOK
of
MORTGAGE
and
TAX-SAVINGS
TABLES

The
RANDOM HOUSE
BOOK
of
MORTGAGE
and
TAX-SAVINGS
TABLES

Edited by
ERIC KAPLAN, CPA, JD

RANDOM HOUSE

Library of Congress Cataloging-in-Publication Data

The Random House Book of Mortgage and Tax-Savings Tables /
edited by Eric Kaplan.
    p. cm.
  ISBN 0-679-73210-1
    1. Interest—Tables. 2. Mortgage loans—Tables. 3. Income
tax—United States—Deductions—Interest—Tables. I. Kaplan, Eric.
HG1634.R36   1990
332.8′2—dc20   90-33973
                                                              CIP

Every effort has been made to ensure the accuracy of the tables in
this book, but there is no guarantee of absolute accuracy.

Manufactured in the United States of America

1 2 3 4 5 6 7 8 9

First Edition

CONTENTS

v

CONTENTS

INTRODUCTION

If you want to buy a home, you know that it involves important financial decisions in addition to the critical issues of size, location, schools, and neighborhood. And you know that you need a mortgage.

Chances are that purchasing a home will be one of the most important and expensive financial transactions of your life. Your new mortgage will likely be among the largest debts you will ever assume. Financing considerations are serious issues that require thoughtful analysis.

How you finance your purchase has a direct effect on how much you can spend on your home. Should you get a fixed-rate or an adjustable-rate mortgage? Should the term of your mortgage be fifteen or thirty years? What about points? How can you compare your new mortgage payment to your old rental payment? How much of a down payment must you have? What are closing costs, and how much are they? The answers to these burning questions will greatly affect your decisions as you consider your purchase.

The tables and discussions in this book provide you with the information you will need to consider in light of your circumstances. The examples that accompany the various tables will assist you in gaining an understanding of the mechanics of using the tables. But cold figures in stark rows will not help you make the decisions that are right for you unless you know what they mean. If you have a basic understanding of the general financial considerations that you should take into account when seeking a mortgage, the tables in this book will be an important and useful tool in your search.

What Is a Mortgage?

Most people instinctively believe that they know what a mortgage is: a loan that one takes to buy a home. Well, it is and it isn't.

At the closing of a home purchase, the buyer is asked by the mortgage lender to sign two documents. The first document is a promissory note. The promissory note is a personal promise to repay the amount that is borrowed at the stated rate of interest over the agreed-upon term of years. The amount borrowed is typically a large amount of money, more than the borrower has readily available to repay to the lender in the event of a default.

That's where the second piece of paper comes in. Besides signing a promissory note, the borrower is asked to sign a mortgage agreement. The mortgage agreement grants the lender a security interest in the home being purchased with the loan proceeds. By signing the mortgage agreement, the borrower is agreeing to allow the home to serve as collateral for the loan. In the event of a default, the mortgage agreement allows the lender to take possession of the collateral and sell it to obtain an immediate repayment of the loan and all arrearages. If the sale of the home does not produce an amount sufficient to cover what is owed, the personal nature of the promise to repay the loan will require the borrower to make up the difference. Of course, any amount in excess of what is owed (i.e. the borrower's equity) will be returned to the borrower.

To state things precisely, when you borrow to purchase a home, you will apply for a mortgage loan: a personal loan secured by a mortgage upon what you are buying.

How Does a Mortgage Work?

A mortgage loan works like any other loan. It is a promise to pay a sum certain in money together with an agreed-upon interest rate over a stipulated period of time on an installment basis, usually monthly. The typical mortgage loan provides for equal payments over the term of the loan, although the monthly payment on adjustable-rate loans may change. The Monthly Payment Tables in Part I present the amount of mortgage payments for a wide range of interest rates, and loan amounts and repayment periods.

Each equal monthly payment is comprised of two elements: interest and principal. Interest is the cost you, the borrower, agree to pay for the use of money loaned. Principal is a return of the money borrowed. While monthly payments remain the same over the term of a loan, the allocation of each payment between interest and principal varies. In the early years of the loan-repayment term, much of the original loan balance remains outstanding. Accordingly, the lion's share of your monthly payment is allocated to interest in order to cover the cost of borrowing. As the loan progresses, however, more and more of the principal is repaid, and the allocation of the monthly payment to principal gradually increases.

Given this relationship, it is not surprising that many borrowers who repay their mortgages before maturity through sale or refinancing are shocked to discover they have repaid precious little of their loan, even though they have made large monthly payments.

The Annual Mortgage-Payment Schedules in Part II are a handy tool for you to track the allocation of your payments of interest and principal.

The Mortgage Marketplace

Historically, home buyers seeking a mortgage visited their local savings banks to obtain a mortgage. The banker knew the local citizens and was familiar with the values of property in the area. The bank placed the mortgage into its portfolio of loans and held it until maturity.

In recent times, however, the mortgage-banking business grew from an industry that was the preserve of the local banker into a megamarket largely controlled by international money centers such as Wall Street. While traditional savings institutions continue to originate many of the new mortgage loans in the United States, they no longer do so solely for their own account.

Today, mortgage lenders such as banks or mortgage companies often act as middlemen, arranging mortgages for home buyers and selling the loans to issuers of mortgage-backed bonds sold on Wall Street. As a matter of fact, when you buy a bond such as a Ginnie Mae for your retirement or investment account, you may be buying a piece of the very mortgage loan covering your own home!

The lender that you deal with earns a profit from the application fees and points charged to originate the loan. In addition, the lender's profit margin on your loan will be affected by the difference between the rate you agree to pay on the loan and the general level of interest rates prevailing when your loan closes, at which point the lender is free to sell it on the bond market. A loan with a higher interest rate has a greater market value; a lower interest rate has a lower value. Finally, the lender may earn an additional profit by agreeing to administer your mortgage, collecting your monthly payments for the investors and seeing to the timely payment of insurance and taxes.

Why is this important? A smoothly functioning market is necessary to provide sufficient capital to the home-buying public. An orderly market is required for investors so that there is confidence in the security behind mortgage backed investments. Accordingly, general standards for mortgage loans have been established. While mortgage loans can be arranged privately under negotiated terms, the vast majority of mortgages in the United States are issued in compliance with these general standards.

Qualifying for a Mortgage

The most important lending standard is the limitation upon the amount of your monthly expenditures for interest, principal, insurance, and taxes. The total of these cannot exceed 28 percent of your monthly gross income before taxes. Up to 36 percent of your gross monthly income can be spent on housing costs and other installment debt, such as auto or student loans and credit-card payments. Be prepared to have all sources of your income confirmed; employers will be contacted, and you will typically be required to provide copies of at least two years of income tax returns as well as current pay stubs.

Additional standard requirements include a comprehensive statement of assets and liabilities, a detailed disclosure of the sources of your down payment and closing costs, and confirmation of all bank and investment account balances. Your employer will be contacted to confirm your annual income and that you remain a continuing employee in good standing. Finally, a credit report will be requested so that your payment history can be evaluated. If you have had recent credit problems that cannot be explained by misunderstandings, it is likely that your application will be declined. Even the smallest unresolved dispute with a creditor can stand in the way of a mortgage loan approval.

Generally, your down payment must be at least 10 percent of the contract price of the home. Many lenders require a larger down payment for vacation homes. Your down payment and closing costs usually must be funded out of savings. This means that you usually cannot borrow from relatives or others to pay for these items. Be prepared to explain the source of unusual deposits into your accounts in the period prior to your application.

All is not lost if the cost of your dream house produces monthly payments beyond these percentages. Many lenders offer "no income verification" mortgages. To qualify for a loan on such a basis, a borrower is often required to make a larger down payment, typically 25 percent or more of the contract price, and agrees to pay a higher interest rate to compensate for the higher level of risk associated with these loans. A word to the wise: There are sound reasons why the marketplace considers a loan risky if it requires you to commit more than 28 percent of your income. Overly optimistic borrowers often find themselves in a serious cash-flow bind that requires them to cut back significantly on their lifestyles to avoid default and foreclosure.

Take Your Pick: Fixed or Variable?

In the 1980s, another mortgage product became widely available that offered borrowers a chance at a mortgage with lower-than-average interest rates: the variable or adjustable-rate mortgage. Adjustable-rate mortgages, or ARMs, are loans in which the interest rate paid by the borrower can vary based on the prevailing interest rates. Whether you should apply for a traditional fixed-rate mortgage or a variable-rate mortgage depends on both your individual circumstances and your temperament.

A fixed-rate mortgage locks in your monthly payments of interest and principal. The payments remain even and level throughout the term of your loan. While your monthly payment is static, the proportion of each payment credited to principal repayment starts out very low and the proportion credited to interest starts out high. The proportion of principal gradually increases so that the loan is completely repaid when the term expires.

The interest rate and the monthly payment for a variable-rate mortgage, on the other hand, are adjusted at stated periods throughout the term of the loan. The length of adjustment period varies from loan to loan; typical adjustment periods are six months, one year, two years, three years, and five years. The adjustment period for a given loan is usually fixed. Interest-rate changes are based on certain benchmark interest rates, which are generally expressed as some number of percentage points over and above the rates applicable to such widely quoted financial instruments as federal Treasury securities and prime-rate loans. The interest rate is commonly capped at a maximum point beyond which it cannot increase, on both an annual basis as well as over the term of the loan regardless of the prevailing level of interest rates. Depending on the interest-rate level at the time of your loan adjustment, your monthly payment can either go up or go down. Thus, for example, an adjustable rate mortgage loan may include terms whereby the interest rate is adjusted every three years so that it is 2 percent or more over U.S. Treasury securities maturing within three years, with maximum increases of 2 percent per year and 6 percent over the term of the loan above the initial interest rate of the loan.

In evaluating a variable-rate mortgage, it is important to focus on the method by which the adjustment is computed. While some lenders offer loans whose rate adjustments are measured in terms of changes in the benchmark rate, most peg their adjustment to the benchmark itself. When lenders offer low "teaser" rates applicable only for the first adjustment period, the initial rate is often lower than the benchmark. If the interest rate is to be set a few percent above the benchmark, the loan will have a built-in increase at the time of the first adjustment. Thus, it is possible that while the benchmark interest rate is stable or even decreasing during the first adjustment period, a borrower's interest rate can actually increase! Obviously, this would not result for a variable-rate loan with adjustments based on the change in the benchmark, rather than on the benchmark itself.

Many borrowers prefer fixed-rate mortgages since it locks in their monthly payment for the entire period of the loan. They have the comfort of knowing that changes in prevailing interest rates will not result in sudden increases in their monthly housing costs. This level of certainty can be a very valuable edge, considering that mortgages are typically repaid over a fifteen- or thirty-year term. Historically, interest rates fluctuate in cycles. There will likely be at least a peak or two in rates during the term of most loans. An adjustment period that happens to coincide with such a peak can produce a significant increase in the monthly payment of a variable-rate mortgage. Indeed, the greatest danger with such loans lies in their use by aggressive borrowers who qualify for their loans based on low initial rates but lack the ability to sustain increases in their monthly carrying charges when their rates are adjusted.

Variable-rate mortgages can be a good choice for buyers who expect to sell in the short term. The initial rates charged on variable-rate mortgages are typically lower than those charged on fixed-rate loans since the lender is not subject to extended interest-rate risks. Over the shorter period these buyers expect to hold their homes, the lower initial rates of the variable rate mortgage may well be lower on average than that for a fixed-rate product.

How Much of a Mortgage Should You Apply For?

Since the amount you can borrow has a direct effect on the amount you can spend, figuring out the maximum you may borrow is of paramount importance. Computing your maximum allowable monthly payment for mortgage and taxes is a relatively straightforward task, but figuring out how much you can borrow is not. It depends upon a few variables.

Monthly loan payment amounts depend on the principal amount of the loan, the interest rate, and the term. The higher the interest rate, the smaller the debt that your maximum monthly payment can support, since more of your budgeted monthly payment must go towards paying interest. For example, a budgeted monthly payment of $1,500 will support a loan of $160,000 at 10.75 percent interest and a thirty-year term. (You can look this up in the Monthly Payment Tables in Part I.) If the interest rate on a thirty-year loan were to increase to 14 percent, the same $1,500 payment would support a loan of only $127,000.

The reality is that you are a very small factor in an enormous market. You will not have a great deal of flexibility in the interest rate you can obtain. About the only way to maximize the amount you can affordably borrow is to stretch out the repayment period or to take out a variable-rate mortgage with lower initial interest rates.

However, there is another, more exotic product that helps buyers increase the size of a loan they can afford: the negative-amortization loan. Negative-amortization loans are typically adjustable-rate mortgages that fix monthly payments in an affordable range. Rather than having your monthly payment rise to make up for interest-rate increases, your payment remains relatively stable over the term of the loan. The shortfall is added to the amount you owe. Be careful with these loans; depending on the direction of interest rate changes, you can end up owing the lender more than you borrowed in the first place!

What Should Your Mortgage Term Be?

The factor that you have most control over is the term of the mortgage. If your loan is repayable in a shorter time, a larger proportion of your monthly payment must go toward principal repayment and less is available to pay interest. The less interest you can afford to pay, the less you can borrow. The converse is also true. Stretching out the period over which you repay your loan leaves more of your monthly budgeted amount available to pay interest, increasing the amount you can afford to borrow.

Home buyers often try to stretch out their loan terms so that they can buy more expensive homes. That's why thirty-year mortgages are the loans home buyers predominantly apply for. Ultimately, however, the interest expense can be greater for a longer-term loan.

For example, with the loan of $160,000 at 10.75 percent interest discussed above, the borrower will pay $215,000 more in interest over thirty years than for the same loan with a fifteen-year term. The big difference is that the fifteen-year loan requires a monthly payment of $1,800, which is $300 more each month than for the thirty-year loan. A budgeted monthly payment of $1,500 will support a fifteen-year loan of only $134,000 at the same interest rate, or $26,000 less than what the borrower could afford with a thirty-year loan. (See the appropriate Monthly Payment Table in Part I.)

Should you apply for a fifteen-year loan or a thirty-year loan? The answer is a function of your circumstances and your attitudes. Does it bother you to pay so much more interest over the course of your loan? Perhaps the tax deductibility of home-mortgage interest will soften the blow for you. Will you be assuming additional expenses in ten to fifteen years for college tuition? Having paid off your mortgage in fifteen years will help you do it. Do you have excess cash available in your monthly budget so that you can afford the increased monthly payment necessary to pay off the loan sooner? Generally, the rate that you can earn on your invested excess cash is lower than the rate you can earn investing the excess cash. This results since there is a spread representing the lender's profit between a lender's cost of funds (the interest rate paid to you on your invested funds) and what is charged to borrowers. If you can afford the higher monthly payment required under a fifteen-year loan the shorter loan may be a wise choice for you.

A middle ground may well be the answer for you. If you are anxious to avoid some of the additional interest but you worry that you won't always be able to make the higher monthly payments required of a shorter loan, perhaps you should get a thirty-year mortgage with no prepayment-penalty provisions. This will allow you the flexibility of voluntarily making additional principal payments when you can afford it thereby reducing the term of your mortgage.

How Much Can You Spend?

Having done the arithmetic to calculate your allowable monthly payment, you can now determine how much you can afford to spend on your home. After making a proper allowance for the monthly cost of taxes and insurance, a review of the Monthly Payment Tables in Part I of this book will quickly disclose how large a mortgage you can support given your maximum allowable monthly payment at current interest rates. Adding the mortgage amount to your down payment will tell you how much to spend.

For example, let's assume your monthly gross income is $6,250 ($75,000 annually). According to the general standard, your maximum allowable monthly payment is 28 percent of your income, or $1,750. The home you'd like to buy is subject to monthly property taxes and insurance costs of $250 ($3,000 annually), leaving you with an allowable mortgage payment of $1,500 a month. Suppose you have $45,000 for your down payment and closing costs. If closing costs are $5,000, you have $40,000 left for the down payment. Interest rates for thirty-year fixed rate mortgages are 10.75 percent. Looking up the payment table in Part I for 10.75 percent interest, you find an affordable monthly payment of $1,493.57 for a $160,000 loan with a thirty-year term. Under the general formula, then, you can afford a $160,000 loan and a $40,000 down payment, or a total of $200,000 for your new home.

A word to the wise is in order. First time homebuyers accustomed to renting fully maintained residences often overlook the substantial initial investment necessary for tools, equipment and furnishings such as window treatments, carpets, lawn mowers, snow blowers, shovels, rakes, etc., which can add up to hundreds (if not thousands) of dollars. Plan to set aside sufficient funds to take care of these items.

How much you *can* spend may be a vastly different question from how much you *should* spend. Your household budget is very personal. The financial formulas that lenders use to qualify borrowers for mortgage loans are broad standards that apply to everyone. Lenders are not able to customize these standards on a personal basis. Only you know your personal spending patterns and how much you can comfortably allocate to monthly housing costs. Many home buyers subscribe to the credo "Buy until it hurts"— that is, to pay as much as one can possibly afford. The theory is that gradual increases in income will allow the home buyer to "grow into a mortgage" and soften the pain of initially burdensome monthly payments. However, this is not necessarily wise. You must know your own limits. While owning your home may be the American dream, losing it is surely one of America's worst nightmares.

PART 1

Monthly
Mortgage
Payment
Tables

HOW TO USE THE MONTHLY MORTGAGE PAYMENT TABLES

These tables show the combined monthly payments of interest and principal necessary to repay a mortgage. They cover a wide range of loan amounts and mortgage-interest rates. This set of tables answers the question that most borrowers instinctively ask first, "How much is my monthly payment?" Since most people generally run their households on a monthly budget, formal or otherwise, monthly payment amounts are important.

The amount of your monthly payment is a function of three variables: the amount of your loan, the interest rate you agree to pay, and the term over which you will repay the loan. The larger the amount that you borrow, the larger the monthly payment will be necessary to retire the loan by the end of its term. Similarly, the higher the interest rate, the larger your monthly expense. On the other the hand, the longer the term of your loan, the smaller your monthly payment since you have more time to repay the same debt.

Your monthly mortgage payment includes both interest (the cost that you agree to pay for the use of money) and principal (a return of the money borrowed). Only mortgage interest can be deductible; the repayment of your debts does not produce any tax benefits.

Given the tax deductibility of mortgage-loan interest in evaluating what you can afford, you should take the expected tax savings into account. Since the remaining unpaid loan balance is higher in the early years of your loan, the proportions of your monthly payment representing tax-deductible interest and nondeductible principal repayment vary as your loan ages. Thus it is not possible to make a blanket statement about the net after-tax cost of your fixed monthly payment. You should consult the Annual Mortgage Payment Schedules and accompanying Tax-Savings Tables in Part II in order to understand the tax savings over the life of your loan.

A word of caution: In evaluating your monthly mortgage payment, you should keep in mind your monthly costs for real estate taxes and hazard insurance. To ensure that their security (collateral) interest in your home is protected, lenders often require you to pay your real estate taxes and insurance premiums into an escrow account, from which they disburse the required payments. Generally, one twelfth of the annual expense is deposited into the escrow account each month. In addition to protecting the lender, this arrangement is a handy way for borrowers to smooth out their cash requirements and avoid the seasonal peaks that would otherwise result from quarterly or semiannual real estate tax and insurance payments.

The following two examples illustrate how to use these tables. You could also use these tables to find an adjusted payment for an adjustable-rate mortgage; see Example 5 on p. 103 in Part II.

Example 1—Finding Your Monthly Payment

Suppose you want to know what the monthly payment would be on an $80,000 mortgage at 11 percent interest over thirty years. First, turn to the table covering 11 percent interest rates, clearly marked in the corner of the page. Find the column for thirty-year terms. Scan down the thirty-year column until you arrive at the payment corresponding to a mortgage of $80,000. As you can see, the monthly payment on your loan will be $761.86.

11.00% INTEREST	**MONTHLY PAYMENT** needed to pay back a mortgage					
Term	26 Years	27 Years	28 Years	29 Years	30 Years	31 Years
AMOUNT						
30 000	291.94	290.09	288.44	286.99	285.70	281.09
40 000	389.25	386.78	384.59	382.65	380.93	374.78
50 000	486.56	483.48	480.74	478.31	476.16	468.48
55 000	535.22	531.82	528.81	526.15	523.78	515.33
60 000	583.88	580.17	576.89	573.98	571.39	562.17
65 000	632.53	628.52	624.96	621.81	619.01	609.02
70 000	681.19	676.87	673.04	669.64	666.63	655.87
75 000	729.85	725.21	721.11	717.47	714.24	702.72
80 000	778.50	773.56	769.18	765.30	761.86	749.57
85 000	827.16	821.91	817.26	813.14	809.47	796.41
90 000	875.81	870.26	865.33	860.97	857.09	843.26

Example 2—How Much You Can Borrow

Suppose you know you can afford a monthly payment of $1,000 toward interest and principal. The current interest rate is 11 percent, and you prefer to pay your loan over fifteen years. Again, find the table covering 11 percent interest rates. Scan the column for fifteen-year loans until you find a monthly payment of $1,000. In this case, the closest amount is $966.11. Looking across the horizontal row, you see that this is the monthly payment corresponding to an $85,000 loan.

			MONTHLY PAYMENT		**11.00%** INTEREST	
			needed to pay back a mortgage			
Term	14 Years	15 Years	16 Years	17 Years	18 Years	19 Years
AMOUNT						
30 000	350.72	340.98	332.70	325.61	319.51	314.24
40 000	467.62	454.64	443.60	434.15	426.02	418.99
50 000	584.53	568.30	554.50	542.69	532.52	523.73
55 000	642.98	625.13	609.95	596.96	588.75	576.11
60 000	701.43	681.96	665.40	651.23	639.03	628.48
65 000	759.89	738.79	720.85	705.50	692.28	680.85
70 000	818.34	795.62	776.30	759.77	745.53	733.22
75 000	876.79	852.45	831.75	814.04	798.79	785.60
80 000	935.24	909.28	887.20	868.30	852.04	837.97
85 000	993.70	966.11	942.65	922.57	905.29	890.34
90 000	1052.15	1022.94	998.10	976.84	958.54	942.72

		needed to pay back a mortgage				
Term	1 Year	5 Years	10 Years	11 Years	12 Years	13 Years
AMOUNT						
30 000	2609.65	608.29	363.98	342.46	324.74	309.92
40 000	3479.54	811.06	485.31	456.62	432.98	413.23
50 000	4349.42	1013.82	606.64	570.77	541.23	516.54
55 000	4784.36	1115.20	667.30	627.85	595.35	568.19
60 000	5219.31	1216.58	727.97	684.93	649.47	619.84
65 000	5654.25	1317.97	788.63	742.00	703.59	671.50
70 000	6089.19	1419.35	849.29	799.08	757.72	723.15
75 000	6524.13	1520.73	909.96	856.16	811.84	774.81
80 000	6959.07	1622.11	970.62	913.24	865.96	826.46
85 000	7394.02	1723.49	1031.28	970.31	920.08	878.11
90 000	7828.96	1824.88	1091.95	1027.39	974.21	929.77
95 000	8263.90	1926.26	1152.61	1084.47	1028.33	981.42
100 000	8698.84	2027.64	1213.28	1141.54	1082.45	1033.07
105 000	9133.79	2129.02	1273.94	1198.62	1136.58	1084.73
110 000	9568.73	2230.40	1334.60	1255.70	1190.70	1136.38
115 000	10003.67	2331.79	1395.27	1312.78	1244.82	1188.03
120 000	10438.61	2433.17	1455.93	1369.85	1298.94	1239.69
125 000	10873.55	2534.55	1516.59	1426.93	1353.07	1291.34
130 000	11308.50	2635.93	1577.26	1484.01	1407.19	1343.00
135 000	11743.44	2737.31	1637.92	1541.09	1461.31	1394.65
140 000	12178.38	2838.70	1698.59	1598.16	1515.43	1446.30
145 000	12613.32	2940.08	1759.25	1655.24	1569.56	1497.96
150 000	13048.26	3041.46	1819.91	1712.32	1623.68	1549.61
155 000	13483.21	3142.84	1880.58	1769.39	1677.80	1601.26
160 000	13918.15	3244.22	1941.24	1826.47	1731.92	1652.92
165 000	14353.09	3345.61	2001.91	1883.55	1786.05	1704.57
170 000	14788.03	3446.99	2062.57	1940.63	1840.17	1756.23
175 000	15222.98	3548.37	2123.23	1997.70	1894.29	1807.88
180 000	15657.92	3649.75	2183.90	2054.78	1948.41	1859.53
185 000	16092.86	3751.13	2244.56	2111.86	2002.54	1911.19
190 000	16527.80	3852.51	2305.22	2168.93	2056.66	1962.84
195 000	16962.74	3953.90	2365.89	2226.01	2110.78	2014.49
200 000	17397.69	4055.28	2426.55	2283.09	2164.91	2066.15
205 000	17832.63	4156.66	2487.22	2340.17	2219.03	2117.80
210 000	18267.57	4258.04	2547.88	2397.24	2273.15	2169.46
215 000	18702.51	4359.42	2608.54	2454.32	2327.27	2221.11
220 000	19137.45	4460.81	2669.21	2511.40	2381.40	2272.76
225 000	19572.40	4562.19	2729.87	2568.48	2435.52	2324.42
230 000	20007.34	4663.57	2790.53	2625.55	2489.64	2376.07
235 000	20442.28	4764.95	2851.20	2682.63	2543.76	2427.72
240 000	20877.22	4866.33	2911.86	2739.71	2597.89	2479.38
245 000	21312.17	4967.72	2972.53	2796.78	2652.01	2531.03
250 000	21747.11	5069.10	3033.19	2853.86	2706.13	2582.68
260 000	22616.99	5271.86	3154.52	2968.02	2814.38	2685.99
270 000	23486.88	5474.63	3275.85	3082.17	2922.62	2789.30
280 000	24356.76	5677.39	3397.17	3196.33	3030.87	2892.61
290 000	25226.64	5880.15	3518.50	3310.48	3139.11	2995.91
300 000	26096.53	6082.92	3639.83	3424.63	3247.36	3099.22
400 000	34795.37	8110.56	4853.10	4566.18	4329.81	4132.30
500 000	43494.21	10138.20	6066.38	5707.72	5412.26	5165.37

needed to pay back a mortgage

Term	14 Years	15 Years	16 Years	17 Years	18 Years	19 Years
AMOUNT						
30 000	297.40	286.70	277.48	269.48	262.49	256.35
40 000	396.53	382.26	369.97	359.30	349.99	341.80
50 000	495.66	477.83	462.46	449.13	437.48	427.25
55 000	545.23	525.61	508.71	494.04	481.23	469.98
60 000	594.79	573.39	554.96	538.95	524.98	512.70
65 000	644.36	621.17	601.20	583.87	568.73	555.43
70 000	693.92	668.96	647.45	628.78	612.47	598.15
75 000	743.49	716.74	693.69	673.69	656.22	640.88
80 000	793.05	764.52	739.94	718.61	699.97	683.60
85 000	842.62	812.30	786.19	763.52	743.72	726.33
90 000	892.19	860.09	832.43	808.43	787.47	769.05
95 000	941.75	907.87	878.68	853.34	831.21	811.78
100 000	991.32	955.65	924.93	898.26	874.96	854.50
105 000	1040.88	1003.43	971.17	943.17	918.71	897.23
110 000	1090.45	1051.22	1017.42	988.08	962.46	939.95
115 000	1140.02	1099.00	1063.66	1033.00	1006.21	982.68
120 000	1189.58	1146.78	1109.91	1077.91	1049.96	1025.40
125 000	1239.15	1194.57	1156.16	1122.82	1093.70	1068.13
130 000	1288.71	1242.35	1202.40	1167.73	1137.45	1110.85
135 000	1338.28	1290.13	1248.65	1212.65	1181.20	1153.58
140 000	1387.85	1337.91	1294.90	1257.56	1224.95	1196.30
145 000	1437.41	1385.70	1341.14	1302.47	1268.70	1239.03
150 000	1486.98	1433.48	1387.39	1347.39	1312.44	1281.75
155 000	1536.54	1481.26	1433.63	1392.30	1356.19	1324.48
160 000	1586.11	1529.04	1479.88	1437.21	1399.94	1367.20
165 000	1635.68	1576.83	1526.13	1482.12	1443.69	1409.93
170 000	1685.24	1624.61	1572.37	1527.04	1487.44	1452.65
175 000	1734.81	1672.39	1618.62	1571.95	1531.18	1495.38
180 000	1784.37	1720.17	1664.87	1616.86	1574.93	1538.10
185 000	1833.94	1767.96	1711.11	1661.78	1618.68	1580.83
190 000	1883.50	1815.74	1757.36	1706.69	1662.43	1623.55
195 000	1933.07	1863.52	1803.60	1751.60	1706.18	1666.28
200 000	1982.64	1911.30	1849.85	1796.51	1749.93	1709.00
205 000	2032.20	1959.09	1896.10	1841.43	1793.67	1751.73
210 000	2081.77	2006.87	1942.34	1886.34	1837.42	1794.45
215 000	2131.33	2054.65	1988.59	1931.25	1881.17	1837.18
220 000	2180.90	2102.43	2034.84	1976.17	1924.92	1879.90
225 000	2230.47	2150.22	2081.08	2021.08	1968.67	1922.63
230 000	2280.03	2198.00	2127.33	2065.99	2012.41	1965.35
235 000	2329.60	2245.78	2173.57	2110.90	2056.16	2008.08
240 000	2379.16	2293.57	2219.82	2155.82	2099.91	2050.80
245 000	2428.73	2341.35	2266.07	2200.73	2143.66	2093.53
250 000	2478.30	2389.13	2312.31	2245.64	2187.41	2136.25
260 000	2577.43	2484.70	2404.81	2335.47	2274.90	2221.70
270 000	2676.56	2580.26	2497.30	2425.29	2362.40	2307.15
280 000	2775.69	2675.83	2589.79	2515.12	2449.90	2392.60
290 000	2874.82	2771.39	2682.28	2604.94	2537.39	2478.05
300 000	2973.95	2866.96	2774.78	2694.77	2624.89	2563.50
400 000	3965.27	3822.61	3699.70	3593.03	3499.85	3418.01
500 000	4956.59	4778.26	4624.63	4491.28	4374.81	4272.51

MONTHLY PAYMENT
needed to pay back a mortgage

Term	20 Years	21 Years	22 Years	23 Years	24 Years	25 Years
AMOUNT						
30 000	250.93	246.13	241.85	238.04	234.62	231.54
40 000	334.58	328.17	322.47	317.38	312.82	308.73
50 000	418.22	410.21	403.09	396.73	391.03	385.91
55 000	460.04	451.24	443.40	436.40	430.13	424.50
60 000	501.86	492.26	483.71	476.07	469.23	463.09
65 000	543.69	533.28	524.02	515.74	508.34	501.68
70 000	585.51	574.30	564.32	555.42	547.44	540.27
75 000	627.33	615.32	604.63	595.09	586.54	578.86
80 000	669.15	656.34	644.94	634.76	625.64	617.45
85 000	710.97	697.36	685.25	674.43	664.75	656.04
90 000	752.80	738.39	725.56	714.11	703.85	694.63
95 000	794.62	779.41	765.87	753.78	742.95	733.23
100 000	836.44	820.43	806.18	793.45	782.05	771.82
105 000	878.26	861.45	846.49	833.13	821.16	810.41
110 000	920.08	902.47	886.80	872.80	860.26	849.00
115 000	961.91	943.49	927.10	912.47	899.36	887.59
120 000	1003.73	984.51	967.41	952.14	938.46	926.18
125 000	1045.55	1025.53	1007.72	991.82	977.57	964.77
130 000	1087.37	1066.56	1048.03	1031.49	1016.67	1003.36
135 000	1129.19	1107.58	1088.34	1071.16	1055.77	1041.95
140 000	1171.02	1148.60	1128.65	1110.83	1094.88	1080.54
145 000	1212.84	1189.62	1168.96	1150.51	1133.98	1119.13
150 000	1254.66	1230.64	1209.27	1190.18	1173.08	1157.72
155 000	1296.48	1271.66	1249.58	1229.85	1212.18	1196.32
160 000	1338.30	1312.68	1289.88	1269.52	1251.29	1234.91
165 000	1380.13	1353.71	1330.19	1309.20	1290.39	1273.50
170 000	1421.95	1394.73	1370.50	1348.87	1329.49	1312.09
175 000	1463.77	1435.75	1410.81	1388.54	1368.59	1350.68
180 000	1505.59	1476.77	1451.12	1428.21	1407.70	1389.27
185 000	1547.41	1517.79	1491.43	1467.89	1446.80	1427.86
190 000	1589.24	1558.81	1531.74	1507.56	1485.90	1466.45
195 000	1631.06	1599.83	1572.05	1547.23	1525.01	1505.04
200 000	1672.88	1640.86	1612.36	1586.91	1564.11	1543.63
205 000	1714.70	1681.88	1652.66	1626.58	1603.21	1582.22
210 000	1756.52	1722.90	1692.97	1666.25	1642.31	1620.81
215 000	1798.35	1763.92	1733.28	1705.92	1681.42	1659.40
220 000	1840.17	1804.94	1773.59	1745.60	1720.52	1698.00
225 000	1881.99	1845.96	1813.90	1785.27	1759.62	1736.59
230 000	1923.81	1886.98	1854.21	1824.94	1798.72	1775.18
235 000	1965.63	1928.01	1894.52	1864.61	1837.83	1813.77
240 000	2007.46	1969.03	1934.83	1904.29	1876.93	1852.36
245 000	2049.28	2010.05	1975.14	1943.96	1916.03	1890.95
250 000	2091.10	2051.07	2015.44	1983.63	1955.14	1929.54
260 000	2174.74	2133.11	2096.06	2062.98	2033.34	2006.72
270 000	2258.39	2215.16	2176.68	2142.32	2111.55	2083.90
280 000	2342.03	2297.20	2257.30	2221.67	2189.75	2161.09
290 000	2425.68	2379.24	2337.92	2301.01	2267.96	2238.27
300 000	2509.32	2461.28	2418.53	2380.36	2346.16	2315.45
400 000	3345.76	3281.71	3224.71	3173.81	3128.22	3087.26
500 000	4182.20	4102.14	4030.89	3967.26	3910.27	3859.08

	MONTHLY PAYMENT				**8.00%** INTEREST	
	needed to pay back a mortgage					
Term	26 Years	27 Years	28 Years	29 Years	30 Years	35 Years
AMOUNT						
30 000	228.78	226.28	224.03	221.98	220.13	213.08
40 000	305.04	301.71	298.70	295.98	293.51	284.10
50 000	381.30	377.14	373.38	369.97	366.88	355.13
55 000	419.43	414.85	410.72	406.97	403.57	390.64
60 000	457.56	452.57	448.06	443.97	440.26	426.16
65 000	495.69	490.28	485.39	480.96	476.95	461.67
70 000	533.82	528.00	522.73	517.96	513.64	497.18
75 000	571.95	565.71	560.07	554.96	550.32	532.70
80 000	610.08	603.42	597.41	591.96	587.01	568.21
85 000	648.21	641.14	634.74	628.95	623.70	603.72
90 000	686.34	678.85	672.08	665.95	660.39	639.23
95 000	724.47	716.57	709.42	702.95	697.08	674.75
100 000	762.60	754.28	746.76	739.95	733.76	710.26
105 000	800.73	791.99	784.10	776.94	770.45	745.77
110 000	838.86	829.71	821.43	813.94	807.14	781.29
115 000	876.99	867.42	858.77	850.94	843.83	816.80
120 000	915.12	905.14	896.11	887.93	880.52	852.31
125 000	953.25	942.85	933.45	924.93	917.21	887.83
130 000	991.38	980.56	970.79	961.93	953.89	923.34
135 000	1029.51	1018.28	1008.12	998.93	990.58	958.85
140 000	1067.64	1055.99	1045.46	1035.92	1027.27	994.37
145 000	1105.77	1093.71	1082.80	1072.92	1063.96	1029.88
150 000	1143.90	1131.42	1120.14	1109.92	1100.65	1065.39
155 000	1182.03	1169.13	1157.48	1146.92	1137.34	1100.90
160 000	1220.16	1206.85	1194.81	1183.91	1174.02	1136.42
165 000	1258.29	1244.56	1232.15	1220.91	1210.71	1171.93
170 000	1296.42	1282.28	1269.49	1257.91	1247.40	1207.44
175 000	1334.55	1319.99	1306.83	1294.91	1284.09	1242.96
180 000	1372.68	1357.70	1344.17	1331.90	1320.78	1278.47
185 000	1410.81	1395.42	1381.50	1368.90	1357.46	1313.98
190 000	1448.94	1433.13	1418.84	1405.90	1394.15	1349.50
195 000	1487.07	1470.85	1456.18	1442.89	1430.84	1385.01
200 000	1525.20	1508.56	1493.52	1479.89	1467.53	1420.52
205 000	1563.33	1546.27	1530.86	1516.89	1504.22	1456.03
210 000	1601.46	1583.99	1568.19	1553.89	1540.91	1491.55
215 000	1639.59	1621.70	1605.53	1590.88	1577.59	1527.06
220 000	1677.72	1659.42	1642.87	1627.88	1614.28	1562.57
225 000	1715.85	1697.13	1680.21	1664.88	1650.97	1598.09
230 000	1753.98	1734.84	1717.54	1701.88	1687.66	1633.60
235 000	1792.11	1772.56	1754.88	1738.87	1724.35	1669.11
240 000	1830.24	1810.27	1792.22	1775.87	1761.03	1704.63
245 000	1868.37	1847.99	1829.56	1812.87	1797.72	1740.14
250 000	1906.50	1885.70	1866.90	1849.86	1834.41	1775.65
260 000	1982.76	1961.13	1941.57	1923.86	1907.79	1846.68
270 000	2059.01	2036.56	2016.25	1997.85	1981.16	1917.70
280 000	2135.27	2111.98	2090.92	2071.85	2054.54	1988.73
290 000	2211.53	2187.41	2165.60	2145.84	2127.92	2059.76
300 000	2287.79	2262.84	2240.28	2219.84	2201.29	2130.78
400 000	3050.39	3017.12	2987.03	2959.78	2935.06	2841.04
500 000	3812.99	3771.40	3733.79	3699.73	3668.82	3551.30

8.50% INTEREST	\multicolumn{6}{c}{MONTHLY PAYMENT needed to pay back a mortgage}					

Term	1 Year	5 Years	10 Years	11 Years	12 Years	13 Years
AMOUNT						
30 000	2616.59	615.50	371.96	350.59	333.02	318.35
40 000	3488.79	820.66	495.94	467.46	444.02	424.47
50 000	4360.99	1025.83	619.93	584.32	555.03	530.59
55 000	4797.09	1128.41	681.92	642.75	610.53	583.65
60 000	5233.19	1230.99	743.91	701.18	666.03	636.71
65 000	5669.29	1333.57	805.91	759.62	721.54	689.77
70 000	6105.38	1436.16	867.90	818.05	777.04	742.83
75 000	6541.48	1538.74	929.89	876.48	832.54	795.88
80 000	6977.58	1641.32	991.89	934.91	888.04	848.94
85 000	7413.68	1743.91	1053.88	993.34	943.55	902.00
90 000	7849.78	1846.49	1115.87	1051.78	999.05	955.06
95 000	8285.88	1949.07	1177.86	1110.21	1054.55	1008.12
100 000	8721.98	2051.65	1239.86	1168.64	1110.06	1061.18
105 000	9158.08	2154.24	1301.85	1227.07	1165.56	1114.24
110 000	9594.18	2256.82	1363.84	1285.50	1221.06	1167.30
115 000	10030.27	2359.40	1425.84	1343.94	1276.56	1220.36
120 000	10466.37	2461.98	1487.83	1402.37	1332.07	1273.41
125 000	10902.47	2564.57	1549.82	1460.80	1387.57	1326.47
130 000	11338.57	2667.15	1611.81	1519.23	1443.07	1379.53
135 000	11774.67	2769.73	1673.81	1577.66	1498.58	1432.59
140 000	12210.77	2872.31	1735.80	1636.09	1554.08	1485.65
145 000	12646.87	2974.90	1797.79	1694.53	1609.58	1538.71
150 000	13082.97	3077.48	1859.79	1752.96	1665.08	1591.77
155 000	13519.07	3180.06	1921.78	1811.39	1720.59	1644.83
160 000	13955.17	3282.65	1983.77	1869.82	1776.09	1697.89
165 000	14391.26	3385.23	2045.76	1928.25	1831.59	1750.95
170 000	14827.36	3487.81	2107.76	1986.69	1887.09	1804.00
175 000	15263.46	3590.39	2169.75	2045.12	1942.60	1857.06
180 000	15699.56	3692.98	2231.74	2103.55	1998.10	1910.12
185 000	16135.66	3795.56	2293.74	2161.98	2053.60	1963.18
190 000	16571.76	3898.14	2355.73	2220.41	2109.11	2016.24
195 000	17007.86	4000.72	2417.72	2278.85	2164.61	2069.30
200 000	17443.96	4103.31	2479.71	2337.28	2220.11	2122.36
205 000	17880.06	4205.89	2541.71	2395.71	2275.61	2175.42
210 000	18316.15	4308.47	2603.70	2454.14	2331.12	2228.48
215 000	18752.25	4411.05	2665.69	2512.57	2386.62	2281.54
220 000	19188.35	4513.64	2727.69	2571.01	2442.12	2334.59
225 000	19624.45	4616.22	2789.68	2629.44	2497.63	2387.65
230 000	20060.55	4718.80	2851.67	2687.87	2553.13	2440.71
235 000	20496.65	4821.38	2913.66	2746.30	2608.63	2493.77
240 000	20932.75	4923.97	2975.66	2804.73	2664.13	2546.83
245 000	21368.85	5026.55	3037.65	2863.17	2719.64	2599.89
250 000	21804.95	5129.13	3099.64	2921.60	2775.14	2652.95
260 000	22677.14	5334.30	3223.63	3038.46	2886.14	2759.07
270 000	23549.34	5539.46	3347.61	3155.33	2997.15	2865.18
280 000	24421.54	5744.63	3471.60	3272.19	3108.16	2971.30
290 000	25293.74	5949.79	3595.58	3389.05	3219.16	3077.42
300 000	26165.93	6154.96	3719.57	3505.92	3330.17	3183.54
400 000	34887.91	8206.61	4959.43	4674.56	4440.22	4244.72
500 000	43609.89	10258.27	6199.28	5843.20	5550.28	5305.90

			MONTHLY PAYMENT		**8.50%** INTEREST	
			needed to pay back a mortgage			
Term	**14** Years	**15** Years	**16** Years	**17** Years	**18** Years	**19** Years
AMOUNT						
30 000	305.98	295.42	286.35	278.49	271.64	265.63
40 000	407.97	393.90	381.80	371.32	362.18	354.18
50 000	509.96	492.37	477.25	464.15	452.73	442.72
55 000	560.96	541.61	524.97	510.56	498.00	487.00
60 000	611.95	590.84	572.69	556.98	543.27	531.27
65 000	662.95	640.08	620.42	603.39	588.55	575.54
70 000	713.94	689.32	668.14	649.80	633.82	619.81
75 000	764.94	738.55	715.87	696.22	679.09	664.08
80 000	815.93	787.79	763.59	742.63	724.37	708.36
85 000	866.93	837.03	811.32	789.05	769.64	752.63
90 000	917.93	886.27	859.04	835.46	814.91	796.90
95 000	968.92	935.50	906.77	881.88	860.18	841.17
100 000	1019.92	984.74	954.49	928.29	905.46	885.45
105 000	1070.91	1033.98	1002.22	974.71	950.73	929.72
110 000	1121.91	1083.21	1049.94	1021.12	996.00	973.99
115 000	1172.91	1132.45	1097.66	1067.54	1041.28	1018.26
120 000	1223.90	1181.69	1145.39	1113.95	1086.55	1062.53
125 000	1274.90	1230.92	1193.11	1160.37	1131.82	1106.81
130 000	1325.89	1280.16	1240.84	1206.78	1177.09	1151.08
135 000	1376.89	1329.40	1288.56	1253.19	1222.37	1195.35
140 000	1427.89	1378.64	1336.29	1299.61	1267.64	1239.62
145 000	1478.88	1427.87	1384.01	1346.02	1312.91	1283.90
150 000	1529.88	1477.11	1431.74	1392.44	1358.19	1328.17
155 000	1580.87	1526.35	1479.46	1438.85	1403.46	1372.44
160 000	1631.87	1575.58	1527.19	1485.27	1448.73	1416.71
165 000	1682.87	1624.82	1574.91	1531.68	1494.00	1460.99
170 000	1733.86	1674.06	1622.63	1578.10	1539.28	1505.26
175 000	1784.86	1723.29	1670.36	1624.51	1584.55	1549.53
180 000	1835.85	1772.53	1718.08	1670.93	1629.82	1593.80
185 000	1886.85	1821.77	1765.81	1717.34	1675.10	1638.07
190 000	1937.85	1871.01	1813.53	1763.75	1720.37	1682.35
195 000	1988.84	1920.24	1861.26	1810.17	1765.64	1726.62
200 000	2039.84	1969.48	1908.98	1856.58	1810.91	1770.89
205 000	2090.83	2018.72	1956.71	1903.00	1856.19	1815.16
210 000	2141.83	2067.95	2004.43	1949.41	1901.46	1859.44
215 000	2192.82	2117.19	2052.16	1995.83	1946.73	1903.71
220 000	2243.82	2166.43	2099.88	2042.24	1992.01	1947.98
225 000	2294.82	2215.66	2147.60	2088.66	2037.28	1992.25
230 000	2345.81	2264.90	2195.33	2135.07	2082.55	2036.52
235 000	2396.81	2314.14	2243.05	2181.49	2127.83	2080.80
240 000	2447.80	2363.37	2290.78	2227.90	2173.10	2125.07
245 000	2498.80	2412.61	2338.50	2274.32	2218.37	2169.34
250 000	2549.80	2461.85	2386.23	2320.73	2263.64	2213.61
260 000	2651.79	2560.32	2481.68	2413.56	2354.19	2302.16
270 000	2753.78	2658.80	2577.13	2506.39	2444.74	2390.70
280 000	2855.77	2757.27	2672.57	2599.22	2535.28	2479.25
290 000	2957.76	2855.74	2768.02	2692.05	2625.83	2567.79
300 000	3059.76	2954.22	2863.47	2784.88	2716.37	2656.34
400 000	4079.67	3938.96	3817.96	3713.17	3621.83	3541.78
500 000	5099.59	4923.70	4772.46	4641.46	4527.29	4427.23

13

MONTHLY PAYMENT
needed to pay back a mortgage

Term	20 Years	21 Years	22 Years	23 Years	24 Years	25 Years
AMOUNT						
30 000	260.35	255.67	251.52	247.83	244.52	241.57
40 000	347.13	340.90	335.36	330.43	326.03	322.09
50 000	433.91	426.12	419.20	413.04	407.54	402.61
55 000	477.30	468.73	461.12	454.35	448.30	442.87
60 000	520.69	511.34	503.04	495.65	489.05	483.14
65 000	564.09	553.96	544.96	536.96	529.80	523.40
70 000	607.48	596.57	586.88	578.26	570.56	563.66
75 000	650.87	639.18	628.80	619.56	611.31	603.92
80 000	694.26	681.79	670.72	660.87	652.07	644.18
85 000	737.65	724.40	712.65	702.17	692.82	684.44
90 000	781.04	767.02	754.57	743.48	733.57	724.70
95 000	824.43	809.63	796.49	784.78	774.33	764.97
100 000	867.82	852.24	838.41	826.09	815.08	805.23
105 000	911.21	894.85	880.33	867.39	855.84	845.49
110 000	954.61	937.46	922.25	908.70	896.59	885.75
115 000	998.00	980.08	964.17	950.00	937.34	926.01
120 000	1041.39	1022.69	1006.09	991.30	978.10	966.27
125 000	1084.78	1065.30	1048.01	1032.61	1018.85	1006.53
130 000	1128.17	1107.91	1089.93	1073.91	1059.61	1046.80
135 000	1171.56	1150.52	1131.85	1115.22	1100.36	1087.06
140 000	1214.95	1193.13	1173.77	1156.52	1141.12	1127.32
145 000	1258.34	1235.75	1215.69	1197.83	1181.87	1167.58
150 000	1301.73	1278.36	1257.61	1239.13	1222.62	1207.84
155 000	1345.13	1320.97	1299.53	1280.43	1263.38	1248.10
160 000	1388.52	1363.58	1341.45	1321.74	1304.13	1288.36
165 000	1431.91	1406.19	1383.37	1363.04	1344.89	1328.62
170 000	1475.30	1448.81	1425.29	1404.35	1385.64	1368.89
175 000	1518.69	1491.42	1467.21	1445.65	1426.39	1409.15
180 000	1562.08	1534.03	1509.13	1486.96	1467.15	1449.41
185 000	1605.47	1576.64	1551.05	1528.26	1507.90	1489.67
190 000	1648.86	1619.25	1592.97	1569.56	1548.66	1529.93
195 000	1692.26	1661.87	1634.89	1610.87	1589.41	1570.19
200 000	1735.65	1704.48	1676.81	1652.17	1630.16	1610.45
205 000	1779.04	1747.09	1718.73	1693.48	1670.92	1650.72
210 000	1822.43	1789.70	1760.65	1734.78	1711.67	1690.98
215 000	1865.82	1832.31	1802.57	1776.09	1752.43	1731.24
220 000	1909.21	1874.93	1844.49	1817.39	1793.18	1771.50
225 000	1952.60	1917.54	1886.41	1858.69	1833.94	1811.76
230 000	1995.99	1960.15	1928.33	1900.00	1874.69	1852.02
235 000	2039.38	2002.76	1970.25	1941.30	1915.44	1892.28
240 000	2082.78	2045.37	2012.17	1982.61	1956.20	1932.55
245 000	2126.17	2087.99	2054.10	2023.91	1996.95	1972.81
250 000	2169.56	2130.60	2096.02	2065.22	2037.71	2013.07
260 000	2256.34	2215.82	2179.86	2147.83	2119.21	2093.59
270 000	2343.12	2301.05	2263.70	2230.43	2200.72	2174.11
280 000	2429.91	2386.27	2347.54	2313.04	2282.23	2254.64
290 000	2516.69	2471.49	2431.38	2395.65	2363.74	2335.16
300 000	2603.47	2556.72	2515.22	2478.26	2445.25	2415.68
400 000	3471.29	3408.96	3353.62	3304.35	3260.33	3220.91
500 000	4339.12	4261.20	4192.03	4130.43	4075.41	4026.14

Term	26 Years	27 Years	28 Years	29 Years	30 Years	35 Years
AMOUNT						
30 000	238.91	236.53	234.37	232.43	230.67	224.06
40 000	318.55	315.37	312.50	309.91	307.57	298.74
50 000	398.19	394.21	390.62	387.39	384.46	373.43
55 000	438.01	433.63	429.69	426.12	422.90	410.77
60 000	477.83	473.05	468.75	464.86	461.35	448.12
65 000	517.65	512.47	507.81	503.60	499.79	485.46
70 000	557.47	551.89	546.87	542.34	538.24	522.80
75 000	597.28	591.32	585.94	581.08	576.69	560.15
80 000	637.10	630.74	625.00	619.82	615.13	597.49
85 000	676.92	670.16	664.06	658.55	653.58	634.83
90 000	716.74	709.58	703.12	697.29	692.02	672.17
95 000	756.56	749.00	742.19	736.03	730.47	709.52
100 000	796.38	788.42	781.25	774.77	768.91	746.86
105 000	836.20	827.84	820.31	813.51	807.36	784.20
110 000	876.02	867.26	859.37	852.25	845.80	821.55
115 000	915.84	906.68	898.43	890.99	884.25	858.89
120 000	955.66	946.11	937.50	929.72	922.70	896.23
125 000	995.47	985.53	976.56	968.46	961.14	933.58
130 000	1035.29	1024.95	1015.62	1007.20	999.59	970.92
135 000	1075.11	1064.37	1054.68	1045.94	1038.03	1008.26
140 000	1114.93	1103.79	1093.75	1084.68	1076.48	1045.60
145 000	1154.75	1143.21	1132.81	1123.42	1114.92	1082.95
150 000	1194.57	1182.63	1171.87	1162.16	1153.37	1120.29
155 000	1234.39	1222.06	1210.93	1200.89	1191.82	1157.63
160 000	1274.21	1261.47	1250.00	1239.63	1230.26	1194.98
165 000	1314.03	1300.89	1289.06	1278.37	1268.71	1232.32
170 000	1353.85	1340.32	1328.12	1317.11	1307.15	1269.66
175 000	1393.66	1379.74	1367.18	1355.85	1345.60	1307.01
180 000	1433.48	1419.16	1406.25	1394.59	1384.04	1344.35
185 000	1473.30	1458.58	1445.31	1433.33	1422.49	1381.69
190 000	1513.12	1498.00	1484.37	1472.06	1460.94	1419.04
195 000	1552.94	1537.42	1523.43	1510.80	1499.38	1456.38
200 000	1592.76	1576.84	1562.49	1549.54	1537.83	1493.72
205 000	1632.58	1616.26	1601.56	1588.28	1576.27	1531.06
210 000	1672.40	1655.68	1640.62	1627.02	1614.72	1568.41
215 000	1712.22	1695.11	1679.68	1665.76	1653.16	1605.75
220 000	1752.04	1734.53	1718.74	1704.50	1691.61	1643.09
225 000	1791.85	1773.95	1757.81	1743.23	1730.06	1680.44
230 000	1831.67	1813.37	1796.87	1781.97	1768.50	1717.78
235 000	1871.49	1852.79	1835.93	1820.71	1806.95	1755.12
240 000	1911.31	1892.21	1874.99	1859.45	1845.39	1792.47
245 000	1951.13	1931.63	1914.06	1898.19	1883.84	1829.81
250 000	1990.95	1971.05	1953.12	1936.93	1922.28	1867.15
260 000	2070.59	2049.89	2031.24	2014.40	1999.18	1941.84
270 000	2150.23	2128.74	2109.37	2091.88	2076.07	2016.52
280 000	2229.86	2207.58	2187.49	2169.36	2152.96	2091.21
290 000	2309.50	2286.42	2265.62	2246.83	2229.85	2165.90
300 000	2389.14	2365.26	2343.74	2324.31	2306.74	2240.58
400 000	3185.52	3153.68	3124.99	3099.08	3075.65	2987.44
500 000	3981.90	3942.11	3906.24	3873.85	3844.57	3734.30

9.00% INTEREST	**MONTHLY PAYMENT** needed to pay back a mortgage					
Term	1 Year	5 Years	10 Years	11 Years	12 Years	13 Years
AMOUNT						
30 000	2623.54	622.75	380.03	358.82	341.41	326.90
40 000	3498.06	830.33	506.70	478.43	455.21	435.87
50 000	4372.57	1037.92	633.38	598.04	569.02	544.84
55 000	4809.83	1141.71	696.72	657.84	625.92	599.32
60 000	5247.09	1245.50	760.05	717.65	682.82	653.81
65 000	5684.35	1349.29	823.39	777.45	739.72	708.29
70 000	6121.60	1453.08	886.73	837.26	796.62	762.78
75 000	6558.86	1556.88	950.07	897.06	853.52	817.26
80 000	6996.12	1660.67	1013.41	956.86	910.42	871.74
85 000	7433.38	1764.46	1076.74	1016.67	967.33	926.23
90 000	7870.63	1868.25	1140.08	1076.47	1024.23	980.71
95 000	8307.89	1972.04	1203.42	1136.28	1081.13	1035.20
100 000	8745.15	2075.84	1266.76	1196.08	1138.03	1089.68
105 000	9182.41	2179.63	1330.10	1255.88	1194.93	1144.16
110 000	9619.66	2283.42	1393.43	1315.69	1251.83	1198.65
115 000	10056.92	2387.21	1456.77	1375.49	1308.74	1253.13
120 000	10494.18	2491.00	1520.11	1435.30	1365.64	1307.62
125 000	10931.43	2594.79	1583.45	1495.10	1422.54	1362.10
130 000	11368.69	2698.59	1646.79	1554.90	1479.44	1416.58
135 000	11805.95	2802.38	1710.12	1614.71	1536.34	1471.07
140 000	12243.21	2906.17	1773.46	1674.51	1593.24	1525.55
145 000	12680.46	3009.96	1836.80	1734.32	1650.14	1580.04
150 000	13117.72	3113.75	1900.14	1794.12	1707.05	1634.52
155 000	13554.98	3217.55	1963.47	1853.92	1763.95	1689.00
160 000	13992.24	3321.34	2026.81	1913.73	1820.85	1743.49
165 000	14429.49	3425.13	2090.15	1973.53	1877.75	1797.97
170 000	14866.75	3528.92	2153.49	2033.34	1934.65	1852.46
175 000	15304.01	3632.71	2216.83	2093.14	1991.55	1906.94
180 000	15741.27	3736.50	2280.16	2152.94	2048.46	1961.42
185 000	16178.52	3840.30	2343.50	2212.75	2105.36	2015.91
190 000	16615.78	3944.09	2406.84	2272.55	2162.26	2070.39
195 000	17053.04	4047.88	2470.18	2332.36	2219.16	2124.88
200 000	17490.30	4151.67	2533.52	2392.16	2276.06	2179.36
205 000	17927.55	4255.46	2596.85	2451.96	2332.96	2233.85
210 000	18364.81	4359.25	2660.19	2511.77	2389.86	2288.33
215 000	18802.07	4463.05	2723.53	2571.57	2446.77	2342.81
220 000	19239.32	4566.84	2786.87	2631.38	2503.67	2397.30
225 000	19676.58	4670.63	2850.20	2691.18	2560.57	2451.78
230 000	20113.84	4774.42	2913.54	2750.98	2617.47	2506.27
235 000	20551.10	4878.21	2976.88	2810.79	2674.37	2560.75
240 000	20988.35	4982.01	3040.22	2870.59	2731.27	2615.23
245 000	21425.61	5085.80	3103.56	2930.40	2788.18	2669.72
250 000	21862.87	5189.59	3166.89	2990.20	2845.08	2724.20
260 000	22737.38	5397.17	3293.57	3109.81	2958.88	2833.17
270 000	23611.90	5604.76	3420.25	3229.42	3072.68	2942.14
280 000	24486.41	5812.34	3546.92	3349.03	3186.49	3051.11
290 000	25360.93	6019.92	3673.60	3468.63	3300.29	3160.07
300 000	26235.44	6227.51	3800.27	3588.24	3414.09	3269.04
400 000	34980.59	8303.34	5067.03	4784.32	4552.12	4358.72
500 000	43725.74	10379.18	6333.79	5980.40	5690.15	5448.40

Term	14 Years	15 Years	16 Years	17 Years	18 Years	19 Years
AMOUNT						
30 000	314.68	304.28	295.35	287.64	280.93	275.07
40 000	419.58	405.71	393.81	383.52	374.58	366.76
50 000	524.47	507.13	492.26	479.40	468.22	458.45
55 000	576.92	557.85	541.48	527.34	515.04	504.29
60 000	629.36	608.56	590.71	575.28	561.87	550.14
65 000	681.81	659.27	639.94	623.22	608.69	595.98
70 000	734.26	709.99	689.16	671.16	655.51	641.83
75 000	786.70	760.70	738.39	719.10	702.33	687.67
80 000	839.15	811.41	787.61	767.04	749.16	733.52
85 000	891.60	862.13	836.84	814.98	795.98	779.36
90 000	944.04	912.84	886.06	862.92	842.80	825.21
95 000	996.49	963.55	935.29	910.86	889.62	871.05
100 000	1048.94	1014.27	984.52	958.80	936.44	916.90
105 000	1101.38	1064.98	1033.74	1006.74	983.27	962.74
110 000	1153.83	1115.69	1082.97	1054.68	1030.09	1008.59
115 000	1206.28	1166.41	1132.19	1102.62	1076.91	1054.43
120 000	1258.73	1217.12	1181.42	1150.56	1123.73	1100.28
125 000	1311.17	1267.83	1230.64	1198.50	1170.56	1146.12
130 000	1363.62	1318.55	1279.87	1246.45	1217.38	1191.97
135 000	1416.07	1369.26	1329.10	1294.39	1264.20	1237.81
140 000	1468.51	1419.97	1378.32	1342.33	1311.02	1283.66
145 000	1520.96	1470.69	1427.55	1390.27	1357.85	1329.50
150 000	1573.41	1521.40	1476.77	1438.21	1404.67	1375.35
155 000	1625.85	1572.11	1526.00	1486.15	1451.49	1421.19
160 000	1678.30	1622.83	1575.23	1534.09	1498.31	1467.03
165 000	1730.75	1673.54	1624.45	1582.03	1545.13	1512.88
170 000	1783.19	1724.25	1673.68	1629.97	1591.96	1558.72
175 000	1835.64	1774.97	1722.90	1677.91	1638.78	1604.57
180 000	1888.09	1825.68	1772.13	1725.85	1685.60	1650.41
185 000	1940.53	1876.39	1821.35	1773.79	1732.42	1696.26
190 000	1992.98	1927.11	1870.58	1821.73	1779.25	1742.10
195 000	2045.43	1977.82	1919.81	1869.67	1826.07	1787.95
200 000	2097.88	2028.53	1969.03	1917.61	1872.89	1833.79
205 000	2150.32	2079.25	2018.26	1965.55	1919.71	1879.64
210 000	2202.77	2129.96	2067.48	2013.49	1966.53	1925.48
215 000	2255.22	2180.67	2116.71	2061.43	2013.36	1971.33
220 000	2307.66	2231.39	2165.93	2109.37	2060.18	2017.17
225 000	2360.11	2282.10	2215.16	2157.31	2107.00	2063.02
230 000	2412.56	2332.81	2264.39	2205.25	2153.82	2108.86
235 000	2465.00	2383.53	2313.61	2253.19	2200.65	2154.71
240 000	2517.45	2434.24	2362.84	2301.13	2247.47	2200.55
245 000	2569.90	2484.95	2412.06	2349.07	2294.29	2246.40
250 000	2622.34	2535.67	2461.29	2397.01	2341.11	2292.24
260 000	2727.24	2637.09	2559.74	2492.89	2434.76	2383.93
270 000	2832.13	2738.52	2658.19	2588.77	2528.40	2475.62
280 000	2937.03	2839.95	2756.64	2684.65	2622.05	2567.31
290 000	3041.92	2941.37	2855.10	2780.53	2715.69	2659.00
300 000	3146.81	3042.80	2953.55	2876.41	2809.33	2750.69
400 000	4195.75	4057.07	3938.06	3835.22	3745.78	3667.59
500 000	5244.69	5071.33	4922.58	4794.02	4682.22	4584.48

9.00% INTEREST	**MONTHLY PAYMENT** needed to pay back a mortgage				
Term	**20** Years	**21** Years	**22** Years	**23** Years	**24** Years	**25** Years
AMOUNT						
30 000	269.92	265.37	261.35	257.78	254.60	251.76
40 000	359.89	353.83	348.47	343.71	339.47	335.68
50 000	449.86	442.29	435.59	429.63	424.33	419.60
55 000	494.85	486.52	479.15	472.60	466.77	461.56
60 000	539.84	530.75	522.70	515.56	509.20	503.52
65 000	584.82	574.98	566.26	558.52	551.63	545.48
70 000	629.81	619.21	609.82	601.49	594.07	587.44
75 000	674.79	663.44	653.38	644.45	636.50	629.40
80 000	719.78	707.66	696.94	687.41	678.93	671.36
85 000	764.77	751.89	740.50	730.38	721.36	713.32
90 000	809.75	796.12	784.06	773.34	763.80	755.28
95 000	854.74	840.35	827.62	816.30	806.23	797.24
100 000	899.73	884.58	871.17	859.27	848.66	839.20
105 000	944.71	928.81	914.73	902.23	891.10	881.16
110 000	989.70	973.04	958.29	945.19	933.53	923.12
115 000	1034.68	1017.27	1001.85	988.16	975.96	965.08
120 000	1079.67	1061.50	1045.41	1031.12	1018.40	1007.04
125 000	1124.66	1105.73	1088.97	1074.09	1060.83	1049.00
130 000	1169.64	1149.96	1132.53	1117.05	1103.26	1090.96
135 000	1214.63	1194.18	1176.09	1160.01	1145.70	1132.92
140 000	1259.62	1238.41	1219.64	1202.98	1188.13	1174.87
145 000	1304.60	1282.64	1263.20	1245.94	1230.56	1216.83
150 000	1349.59	1326.87	1306.76	1288.90	1273.00	1258.79
155 000	1394.58	1371.10	1350.32	1331.87	1315.43	1300.75
160 000	1439.56	1415.33	1393.88	1374.83	1357.86	1342.71
165 000	1484.55	1459.56	1437.44	1417.79	1400.30	1384.67
170 000	1529.53	1503.79	1481.00	1460.76	1442.73	1426.63
175 000	1574.52	1548.02	1524.56	1503.72	1485.16	1468.59
180 000	1619.51	1592.25	1568.11	1546.68	1527.60	1510.55
185 000	1664.49	1636.47	1611.67	1589.65	1570.03	1552.51
190 000	1709.48	1680.70	1655.23	1632.61	1612.46	1594.47
195 000	1754.47	1724.93	1698.79	1675.57	1654.90	1636.43
200 000	1799.45	1769.16	1742.35	1718.54	1697.33	1678.39
205 000	1844.44	1813.39	1785.91	1761.50	1739.76	1720.35
210 000	1889.42	1857.62	1829.47	1804.46	1782.20	1762.31
215 000	1934.41	1901.85	1873.02	1847.43	1824.63	1804.27
220 000	1979.40	1946.08	1916.58	1890.39	1867.06	1846.23
225 000	2024.38	1990.31	1960.14	1933.35	1909.49	1888.19
230 000	2069.37	2034.54	2003.70	1976.32	1951.93	1930.15
235 000	2114.36	2078.77	2047.26	2019.28	1994.36	1972.11
240 000	2159.34	2122.99	2090.82	2062.24	2036.79	2014.07
245 000	2204.33	2167.22	2134.38	2105.21	2079.23	2056.03
250 000	2249.31	2211.45	2177.94	2148.17	2121.66	2097.99
260 000	2339.29	2299.91	2265.05	2234.10	2206.53	2181.91
270 000	2429.26	2388.37	2352.17	2320.02	2291.39	2265.83
280 000	2519.23	2476.83	2439.29	2405.95	2376.26	2349.75
290 000	2609.21	2565.28	2526.41	2491.88	2461.13	2433.67
300 000	2699.18	2653.74	2613.52	2577.80	2545.99	2517.59
400 000	3598.90	3538.32	3484.70	3437.07	3394.66	3356.79
500 000	4498.63	4422.91	4355.87	4296.34	4243.32	4195.98

Term	26 Years	27 Years	28 Years	29 Years	30 Years	35 Years
AMOUNT						
30 000	249.22	246.94	244.89	243.05	241.39	235.20
40 000	332.29	329.25	326.52	324.06	321.85	313.60
50 000	415.36	411.56	408.15	405.08	402.31	392.00
55 000	456.90	452.72	448.96	445.59	442.54	431.20
60 000	498.43	493.88	489.78	486.09	482.77	470.40
65 000	539.97	535.03	530.59	526.60	523.00	509.60
70 000	581.51	576.19	571.41	567.11	563.24	548.80
75 000	623.04	617.34	612.22	607.62	603.47	587.99
80 000	664.58	658.50	653.04	648.13	643.70	627.19
85 000	706.11	699.66	693.85	688.63	683.93	666.39
90 000	747.65	740.81	734.67	729.14	724.16	705.59
95 000	789.19	781.97	775.48	769.65	764.39	744.79
100 000	830.72	823.13	816.30	810.16	804.62	783.99
105 000	872.26	864.28	857.11	850.67	844.85	823.19
110 000	913.80	905.44	897.93	891.17	885.08	862.39
115 000	955.33	946.59	938.74	931.68	925.32	901.59
120 000	996.87	987.75	979.56	972.19	965.55	940.79
125 000	1038.40	1028.91	1020.37	1012.70	1005.78	979.99
130 000	1079.94	1070.06	1061.19	1053.20	1046.01	1019.19
135 000	1121.48	1111.22	1102.00	1093.71	1086.24	1058.39
140 000	1163.01	1152.38	1142.82	1134.22	1126.47	1097.59
145 000	1204.55	1193.53	1183.63	1174.73	1166.70	1136.79
150 000	1246.09	1234.69	1224.45	1215.24	1206.93	1175.99
155 000	1287.62	1275.84	1265.26	1255.74	1247.17	1215.19
160 000	1329.16	1317.00	1306.08	1296.25	1287.40	1254.39
165 000	1370.69	1358.16	1346.89	1336.76	1327.63	1293.59
170 000	1412.23	1399.31	1387.71	1377.27	1367.86	1332.79
175 000	1453.77	1440.47	1428.52	1417.78	1408.09	1371.99
180 000	1495.30	1481.63	1469.34	1458.28	1448.32	1411.19
185 000	1536.84	1522.78	1510.15	1498.79	1488.55	1450.39
190 000	1578.37	1563.94	1550.97	1539.30	1528.78	1489.59
195 000	1619.91	1605.09	1591.78	1579.81	1569.01	1528.79
200 000	1661.45	1646.25	1632.60	1620.32	1609.25	1567.99
205 000	1702.98	1687.41	1673.41	1660.82	1649.48	1607.19
210 000	1744.52	1728.56	1714.23	1701.33	1689.71	1646.39
215 000	1786.06	1769.72	1755.04	1741.84	1729.94	1685.58
220 000	1827.59	1810.88	1795.86	1782.35	1770.17	1724.78
225 000	1869.13	1852.03	1836.67	1822.85	1810.40	1763.98
230 000	1910.66	1893.19	1877.49	1863.36	1850.63	1803.18
235 000	1952.20	1934.34	1918.30	1903.87	1890.86	1842.38
240 000	1993.74	1975.50	1959.12	1944.38	1931.09	1881.58
245 000	2035.27	2016.66	1999.93	1984.89	1971.33	1920.78
250 000	2076.81	2057.81	2040.75	2025.39	2011.56	1959.98
260 000	2159.88	2140.13	2122.38	2106.41	2092.02	2038.38
270 000	2242.95	2222.44	2204.01	2187.43	2172.48	2116.78
280 000	2326.03	2304.75	2285.64	2268.44	2252.94	2195.18
290 000	2409.10	2387.06	2367.27	2349.46	2333.41	2273.58
300 000	2492.17	2469.38	2448.90	2430.47	2413.87	2351.98
400 000	3322.89	3292.50	3265.20	3240.63	3218.49	3135.97
500 000	4153.62	4115.63	4081.50	4050.79	4023.11	3919.96

9.50% INTEREST	MONTHLY PAYMENT needed to pay back a mortgage					
Term	1 Year	5 Years	10 Years	11 Years	12 Years	13 Years
AMOUNT						
30 000	2630.51	630.06	388.19	367.16	349.91	335.57
40 000	3507.34	840.07	517.59	489.55	466.55	447.43
50 000	4384.18	1050.09	646.99	611.93	583.19	559.29
55 000	4822.59	1155.10	711.69	673.13	641.51	615.21
60 000	5261.01	1260.11	776.39	734.32	699.82	671.14
65 000	5699.43	1365.12	841.08	795.51	758.14	727.07
70 000	6137.85	1470.13	905.78	856.71	816.46	783.00
75 000	6576.26	1575.14	970.48	917.90	874.78	838.93
80 000	7014.68	1680.15	1035.18	979.09	933.10	894.86
85 000	7453.10	1785.16	1099.88	1040.28	991.42	950.79
90 000	7891.52	1890.17	1164.58	1101.48	1049.74	1006.71
95 000	8329.93	1995.18	1229.28	1162.67	1108.05	1062.64
100 000	8768.35	2100.19	1293.98	1223.86	1166.37	1118.57
105 000	9206.77	2205.20	1358.67	1285.06	1224.69	1174.50
110 000	9645.19	2310.20	1423.37	1346.25	1283.01	1230.43
115 000	10083.60	2415.21	1488.07	1407.44	1341.33	1286.36
120 000	10522.02	2520.22	1552.77	1468.64	1399.65	1342.29
125 000	10960.44	2625.23	1617.47	1529.83	1457.97	1398.22
130 000	11398.86	2730.24	1682.17	1591.02	1516.29	1454.14
135 000	11837.27	2835.25	1746.87	1652.22	1574.60	1510.07
140 000	12275.69	2940.26	1811.57	1713.41	1632.92	1566.00
145 000	12714.11	3045.27	1876.26	1774.60	1691.24	1621.93
150 000	13152.53	3150.28	1940.96	1835.80	1749.56	1677.86
155 000	13590.94	3255.29	2005.66	1896.99	1807.88	1733.79
160 000	14029.36	3360.30	2070.36	1958.18	1866.20	1789.72
165 000	14467.78	3465.31	2135.06	2019.38	1924.52	1845.64
170 000	14906.20	3570.32	2199.76	2080.57	1982.83	1901.57
175 000	15344.61	3675.33	2264.46	2141.76	2041.15	1957.50
180 000	15783.03	3780.34	2329.16	2202.96	2099.47	2013.43
185 000	16221.45	3885.34	2393.85	2264.15	2157.79	2069.36
190 000	16659.87	3990.35	2458.55	2325.34	2216.11	2125.29
195 000	17098.28	4095.36	2523.25	2386.54	2274.43	2181.22
200 000	17536.70	4200.37	2587.95	2447.73	2332.75	2237.14
205 000	17975.12	4305.38	2652.65	2508.92	2391.07	2293.07
210 000	18413.54	4410.39	2717.35	2570.12	2449.38	2349.00
215 000	18851.96	4515.40	2782.05	2631.31	2507.70	2404.93
220 000	19290.37	4620.41	2846.75	2692.50	2566.02	2460.86
225 000	19728.79	4725.42	2911.45	2753.70	2624.34	2516.79
230 000	20167.21	4830.43	2976.14	2814.89	2682.66	2572.72
235 000	20605.63	4935.44	3040.84	2876.08	2740.98	2628.64
240 000	21044.04	5040.45	3105.54	2937.27	2799.30	2684.57
245 000	21482.46	5145.46	3170.24	2998.47	2857.61	2740.50
250 000	21920.88	5250.47	3234.94	3059.66	2915.93	2796.43
260 000	22797.71	5460.48	3364.34	3182.05	3032.57	2908.29
270 000	23674.55	5670.50	3493.73	3304.43	3149.21	3020.14
280 000	24551.38	5880.52	3623.13	3426.82	3265.85	3132.00
290 000	25428.22	6090.54	3752.53	3549.21	3382.48	3243.86
300 000	26305.05	6300.56	3881.93	3671.59	3499.12	3355.72
400 000	35073.40	8400.74	5175.90	4895.46	4665.49	4474.29
500 000	43841.76	10500.93	6469.88	6119.32	5831.87	5592.86

Term	14 Years	15 Years	16 Years	17 Years	18 Years	19 Years
AMOUNT						
30 000	323.51	313.27	304.50	296.93	290.37	284.65
40 000	431.35	417.69	406.00	395.91	387.16	379.54
50 000	539.18	522.11	507.49	494.89	483.96	474.42
55 000	593.10	574.32	558.24	544.38	532.35	521.86
60 000	647.02	626.53	608.99	593.87	580.75	569.30
65 000	700.94	678.75	659.74	643.36	629.14	616.75
70 000	754.86	730.96	710.49	692.85	677.54	664.19
75 000	808.78	783.17	761.24	742.34	725.93	711.63
80 000	862.69	835.38	811.99	791.82	774.33	759.07
85 000	916.61	887.59	862.74	841.31	822.72	806.51
90 000	970.53	939.80	913.49	890.80	871.12	853.96
95 000	1024.45	992.01	964.24	940.29	919.52	901.40
100 000	1078.37	1044.22	1014.99	989.78	967.91	948.84
105 000	1132.29	1096.44	1065.74	1039.27	1016.31	996.28
110 000	1186.20	1148.65	1116.49	1088.76	1064.70	1043.72
115 000	1240.12	1200.86	1167.24	1138.25	1113.10	1091.17
120 000	1294.04	1253.07	1217.99	1187.74	1161.49	1138.61
125 000	1347.96	1305.28	1268.74	1237.23	1209.89	1186.05
130 000	1401.88	1357.49	1319.49	1286.71	1258.28	1233.49
135 000	1455.80	1409.70	1370.24	1336.20	1306.68	1280.93
140 000	1509.72	1461.91	1420.99	1385.69	1355.08	1328.38
145 000	1563.63	1514.13	1471.73	1435.18	1403.47	1375.82
150 000	1617.55	1566.34	1522.48	1484.67	1451.87	1423.26
155 000	1671.47	1618.55	1573.23	1534.16	1500.26	1470.70
160 000	1725.39	1670.76	1623.98	1583.65	1548.66	1518.14
165 000	1779.31	1722.97	1674.73	1633.14	1597.05	1565.59
170 000	1833.23	1775.18	1725.48	1682.63	1645.45	1613.03
175 000	1887.14	1827.39	1776.23	1732.12	1693.85	1660.47
180 000	1941.06	1879.60	1826.98	1781.61	1742.24	1707.91
185 000	1994.98	1931.82	1877.73	1831.09	1790.64	1755.35
190 000	2048.90	1984.03	1928.48	1880.58	1839.03	1802.80
195 000	2102.82	2036.24	1979.23	1930.07	1887.43	1850.24
200 000	2156.74	2088.45	2029.98	1979.56	1935.82	1897.68
205 000	2210.65	2140.66	2080.73	2029.05	1984.22	1945.12
210 000	2264.57	2192.87	2131.48	2078.54	2032.61	1992.56
215 000	2318.49	2245.08	2182.23	2128.03	2081.01	2040.01
220 000	2372.41	2297.29	2232.98	2177.52	2129.41	2087.45
225 000	2426.33	2349.51	2283.73	2227.01	2177.80	2134.89
230 000	2480.25	2401.72	2334.48	2276.50	2226.20	2182.33
235 000	2534.16	2453.93	2385.23	2325.98	2274.59	2229.77
240 000	2588.08	2506.14	2435.97	2375.47	2322.99	2277.22
245 000	2642.00	2558.35	2486.72	2424.96	2371.38	2324.66
250 000	2695.92	2610.56	2537.47	2474.45	2419.78	2372.10
260 000	2803.76	2714.98	2638.97	2573.43	2516.57	2466.98
270 000	2911.59	2819.41	2740.47	2672.41	2613.36	2561.87
280 000	3019.43	2923.83	2841.97	2771.39	2710.15	2656.75
290 000	3127.27	3028.25	2943.47	2870.36	2806.94	2751.64
300 000	3235.10	3132.67	3044.97	2969.34	2903.73	2846.52
400 000	4313.47	4176.90	4059.96	3959.12	3871.65	3795.36
500 000	5391.84	5221.12	5074.95	4948.90	4839.56	4744.20

	9.50% INTEREST	MONTHLY PAYMENT

MONTHLY PAYMENT
needed to pay back a mortgage

Term	20 Years	21 Years	22 Years	23 Years	24 Years	25 Years
AMOUNT						
30 000	279.64	275.23	271.34	267.89	264.83	262.11
40 000	372.85	366.97	361.78	357.19	353.11	349.48
50 000	466.07	458.72	452.23	446.49	441.39	436.85
55 000	512.67	504.59	497.45	491.14	485.53	480.53
60 000	559.28	550.46	542.68	535.78	529.66	524.22
65 000	605.89	596.33	587.90	580.43	573.80	567.90
70 000	652.49	642.20	633.12	625.08	617.94	611.59
75 000	699.10	688.08	678.35	669.73	662.08	655.27
80 000	745.70	733.95	723.57	714.38	706.22	698.96
85 000	792.31	779.82	768.79	759.03	750.36	742.64
90 000	838.92	825.69	814.02	803.68	794.50	786.33
95 000	885.52	871.56	859.24	848.33	838.64	830.01
100 000	932.13	917.43	904.46	892.97	882.77	873.70
105 000	978.74	963.31	949.68	937.62	926.91	917.38
110 000	1025.34	1009.18	994.91	982.27	971.05	961.07
115 000	1071.95	1055.05	1040.13	1026.92	1015.19	1004.75
120 000	1118.56	1100.92	1085.35	1071.57	1059.33	1048.44
125 000	1165.16	1146.79	1130.58	1116.22	1103.47	1092.12
130 000	1211.77	1192.66	1175.80	1160.87	1147.61	1135.81
135 000	1258.38	1238.54	1221.02	1205.52	1191.75	1179.49
140 000	1304.98	1284.41	1266.25	1250.16	1235.88	1223.18
145 000	1351.59	1330.28	1311.47	1294.81	1280.02	1266.86
150 000	1398.20	1376.15	1356.69	1339.46	1324.16	1310.54
155 000	1444.80	1422.02	1401.92	1384.11	1368.30	1354.23
160 000	1491.41	1467.89	1447.14	1428.76	1412.44	1397.91
165 000	1538.02	1513.77	1492.36	1473.41	1456.58	1441.60
170 000	1584.62	1559.64	1537.58	1518.06	1500.72	1485.28
175 000	1631.23	1605.51	1582.81	1562.70	1544.86	1528.97
180 000	1677.84	1651.38	1628.03	1607.35	1588.99	1572.65
185 000	1724.44	1697.25	1673.25	1652.00	1633.13	1616.34
190 000	1771.05	1743.13	1718.48	1696.65	1677.27	1660.02
195 000	1817.66	1789.00	1763.70	1741.30	1721.41	1703.71
200 000	1864.26	1834.87	1808.92	1785.95	1765.55	1747.39
205 000	1910.87	1880.74	1854.15	1830.60	1809.69	1791.08
210 000	1957.48	1926.61	1899.37	1875.25	1853.83	1834.76
215 000	2004.08	1972.48	1944.59	1919.89	1897.97	1878.45
220 000	2050.69	2018.36	1989.81	1964.54	1942.10	1922.13
225 000	2097.30	2064.23	2035.04	2009.19	1986.24	1965.82
230 000	2143.90	2110.10	2080.26	2053.84	2030.38	2009.50
235 000	2190.51	2155.97	2125.48	2098.49	2074.52	2053.19
240 000	2237.11	2201.84	2170.71	2143.14	2118.66	2096.87
245 000	2283.72	2247.71	2215.93	2187.79	2162.80	2140.56
250 000	2330.33	2293.59	2261.15	2232.44	2206.94	2184.24
260 000	2423.54	2385.33	2351.60	2321.73	2295.21	2271.61
270 000	2516.75	2477.07	2442.05	2411.03	2383.49	2358.98
280 000	2609.97	2568.82	2532.49	2500.33	2471.77	2446.35
290 000	2703.18	2660.56	2622.94	2589.63	2560.05	2533.72
300 000	2796.39	2752.30	2713.38	2678.92	2648.32	2621.09
400 000	3728.52	3669.74	3617.85	3571.90	3531.10	3494.79
500 000	4660.66	4587.17	4522.31	4464.87	4413.87	4368.48

Term	26 Years	27 Years	28 Years	29 Years	30 Years	35 Years
AMOUNT						
30 000	259.68	257.51	255.56	253.82	252.26	246.48
40 000	346.24	343.34	340.75	338.43	336.34	328.64
50 000	432.80	429.18	425.94	423.04	420.43	410.81
55 000	476.08	472.10	468.53	465.34	462.47	451.89
60 000	519.36	515.02	511.13	507.64	504.51	492.97
65 000	562.64	557.93	553.72	549.95	546.56	534.05
70 000	605.92	600.85	596.32	592.25	588.60	575.13
75 000	649.20	643.77	638.91	634.55	630.64	616.21
80 000	692.48	686.69	681.51	676.86	672.68	657.29
85 000	735.76	729.61	724.10	719.16	714.73	698.37
90 000	779.04	772.53	766.69	761.46	756.77	739.45
95 000	822.32	815.44	809.29	803.77	798.81	780.53
100 000	865.60	858.36	851.88	846.07	840.85	821.61
105 000	908.88	901.28	894.48	888.38	882.90	862.69
110 000	952.16	944.20	937.07	930.68	924.94	903.77
115 000	995.44	987.12	979.66	972.98	966.98	944.85
120 000	1038.72	1030.03	1022.26	1015.29	1009.03	985.93
125 000	1082.00	1072.95	1064.85	1057.59	1051.07	1027.01
130 000	1125.28	1115.87	1107.45	1099.89	1093.11	1068.10
135 000	1168.56	1158.79	1150.04	1142.20	1135.15	1109.18
140 000	1211.84	1201.71	1192.63	1184.50	1177.20	1150.26
145 000	1255.12	1244.62	1235.23	1226.80	1219.24	1191.34
150 000	1298.40	1287.54	1277.82	1269.11	1261.28	1232.42
155 000	1341.68	1330.46	1320.42	1311.41	1303.32	1273.50
160 000	1384.96	1373.38	1363.01	1353.71	1345.37	1314.58
165 000	1428.24	1416.30	1405.60	1396.02	1387.41	1355.66
170 000	1471.52	1459.21	1448.20	1438.32	1429.45	1396.74
175 000	1514.80	1502.13	1490.79	1480.63	1471.49	1437.82
180 000	1558.08	1545.05	1533.39	1522.93	1513.54	1478.90
185 000	1601.36	1587.97	1575.98	1565.23	1555.58	1519.98
190 000	1644.64	1630.89	1618.58	1607.54	1597.62	1561.06
195 000	1687.92	1673.80	1661.17	1649.84	1639.67	1602.14
200 000	1731.20	1716.72	1703.76	1692.14	1681.71	1643.22
205 000	1774.48	1759.64	1746.36	1734.45	1723.75	1684.30
210 000	1817.76	1802.56	1788.95	1776.75	1765.79	1725.38
215 000	1861.04	1845.48	1831.55	1819.05	1807.84	1766.46
220 000	1904.32	1888.39	1874.14	1861.36	1849.88	1807.55
225 000	1947.60	1931.31	1916.73	1903.66	1891.92	1848.63
230 000	1990.88	1974.23	1959.33	1945.96	1933.96	1889.71
235 000	2034.16	2017.15	2001.92	1988.27	1976.01	1930.79
240 000	2077.44	2060.07	2044.52	2030.57	2018.05	1971.87
245 000	2120.72	2102.99	2087.11	2072.88	2060.09	2012.95
250 000	2164.00	2145.90	2129.70	2115.18	2102.14	2054.03
260 000	2250.56	2231.74	2214.89	2199.79	2186.22	2136.19
270 000	2337.12	2317.58	2300.08	2284.39	2270.31	2218.35
280 000	2423.68	2403.41	2385.27	2369.00	2354.39	2300.51
290 000	2510.24	2489.25	2470.46	2453.61	2438.48	2382.67
300 000	2596.80	2575.08	2555.65	2538.21	2522.56	2464.83
400 000	3462.40	3433.45	3407.53	3384.29	3363.42	3286.45
500 000	4327.99	4291.81	4259.41	4230.36	4204.27	4108.06

10.00% INTEREST	**MONTHLY PAYMENT** needed to pay back a mortgage				
Term	**1** Year	**5** Years	**10** Years	**11** Years	**12** Years	**13** Years
AMOUNT						
30 000	2637.48	637.41	396.45	375.60	358.52	344.35
40 000	3516.64	849.88	528.60	500.80	478.03	459.14
50 000	4395.79	1062.35	660.75	625.99	597.54	573.92
55 000	4835.37	1168.59	726.83	688.59	657.29	631.32
60 000	5274.95	1274.82	792.90	751.19	717.05	688.71
65 000	5714.53	1381.06	858.98	813.79	776.80	746.10
70 000	6154.11	1487.29	925.06	876.39	836.55	803.49
75 000	6593.69	1593.53	991.13	938.99	896.31	860.89
80 000	7033.27	1699.76	1057.21	1001.59	956.06	918.28
85 000	7472.85	1806.00	1123.28	1064.19	1015.82	975.67
90 000	7912.43	1912.23	1189.36	1126.79	1075.57	1033.06
95 000	8352.01	2018.47	1255.43	1189.39	1135.32	1090.46
100 000	8791.59	2124.70	1321.51	1251.99	1195.08	1147.85
105 000	9231.17	2230.94	1387.58	1314.59	1254.83	1205.24
110 000	9670.75	2337.17	1453.66	1377.19	1314.59	1262.63
115 000	10110.33	2443.41	1519.73	1439.79	1374.34	1320.03
120 000	10549.91	2549.65	1585.81	1502.39	1434.09	1377.42
125 000	10989.49	2655.88	1651.88	1564.98	1493.85	1434.81
130 000	11429.07	2762.12	1717.96	1627.58	1553.60	1492.20
135 000	11868.64	2868.35	1784.03	1690.18	1613.36	1549.59
140 000	12308.22	2974.59	1850.11	1752.78	1673.11	1606.99
145 000	12747.80	3080.82	1916.19	1815.38	1732.86	1664.38
150 000	13187.38	3187.06	1982.26	1877.98	1792.62	1721.77
155 000	13626.96	3293.29	2048.34	1940.58	1852.37	1779.16
160 000	14066.54	3399.53	2114.41	2003.18	1912.13	1836.56
165 000	14506.12	3505.76	2180.49	2065.78	1971.88	1893.95
170 000	14945.70	3612.00	2246.56	2128.38	2031.63	1951.34
175 000	15385.28	3718.23	2312.64	2190.98	2091.39	2008.73
180 000	15824.86	3824.47	2378.71	2253.58	2151.14	2066.13
185 000	16264.44	3930.70	2444.79	2316.18	2210.89	2123.52
190 000	16704.02	4036.94	2510.86	2378.78	2270.65	2180.91
195 000	17143.60	4143.17	2576.94	2441.38	2330.40	2238.30
200 000	17583.18	4249.41	2643.01	2503.98	2390.16	2295.70
205 000	18022.76	4355.64	2709.09	2566.57	2449.91	2353.09
210 000	18462.34	4461.88	2775.17	2629.17	2509.66	2410.48
215 000	18901.92	4568.11	2841.24	2691.77	2569.42	2467.87
220 000	19341.50	4674.35	2907.32	2754.37	2629.17	2525.27
225 000	19781.07	4780.59	2973.39	2816.97	2688.93	2582.66
230 000	20220.65	4886.82	3039.47	2879.57	2748.68	2640.05
235 000	20660.23	4993.06	3105.54	2942.17	2808.43	2697.44
240 000	21099.81	5099.29	3171.62	3004.77	2868.19	2754.84
245 000	21539.39	5205.53	3237.69	3067.37	2927.94	2812.23
250 000	21978.97	5311.76	3303.77	3129.97	2987.70	2869.62
260 000	22858.13	5524.23	3435.92	3255.17	3107.20	2984.41
270 000	23737.29	5736.70	3568.07	3380.37	3226.71	3099.19
280 000	24616.45	5949.17	3700.22	3505.57	3346.22	3213.97
290 000	25495.61	6161.64	3832.37	3630.76	3465.73	3328.76
300 000	26374.77	6374.11	3964.52	3755.96	3585.23	3443.54
400 000	35166.35	8498.82	5286.03	5007.95	4780.31	4591.39
500 000	43957.94	10623.52	6607.54	6259.94	5975.39	5739.24

Term	14 Years	15 Years	16 Years	17 Years	18 Years	19 Years
AMOUNT						
30 000	332.46	322.38	313.77	306.36	299.95	294.38
40 000	443.28	429.84	418.36	408.48	399.94	392.50
50 000	554.10	537.30	522.95	510.61	499.92	490.63
55 000	609.51	591.03	575.25	561.67	549.91	539.69
60 000	664.92	644.76	627.54	612.73	599.91	588.76
65 000	720.33	698.49	679.84	663.79	649.90	637.82
70 000	775.74	752.22	732.13	714.85	699.89	686.88
75 000	831.15	805.95	784.43	765.91	749.88	735.94
80 000	886.56	859.68	836.72	816.97	799.87	785.01
85 000	941.97	913.41	889.02	868.03	849.87	834.07
90 000	997.38	967.14	941.31	919.09	899.86	883.13
95 000	1052.79	1020.87	993.61	970.15	949.85	932.20
100 000	1108.20	1074.61	1045.90	1021.21	999.84	981.26
105 000	1163.61	1128.34	1098.20	1072.27	1049.84	1030.32
110 000	1219.02	1182.07	1150.49	1123.33	1099.83	1079.38
115 000	1274.43	1235.80	1202.79	1174.39	1149.82	1128.45
120 000	1329.84	1289.53	1255.08	1225.45	1199.81	1177.51
125 000	1385.25	1343.26	1307.38	1276.51	1249.80	1226.57
130 000	1440.66	1396.99	1359.67	1327.57	1299.80	1275.64
135 000	1496.07	1450.72	1411.97	1378.63	1349.79	1324.70
140 000	1551.48	1504.45	1464.26	1429.69	1399.78	1373.76
145 000	1606.89	1558.18	1516.56	1480.76	1449.77	1422.83
150 000	1662.30	1611.91	1568.85	1531.82	1499.77	1471.89
155 000	1717.71	1665.64	1621.15	1582.88	1549.76	1520.95
160 000	1773.12	1719.37	1673.44	1633.94	1599.75	1570.01
165 000	1828.53	1773.10	1725.74	1685.00	1649.74	1619.08
170 000	1883.94	1826.83	1778.03	1736.06	1699.73	1668.14
175 000	1939.35	1880.56	1830.33	1787.12	1749.73	1717.20
180 000	1994.76	1934.29	1882.62	1838.18	1799.72	1766.27
185 000	2050.17	1988.02	1934.92	1889.24	1849.71	1815.33
190 000	2105.59	2041.75	1987.21	1940.30	1899.70	1864.39
195 000	2161.00	2095.48	2039.51	1991.36	1949.70	1913.45
200 000	2216.41	2149.21	2091.80	2042.42	1999.69	1962.52
205 000	2271.82	2202.94	2144.10	2093.48	2049.68	2011.58
210 000	2327.23	2256.67	2196.39	2144.54	2099.67	2060.64
215 000	2382.64	2310.40	2248.69	2195.60	2149.66	2109.71
220 000	2438.05	2364.13	2300.98	2246.66	2199.66	2158.77
225 000	2493.46	2417.86	2353.28	2297.72	2249.65	2207.83
230 000	2548.87	2471.59	2405.57	2348.78	2299.64	2256.90
235 000	2604.28	2525.32	2457.87	2399.84	2349.63	2305.96
240 000	2659.69	2579.05	2510.16	2450.91	2399.62	2355.02
245 000	2715.10	2632.78	2562.46	2501.97	2449.62	2404.08
250 000	2770.51	2686.51	2614.75	2553.03	2499.61	2453.15
260 000	2881.33	2793.97	2719.35	2655.15	2599.59	2551.27
270 000	2992.15	2901.43	2823.94	2757.27	2699.58	2649.40
280 000	3102.97	3008.89	2928.53	2859.39	2799.56	2747.52
290 000	3213.79	3116.35	3033.12	2961.51	2899.55	2845.65
300 000	3324.61	3223.82	3137.71	3063.63	2999.53	2943.78
400 000	4432.81	4298.42	4183.61	4084.84	3999.37	3925.04
500 000	5541.01	5373.03	5229.51	5106.05	4999.22	4906.29

10.00% INTEREST	**MONTHLY PAYMENT** needed to pay back a mortgage				
Term	**20** Years	**21** Years	**22** Years	**23** Years	**24** Years	**25** Years
AMOUNT						
30 000	289.51	285.23	281.47	278.15	275.22	272.61
40 000	386.01	380.31	375.30	370.87	366.96	363.48
50 000	482.51	475.39	469.12	463.59	458.69	454.35
55 000	530.76	522.93	516.04	509.95	504.56	499.79
60 000	579.01	570.47	562.95	556.31	550.43	545.22
65 000	627.26	618.01	609.86	602.67	596.30	590.66
70 000	675.52	665.55	656.77	649.03	642.17	636.09
75 000	723.77	713.09	703.68	695.39	688.04	681.53
80 000	772.02	760.62	750.60	741.75	733.91	726.96
85 000	820.27	808.16	797.51	788.10	779.78	772.40
90 000	868.52	855.70	844.42	834.46	825.65	817.83
95 000	916.77	903.24	891.33	880.82	871.52	863.27
100 000	965.02	950.78	938.25	927.18	917.39	908.70
105 000	1013.27	998.32	985.16	973.54	963.26	954.14
110 000	1061.52	1045.86	1032.07	1019.90	1009.13	999.57
115 000	1109.77	1093.40	1078.98	1066.26	1055.00	1045.01
120 000	1158.03	1140.94	1125.90	1112.62	1100.87	1090.44
125 000	1206.28	1188.48	1172.81	1158.98	1146.74	1135.88
130 000	1254.53	1236.01	1219.72	1205.34	1192.61	1181.31
135 000	1302.78	1283.55	1266.63	1251.70	1238.47	1226.75
140 000	1351.03	1331.09	1313.54	1298.05	1284.34	1272.18
145 000	1399.28	1378.63	1360.46	1344.41	1330.21	1317.62
150 000	1447.53	1426.17	1407.37	1390.77	1376.08	1363.05
155 000	1495.78	1473.71	1454.28	1437.13	1421.95	1408.49
160 000	1544.03	1521.25	1501.19	1483.49	1467.82	1453.92
165 000	1592.29	1568.79	1548.11	1529.85	1513.69	1499.36
170 000	1640.54	1616.33	1595.02	1576.21	1559.56	1544.79
175 000	1688.79	1663.87	1641.93	1622.57	1605.43	1590.23
180 000	1737.04	1711.40	1688.84	1668.93	1651.30	1635.66
185 000	1785.29	1758.94	1735.76	1715.29	1697.17	1681.10
190 000	1833.54	1806.48	1782.67	1761.65	1743.04	1726.53
195 000	1881.79	1854.02	1829.58	1808.00	1788.91	1771.97
200 000	1930.04	1901.56	1876.49	1854.36	1834.78	1817.40
205 000	1978.29	1949.10	1923.40	1900.72	1880.65	1862.84
210 000	2026.55	1996.64	1970.32	1947.08	1926.52	1908.27
215 000	2074.80	2044.18	2017.23	1993.44	1972.39	1953.71
220 000	2123.05	2091.72	2064.14	2039.80	2018.26	1999.14
225 000	2171.30	2139.26	2111.05	2086.16	2064.12	2044.58
230 000	2219.55	2186.79	2157.97	2132.52	2109.99	2090.01
235 000	2267.80	2234.33	2204.88	2178.88	2155.86	2135.45
240 000	2316.05	2281.87	2251.79	2225.24	2201.73	2180.88
245 000	2364.30	2329.41	2298.70	2271.60	2247.60	2226.32
250 000	2412.55	2376.95	2345.61	2317.95	2293.47	2271.75
260 000	2509.06	2472.03	2439.44	2410.67	2385.21	2362.62
270 000	2605.56	2567.11	2533.26	2503.39	2476.95	2453.49
280 000	2702.06	2662.18	2627.09	2596.11	2568.69	2544.36
290 000	2798.56	2757.26	2720.91	2688.83	2660.43	2635.23
300 000	2895.06	2852.34	2814.74	2781.54	2752.17	2726.10
400 000	3860.09	3803.12	3752.98	3708.73	3669.55	3634.80
500 000	4825.11	4753.90	4691.23	4635.91	4586.94	4543.50

| | | needed to pay back a mortgage | | | INTEREST |
Term	26 Years	27 Years	28 Years	29 Years	30 Years	35 Years
AMOUNT						
30 000	270.29	268.23	266.39	264.74	263.27	257.90
40 000	360.39	357.64	355.18	352.99	351.03	343.87
50 000	450.49	447.05	443.98	441.24	438.79	429.84
55 000	495.54	491.75	488.38	485.36	482.66	472.82
60 000	540.59	536.46	532.78	529.49	526.54	515.80
65 000	585.64	581.16	577.17	573.61	570.42	558.79
70 000	630.68	625.87	621.57	617.73	614.30	601.77
75 000	675.73	670.57	665.97	661.86	658.18	644.75
80 000	720.78	715.28	710.37	705.98	702.06	687.74
85 000	765.83	759.98	754.77	750.11	745.94	730.72
90 000	810.88	804.69	799.16	794.23	789.81	773.71
95 000	855.93	849.39	843.56	838.35	833.69	816.69
100 000	900.98	894.10	887.96	882.48	877.57	859.67
105 000	946.03	938.80	932.36	926.60	921.45	902.66
110 000	991.07	983.51	976.76	970.72	965.33	945.64
115 000	1036.12	1028.21	1021.15	1014.85	1009.21	988.62
120 000	1081.17	1072.92	1065.55	1058.97	1053.09	1031.61
125 000	1126.22	1117.62	1109.95	1103.10	1096.96	1074.59
130 000	1171.27	1162.33	1154.35	1147.22	1140.84	1117.57
135 000	1216.32	1207.03	1198.75	1191.34	1184.72	1160.56
140 000	1261.37	1251.74	1243.14	1235.47	1228.60	1203.54
145 000	1306.42	1296.44	1287.54	1279.59	1272.48	1246.53
150 000	1351.47	1341.15	1331.94	1323.72	1316.36	1289.51
155 000	1396.51	1385.85	1376.34	1367.84	1360.24	1332.49
160 000	1441.56	1430.56	1420.74	1411.96	1404.11	1375.48
165 000	1486.61	1475.26	1465.13	1456.09	1447.99	1418.46
170 000	1531.66	1519.97	1509.53	1500.21	1491.87	1461.44
175 000	1576.71	1564.67	1553.93	1544.33	1535.75	1504.43
180 000	1621.76	1609.38	1598.33	1588.46	1579.63	1547.41
185 000	1666.81	1654.08	1642.73	1632.58	1623.51	1590.39
190 000	1711.86	1698.79	1687.12	1676.71	1667.39	1633.38
195 000	1756.91	1743.49	1731.52	1720.83	1711.26	1676.36
200 000	1801.95	1788.20	1775.92	1764.95	1755.14	1719.34
205 000	1847.00	1832.90	1820.32	1809.08	1799.02	1762.33
210 000	1892.05	1877.61	1864.72	1853.20	1842.90	1805.31
215 000	1937.10	1922.31	1909.11	1897.33	1886.78	1848.30
220 000	1982.15	1967.01	1953.51	1941.45	1930.66	1891.28
225 000	2027.20	2011.72	1997.91	1985.57	1974.54	1934.26
230 000	2072.25	2056.42	2042.31	2029.70	2018.41	1977.25
235 000	2117.30	2101.13	2086.71	2073.82	2062.29	2020.23
240 000	2162.34	2145.83	2131.10	2117.94	2106.17	2063.21
245 000	2207.39	2190.54	2175.50	2162.07	2150.05	2106.20
250 000	2252.44	2235.24	2219.90	2206.19	2193.93	2149.18
260 000	2342.54	2324.65	2308.70	2294.44	2281.69	2235.15
270 000	2432.64	2414.06	2397.49	2382.69	2369.44	2321.12
280 000	2522.74	2503.47	2486.29	2470.94	2457.20	2407.08
290 000	2612.83	2592.88	2575.09	2559.18	2544.96	2493.05
300 000	2702.93	2682.29	2663.88	2647.43	2632.71	2579.02
400 000	3603.91	3576.39	3551.84	3529.91	3510.29	3438.69
500 000	4504.88	4470.49	4439.80	4412.39	4387.86	4298.36

10.50% INTEREST

MONTHLY PAYMENT
needed to pay back a mortgage

Term	1 Year	5 Years	10 Years	11 Years	12 Years	13 Years
AMOUNT						
30 000	2644.46	644.82	404.80	384.13	367.24	353.25
40 000	3525.94	859.76	539.74	512.18	489.66	471.00
50 000	4407.43	1074.70	674.67	640.22	612.07	588.75
55 000	4848.17	1182.16	742.14	704.25	673.28	647.63
60 000	5288.92	1289.63	809.61	768.27	734.48	706.50
65 000	5729.66	1397.10	877.08	832.29	795.69	765.38
70 000	6170.40	1504.57	944.54	896.31	856.90	824.25
75 000	6611.15	1612.04	1012.01	960.33	918.11	883.13
80 000	7051.89	1719.51	1079.48	1024.36	979.31	942.00
85 000	7492.63	1826.98	1146.95	1088.38	1040.52	1000.88
90 000	7933.37	1934.45	1214.41	1152.40	1101.73	1059.75
95 000	8374.12	2041.92	1281.88	1216.42	1162.93	1118.63
100 000	8814.86	2149.39	1349.35	1280.45	1224.14	1177.50
105 000	9255.60	2256.86	1416.82	1344.47	1285.35	1236.38
110 000	9696.35	2364.33	1484.28	1408.49	1346.55	1295.25
115 000	10137.09	2471.80	1551.75	1472.51	1407.76	1354.13
120 000	10577.83	2579.27	1619.22	1536.54	1468.97	1413.00
125 000	11018.58	2686.74	1686.69	1600.56	1530.18	1471.88
130 000	11459.32	2794.21	1754.15	1664.58	1591.38	1530.75
135 000	11900.06	2901.68	1821.62	1728.60	1652.59	1589.63
140 000	12340.80	3009.15	1889.09	1792.62	1713.80	1648.50
145 000	12781.55	3116.62	1956.56	1856.65	1775.00	1707.38
150 000	13222.29	3224.09	2024.02	1920.67	1836.21	1766.25
155 000	13663.03	3331.55	2091.49	1984.69	1897.42	1825.13
160 000	14103.78	3439.02	2158.96	2048.71	1958.63	1884.00
165 000	14544.52	3546.49	2226.43	2112.74	2019.83	1942.88
170 000	14985.26	3653.96	2293.89	2176.76	2081.04	2001.75
175 000	15426.01	3761.43	2361.36	2240.78	2142.25	2060.63
180 000	15866.75	3868.90	2428.83	2304.80	2203.45	2119.50
185 000	16307.49	3976.37	2496.30	2368.82	2264.66	2178.38
190 000	16748.23	4083.84	2563.76	2432.85	2325.87	2237.25
195 000	17188.98	4191.31	2631.23	2496.87	2387.07	2296.13
200 000	17629.72	4298.78	2698.70	2560.89	2448.28	2355.00
205 000	18070.46	4406.25	2766.17	2624.91	2509.49	2413.88
210 000	18511.21	4513.72	2833.63	2688.94	2570.70	2472.75
215 000	18951.95	4621.19	2901.10	2752.96	2631.90	2531.63
220 000	19392.69	4728.66	2968.57	2816.98	2693.11	2590.50
225 000	19833.44	4836.13	3036.04	2881.00	2754.32	2649.38
230 000	20274.18	4943.60	3103.50	2945.03	2815.52	2708.25
235 000	20714.92	5051.07	3170.97	3009.05	2876.73	2767.13
240 000	21155.66	5158.54	3238.44	3073.07	2937.94	2826.00
245 000	21596.41	5266.01	3305.91	3137.09	2999.14	2884.88
250 000	22037.15	5373.48	3373.37	3201.11	3060.35	2943.75
260 000	22918.64	5588.41	3508.31	3329.16	3182.77	3061.51
270 000	23800.12	5803.35	3643.24	3457.20	3305.18	3179.26
280 000	24681.61	6018.29	3778.18	3585.25	3427.59	3297.01
290 000	25563.09	6233.23	3913.11	3713.29	3550.01	3414.76
300 000	26444.58	6448.17	4048.05	3841.34	3672.42	3532.51
400 000	35259.44	8597.56	5397.40	5121.78	4896.56	4710.01
500 000	44074.30	10746.95	6746.75	6402.23	6120.70	5887.51

Term	14 Years	15 Years	16 Years	17 Years	18 Years	19 Years
AMOUNT						
30 000	341.53	331.62	323.17	315.92	309.67	304.24
40 000	455.37	442.16	430.90	421.23	412.89	405.66
50 000	569.22	552.70	538.62	526.54	516.11	507.07
55 000	626.14	607.97	592.48	579.19	567.73	557.78
60 000	683.06	663.24	646.35	631.85	619.34	608.48
65 000	739.98	718.51	700.21	684.50	670.95	659.19
70 000	796.90	773.78	754.07	737.16	722.56	709.90
75 000	853.83	829.05	807.93	789.81	774.17	760.60
80 000	910.75	884.32	861.79	842.46	825.78	811.31
85 000	967.67	939.59	915.66	895.12	877.39	862.02
90 000	1024.59	994.86	969.52	947.77	929.00	912.73
95 000	1081.51	1050.13	1023.38	1000.43	980.62	963.43
100 000	1138.43	1105.40	1077.24	1053.08	1032.23	1014.14
105 000	1195.36	1160.67	1131.10	1105.74	1083.84	1064.85
110 000	1252.28	1215.94	1184.97	1158.39	1135.45	1115.55
115 000	1309.20	1271.21	1238.83	1211.04	1187.06	1166.26
120 000	1366.12	1326.48	1292.69	1263.70	1238.67	1216.97
125 000	1423.04	1381.75	1346.55	1316.35	1290.28	1267.67
130 000	1479.96	1437.02	1400.42	1369.01	1341.90	1318.38
135 000	1536.89	1492.29	1454.28	1421.66	1393.51	1369.09
140 000	1593.81	1547.56	1508.14	1474.31	1445.12	1419.79
145 000	1650.73	1602.83	1562.00	1526.97	1496.73	1470.50
150 000	1707.65	1658.10	1615.86	1579.62	1548.34	1521.21
155 000	1764.57	1713.37	1669.73	1632.28	1599.95	1571.92
160 000	1821.49	1768.64	1723.59	1684.93	1651.56	1622.62
165 000	1878.42	1823.91	1777.45	1737.58	1703.18	1673.33
170 000	1935.34	1879.18	1831.31	1790.24	1754.79	1724.04
175 000	1992.26	1934.45	1885.17	1842.89	1806.40	1774.74
180 000	2049.18	1989.72	1939.04	1895.55	1858.01	1825.45
185 000	2106.10	2044.99	1992.90	1948.20	1909.62	1876.16
190 000	2163.02	2100.26	2046.76	2000.85	1961.23	1926.86
195 000	2219.95	2155.53	2100.62	2053.51	2012.84	1977.57
200 000	2276.87	2210.80	2154.48	2106.16	2064.46	2028.28
205 000	2333.79	2266.07	2208.35	2158.82	2116.07	2078.98
210 000	2390.71	2321.34	2262.21	2211.47	2167.68	2129.69
215 000	2447.63	2376.61	2316.07	2264.12	2219.29	2180.40
220 000	2504.55	2431.88	2369.93	2316.78	2270.90	2231.11
225 000	2561.48	2487.15	2423.80	2369.43	2322.51	2281.81
230 000	2618.40	2542.42	2477.66	2422.09	2374.12	2332.52
235 000	2675.32	2597.69	2531.52	2474.74	2425.74	2383.23
240 000	2732.24	2652.96	2585.38	2527.39	2477.35	2433.93
245 000	2789.16	2708.23	2639.24	2580.05	2528.96	2484.64
250 000	2846.09	2763.50	2693.11	2632.70	2580.57	2535.35
260 000	2959.93	2874.04	2800.83	2738.01	2683.79	2636.76
270 000	3073.77	2984.58	2908.55	2843.32	2787.01	2738.18
280 000	3187.62	3095.12	3016.28	2948.63	2890.24	2839.59
290 000	3301.46	3205.66	3124.00	3053.94	2993.46	2941.00
300 000	3415.30	3316.20	3231.73	3159.24	3096.68	3042.42
400 000	4553.74	4421.60	4308.97	4212.32	4128.91	4056.56
500 000	5692.17	5526.99	5386.21	5265.41	5161.14	5070.69

29

Term	20 Years	21 Years	22 Years	23 Years	24 Years	25 Years
AMOUNT						
30 000	299.51	295.38	291.75	288.56	285.74	283.25
40 000	399.35	393.84	389.00	384.75	380.99	377.67
50 000	499.19	492.30	486.25	480.93	476.24	472.09
55 000	549.11	541.53	534.88	529.03	523.86	519.30
60 000	599.03	590.76	583.50	577.12	571.49	566.51
65 000	648.95	639.99	632.13	625.21	619.11	613.72
70 000	698.87	689.22	680.75	673.31	666.74	660.93
75 000	748.78	738.45	729.38	721.40	714.36	708.14
80 000	798.70	787.68	778.01	769.49	761.98	755.35
85 000	848.62	836.91	826.63	817.59	809.61	802.55
90 000	898.54	886.14	875.26	865.68	857.23	849.76
95 000	948.46	935.37	923.88	913.77	904.86	896.97
100 000	998.38	984.60	972.51	961.87	952.48	944.18
105 000	1048.30	1033.83	1021.13	1009.96	1000.10	991.39
110 000	1098.22	1083.06	1069.76	1058.05	1047.73	1038.60
115 000	1148.14	1132.29	1118.38	1106.15	1095.35	1085.81
120 000	1198.06	1181.52	1167.01	1154.24	1142.98	1133.02
125 000	1247.97	1230.75	1215.63	1202.33	1190.60	1180.23
130 000	1297.89	1279.98	1264.26	1250.43	1238.23	1227.44
135 000	1347.81	1329.21	1312.88	1298.52	1285.85	1274.65
140 000	1397.73	1378.44	1361.51	1346.61	1333.47	1321.85
145 000	1447.65	1427.67	1410.14	1394.71	1381.10	1369.06
150 000	1497.57	1476.90	1458.76	1442.80	1428.72	1416.27
155 000	1547.49	1526.13	1507.39	1490.89	1476.35	1463.48
160 000	1597.41	1575.36	1556.01	1538.99	1523.97	1510.69
165 000	1647.33	1624.59	1604.64	1587.08	1571.59	1557.90
170 000	1697.25	1673.82	1653.26	1635.17	1619.22	1605.11
175 000	1747.16	1723.05	1701.89	1683.27	1666.84	1652.32
180 000	1797.08	1772.28	1750.51	1731.36	1714.47	1699.53
185 000	1847.00	1821.51	1799.14	1779.45	1762.09	1746.74
190 000	1896.92	1870.74	1847.76	1827.55	1809.71	1793.95
195 000	1946.84	1919.97	1896.39	1875.64	1857.34	1841.15
200 000	1996.76	1969.20	1945.01	1923.73	1904.96	1888.36
205 000	2046.68	2018.43	1993.64	1971.83	1952.59	1935.57
210 000	2096.60	2067.66	2042.26	2019.92	2000.21	1982.78
215 000	2146.52	2116.89	2090.89	2068.01	2047.83	2029.99
220 000	2196.44	2166.12	2139.52	2116.11	2095.46	2077.20
225 000	2246.35	2215.35	2188.14	2164.20	2143.08	2124.41
230 000	2296.27	2264.58	2236.77	2212.29	2190.71	2171.62
235 000	2346.19	2313.81	2285.39	2260.39	2238.33	2218.83
240 000	2396.11	2363.04	2334.02	2308.48	2285.95	2266.04
245 000	2446.03	2412.27	2382.64	2356.57	2333.58	2313.25
250 000	2495.95	2461.50	2431.27	2404.67	2381.20	2360.45
260 000	2595.79	2559.96	2528.52	2500.85	2476.45	2454.87
270 000	2695.63	2658.42	2625.77	2597.04	2571.70	2549.29
280 000	2795.46	2756.88	2723.02	2693.23	2666.95	2643.71
290 000	2895.30	2855.34	2820.27	2789.41	2762.19	2738.13
300 000	2995.14	2953.80	2917.52	2885.60	2857.44	2832.55
400 000	3993.52	3938.39	3890.03	3847.47	3809.92	3776.73
500 000	4991.90	4922.99	4862.54	4809.34	4762.40	4720.91

Term	26 Years	27 Years	28 Years	29 Years	30 Years	35 Years
AMOUNT						
30 000	281.05	279.09	277.35	275.80	274.42	269.44
40 000	374.73	372.12	369.80	367.74	365.90	359.25
50 000	468.41	465.15	462.25	459.67	457.37	449.07
55 000	515.26	511.67	508.48	505.64	503.11	493.97
60 000	562.10	558.18	554.70	551.60	548.84	538.88
65 000	608.94	604.70	600.93	597.57	594.58	583.79
70 000	655.78	651.21	647.15	643.54	640.32	628.69
75 000	702.62	697.73	693.38	689.51	686.05	673.60
80 000	749.46	744.24	739.60	735.47	731.79	718.51
85 000	796.30	790.76	785.83	781.44	777.53	763.41
90 000	843.15	837.27	832.05	827.41	823.27	808.32
95 000	889.99	883.79	878.28	873.37	869.00	853.23
100 000	936.83	930.30	924.50	919.34	914.74	898.13
105 000	983.67	976.82	970.73	965.31	960.48	943.04
110 000	1030.51	1023.33	1016.95	1011.27	1006.21	987.95
115 000	1077.35	1069.85	1063.18	1057.24	1051.95	1032.85
120 000	1124.20	1116.36	1109.40	1103.21	1097.69	1077.76
125 000	1171.04	1162.88	1155.63	1149.18	1143.42	1122.67
130 000	1217.88	1209.40	1201.85	1195.14	1189.16	1167.57
135 000	1264.72	1255.91	1248.08	1241.11	1234.90	1212.48
140 000	1311.56	1302.43	1294.31	1287.08	1280.64	1257.39
145 000	1358.40	1348.94	1340.53	1333.04	1326.37	1302.29
150 000	1405.24	1395.46	1386.76	1379.01	1372.11	1347.20
155 000	1452.09	1441.97	1432.98	1424.98	1417.85	1392.11
160 000	1498.93	1488.49	1479.21	1470.95	1463.58	1437.01
165 000	1545.77	1535.00	1525.43	1516.91	1509.32	1481.92
170 000	1592.61	1581.52	1571.66	1562.88	1555.06	1526.83
175 000	1639.45	1628.03	1617.88	1608.85	1600.79	1571.73
180 000	1686.29	1674.55	1664.11	1654.81	1646.53	1616.64
185 000	1733.13	1721.06	1710.33	1700.78	1692.27	1661.55
190 000	1779.98	1767.58	1756.56	1746.75	1738.00	1706.45
195 000	1826.82	1814.09	1802.78	1792.71	1783.74	1751.36
200 000	1873.66	1860.61	1849.01	1838.68	1829.48	1796.27
205 000	1920.50	1907.12	1895.23	1884.65	1875.22	1841.17
210 000	1967.34	1953.64	1941.46	1930.62	1920.95	1886.08
215 000	2014.18	2000.15	1987.68	1976.58	1966.69	1930.99
220 000	2061.02	2046.67	2033.91	2022.55	2012.43	1975.89
225 000	2107.87	2093.18	2080.13	2068.52	2058.16	2020.80
230 000	2154.71	2139.70	2126.36	2114.48	2103.90	2065.71
235 000	2201.55	2186.21	2172.58	2160.45	2149.64	2110.61
240 000	2248.39	2232.73	2218.81	2206.42	2195.37	2155.52
245 000	2295.23	2279.24	2265.03	2252.38	2241.11	2200.43
250 000	2342.07	2325.76	2311.26	2298.35	2286.85	2245.34
260 000	2435.76	2418.79	2403.71	2390.29	2378.32	2335.15
270 000	2529.44	2511.82	2496.16	2482.22	2469.80	2424.96
280 000	2623.12	2604.85	2588.61	2574.15	2561.27	2514.78
290 000	2716.80	2697.88	2681.06	2666.09	2652.74	2604.59
300 000	2810.49	2790.91	2773.51	2758.02	2744.22	2694.40
400 000	3747.32	3721.22	3698.01	3677.36	3658.96	3592.54
500 000	4684.15	4651.52	4622.52	4596.70	4573.70	4490.67

11.00% INTEREST	MONTHLY PAYMENT needed to pay back a mortgage				
Term	1 Year	5 Years	10 Years	11 Years	12 Years	13 Years

AMOUNT	1 Year	5 Years	10 Years	11 Years	12 Years	13 Years
30 000	2651.45	652.27	413.25	392.77	376.07	362.26
40 000	3535.27	869.70	551.00	523.69	501.42	483.01
50 000	4419.08	1087.12	688.75	654.62	626.78	603.76
55 000	4860.99	1195.83	757.63	720.08	689.46	664.14
60 000	5302.90	1304.55	826.50	785.54	752.13	724.52
65 000	5744.81	1413.26	895.38	851.00	814.81	784.89
70 000	6186.72	1521.97	964.25	916.46	877.49	845.27
75 000	6628.62	1630.68	1033.13	981.93	940.17	905.65
80 000	7070.53	1739.39	1102.00	1047.39	1002.84	966.02
85 000	7512.44	1848.11	1170.88	1112.85	1065.52	1026.40
90 000	7954.35	1956.82	1239.75	1178.31	1128.20	1086.77
95 000	8396.26	2065.53	1308.63	1243.77	1190.88	1147.15
100 000	8838.17	2174.24	1377.50	1309.23	1253.56	1207.53
105 000	9280.07	2282.95	1446.38	1374.70	1316.23	1267.90
110 000	9721.98	2391.67	1515.25	1440.16	1378.91	1328.28
115 000	10163.89	2500.38	1584.13	1505.62	1441.59	1388.66
120 000	10605.80	2609.09	1653.00	1571.08	1504.27	1449.03
125 000	11047.71	2717.80	1721.88	1636.54	1566.94	1509.41
130 000	11489.62	2826.51	1790.75	1702.01	1629.62	1569.79
135 000	11931.52	2935.23	1859.63	1767.47	1692.30	1630.16
140 000	12373.43	3043.94	1928.50	1832.93	1754.98	1690.54
145 000	12815.34	3152.65	1997.38	1898.39	1817.66	1750.91
150 000	13257.25	3261.36	2066.25	1963.85	1880.33	1811.29
155 000	13699.16	3370.08	2135.13	2029.31	1943.01	1871.67
160 000	14141.07	3478.79	2204.00	2094.78	2005.69	1932.04
165 000	14582.97	3587.50	2272.88	2160.24	2068.37	1992.42
170 000	15024.88	3696.21	2341.75	2225.70	2131.04	2052.80
175 000	15466.79	3804.92	2410.63	2291.16	2193.72	2113.17
180 000	15908.70	3913.64	2479.50	2356.62	2256.40	2173.55
185 000	16350.61	4022.35	2548.38	2422.08	2319.08	2233.93
190 000	16792.52	4131.06	2617.25	2487.55	2381.75	2294.30
195 000	17234.42	4239.77	2686.13	2553.01	2444.43	2354.68
200 000	17676.33	4348.48	2755.00	2618.47	2507.11	2415.05
205 000	18118.24	4457.20	2823.88	2683.93	2569.79	2475.43
210 000	18560.15	4565.91	2892.75	2749.39	2632.47	2535.81
215 000	19002.06	4674.62	2961.63	2814.86	2695.14	2596.18
220 000	19443.96	4783.33	3030.50	2880.32	2757.82	2656.56
225 000	19885.87	4892.05	3099.38	2945.78	2820.50	2716.94
230 000	20327.78	5000.76	3168.25	3011.24	2883.18	2777.31
235 000	20769.69	5109.47	3237.13	3076.70	2945.85	2837.69
240 000	21211.60	5218.18	3306.00	3142.16	3008.53	2898.07
245 000	21653.51	5326.89	3374.88	3207.63	3071.21	2958.44
250 000	22095.41	5435.61	3443.75	3273.09	3133.89	3018.82
260 000	22979.23	5653.03	3581.50	3404.01	3259.24	3139.57
270 000	23863.05	5870.45	3719.25	3534.93	3384.60	3260.32
280 000	24746.86	6087.88	3857.00	3665.86	3509.95	3381.08
290 000	25630.68	6305.30	3994.75	3796.78	3635.31	3501.83
300 000	26514.50	6522.73	4132.50	3927.70	3760.67	3622.58
400 000	35352.66	8696.97	5510.00	5236.94	5014.22	4830.11
500 000	44190.83	10871.21	6887.50	6546.17	6267.78	6037.64

Term	14 Years	15 Years	16 Years	17 Years	18 Years	19 Years
AMOUNT						
30 000	350.72	340.98	332.70	325.61	319.51	314.24
40 000	467.62	454.64	443.60	434.15	426.02	418.99
50 000	584.53	568.30	554.50	542.69	532.52	523.73
55 000	642.98	625.13	609.95	596.96	585.78	576.11
60 000	701.43	681.96	665.40	651.23	639.03	628.48
65 000	759.89	738.79	720.85	705.50	692.28	680.85
70 000	818.34	795.62	776.30	759.77	745.53	733.22
75 000	876.79	852.45	831.75	814.04	798.79	785.60
80 000	935.24	909.28	887.20	868.30	852.04	837.97
85 000	993.70	966.11	942.65	922.57	905.29	890.34
90 000	1052.15	1022.94	998.10	976.84	958.54	942.72
95 000	1110.60	1079.77	1053.55	1031.11	1011.80	995.09
100 000	1169.05	1136.60	1109.00	1085.38	1065.05	1047.46
105 000	1227.51	1193.43	1164.45	1139.65	1118.30	1099.84
110 000	1285.96	1250.26	1219.90	1193.92	1171.55	1152.21
115 000	1344.41	1307.09	1275.35	1248.19	1224.81	1204.58
120 000	1402.87	1363.92	1330.80	1302.46	1278.06	1256.96
125 000	1461.32	1420.75	1386.25	1356.73	1331.31	1309.33
130 000	1519.77	1477.58	1441.70	1410.99	1384.56	1361.70
135 000	1578.22	1534.41	1497.15	1465.26	1437.82	1414.08
140 000	1636.68	1591.24	1552.60	1519.53	1491.07	1466.45
145 000	1695.13	1648.07	1608.05	1573.80	1544.32	1518.82
150 000	1753.58	1704.90	1663.50	1628.07	1597.57	1571.20
155 000	1812.03	1761.73	1718.95	1682.34	1650.83	1623.57
160 000	1870.49	1818.56	1774.40	1736.61	1704.08	1675.94
165 000	1928.94	1875.38	1829.85	1790.88	1757.33	1728.32
170 000	1987.39	1932.21	1885.30	1845.15	1810.58	1780.69
175 000	2045.84	1989.04	1940.75	1899.42	1863.84	1833.06
180 000	2104.30	2045.87	1996.20	1953.69	1917.09	1885.44
185 000	2162.75	2102.70	2051.65	2007.95	1970.34	1937.81
190 000	2221.20	2159.53	2107.10	2062.22	2023.59	1990.18
195 000	2279.66	2216.36	2162.55	2116.49	2076.85	2042.55
200 000	2338.11	2273.19	2218.00	2170.76	2130.10	2094.93
205 000	2396.56	2330.02	2273.45	2225.03	2183.35	2147.30
210 000	2455.01	2386.85	2328.90	2279.30	2236.60	2199.67
215 000	2513.47	2443.68	2384.35	2333.57	2289.86	2252.05
220 000	2571.92	2500.51	2439.80	2387.84	2343.11	2304.42
225 000	2630.37	2557.34	2495.25	2442.11	2396.36	2356.79
230 000	2688.82	2614.17	2550.70	2496.38	2449.61	2409.17
235 000	2747.28	2671.00	2606.15	2550.64	2502.87	2461.54
240 000	2805.73	2727.83	2661.60	2604.91	2556.12	2513.91
245 000	2864.18	2784.66	2717.05	2659.18	2609.37	2566.29
250 000	2922.64	2841.49	2772.50	2713.45	2662.62	2618.66
260 000	3039.54	2955.15	2883.40	2821.99	2769.13	2723.41
270 000	3156.45	3068.81	2994.30	2930.53	2875.63	2828.15
280 000	3273.35	3182.47	3105.20	3039.07	2982.14	2932.90
290 000	3390.26	3296.13	3216.10	3147.60	3088.64	3037.65
300 000	3507.16	3409.79	3327.00	3256.14	3195.15	3142.39
400 000	4676.22	4546.39	4436.00	4341.52	4260.20	4189.86
500 000	5845.27	5682.98	5545.00	5426.90	5325.25	5237.32

11.00% INTEREST	MONTHLY PAYMENT needed to pay back a mortgage					
Term	20 Years	21 Years	22 Years	23 Years	24 Years	25 Years
AMOUNT						
30 000	309.66	305.66	302.17	299.10	296.41	294.03
40 000	412.88	407.55	402.89	398.80	395.21	392.05
50 000	516.09	509.44	503.61	498.50	494.01	490.06
55 000	567.70	560.38	553.97	548.35	543.41	539.06
60 000	619.31	611.32	604.33	598.20	592.82	588.07
65 000	670.92	662.27	654.70	648.06	642.22	637.07
70 000	722.53	713.21	705.06	697.91	691.62	686.08
75 000	774.14	764.15	755.42	747.76	741.02	735.08
80 000	825.75	815.10	805.78	797.61	790.42	784.09
85 000	877.36	866.04	856.14	847.46	839.82	833.10
90 000	928.97	916.98	906.50	897.31	889.22	882.10
95 000	980.58	967.93	956.86	947.16	938.63	931.11
100 000	1032.19	1018.87	1007.22	997.01	988.03	980.11
105 000	1083.80	1069.81	1057.58	1046.86	1037.43	1029.12
110 000	1135.41	1120.76	1107.95	1096.71	1086.83	1078.12
115 000	1187.02	1171.70	1158.31	1146.56	1136.23	1127.13
120 000	1238.63	1222.65	1208.67	1196.41	1185.63	1176.14
125 000	1290.24	1273.59	1259.03	1246.26	1235.03	1225.14
130 000	1341.84	1324.53	1309.39	1296.11	1284.43	1274.15
135 000	1393.45	1375.48	1359.75	1345.96	1333.84	1323.15
140 000	1445.06	1426.42	1410.11	1395.81	1383.24	1372.16
145 000	1496.67	1477.36	1460.47	1445.66	1432.64	1421.16
150 000	1548.28	1528.31	1510.84	1495.51	1482.04	1470.17
155 000	1599.89	1579.25	1561.20	1545.36	1531.44	1519.18
160 000	1651.50	1630.19	1611.56	1595.21	1580.84	1568.18
165 000	1703.11	1681.14	1661.92	1645.06	1630.24	1617.19
170 000	1754.72	1732.08	1712.28	1694.91	1679.65	1666.19
175 000	1806.33	1783.02	1762.64	1744.76	1729.05	1715.20
180 000	1857.94	1833.97	1813.00	1794.61	1778.45	1764.20
185 000	1909.55	1884.91	1863.36	1844.46	1827.85	1813.21
190 000	1961.16	1935.85	1913.72	1894.32	1877.25	1862.21
195 000	2012.77	1986.80	1964.09	1944.17	1926.65	1911.22
200 000	2064.38	2037.74	2014.45	1994.02	1976.05	1960.23
205 000	2115.99	2088.69	2064.81	2043.87	2025.45	2009.23
210 000	2167.60	2139.63	2115.17	2093.72	2074.86	2058.24
215 000	2219.21	2190.57	2165.53	2143.57	2124.26	2107.24
220 000	2270.81	2241.52	2215.89	2193.42	2173.66	2156.25
225 000	2322.42	2292.46	2266.25	2243.27	2223.06	2205.25
230 000	2374.03	2343.40	2316.61	2293.12	2272.46	2254.26
235 000	2425.64	2394.35	2366.98	2342.97	2321.86	2303.27
240 000	2477.25	2445.29	2417.34	2392.82	2371.26	2352.27
245 000	2528.86	2496.23	2467.70	2442.67	2420.67	2401.28
250 000	2580.47	2547.18	2518.06	2492.52	2470.07	2450.28
260 000	2683.69	2649.06	2618.78	2592.22	2568.87	2548.29
270 000	2786.91	2750.95	2719.50	2691.92	2667.67	2646.31
280 000	2890.13	2852.84	2820.23	2791.62	2766.47	2744.32
290 000	2993.35	2954.73	2920.95	2891.32	2865.28	2842.33
300 000	3096.57	3056.61	3021.67	2991.02	2964.08	2940.34
400 000	4128.75	4075.48	4028.89	3988.03	3952.11	3920.45
500 000	5160.94	5094.35	5036.12	4985.04	4940.13	4900.57

Term	26 Years	27 Years	28 Years	29 Years	30 Years	35 Years
AMOUNT						
30 000	291.94	290.09	288.44	286.99	285.70	281.09
40 000	389.25	386.78	384.59	382.65	380.93	374.78
50 000	486.56	483.48	480.74	478.31	476.16	468.48
55 000	535.22	531.82	528.81	526.15	523.78	515.33
60 000	583.88	580.17	576.89	573.98	571.39	562.17
65 000	632.53	628.52	624.96	621.81	619.01	609.02
70 000	681.19	676.87	673.04	669.64	666.63	655.87
75 000	729.85	725.21	721.11	717.47	714.24	702.72
80 000	778.50	773.56	769.18	765.30	761.86	749.57
85 000	827.16	821.91	817.26	813.14	809.47	796.41
90 000	875.81	870.26	865.33	860.97	857.09	843.26
95 000	924.47	918.60	913.41	908.80	904.71	890.11
100 000	973.13	966.95	961.48	956.63	952.32	936.96
105 000	1021.78	1015.30	1009.55	1004.46	999.94	983.81
110 000	1070.44	1063.65	1057.63	1052.29	1047.56	1030.65
115 000	1119.10	1111.99	1105.70	1100.12	1095.17	1077.50
120 000	1167.75	1160.34	1153.78	1147.96	1142.79	1124.35
125 000	1216.41	1208.69	1201.85	1195.79	1190.40	1171.20
130 000	1265.07	1257.04	1249.92	1243.62	1238.02	1218.04
135 000	1313.72	1305.38	1298.00	1291.45	1285.64	1264.89
140 000	1362.38	1353.73	1346.07	1339.28	1333.25	1311.74
145 000	1411.03	1402.08	1394.15	1387.11	1380.87	1358.59
150 000	1459.69	1450.43	1442.22	1434.94	1428.49	1405.44
155 000	1508.35	1498.77	1490.29	1482.78	1476.10	1452.28
160 000	1557.00	1547.12	1538.37	1530.61	1523.72	1499.13
165 000	1605.66	1595.47	1586.44	1578.44	1571.33	1545.98
170 000	1654.32	1643.82	1634.52	1626.27	1618.95	1592.83
175 000	1702.97	1692.16	1682.59	1674.10	1666.57	1639.68
180 000	1751.63	1740.51	1730.66	1721.93	1714.18	1686.52
185 000	1800.29	1788.86	1778.74	1769.76	1761.80	1733.37
190 000	1848.94	1837.21	1826.81	1817.60	1809.41	1780.22
195 000	1897.60	1885.55	1874.89	1865.43	1857.03	1827.07
200 000	1946.25	1933.90	1922.96	1913.26	1904.65	1873.92
205 000	1994.91	1982.25	1971.03	1961.09	1952.26	1920.76
210 000	2043.57	2030.60	2019.11	2008.92	1999.88	1967.61
215 000	2092.22	2078.94	2067.18	2056.75	2047.50	2014.46
220 000	2140.88	2127.29	2115.26	2104.58	2095.11	2061.31
225 000	2189.54	2175.64	2163.33	2152.42	2142.73	2108.15
230 000	2238.19	2223.99	2211.40	2200.25	2190.34	2155.00
235 000	2286.85	2272.33	2259.48	2248.08	2237.96	2201.85
240 000	2335.51	2320.68	2307.55	2295.91	2285.58	2248.70
245 000	2384.16	2369.03	2355.63	2343.74	2333.19	2295.55
250 000	2432.82	2417.38	2403.70	2391.57	2380.81	2342.39
260 000	2530.13	2514.07	2499.85	2487.24	2476.04	2436.09
270 000	2627.44	2610.77	2596.00	2582.90	2571.27	2529.79
280 000	2724.76	2707.46	2692.14	2678.56	2666.51	2623.48
290 000	2822.07	2804.16	2788.29	2774.23	2761.74	2717.18
300 000	2919.38	2900.85	2884.44	2869.89	2856.97	2810.87
400 000	3892.51	3867.80	3845.92	3826.52	3809.29	3747.83
500 000	4865.64	4834.75	4807.40	4783.15	4761.62	4684.79

11.50% INTEREST	**MONTHLY PAYMENT** needed to pay back a mortgage				
Term	1 Year	5 Years	10 Years	11 Years	12 Years	13 Years
AMOUNT						
30 000	2658.45	659.78	421.79	401.51	384.99	371.38
40 000	3544.60	879.70	562.38	535.34	513.33	495.17
50 000	4430.75	1099.63	702.98	669.18	641.66	618.96
55 000	4873.83	1209.59	773.27	736.09	705.82	680.85
60 000	5316.90	1319.56	843.57	803.01	769.99	742.75
65 000	5759.98	1429.52	913.87	869.93	834.16	804.65
70 000	6203.05	1539.48	984.17	936.85	898.32	866.54
75 000	6646.13	1649.45	1054.47	1003.76	962.49	928.44
80 000	7089.20	1759.41	1124.76	1070.68	1026.65	990.33
85 000	7532.28	1869.37	1195.06	1137.60	1090.82	1052.23
90 000	7975.35	1979.33	1265.36	1204.52	1154.98	1114.13
95 000	8418.43	2089.30	1335.66	1271.43	1219.15	1176.02
100 000	8861.51	2199.26	1405.95	1338.35	1283.32	1237.92
105 000	9304.58	2309.22	1476.25	1405.27	1347.48	1299.81
110 000	9747.66	2419.19	1546.55	1472.19	1411.65	1361.71
115 000	10190.73	2529.15	1616.85	1539.10	1475.81	1423.61
120 000	10633.81	2639.11	1687.15	1606.02	1539.98	1485.50
125 000	11076.88	2749.08	1757.44	1672.94	1604.15	1547.40
130 000	11519.96	2859.04	1827.74	1739.86	1668.31	1609.29
135 000	11963.03	2969.00	1898.04	1806.77	1732.48	1671.19
140 000	12406.11	3078.97	1968.34	1873.69	1796.64	1733.08
145 000	12849.18	3188.93	2038.63	1940.61	1860.81	1794.98
150 000	13292.26	3298.89	2108.93	2007.53	1924.97	1856.88
155 000	13735.33	3408.85	2179.23	2074.44	1989.14	1918.77
160 000	14178.41	3518.82	2249.53	2141.36	2053.31	1980.67
165 000	14621.48	3628.78	2319.82	2208.28	2117.47	2042.56
170 000	15064.56	3738.74	2390.12	2275.20	2181.64	2104.46
175 000	15507.63	3848.71	2460.42	2342.11	2245.80	2166.36
180 000	15950.71	3958.67	2530.72	2409.03	2309.97	2228.25
185 000	16393.78	4068.63	2601.02	2475.95	2374.14	2290.15
190 000	16836.86	4178.60	2671.31	2542.87	2438.30	2352.04
195 000	17279.94	4288.56	2741.61	2609.78	2502.47	2413.94
200 000	17723.01	4398.52	2811.91	2676.70	2566.63	2475.84
205 000	18166.09	4508.48	2882.21	2743.62	2630.80	2537.73
210 000	18609.16	4618.45	2952.50	2810.54	2694.96	2599.63
215 000	19052.24	4728.41	3022.80	2877.45	2759.13	2661.52
220 000	19495.31	4838.37	3093.10	2944.37	2823.30	2723.42
225 000	19938.39	4948.34	3163.40	3011.29	2887.46	2785.31
230 000	20381.46	5058.30	3233.70	3078.21	2951.63	2847.21
235 000	20824.54	5168.26	3303.99	3145.12	3015.79	2909.11
240 000	21267.61	5278.23	3374.29	3212.04	3079.96	2971.00
245 000	21710.69	5388.19	3444.59	3278.96	3144.13	3032.90
250 000	22153.76	5498.15	3514.89	3345.88	3208.29	3094.79
260 000	23039.91	5718.08	3655.48	3479.71	3336.62	3218.59
270 000	23926.06	5938.00	3796.08	3613.55	3464.95	3342.38
280 000	24812.22	6157.93	3936.67	3747.38	3593.29	3466.17
290 000	25698.37	6377.86	4077.27	3881.22	3721.62	3589.96
300 000	26584.52	6597.78	4217.86	4015.05	3849.95	3713.75
400 000	35446.02	8797.04	5623.82	5353.40	5133.27	4951.67
500 000	44307.53	10996.30	7029.77	6691.75	6416.58	6189.59

Term	14 Years	15 Years	16 Years	17 Years	18 Years	19 Years
AMOUNT						
30 000	360.02	350.46	342.35	335.43	329.49	324.37
40 000	480.02	467.28	456.47	447.24	439.32	432.49
50 000	600.03	584.09	570.58	559.05	549.15	540.61
55 000	660.03	642.50	627.64	614.95	604.06	594.67
60 000	720.03	700.91	684.70	670.86	658.98	648.73
65 000	780.04	759.32	741.76	726.76	713.89	702.79
70 000	840.04	817.73	798.82	782.67	768.81	756.85
75 000	900.04	876.14	855.87	838.57	823.72	810.91
80 000	960.04	934.55	912.93	894.48	878.64	864.97
85 000	1020.05	992.96	969.99	950.38	933.55	919.04
90 000	1080.05	1051.37	1027.05	1006.29	988.47	973.10
95 000	1140.05	1109.78	1084.11	1062.19	1043.38	1027.16
100 000	1200.06	1168.19	1141.16	1118.10	1098.30	1081.22
105 000	1260.06	1226.60	1198.22	1174.00	1153.21	1135.28
110 000	1320.06	1285.01	1255.28	1229.91	1208.12	1189.34
115 000	1380.06	1343.42	1312.34	1285.81	1263.04	1243.40
120 000	1440.07	1401.83	1369.40	1341.72	1317.95	1297.46
125 000	1500.07	1460.24	1426.46	1397.62	1372.87	1351.52
130 000	1560.07	1518.65	1483.51	1453.53	1427.78	1405.58
135 000	1620.07	1577.06	1540.57	1509.43	1482.70	1459.64
140 000	1680.08	1635.47	1597.63	1565.33	1537.61	1513.71
145 000	1740.08	1693.88	1654.69	1621.24	1592.53	1567.77
150 000	1800.08	1752.28	1711.75	1677.14	1647.44	1621.83
155 000	1860.09	1810.69	1768.81	1733.05	1702.36	1675.89
160 000	1920.09	1869.10	1825.86	1788.95	1757.27	1729.95
165 000	1980.09	1927.51	1882.92	1844.86	1812.19	1784.01
170 000	2040.09	1985.92	1939.98	1900.76	1867.10	1838.07
175 000	2100.10	2044.33	1997.04	1956.67	1922.02	1892.13
180 000	2160.10	2102.74	2054.10	2012.57	1976.93	1946.19
185 000	2220.10	2161.15	2111.16	2068.48	2031.85	2000.25
190 000	2280.11	2219.56	2168.21	2124.38	2086.76	2054.31
195 000	2340.11	2277.97	2225.27	2180.29	2141.68	2108.38
200 000	2400.11	2336.38	2282.33	2236.19	2196.59	2162.44
205 000	2460.11	2394.79	2339.39	2292.10	2251.51	2216.50
210 000	2520.12	2453.20	2396.45	2348.00	2306.42	2270.56
215 000	2580.12	2511.61	2453.50	2403.91	2361.33	2324.62
220 000	2640.12	2570.02	2510.56	2459.81	2416.25	2378.68
225 000	2700.12	2628.43	2567.62	2515.72	2471.16	2432.74
230 000	2760.13	2686.84	2624.68	2571.62	2526.08	2486.80
235 000	2820.13	2745.25	2681.74	2627.53	2580.99	2540.86
240 000	2880.13	2803.66	2738.80	2683.43	2635.91	2594.92
245 000	2940.14	2862.07	2795.85	2739.34	2690.82	2648.98
250 000	3000.14	2920.47	2852.91	2795.24	2745.74	2703.05
260 000	3120.14	3037.29	2967.03	2907.05	2855.57	2811.17
270 000	3240.15	3154.11	3081.15	3018.86	2965.40	2919.29
280 000	3360.16	3270.93	3195.26	3130.67	3075.23	3027.41
290 000	3480.16	3387.75	3309.38	3242.48	3185.06	3135.53
300 000	3600.17	3504.57	3423.49	3354.29	3294.89	3243.65
400 000	4800.22	4672.76	4564.66	4472.39	4393.18	4324.87
500 000	6000.28	5840.95	5705.82	5590.48	5491.48	5406.09

MONTHLY PAYMENT
needed to pay back a mortgage

Term	20 Years	21 Years	22 Years	23 Years	24 Years	25 Years
AMOUNT						
30 000	319.93	316.07	312.71	309.77	307.20	304.94
40 000	426.57	421.43	416.95	413.03	409.60	406.59
50 000	533.21	526.79	521.19	516.29	512.00	508.23
55 000	586.54	579.47	573.31	567.92	563.20	559.06
60 000	639.86	632.15	625.42	619.55	614.40	609.88
65 000	693.18	684.83	677.54	671.18	665.60	660.70
70 000	746.50	737.50	729.66	722.81	716.80	711.53
75 000	799.82	790.18	781.78	774.44	768.00	762.35
80 000	853.14	842.86	833.90	826.07	819.20	813.18
85 000	906.47	895.54	886.02	877.69	870.40	864.00
90 000	959.79	948.22	938.14	929.32	921.60	914.82
95 000	1013.11	1000.90	990.26	980.95	972.80	965.65
100 000	1066.43	1053.58	1042.37	1032.58	1024.00	1016.47
105 000	1119.75	1106.26	1094.49	1084.21	1075.20	1067.29
110 000	1173.07	1158.94	1146.61	1135.84	1126.40	1118.12
115 000	1226.39	1211.61	1198.73	1187.47	1177.60	1168.94
120 000	1279.72	1264.29	1250.85	1239.10	1228.80	1219.76
125 000	1333.04	1316.97	1302.97	1290.73	1280.00	1270.59
130 000	1386.36	1369.65	1355.09	1342.36	1331.20	1321.41
135 000	1439.68	1422.33	1407.21	1393.98	1382.40	1372.23
140 000	1493.00	1475.01	1459.32	1445.61	1433.60	1423.06
145 000	1546.32	1527.69	1511.44	1497.24	1484.80	1473.88
150 000	1599.64	1580.37	1563.56	1548.87	1536.00	1524.70
155 000	1652.97	1633.05	1615.68	1600.50	1587.20	1575.53
160 000	1706.29	1685.72	1667.80	1652.13	1638.40	1626.35
165 000	1759.61	1738.40	1719.92	1703.76	1689.60	1677.17
170 000	1812.93	1791.08	1772.04	1755.39	1740.80	1728.00
175 000	1866.25	1843.76	1824.15	1807.02	1792.00	1778.82
180 000	1919.57	1896.44	1876.27	1858.65	1843.20	1829.64
185 000	1972.89	1949.12	1928.39	1910.28	1894.40	1880.47
190 000	2026.22	2001.80	1980.51	1961.90	1945.60	1931.29
195 000	2079.54	2054.48	2032.63	2013.53	1996.80	1982.11
200 000	2132.86	2107.16	2084.75	2065.16	2048.00	2032.94
205 000	2186.18	2159.83	2136.87	2116.79	2099.20	2083.76
210 000	2239.50	2212.51	2188.99	2168.42	2150.40	2134.58
215 000	2292.82	2265.19	2241.10	2220.05	2201.60	2185.41
220 000	2346.15	2317.87	2293.22	2271.68	2252.80	2236.23
225 000	2399.47	2370.55	2345.34	2323.31	2304.00	2287.06
230 000	2452.79	2423.23	2397.46	2374.94	2355.20	2337.88
235 000	2506.11	2475.91	2449.58	2426.57	2406.40	2388.70
240 000	2559.43	2528.59	2501.70	2478.20	2457.60	2439.53
245 000	2612.75	2581.27	2553.82	2529.82	2508.80	2490.35
250 000	2666.07	2633.94	2605.94	2581.45	2560.00	2541.17
260 000	2772.72	2739.30	2710.17	2684.71	2662.40	2642.82
270 000	2879.36	2844.66	2814.41	2787.97	2764.80	2744.47
280 000	2986.00	2950.02	2918.65	2891.23	2867.20	2846.11
290 000	3092.65	3055.38	3022.89	2994.49	2969.60	2947.76
300 000	3199.29	3160.73	3127.12	3097.74	3072.00	3049.41
400 000	4265.72	4214.31	4169.50	4130.33	4096.01	4065.88
500 000	5332.15	5267.89	5211.87	5162.91	5120.01	5082.34

needed to pay back a mortgage

Term	26 Years	27 Years	28 Years	29 Years	30 Years	35 Years
AMOUNT						
30 000	302.95	301.20	299.66	298.29	297.09	292.83
40 000	403.94	401.60	399.54	397.72	396.12	390.44
50 000	504.92	502.00	499.43	497.16	495.15	488.05
55 000	555.41	552.20	549.37	546.87	544.66	536.86
60 000	605.91	602.40	599.32	596.59	594.17	585.66
65 000	656.40	652.61	649.26	646.30	643.69	634.47
70 000	706.89	702.81	699.20	696.02	693.20	683.28
75 000	757.38	753.01	749.14	745.73	742.72	732.08
80 000	807.88	803.21	799.09	795.45	792.23	780.89
85 000	858.37	853.41	849.03	845.17	841.75	829.69
90 000	908.86	903.61	898.97	894.88	891.26	878.50
95 000	959.35	953.81	948.92	944.60	940.78	927.30
100 000	1009.84	1004.01	998.86	994.31	990.29	976.11
105 000	1060.34	1054.21	1048.80	1044.03	1039.81	1024.91
110 000	1110.83	1104.41	1098.75	1093.74	1089.32	1073.72
115 000	1161.32	1154.61	1148.69	1143.46	1138.84	1122.52
120 000	1211.81	1204.81	1198.63	1193.17	1188.35	1171.33
125 000	1262.30	1255.01	1248.57	1242.89	1237.86	1220.13
130 000	1312.80	1305.21	1298.52	1292.61	1287.38	1268.94
135 000	1363.29	1355.41	1348.46	1342.32	1336.89	1317.74
140 000	1413.78	1405.61	1398.40	1392.04	1386.41	1366.55
145 000	1464.27	1455.81	1448.35	1441.75	1435.92	1415.36
150 000	1514.77	1506.01	1498.29	1491.47	1485.44	1464.16
155 000	1565.26	1556.21	1548.23	1541.18	1534.95	1512.97
160 000	1615.75	1606.41	1598.18	1590.90	1584.47	1561.77
165 000	1666.24	1656.61	1648.12	1640.62	1633.98	1610.58
170 000	1716.73	1706.81	1698.06	1690.33	1683.50	1659.38
175 000	1767.23	1757.01	1748.00	1740.05	1733.01	1708.19
180 000	1817.72	1807.21	1797.95	1789.76	1782.52	1756.99
185 000	1868.21	1857.41	1847.89	1839.48	1832.04	1805.80
190 000	1918.70	1907.61	1897.83	1889.19	1881.55	1854.60
195 000	1969.20	1957.82	1947.78	1938.91	1931.07	1903.41
200 000	2019.69	2008.02	1997.72	1988.62	1980.58	1952.21
205 000	2070.18	2058.22	2047.66	2038.34	2030.10	2001.02
210 000	2120.67	2108.42	2097.60	2088.06	2079.61	2049.83
215 000	2171.16	2158.62	2147.55	2137.77	2129.13	2098.63
220 000	2221.66	2208.82	2197.49	2187.49	2178.64	2147.44
225 000	2272.15	2259.02	2247.43	2237.20	2228.16	2196.24
230 000	2322.64	2309.22	2297.38	2286.92	2277.67	2245.05
235 000	2373.13	2359.42	2347.32	2336.63	2327.18	2293.85
240 000	2423.63	2409.62	2397.26	2386.35	2376.70	2342.66
245 000	2474.12	2459.82	2447.21	2436.06	2426.21	2391.46
250 000	2524.61	2510.02	2497.15	2485.78	2475.73	2440.27
260 000	2625.59	2610.42	2597.03	2585.21	2574.76	2537.88
270 000	2726.58	2710.82	2696.92	2684.64	2673.79	2635.49
280 000	2827.56	2811.22	2796.81	2784.07	2772.82	2733.10
290 000	2928.55	2911.62	2896.69	2883.51	2871.85	2830.71
300 000	3029.53	3012.02	2996.58	2982.94	2970.87	2928.32
400 000	4039.38	4016.03	3995.44	3977.25	3961.17	3904.43
500 000	5049.22	5020.04	4994.30	4971.56	4951.46	4880.54

12.00% INTEREST	**MONTHLY PAYMENT** needed to pay back a mortgage				
Term	**1** Year	**5** Years	**10** Years	**11** Years	**12** Years	**13** Years
AMOUNT						
30 000	2665.46	667.33	430.41	410.34	394.03	380.60
40 000	3553.95	889.78	573.88	547.12	525.37	507.47
50 000	4442.44	1112.22	717.35	683.89	656.71	634.33
55 000	4886.68	1223.44	789.09	752.28	722.38	697.77
60 000	5330.93	1334.67	860.83	820.67	788.05	761.20
65 000	5775.17	1445.89	932.56	889.06	853.72	824.63
70 000	6219.42	1557.11	1004.30	957.45	919.39	888.07
75 000	6663.66	1668.33	1076.03	1025.84	985.06	951.50
80 000	7107.90	1779.56	1147.77	1094.23	1050.74	1014.93
85 000	7552.15	1890.78	1219.50	1162.62	1116.41	1078.37
90 000	7996.39	2002.00	1291.24	1231.01	1182.08	1141.80
95 000	8440.63	2113.22	1362.97	1299.40	1247.75	1205.23
100 000	8884.88	2224.44	1434.71	1367.79	1313.42	1268.67
105 000	9329.12	2335.67	1506.44	1436.18	1379.09	1332.10
110 000	9773.37	2446.89	1578.18	1504.57	1444.76	1395.53
115 000	10217.61	2558.11	1649.92	1572.96	1510.43	1458.97
120 000	10661.85	2669.33	1721.65	1641.35	1576.10	1522.40
125 000	11106.10	2780.56	1793.39	1709.73	1641.77	1585.83
130 000	11550.34	2891.78	1865.12	1778.12	1707.44	1649.27
135 000	11994.59	3003.00	1936.86	1846.51	1773.12	1712.70
140 000	12438.83	3114.22	2008.59	1914.90	1838.79	1776.13
145 000	12883.07	3225.44	2080.33	1983.29	1904.46	1839.57
150 000	13327.32	3336.67	2152.06	2051.68	1970.13	1903.00
155 000	13771.56	3447.89	2223.80	2120.07	2035.80	1966.43
160 000	14215.81	3559.11	2295.54	2188.46	2101.47	2029.87
165 000	14660.05	3670.33	2367.27	2256.85	2167.14	2093.30
170 000	15104.29	3781.56	2439.01	2325.24	2232.81	2156.73
175 000	15548.54	3892.78	2510.74	2393.63	2298.48	2220.17
180 000	15992.78	4004.00	2582.48	2462.02	2364.15	2283.60
185 000	16437.03	4115.22	2654.21	2530.41	2429.83	2347.03
190 000	16881.27	4226.45	2725.95	2598.80	2495.50	2410.47
195 000	17325.51	4337.67	2797.68	2667.19	2561.17	2473.90
200 000	17769.76	4448.89	2869.42	2735.58	2626.84	2537.33
205 000	18214.00	4560.11	2941.15	2803.97	2692.51	2600.77
210 000	18658.25	4671.33	3012.89	2872.35	2758.18	2664.20
215 000	19102.49	4782.56	3084.63	2940.74	2823.85	2727.63
220 000	19546.73	4893.78	3156.36	3009.13	2889.52	2791.07
225 000	19990.98	5005.00	3228.10	3077.52	2955.19	2854.50
230 000	20435.22	5116.22	3299.83	3145.91	3020.86	2917.93
235 000	20879.47	5227.45	3371.57	3214.30	3086.53	2981.37
240 000	21323.71	5338.67	3443.30	3282.69	3152.21	3044.80
245 000	21767.95	5449.89	3515.04	3351.08	3217.88	3108.23
250 000	22212.20	5561.11	3586.77	3419.47	3283.55	3171.67
260 000	23100.69	5783.56	3730.24	3556.25	3414.89	3298.53
270 000	23989.17	6006.00	3873.72	3693.03	3546.23	3425.40
280 000	24877.66	6228.45	4017.19	3829.81	3677.57	3552.27
290 000	25766.15	6450.89	4160.66	3966.58	3808.92	3679.13
300 000	26654.64	6673.33	4304.13	4103.36	3940.26	3806.00
400 000	35539.52	8897.78	5738.84	5471.15	5253.68	5074.66
500 000	44424.39	11122.22	7173.55	6838.94	6567.10	6343.33

Term	14 Years	15 Years	16 Years	17 Years	18 Years	19 Years
AMOUNT						
30 000	369.43	360.05	352.12	345.36	339.59	334.62
40 000	492.57	480.07	469.49	460.49	452.78	446.15
50 000	615.71	600.08	586.86	575.61	565.98	557.69
55 000	677.29	660.09	645.55	633.17	622.57	613.46
60 000	738.86	720.10	704.24	690.73	679.17	669.23
65 000	800.43	780.11	762.92	748.29	735.77	725.00
70 000	862.00	840.12	821.61	805.85	792.37	780.77
75 000	923.57	900.13	880.29	863.41	848.96	836.54
80 000	985.14	960.13	938.98	920.97	905.56	892.31
85 000	1046.72	1020.14	997.67	978.53	962.16	948.08
90 000	1108.29	1080.15	1056.35	1036.09	1018.76	1003.85
95 000	1169.86	1140.16	1115.04	1093.65	1075.35	1059.62
100 000	1231.43	1200.17	1173.73	1151.22	1131.95	1115.39
105 000	1293.00	1260.18	1232.41	1208.78	1188.55	1171.15
110 000	1354.57	1320.18	1291.10	1266.34	1245.15	1226.92
115 000	1416.14	1380.19	1349.78	1323.90	1301.74	1282.69
120 000	1477.72	1440.20	1408.47	1381.46	1358.34	1338.46
125 000	1539.29	1500.21	1467.16	1439.02	1414.94	1394.23
130 000	1600.86	1560.22	1525.84	1496.58	1471.54	1450.00
135 000	1662.43	1620.23	1584.53	1554.14	1528.13	1505.77
140 000	1724.00	1680.24	1643.22	1611.70	1584.73	1561.54
145 000	1785.57	1740.24	1701.90	1669.26	1641.33	1617.31
150 000	1847.14	1800.25	1760.59	1726.82	1697.93	1673.08
155 000	1908.72	1860.26	1819.27	1784.38	1754.52	1728.85
160 000	1970.29	1920.27	1877.96	1841.94	1811.12	1784.62
165 000	2031.86	1980.28	1936.65	1899.51	1867.72	1840.39
170 000	2093.43	2040.29	1995.33	1957.07	1924.32	1896.16
175 000	2155.00	2100.29	2054.02	2014.63	1980.91	1951.92
180 000	2216.57	2160.30	2112.71	2072.19	2037.51	2007.69
185 000	2278.14	2220.31	2171.39	2129.75	2094.11	2063.46
190 000	2339.72	2280.32	2230.08	2187.31	2150.71	2119.23
195 000	2401.29	2340.33	2288.76	2244.87	2207.30	2175.00
200 000	2462.86	2400.34	2347.45	2302.43	2263.90	2230.77
205 000	2524.43	2460.34	2406.14	2359.99	2320.50	2286.54
210 000	2586.00	2520.35	2464.82	2417.55	2377.10	2342.31
215 000	2647.57	2580.36	2523.51	2475.11	2433.69	2398.08
220 000	2709.14	2640.37	2582.20	2532.67	2490.29	2453.85
225 000	2770.72	2700.38	2640.88	2590.23	2546.89	2509.62
230 000	2832.29	2760.39	2699.57	2647.80	2603.49	2565.39
235 000	2893.86	2820.39	2758.25	2705.36	2660.08	2621.16
240 000	2955.43	2880.40	2816.94	2762.92	2716.68	2676.93
245 000	3017.00	2940.41	2875.63	2820.48	2773.28	2732.69
250 000	3078.57	3000.42	2934.31	2878.04	2829.88	2788.46
260 000	3201.72	3120.44	3051.69	2993.16	2943.07	2900.00
270 000	3324.86	3240.45	3169.06	3108.28	3056.27	3011.54
280 000	3448.00	3360.47	3286.43	3223.40	3169.46	3123.08
290 000	3571.15	3480.49	3403.80	3338.53	3282.66	3234.62
300 000	3694.29	3600.50	3521.18	3453.65	3395.85	3346.16
400 000	4925.72	4800.67	4694.90	4604.86	4527.80	4461.54
500 000	6157.15	6000.84	5868.63	5756.08	5659.75	5576.93

12.00% INTEREST			**MONTHLY PAYMENT** needed to pay back a mortgage			
Term	20 Years	21 Years	22 Years	23 Years	24 Years	25 Years
AMOUNT						
30 000	330.33	326.61	323.38	320.57	318.11	315.97
40 000	440.43	435.48	431.18	427.43	424.15	421.29
50 000	550.54	544.35	538.97	534.28	530.19	526.61
55 000	605.60	598.78	592.87	587.71	583.21	579.27
60 000	660.65	653.22	646.76	641.14	636.23	631.93
65 000	715.71	707.65	700.66	694.57	689.25	684.60
70 000	770.76	762.09	754.56	748.00	742.27	737.26
75 000	825.81	816.52	808.45	801.42	795.29	789.92
80 000	880.87	870.96	862.35	854.85	848.31	842.58
85 000	935.92	925.39	916.25	908.28	901.32	895.24
90 000	990.98	979.83	970.14	961.71	954.34	947.90
95 000	1046.03	1034.26	1024.04	1015.14	1007.36	1000.56
100 000	1101.09	1088.70	1077.94	1068.56	1060.38	1053.22
105 000	1156.14	1143.13	1131.84	1121.99	1113.40	1105.89
110 000	1211.19	1197.57	1185.73	1175.42	1166.42	1158.55
115 000	1266.25	1252.00	1239.63	1228.85	1219.44	1211.21
120 000	1321.30	1306.44	1293.53	1282.28	1272.46	1263.87
125 000	1376.36	1360.87	1347.42	1335.71	1325.48	1316.53
130 000	1431.41	1415.31	1401.32	1389.13	1378.50	1369.19
135 000	1486.47	1469.74	1455.22	1442.56	1431.52	1421.85
140 000	1541.52	1524.18	1509.11	1495.99	1484.53	1474.51
145 000	1596.57	1578.61	1563.01	1549.42	1537.55	1527.18
150 000	1651.63	1633.05	1616.91	1602.85	1590.57	1579.84
155 000	1706.68	1687.48	1670.80	1656.28	1643.59	1632.50
160 000	1761.74	1741.92	1724.70	1709.70	1696.61	1685.16
165 000	1816.79	1796.35	1778.60	1763.13	1749.63	1737.82
170 000	1871.85	1850.79	1832.50	1816.56	1802.65	1790.48
175 000	1926.90	1905.22	1886.39	1869.99	1855.67	1843.14
180 000	1981.96	1959.66	1940.29	1923.42	1908.69	1895.80
185 000	2037.01	2014.09	1994.19	1976.85	1961.71	1948.46
190 000	2092.06	2068.53	2048.08	2030.27	2014.73	2001.13
195 000	2147.12	2122.96	2101.98	2083.70	2067.74	2053.79
200 000	2202.17	2177.40	2155.88	2137.13	2120.76	2106.45
205 000	2257.23	2231.83	2209.77	2190.56	2173.78	2159.11
210 000	2312.28	2286.27	2263.67	2243.99	2226.80	2211.77
215 000	2367.34	2340.70	2317.57	2297.41	2279.82	2264.43
220 000	2422.39	2395.14	2371.46	2350.84	2332.84	2317.09
225 000	2477.44	2449.57	2425.36	2404.27	2385.86	2369.75
230 000	2532.50	2504.01	2479.26	2457.70	2438.88	2422.42
235 000	2587.55	2558.44	2533.16	2511.13	2491.90	2475.08
240 000	2642.61	2612.88	2587.05	2564.56	2544.92	2527.74
245 000	2697.66	2667.31	2640.95	2617.98	2597.94	2580.40
250 000	2752.72	2721.75	2694.85	2671.41	2650.95	2633.06
260 000	2862.82	2830.62	2802.64	2778.27	2756.99	2738.38
270 000	2972.93	2939.49	2910.43	2885.13	2863.03	2843.71
280 000	3083.04	3048.36	3018.23	2991.98	2969.07	2949.03
290 000	3193.15	3157.23	3126.02	3098.84	3075.11	3054.35
300 000	3303.26	3266.10	3233.82	3205.69	3181.15	3159.67
400 000	4404.34	4354.80	4311.75	4274.26	4241.53	4212.90
500 000	5505.43	5443.50	5389.69	5342.82	5301.91	5266.12

Term	26 Years	27 Years	28 Years	29 Years	30 Years	35 Years
AMOUNT						
30 000	314.09	312.43	310.98	309.71	308.58	304.66
40 000	418.78	416.58	414.65	412.94	411.45	406.22
50 000	523.48	520.72	518.31	516.18	514.31	507.77
55 000	575.82	572.80	570.14	567.80	565.74	558.55
60 000	628.17	624.87	621.97	619.42	617.17	609.33
65 000	680.52	676.94	673.80	671.03	668.60	660.11
70 000	732.87	729.01	725.63	722.65	720.03	710.88
75 000	785.21	781.09	777.46	774.27	771.46	761.66
80 000	837.56	833.16	829.29	825.89	822.89	812.44
85 000	889.91	885.23	881.12	877.50	874.32	863.22
90 000	942.26	937.30	932.95	929.12	925.75	913.99
95 000	994.60	989.38	984.78	980.74	977.18	964.77
100 000	1046.95	1041.45	1036.61	1032.36	1028.61	1015.55
105 000	1099.30	1093.52	1088.44	1083.98	1080.04	1066.33
110 000	1151.65	1145.59	1140.27	1135.59	1131.47	1117.10
115 000	1204.00	1197.67	1192.10	1187.21	1182.90	1167.88
120 000	1256.34	1249.74	1243.94	1238.83	1234.34	1218.66
125 000	1308.69	1301.81	1295.77	1290.45	1285.77	1269.44
130 000	1361.04	1353.88	1347.60	1342.07	1337.20	1320.21
135 000	1413.39	1405.96	1399.43	1393.68	1388.63	1370.99
140 000	1465.73	1458.03	1451.26	1445.30	1440.06	1421.77
145 000	1518.08	1510.10	1503.09	1496.92	1491.49	1472.55
150 000	1570.43	1562.17	1554.92	1548.54	1542.92	1523.32
155 000	1622.78	1614.25	1606.75	1600.16	1594.35	1574.10
160 000	1675.12	1666.32	1658.58	1651.77	1645.78	1624.88
165 000	1727.47	1718.39	1710.41	1703.39	1697.21	1675.66
170 000	1779.82	1770.46	1762.24	1755.01	1748.64	1726.43
175 000	1832.17	1822.54	1814.07	1806.63	1800.07	1777.21
180 000	1884.51	1874.61	1865.90	1858.25	1851.50	1827.99
185 000	1936.86	1926.68	1917.73	1909.86	1902.93	1878.77
190 000	1989.21	1978.75	1969.56	1961.48	1954.36	1929.54
195 000	2041.56	2030.83	2021.40	2013.10	2005.79	1980.32
200 000	2093.90	2082.90	2073.23	2064.72	2057.23	2031.10
205 000	2146.25	2134.97	2125.06	2116.34	2108.66	2081.88
210 000	2198.60	2187.04	2176.89	2167.95	2160.09	2132.65
215 000	2250.95	2239.12	2228.72	2219.57	2211.52	2183.43
220 000	2303.30	2291.19	2280.55	2271.19	2262.95	2234.21
225 000	2355.64	2343.26	2332.38	2322.81	2314.38	2284.99
230 000	2407.99	2395.33	2384.21	2374.43	2365.81	2335.76
235 000	2460.34	2447.40	2436.04	2426.04	2417.24	2386.54
240 000	2512.69	2499.48	2487.87	2477.66	2468.67	2437.32
245 000	2565.03	2551.55	2539.70	2529.28	2520.10	2488.10
250 000	2617.38	2603.62	2591.53	2580.90	2571.53	2538.87
260 000	2722.08	2707.77	2695.19	2684.13	2674.39	2640.43
270 000	2826.77	2811.91	2798.86	2787.37	2777.25	2741.98
280 000	2931.47	2916.06	2902.52	2890.60	2880.12	2843.54
290 000	3036.16	3020.20	3006.18	2993.84	2982.98	2945.09
300 000	3140.86	3124.35	3109.84	3097.08	3085.84	3046.65
400 000	4187.81	4165.80	4146.45	4129.44	4114.45	4062.20
500 000	5234.76	5207.24	5183.06	5161.79	5143.06	5077.75

43

12.50% INTEREST	MONTHLY PAYMENT needed to pay back a mortgage				
Term	**1 Year**	**5 Years**	**10 Years**	**11 Years**	**12 Years**	**13 Years**

AMOUNT	1 Year	5 Years	10 Years	11 Years	12 Years	13 Years
30 000	2672.49	674.94	439.13	419.26	403.16	389.93
40 000	3563.31	899.92	585.50	559.02	537.54	519.91
50 000	4454.14	1124.90	731.88	698.77	671.93	649.88
55 000	4899.56	1237.39	805.07	768.65	739.12	714.87
60 000	5344.97	1349.88	878.26	838.53	806.31	779.86
65 000	5790.39	1462.37	951.45	908.40	873.51	844.85
70 000	6235.80	1574.86	1024.63	978.28	940.70	909.84
75 000	6681.21	1687.35	1097.82	1048.16	1007.89	974.82
80 000	7126.63	1799.84	1171.01	1118.03	1075.09	1039.81
85 000	7572.04	1912.32	1244.20	1187.91	1142.28	1104.80
90 000	8017.46	2024.81	1317.39	1257.79	1209.47	1169.79
95 000	8462.87	2137.30	1390.57	1327.67	1276.66	1234.78
100 000	8908.29	2249.79	1463.76	1397.54	1343.86	1299.77
105 000	9353.70	2362.28	1536.95	1467.42	1411.05	1364.75
110 000	9799.11	2474.77	1610.14	1537.30	1478.24	1429.74
115 000	10244.53	2587.26	1683.33	1607.17	1545.44	1494.73
120 000	10689.94	2699.75	1756.51	1677.05	1612.63	1559.72
125 000	11135.36	2812.24	1829.70	1746.93	1679.82	1624.71
130 000	11580.77	2924.73	1902.89	1816.81	1747.01	1689.70
135 000	12026.19	3037.22	1976.08	1886.68	1814.21	1754.68
140 000	12471.60	3149.71	2049.27	1956.56	1881.40	1819.67
145 000	12917.02	3262.20	2122.45	2026.44	1948.59	1884.66
150 000	13362.43	3374.69	2195.64	2096.31	2015.79	1949.65
155 000	13807.84	3487.18	2268.83	2166.19	2082.98	2014.64
160 000	14253.26	3599.67	2342.02	2236.07	2150.17	2079.63
165 000	14698.67	3712.16	2415.21	2305.95	2217.36	2144.61
170 000	15144.09	3824.65	2488.39	2375.82	2284.56	2209.60
175 000	15589.50	3937.14	2561.58	2445.70	2351.75	2274.59
180 000	16034.92	4049.63	2634.77	2515.58	2418.94	2339.58
185 000	16480.33	4162.12	2707.96	2585.45	2486.14	2404.57
190 000	16925.74	4274.61	2781.15	2655.33	2553.33	2469.56
195 000	17371.16	4387.10	2854.34	2725.21	2620.52	2534.54
200 000	17816.57	4499.59	2927.52	2795.09	2687.71	2599.53
205 000	18261.99	4612.08	3000.71	2864.96	2754.91	2664.52
210 000	18707.40	4724.57	3073.90	2934.84	2822.10	2729.51
215 000	19152.82	4837.06	3147.09	3004.72	2889.29	2794.50
220 000	19598.23	4949.55	3220.28	3074.59	2956.49	2859.49
225 000	20043.64	5062.04	3293.46	3144.47	3023.68	2924.47
230 000	20489.06	5174.53	3366.65	3214.35	3090.87	2989.46
235 000	20934.47	5287.02	3439.84	3284.23	3158.06	3054.45
240 000	21379.89	5399.51	3513.03	3354.10	3225.26	3119.44
245 000	21825.30	5511.99	3586.22	3423.98	3292.45	3184.43
250 000	22270.72	5624.48	3659.40	3493.86	3359.64	3249.42
260 000	23161.54	5849.46	3805.78	3633.61	3494.03	3379.39
270 000	24052.37	6074.44	3952.16	3773.37	3628.41	3509.37
280 000	24943.20	6299.42	4098.53	3913.12	3762.80	3639.35
290 000	25834.03	6524.40	4244.91	4052.87	3897.19	3769.32
300 000	26724.86	6749.38	4391.29	4192.63	4031.57	3899.30
400 000	35633.15	8999.18	5855.05	5590.17	5375.43	5199.06
500 000	44541.43	11248.97	7318.81	6987.71	6719.29	6498.83

Term	14 Years	15 Years	16 Years	17 Years	18 Years	19 Years
AMOUNT						
30 000	378.95	369.76	362.00	355.42	349.80	344.99
40 000	505.27	493.01	482.67	473.89	466.40	459.98
50 000	631.58	616.26	603.33	592.36	583.00	574.98
55 000	694.74	677.89	663.67	651.60	641.30	632.47
60 000	757.90	739.51	724.00	710.84	699.60	689.97
65 000	821.06	801.14	784.34	770.07	757.90	747.47
70 000	884.22	862.77	844.67	829.31	816.20	804.97
75 000	947.38	924.39	905.00	888.54	874.50	862.46
80 000	1010.53	986.02	965.34	947.78	932.80	919.96
85 000	1073.69	1047.64	1025.67	1007.02	991.10	977.46
90 000	1136.85	1109.27	1086.00	1066.25	1049.40	1034.96
95 000	1200.01	1170.90	1146.34	1125.49	1107.70	1092.45
100 000	1263.17	1232.52	1206.67	1184.73	1166.00	1149.95
105 000	1326.33	1294.15	1267.00	1243.96	1224.30	1207.45
110 000	1389.49	1355.77	1327.34	1303.20	1282.60	1264.95
115 000	1452.64	1417.40	1387.67	1362.43	1340.90	1322.44
120 000	1515.80	1479.03	1448.00	1421.67	1399.20	1379.94
125 000	1578.96	1540.65	1508.34	1480.91	1457.50	1437.44
130 000	1642.12	1602.28	1568.67	1540.14	1515.80	1494.94
135 000	1705.28	1663.90	1629.00	1599.38	1574.10	1552.43
140 000	1768.44	1725.53	1689.34	1658.62	1632.40	1609.93
145 000	1831.59	1787.16	1749.67	1717.85	1690.70	1667.43
150 000	1894.75	1848.78	1810.00	1777.09	1749.00	1724.93
155 000	1957.91	1910.41	1870.34	1836.32	1807.30	1782.42
160 000	2021.07	1972.04	1930.67	1895.56	1865.60	1839.92
165 000	2084.23	2033.66	1991.01	1954.80	1923.90	1897.42
170 000	2147.39	2095.29	2051.34	2014.03	1982.20	1954.92
175 000	2210.54	2156.91	2111.67	2073.27	2040.50	2012.41
180 000	2273.70	2218.54	2172.01	2132.51	2098.80	2069.91
185 000	2336.86	2280.17	2232.34	2191.74	2157.10	2127.41
190 000	2400.02	2341.79	2292.67	2250.98	2215.40	2184.91
195 000	2463.18	2403.42	2353.01	2310.22	2273.70	2242.40
200 000	2526.34	2465.04	2413.34	2369.45	2332.00	2299.90
205 000	2589.50	2526.67	2473.67	2428.69	2390.30	2357.40
210 000	2652.65	2588.30	2534.01	2487.92	2448.60	2414.90
215 000	2715.81	2649.92	2594.34	2547.16	2506.90	2472.39
220 000	2778.97	2711.55	2654.67	2606.40	2565.20	2529.89
225 000	2842.13	2773.17	2715.01	2665.63	2623.50	2587.39
230 000	2905.29	2834.80	2775.34	2724.87	2681.80	2644.89
235 000	2968.45	2896.43	2835.67	2784.11	2740.10	2702.38
240 000	3031.60	2958.05	2896.01	2843.34	2798.40	2759.88
245 000	3094.76	3019.68	2956.34	2902.58	2856.70	2817.38
250 000	3157.92	3081.31	3016.67	2961.81	2915.00	2874.88
260 000	3284.24	3204.56	3137.34	3080.29	3031.60	2989.87
270 000	3410.55	3327.81	3258.01	3198.76	3148.20	3104.87
280 000	3536.87	3451.06	3378.68	3317.23	3264.80	3219.86
290 000	3663.19	3574.31	3499.34	3435.70	3381.40	3334.86
300 000	3789.51	3697.57	3620.01	3554.18	3498.00	3449.85
400 000	5052.67	4930.09	4826.68	4738.90	4664.00	4599.80
500 000	6315.84	6162.61	6033.35	5923.63	5830.00	5749.75

12.50% INTEREST	MONTHLY PAYMENT needed to pay back a mortgage					
Term	**20** Years	**21** Years	**22** Years	**23** Years	**24** Years	**25** Years
AMOUNT						
30 000	340.84	337.27	334.17	331.48	329.14	327.11
40 000	454.46	449.69	445.56	441.97	438.86	436.14
50 000	568.07	562.11	556.95	552.47	548.57	545.18
55 000	624.88	618.32	612.64	607.72	603.43	599.69
60 000	681.68	674.53	668.34	662.96	658.29	654.21
65 000	738.49	730.74	724.03	718.21	713.14	708.73
70 000	795.30	786.95	779.73	773.46	768.00	763.25
75 000	852.11	843.16	835.42	828.70	822.86	817.77
80 000	908.91	899.37	891.12	883.95	877.72	872.28
85 000	965.72	955.59	946.81	939.20	932.57	926.80
90 000	1022.53	1011.80	1002.51	994.44	987.43	981.32
95 000	1079.33	1068.01	1058.20	1049.69	1042.29	1035.84
100 000	1136.14	1124.22	1113.90	1104.94	1097.14	1090.35
105 000	1192.95	1180.43	1169.59	1160.18	1152.00	1144.87
110 000	1249.75	1236.64	1225.29	1215.43	1206.86	1199.39
115 000	1306.56	1292.85	1280.98	1270.68	1261.72	1253.91
120 000	1363.37	1349.06	1336.67	1325.92	1316.57	1308.42
125 000	1420.18	1405.27	1392.37	1381.17	1371.43	1362.94
130 000	1476.98	1461.48	1448.06	1436.42	1426.29	1417.46
135 000	1533.79	1517.69	1503.76	1491.66	1481.15	1471.98
140 000	1590.60	1573.91	1559.45	1546.91	1536.00	1526.50
145 000	1647.40	1630.12	1615.15	1602.16	1590.86	1581.01
150 000	1704.21	1686.33	1670.84	1657.41	1645.72	1635.53
155 000	1761.02	1742.54	1726.54	1712.65	1700.57	1690.05
160 000	1817.82	1798.75	1782.23	1767.90	1755.43	1744.57
165 000	1874.63	1854.96	1837.93	1823.15	1810.29	1799.08
170 000	1931.44	1911.17	1893.62	1878.39	1865.15	1853.60
175 000	1988.25	1967.38	1949.32	1933.64	1920.00	1908.12
180 000	2045.05	2023.59	2005.01	1988.89	1974.86	1962.64
185 000	2101.86	2079.80	2060.71	2044.13	2029.72	2017.16
190 000	2158.67	2136.01	2116.40	2099.38	2084.57	2071.67
195 000	2215.47	2192.23	2172.10	2154.63	2139.43	2126.19
200 000	2272.28	2248.44	2227.79	2209.87	2194.29	2180.71
205 000	2329.09	2304.65	2283.49	2265.12	2249.15	2235.23
210 000	2385.90	2360.86	2339.18	2320.37	2304.00	2289.74
215 000	2442.70	2417.07	2394.88	2375.61	2358.86	2344.26
220 000	2499.51	2473.28	2450.57	2430.86	2413.72	2398.78
225 000	2556.32	2529.49	2506.27	2486.11	2468.58	2453.30
230 000	2613.12	2585.70	2561.96	2541.35	2523.43	2507.81
235 000	2669.93	2641.91	2617.66	2596.60	2578.29	2562.33
240 000	2726.74	2698.12	2673.35	2651.85	2633.15	2616.85
245 000	2783.54	2754.33	2729.04	2707.10	2688.00	2671.37
250 000	2840.35	2810.55	2784.74	2762.34	2742.86	2725.89
260 000	2953.97	2922.97	2896.13	2872.84	2852.58	2834.92
270 000	3067.58	3035.39	3007.52	2983.33	2962.29	2943.96
280 000	3181.19	3147.81	3118.91	3093.82	3072.00	3052.99
290 000	3294.81	3260.23	3230.30	3204.32	3181.72	3162.03
300 000	3408.42	3372.65	3341.69	3314.81	3291.43	3271.06
400 000	4544.56	4496.87	4455.58	4419.75	4388.58	4361.42
500 000	5680.70	5621.09	5569.48	5524.68	5485.72	5451.77

46

	MONTHLY PAYMENT				**12.50%**	
	needed to pay back a mortgage				INTEREST	
Term	26 Years	27 Years	28 Years	29 Years	30 Years	35 Years
AMOUNT						
30 000	325.33	323.77	322.41	321.22	320.18	316.58
40 000	433.77	431.70	429.89	428.30	426.90	422.10
50 000	542.21	539.62	537.36	535.37	533.63	527.63
55 000	596.44	593.59	591.09	588.91	586.99	580.39
60 000	650.66	647.55	644.83	642.44	640.35	633.15
65 000	704.88	701.51	698.56	695.98	693.72	685.92
70 000	759.10	755.47	752.30	749.52	747.08	738.68
75 000	813.32	809.44	806.03	803.06	800.44	791.44
80 000	867.54	863.40	859.77	856.59	853.81	844.20
85 000	921.76	917.36	913.51	910.13	907.17	896.97
90 000	975.98	971.32	967.24	963.67	960.53	949.73
95 000	1030.21	1025.28	1020.98	1017.20	1013.89	1002.49
100 000	1084.43	1079.25	1074.71	1070.74	1067.26	1055.25
105 000	1138.65	1133.21	1128.45	1124.28	1120.62	1108.02
110 000	1192.87	1187.17	1182.18	1177.82	1173.98	1160.78
115 000	1247.09	1241.13	1235.92	1231.35	1227.35	1213.54
120 000	1301.31	1295.10	1289.66	1284.89	1280.71	1266.31
125 000	1355.53	1349.06	1343.39	1338.43	1334.07	1319.07
130 000	1409.76	1403.02	1397.13	1391.96	1387.44	1371.83
135 000	1463.98	1456.98	1450.86	1445.50	1440.80	1424.59
140 000	1518.20	1510.95	1504.60	1499.04	1494.16	1477.36
145 000	1572.42	1564.91	1558.33	1552.57	1547.52	1530.12
150 000	1626.64	1618.87	1612.07	1606.11	1600.89	1582.88
155 000	1680.86	1672.83	1665.81	1659.65	1654.25	1635.64
160 000	1735.08	1726.79	1719.54	1713.19	1707.61	1688.41
165 000	1789.31	1780.76	1773.28	1766.72	1760.98	1741.17
170 000	1843.53	1834.72	1827.01	1820.26	1814.34	1793.93
175 000	1897.75	1888.68	1880.75	1873.80	1867.70	1846.70
180 000	1951.97	1942.64	1934.48	1927.33	1921.06	1899.46
185 000	2006.19	1996.61	1988.22	1980.87	1974.43	1952.22
190 000	2060.41	2050.57	2041.95	2034.41	2027.79	2004.98
195 000	2114.63	2104.53	2095.69	2087.94	2081.15	2057.75
200 000	2168.85	2158.49	2149.43	2141.48	2134.52	2110.51
205 000	2223.08	2212.46	2203.16	2195.02	2187.88	2163.27
210 000	2277.30	2266.42	2256.90	2248.56	2241.24	2216.03
215 000	2331.52	2320.38	2310.63	2302.09	2294.60	2268.80
220 000	2385.74	2374.34	2364.37	2355.63	2347.97	2321.56
225 000	2439.96	2428.31	2418.10	2409.17	2401.33	2374.32
230 000	2494.18	2482.27	2471.84	2462.70	2454.69	2427.09
235 000	2548.40	2536.23	2525.58	2516.24	2508.06	2479.85
240 000	2602.63	2590.19	2579.31	2569.78	2561.42	2532.61
245 000	2656.85	2644.15	2633.05	2623.32	2614.78	2585.37
250 000	2711.07	2698.12	2686.78	2676.85	2668.14	2638.14
260 000	2819.51	2806.04	2794.25	2783.93	2774.87	2743.66
270 000	2927.95	2913.97	2901.73	2891.00	2881.60	2849.19
280 000	3036.40	3021.89	3009.20	2998.07	2988.32	2954.71
290 000	3144.84	3129.82	3116.67	3105.15	3095.05	3060.24
300 000	3253.28	3237.74	3224.14	3212.22	3201.77	3165.76
400 000	4337.71	4316.99	4298.85	4282.96	4269.03	4221.02
500 000	5422.14	5396.23	5373.57	5353.71	5336.29	5276.27

MONTHLY PAYMENT

needed to pay back a mortgage

Term	1 Year	5 Years	10 Years	11 Years	12 Years	13 Years
AMOUNT						
30 000	2679.52	682.59	447.93	428.28	412.39	399.36
40 000	3572.69	910.12	597.24	571.04	549.85	532.48
50 000	4465.86	1137.65	746.55	713.81	687.31	665.61
55 000	4912.45	1251.42	821.21	785.19	756.04	732.17
60 000	5359.04	1365.18	895.86	856.57	824.78	798.73
65 000	5805.62	1478.95	970.52	927.95	893.51	865.29
70 000	6252.21	1592.72	1045.18	999.33	962.24	931.85
75 000	6698.80	1706.48	1119.83	1070.71	1030.97	998.41
80 000	7145.38	1820.25	1194.49	1142.09	1099.70	1064.97
85 000	7591.97	1934.01	1269.14	1213.47	1168.43	1131.53
90 000	8038.55	2047.78	1343.80	1284.85	1237.16	1198.09
95 000	8485.14	2161.54	1418.45	1356.23	1305.89	1264.65
100 000	8931.73	2275.31	1493.11	1427.61	1374.63	1331.21
105 000	9378.31	2389.07	1567.76	1498.99	1443.36	1397.77
110 000	9824.90	2502.84	1642.42	1570.37	1512.09	1464.33
115 000	10271.49	2616.60	1717.07	1641.75	1580.82	1530.89
120 000	10718.07	2730.37	1791.73	1713.13	1649.55	1597.45
125 000	11164.66	2844.13	1866.38	1784.51	1718.28	1664.01
130 000	11611.25	2957.90	1941.04	1855.89	1787.01	1730.57
135 000	12057.83	3071.66	2015.69	1927.27	1855.74	1797.13
140 000	12504.42	3185.43	2090.35	1998.66	1924.48	1863.69
145 000	12951.00	3299.20	2165.01	2070.04	1993.21	1930.25
150 000	13397.59	3412.96	2239.66	2141.42	2061.94	1996.82
155 000	13844.18	3526.73	2314.32	2212.80	2130.67	2063.38
160 000	14290.76	3640.49	2388.97	2284.18	2199.40	2129.94
165 000	14737.35	3754.26	2463.63	2355.56	2268.13	2196.50
170 000	15183.94	3868.02	2538.28	2426.94	2336.86	2263.06
175 000	15630.52	3981.79	2612.94	2498.32	2405.59	2329.62
180 000	16077.11	4095.55	2687.59	2569.70	2474.33	2396.18
185 000	16523.70	4209.32	2762.25	2641.08	2543.06	2462.74
190 000	16970.28	4323.08	2836.90	2712.46	2611.79	2529.30
195 000	17416.87	4436.85	2911.56	2783.84	2680.52	2595.86
200 000	17863.46	4550.61	2986.21	2855.22	2749.25	2662.42
205 000	18310.04	4664.38	3060.87	2926.60	2817.98	2728.98
210 000	18756.63	4778.15	3135.53	2997.98	2886.71	2795.54
215 000	19203.21	4891.91	3210.18	3069.36	2955.44	2862.10
220 000	19649.80	5005.68	3284.84	3140.74	3024.18	2928.66
225 000	20096.39	5119.44	3359.49	3212.12	3092.91	2995.22
230 000	20542.97	5233.21	3434.15	3283.50	3161.64	3061.78
235 000	20989.56	5346.97	3508.80	3354.89	3230.37	3128.34
240 000	21436.15	5460.74	3583.46	3426.27	3299.10	3194.90
245 000	21882.73	5574.50	3658.11	3497.65	3367.83	3261.47
250 000	22329.32	5688.27	3732.77	3569.03	3436.56	3328.03
260 000	23222.49	5915.80	3882.08	3711.79	3574.03	3461.15
270 000	24115.66	6143.33	4031.39	3854.55	3711.49	3594.27
280 000	25008.84	6370.86	4180.70	3997.31	3848.95	3727.39
290 000	25902.01	6598.39	4330.01	4140.07	3986.41	3860.51
300 000	26795.18	6825.92	4479.32	4282.83	4123.88	3993.63
400 000	35726.91	9101.23	5972.43	5710.44	5498.50	5324.84
500 000	44658.64	11376.54	7465.54	7138.05	6873.13	6656.05

	MONTHLY PAYMENT				**13.00%**	
	needed to pay back a mortgage				INTEREST	
Term	**14** Years	**15** Years	**16** Years	**17** Years	**18** Years	**19** Years
AMOUNT						
30 000	388.58	379.57	372.00	365.58	360.13	355.47
40 000	518.11	506.10	496.00	487.45	480.17	473.96
50 000	647.63	632.62	619.99	609.31	600.22	592.45
55 000	712.39	695.88	681.99	670.24	660.24	651.69
60 000	777.16	759.15	743.99	731.17	720.26	710.94
65 000	841.92	822.41	805.99	792.10	780.28	770.18
70 000	906.68	885.67	867.99	853.03	840.30	829.43
75 000	971.45	948.93	929.99	913.96	900.32	888.67
80 000	1036.21	1012.19	991.99	974.89	960.35	947.92
85 000	1100.97	1075.46	1053.99	1035.82	1020.37	1007.16
90 000	1165.74	1138.72	1115.99	1096.75	1080.39	1066.41
95 000	1230.50	1201.98	1177.99	1157.68	1140.41	1125.65
100 000	1295.26	1265.24	1239.99	1218.61	1200.43	1184.90
105 000	1360.03	1328.50	1301.99	1279.55	1260.45	1244.14
110 000	1424.79	1391.77	1363.99	1340.48	1320.48	1303.39
115 000	1489.55	1455.03	1425.99	1401.41	1380.50	1362.63
120 000	1554.32	1518.29	1487.99	1462.34	1440.52	1421.88
125 000	1619.08	1581.55	1549.98	1523.27	1500.54	1481.12
130 000	1683.84	1644.81	1611.98	1584.20	1560.56	1540.37
135 000	1748.61	1708.08	1673.98	1645.13	1620.58	1599.61
140 000	1813.37	1771.34	1735.98	1706.06	1680.61	1658.86
145 000	1878.13	1834.60	1797.98	1766.99	1740.63	1718.10
150 000	1942.90	1897.86	1859.98	1827.92	1800.65	1777.35
155 000	2007.66	1961.13	1921.98	1888.85	1860.67	1836.59
160 000	2072.42	2024.39	1983.98	1949.78	1920.69	1895.84
165 000	2137.18	2087.65	2045.98	2010.71	1980.71	1955.08
170 000	2201.95	2150.91	2107.98	2071.64	2040.74	2014.33
175 000	2266.71	2214.17	2169.98	2132.58	2100.76	2073.57
180 000	2331.47	2277.44	2231.98	2193.51	2160.78	2132.82
185 000	2396.24	2340.70	2293.98	2254.44	2220.80	2192.06
190 000	2461.00	2403.96	2355.98	2315.37	2280.82	2251.31
195 000	2525.76	2467.22	2417.98	2376.30	2340.84	2310.55
200 000	2590.53	2530.48	2479.98	2437.23	2400.87	2369.80
205 000	2655.29	2593.75	2541.98	2498.16	2460.89	2429.04
210 000	2720.05	2657.01	2603.97	2559.09	2520.91	2488.29
215 000	2784.82	2720.27	2665.97	2620.02	2580.93	2547.53
220 000	2849.58	2783.53	2727.97	2680.95	2640.95	2606.78
225 000	2914.34	2846.79	2789.97	2741.88	2700.97	2666.02
230 000	2979.11	2910.06	2851.97	2802.81	2760.99	2725.27
235 000	3043.87	2973.32	2913.97	2863.74	2821.02	2784.51
240 000	3108.63	3036.58	2975.97	2924.67	2881.04	2843.76
245 000	3173.40	3099.84	3037.97	2985.61	2941.06	2903.00
250 000	3238.16	3163.11	3099.97	3046.54	3001.08	2962.24
260 000	3367.69	3289.63	3223.97	3168.40	3121.12	3080.73
270 000	3497.21	3416.15	3347.97	3290.26	3241.17	3199.22
280 000	3626.74	3542.68	3471.97	3412.12	3361.21	3317.71
290 000	3756.26	3669.20	3595.96	3533.98	3481.25	3436.20
300 000	3885.79	3795.73	3719.96	3655.84	3601.30	3554.69
400 000	5181.05	5060.97	4959.95	4874.46	4801.73	4739.59
500 000	6476.32	6326.21	6199.94	6093.07	6002.16	5924.49

13.00% INTEREST	MONTHLY PAYMENT					
	needed to pay back a mortgage					
Term	**20 Years**	**21 Years**	**22 Years**	**23 Years**	**24 Years**	**25 Years**
AMOUNT						
30 000	351.47	348.03	345.07	342.50	340.28	338.35
40 000	468.63	464.05	460.09	456.67	453.71	451.13
50 000	585.79	580.06	575.11	570.84	567.13	563.92
55 000	644.37	638.06	632.62	627.92	623.85	620.31
60 000	702.95	696.07	690.14	685.01	680.56	676.70
65 000	761.52	754.07	747.65	742.09	737.27	733.09
70 000	820.10	812.08	805.16	799.17	793.99	789.48
75 000	878.68	870.09	862.67	856.26	850.70	845.88
80 000	937.26	928.09	920.18	913.34	907.41	902.27
85 000	995.84	986.10	977.69	970.42	964.13	958.66
90 000	1054.42	1044.10	1035.20	1027.51	1020.84	1015.05
95 000	1113.00	1102.11	1092.72	1084.59	1077.55	1071.44
100 000	1171.58	1160.11	1150.23	1141.68	1134.27	1127.84
105 000	1230.15	1218.12	1207.74	1198.76	1190.98	1184.23
110 000	1288.73	1276.13	1265.25	1255.84	1247.69	1240.62
115 000	1347.31	1334.13	1322.76	1312.93	1304.41	1297.01
120 000	1405.89	1392.14	1380.27	1370.01	1361.12	1353.40
125 000	1464.47	1450.14	1437.78	1427.09	1417.83	1409.79
130 000	1523.05	1508.15	1495.29	1484.18	1474.55	1466.19
135 000	1581.63	1566.15	1552.81	1541.26	1531.26	1522.58
140 000	1640.21	1624.16	1610.32	1598.35	1587.97	1578.97
145 000	1698.78	1682.17	1667.83	1655.43	1644.69	1635.36
150 000	1757.36	1740.17	1725.34	1712.51	1701.40	1691.75
155 000	1815.94	1798.18	1782.85	1769.60	1758.11	1748.14
160 000	1874.52	1856.18	1840.36	1826.68	1814.83	1804.54
165 000	1933.10	1914.19	1897.87	1883.77	1871.54	1860.93
170 000	1991.68	1972.19	1955.38	1940.85	1928.25	1917.32
175 000	2050.26	2030.20	2012.90	1997.93	1984.97	1973.71
180 000	2108.84	2088.21	2070.41	2055.02	2041.68	2030.10
185 000	2167.42	2146.21	2127.92	2112.10	2098.39	2086.50
190 000	2225.99	2204.22	2185.43	2169.18	2155.11	2142.89
195 000	2284.57	2262.22	2242.94	2226.27	2211.82	2199.28
200 000	2343.15	2320.23	2300.45	2283.35	2268.53	2255.67
205 000	2401.73	2378.23	2357.96	2340.44	2325.25	2312.06
210 000	2460.31	2436.24	2415.48	2397.52	2381.96	2368.45
215 000	2518.89	2494.25	2472.99	2454.60	2438.67	2424.85
220 000	2577.47	2552.25	2530.50	2511.69	2495.39	2481.24
225 000	2636.05	2610.26	2588.01	2568.77	2552.10	2537.63
230 000	2694.62	2668.26	2645.52	2625.85	2608.81	2594.02
235 000	2753.20	2726.27	2703.03	2682.94	2665.53	2650.41
240 000	2811.78	2784.27	2760.54	2740.02	2722.24	2706.80
245 000	2870.36	2842.28	2818.05	2797.11	2778.95	2763.20
250 000	2928.94	2900.29	2875.57	2854.19	2835.67	2819.59
260 000	3046.10	3016.30	2990.59	2968.36	2949.09	2932.37
270 000	3163.25	3132.31	3105.61	3082.52	3062.52	3045.16
280 000	3280.41	3248.32	3220.63	3196.69	3175.95	3157.94
290 000	3397.57	3364.33	3335.66	3310.86	3289.37	3270.72
300 000	3514.73	3480.34	3450.68	3425.03	3402.80	3383.51
400 000	4686.30	4640.46	4600.91	4566.70	4537.07	4511.34
500 000	5857.88	5800.57	5751.13	5708.38	5671.33	5639.18

| | | **MONTHLY PAYMENT** | | | **13.00%** | |
| | | needed to pay back a mortgage | | | INTEREST | |
Term	26 Years	27 Years	28 Years	29 Years	30 Years	35 Years
AMOUNT						
30 000	336.67	335.21	333.94	332.83	331.86	328.56
40 000	448.90	446.95	445.25	443.77	442.48	438.08
50 000	561.12	558.69	556.57	554.72	553.10	547.60
55 000	617.23	614.56	612.22	610.19	608.41	602.36
60 000	673.35	670.43	667.88	665.66	663.72	657.12
65 000	729.46	726.29	723.54	721.13	719.03	711.88
70 000	785.57	782.16	779.19	776.60	774.34	766.64
75 000	841.68	838.03	834.85	832.07	829.65	821.39
80 000	897.80	893.90	890.51	887.55	884.96	876.15
85 000	953.91	949.77	946.16	943.02	940.27	930.91
90 000	1010.02	1005.64	1001.82	998.49	995.58	985.67
95 000	1066.13	1061.51	1057.48	1053.96	1050.89	1040.43
100 000	1122.24	1117.38	1113.13	1109.43	1106.20	1095.19
105 000	1178.36	1173.24	1168.79	1164.90	1161.51	1149.95
110 000	1234.47	1229.11	1224.45	1220.38	1216.82	1204.71
115 000	1290.58	1284.98	1280.10	1275.85	1272.13	1259.47
120 000	1346.69	1340.85	1335.76	1331.32	1327.44	1314.23
125 000	1402.80	1396.72	1391.42	1386.79	1382.75	1368.99
130 000	1458.92	1452.59	1447.07	1442.26	1438.06	1423.75
135 000	1515.03	1508.46	1502.73	1497.73	1493.37	1478.51
140 000	1571.14	1564.33	1558.39	1553.20	1548.68	1533.27
145 000	1627.25	1620.20	1614.04	1608.68	1603.99	1588.03
150 000	1683.37	1676.06	1669.70	1664.15	1659.30	1642.79
155 000	1739.48	1731.93	1725.36	1719.62	1714.61	1697.55
160 000	1795.59	1787.80	1781.01	1775.09	1769.92	1752.31
165 000	1851.70	1843.67	1836.67	1830.56	1825.23	1807.07
170 000	1907.81	1899.54	1892.33	1886.03	1880.54	1861.83
175 000	1963.93	1955.41	1947.98	1941.51	1935.85	1916.59
180 000	2020.04	2011.28	2003.64	1996.98	1991.16	1971.35
185 000	2076.15	2067.15	2059.30	2052.45	2046.47	2026.11
190 000	2132.26	2123.01	2114.95	2107.92	2101.78	2080.87
195 000	2188.38	2178.88	2170.61	2163.39	2157.09	2135.63
200 000	2244.49	2234.75	2226.27	2218.86	2212.40	2190.39
205 000	2300.60	2290.62	2281.92	2274.34	2267.71	2245.15
210 000	2356.71	2346.49	2337.58	2329.81	2323.02	2299.91
215 000	2412.82	2402.36	2393.24	2385.28	2378.33	2354.67
220 000	2468.94	2458.23	2448.89	2440.75	2433.64	2409.42
225 000	2525.05	2514.10	2504.55	2496.22	2488.95	2464.18
230 000	2581.16	2569.96	2560.21	2551.69	2544.26	2518.94
235 000	2637.27	2625.83	2615.86	2607.16	2599.57	2573.70
240 000	2693.39	2681.70	2671.52	2662.64	2654.88	2628.46
245 000	2749.50	2737.57	2727.18	2718.11	2710.19	2683.22
250 000	2805.61	2793.44	2782.83	2773.58	2765.50	2737.98
260 000	2917.83	2905.18	2894.15	2884.52	2876.12	2847.50
270 000	3030.06	3016.92	3005.46	2995.47	2986.74	2957.02
280 000	3142.28	3128.65	3116.77	3106.41	3097.36	3066.54
290 000	3254.51	3240.39	3228.09	3217.35	3207.98	3176.06
300 000	3366.73	3352.13	3339.40	3328.30	3318.60	3285.58
400 000	4488.98	4469.50	4452.53	4437.73	4424.80	4380.77
500 000	5611.22	5586.88	5565.67	5547.16	5531.00	5475.97

13.50% INTEREST	MONTHLY PAYMENT needed to pay back a mortgage					
Term	1 Year	5 Years	10 Years	11 Years	12 Years	13 Years
AMOUNT						
30 000	2686.56	690.30	456.82	437.40	421.72	408.90
40 000	3582.08	920.39	609.10	583.19	562.29	545.20
50 000	4477.60	1150.49	761.37	728.99	702.86	681.50
55 000	4925.36	1265.54	837.51	801.89	773.14	749.65
60 000	5373.12	1380.59	913.65	874.79	843.43	817.80
65 000	5820.88	1495.64	989.78	947.69	913.72	885.94
70 000	6268.64	1610.69	1065.92	1020.59	984.00	954.09
75 000	6716.40	1725.74	1142.06	1093.49	1054.29	1022.24
80 000	7164.16	1840.79	1218.19	1166.39	1124.57	1090.39
85 000	7611.92	1955.84	1294.33	1239.29	1194.86	1158.54
90 000	8059.68	2070.89	1370.47	1312.19	1265.15	1226.69
95 000	8507.44	2185.94	1446.61	1385.09	1335.43	1294.84
100 000	8955.20	2300.98	1522.74	1457.99	1405.72	1362.99
105 000	9402.96	2416.03	1598.88	1530.89	1476.00	1431.14
110 000	9850.72	2531.08	1675.02	1603.79	1546.29	1499.29
115 000	10298.48	2646.13	1751.15	1676.68	1616.57	1567.44
120 000	10746.24	2761.18	1827.29	1749.58	1686.86	1635.59
125 000	11194.00	2876.23	1903.43	1822.48	1757.15	1703.74
130 000	11641.76	2991.28	1979.57	1895.38	1827.43	1771.89
135 000	12089.52	3106.33	2055.70	1968.28	1897.72	1840.04
140 000	12537.28	3221.38	2131.84	2041.18	1968.00	1908.19
145 000	12985.04	3336.43	2207.98	2114.08	2038.29	1976.34
150 000	13432.80	3451.48	2284.11	2186.98	2108.58	2044.49
155 000	13880.56	3566.53	2360.25	2259.88	2178.86	2112.64
160 000	14328.32	3681.58	2436.39	2332.78	2249.15	2180.79
165 000	14776.08	3796.62	2512.53	2405.68	2319.43	2248.94
170 000	15223.84	3911.67	2588.66	2478.58	2389.72	2317.09
175 000	15671.60	4026.72	2664.80	2551.48	2460.01	2385.24
180 000	16119.36	4141.77	2740.94	2624.38	2530.29	2453.39
185 000	16567.13	4256.82	2817.07	2697.28	2600.58	2521.53
190 000	17014.89	4371.87	2893.21	2770.17	2670.86	2589.68
195 000	17462.65	4486.92	2969.35	2843.07	2741.15	2657.83
200 000	17910.41	4601.97	3045.49	2915.97	2811.43	2725.98
205 000	18358.17	4717.02	3121.62	2988.87	2881.72	2794.13
210 000	18805.93	4832.07	3197.76	3061.77	2952.01	2862.28
215 000	19253.69	4947.12	3273.90	3134.67	3022.29	2930.43
220 000	19701.45	5062.17	3350.03	3207.57	3092.58	2998.58
225 000	20149.21	5177.22	3426.17	3280.47	3162.86	3066.73
230 000	20596.97	5292.26	3502.31	3353.37	3233.15	3134.88
235 000	21044.73	5407.31	3578.45	3426.27	3303.44	3203.03
240 000	21492.49	5522.36	3654.58	3499.17	3373.72	3271.18
245 000	21940.25	5637.41	3730.72	3572.07	3444.01	3339.33
250 000	22388.01	5752.46	3806.86	3644.97	3514.29	3407.48
260 000	23283.53	5982.56	3959.13	3790.77	3654.86	3543.78
270 000	24179.05	6212.66	4111.41	3936.56	3795.44	3680.08
280 000	25074.57	6442.76	4263.68	4082.36	3936.01	3816.38
290 000	25970.09	6672.86	4415.95	4228.16	4076.58	3952.68
300 000	26865.61	6902.95	4568.23	4373.96	4217.15	4088.98
400 000	35820.81	9203.94	6090.97	5831.95	5622.87	5451.97
500 000	44776.01	11504.92	7613.71	7289.93	7028.59	6814.96

Term	14 Years	15 Years	16 Years	17 Years	18 Years	19 Years
AMOUNT						
30 000	398.31	389.50	382.10	375.86	370.57	366.06
40 000	531.08	519.33	509.47	501.15	494.09	488.08
50 000	663.85	649.16	636.83	626.43	617.62	610.11
55 000	730.24	714.08	700.52	689.08	679.38	671.12
60 000	796.62	778.99	764.20	751.72	741.14	732.13
65 000	863.01	843.91	827.88	814.36	802.90	793.14
70 000	929.39	908.82	891.57	877.01	864.66	854.15
75 000	995.78	973.74	955.25	939.65	926.42	915.16
80 000	1062.17	1038.65	1018.93	1002.30	988.19	976.17
85 000	1128.55	1103.57	1082.62	1064.94	1049.95	1037.18
90 000	1194.94	1168.49	1146.30	1127.58	1111.71	1098.19
95 000	1261.32	1233.40	1209.98	1190.23	1173.47	1159.20
100 000	1327.71	1298.32	1273.67	1252.87	1235.23	1220.21
105 000	1394.09	1363.23	1337.35	1315.51	1296.99	1281.22
110 000	1460.48	1428.15	1401.03	1378.16	1358.75	1342.23
115 000	1526.86	1493.07	1464.72	1440.80	1420.52	1403.24
120 000	1593.25	1557.98	1528.40	1503.44	1482.28	1464.25
125 000	1659.63	1622.90	1592.09	1566.09	1544.04	1525.26
130 000	1726.02	1687.81	1655.77	1628.73	1605.80	1586.27
135 000	1792.40	1752.73	1719.45	1691.37	1667.56	1647.29
140 000	1858.79	1817.65	1783.14	1754.02	1729.32	1708.30
145 000	1925.17	1882.56	1846.82	1816.66	1791.09	1769.31
150 000	1991.56	1947.48	1910.50	1879.30	1852.85	1830.32
155 000	2057.95	2012.39	1974.19	1941.95	1914.61	1891.33
160 000	2124.33	2077.31	2037.87	2004.59	1976.37	1952.34
165 000	2190.72	2142.23	2101.55	2067.23	2038.13	2013.35
170 000	2257.10	2207.14	2165.24	2129.88	2099.89	2074.36
175 000	2323.49	2272.06	2228.92	2192.52	2161.65	2135.37
180 000	2389.87	2336.97	2292.60	2255.16	2223.42	2196.38
185 000	2456.26	2401.89	2356.29	2317.81	2285.18	2257.39
190 000	2522.64	2466.81	2419.97	2380.45	2346.94	2318.40
195 000	2589.03	2531.72	2483.65	2443.09	2408.70	2379.41
200 000	2655.41	2596.64	2547.34	2505.74	2470.46	2440.42
205 000	2721.80	2661.55	2611.02	2568.38	2532.22	2501.43
210 000	2788.18	2726.47	2674.70	2631.02	2593.99	2562.44
215 000	2854.57	2791.38	2738.39	2693.67	2655.75	2623.45
220 000	2920.96	2856.30	2802.07	2756.31	2717.51	2684.47
225 000	2987.34	2921.22	2865.75	2818.95	2779.27	2745.48
230 000	3053.73	2986.13	2929.44	2881.60	2841.03	2806.49
235 000	3120.11	3051.05	2993.12	2944.24	2902.79	2867.50
240 000	3186.50	3115.96	3056.80	3006.89	2964.56	2928.51
245 000	3252.88	3180.88	3120.49	3069.53	3026.32	2989.52
250 000	3319.27	3245.80	3184.17	3132.17	3088.08	3050.53
260 000	3452.04	3375.63	3311.54	3257.46	3211.60	3172.55
270 000	3584.81	3505.46	3438.90	3382.75	3335.12	3294.57
280 000	3717.58	3635.29	3566.27	3508.04	3458.65	3416.59
290 000	3850.35	3765.12	3693.64	3633.32	3582.17	3538.61
300 000	3983.12	3894.96	3821.00	3758.61	3705.69	3660.63
400 000	5310.83	5193.27	5094.67	5011.48	4940.93	4880.85
500 000	6638.53	6491.59	6368.34	6264.34	6176.16	6101.06

13.50% INTEREST	**MONTHLY PAYMENT** needed to pay back a mortgage				
Term	**20 Years**	**21 Years**	**22 Years**	**23 Years**	**24 Years**	**25 Years**

AMOUNT	20 Years	21 Years	22 Years	23 Years	24 Years	25 Years
30 000	362.21	358.91	356.07	353.63	351.52	349.69
40 000	482.95	478.55	474.76	471.50	468.69	466.26
50 000	603.69	598.18	593.46	589.38	585.86	582.82
55 000	664.06	658.00	652.80	648.32	644.45	641.10
60 000	724.42	717.82	712.15	707.26	703.04	699.39
65 000	784.79	777.64	771.49	766.19	761.62	757.67
70 000	845.16	837.46	830.84	825.13	820.21	815.95
75 000	905.53	897.28	890.18	884.07	878.80	874.23
80 000	965.90	957.10	949.53	943.01	937.38	932.52
85 000	1026.27	1016.91	1008.87	1001.95	995.97	990.80
90 000	1086.64	1076.73	1068.22	1060.89	1054.55	1049.08
95 000	1147.01	1136.55	1127.57	1119.82	1113.14	1107.36
100 000	1207.37	1196.37	1186.91	1178.76	1171.73	1165.64
105 000	1267.74	1256.19	1246.26	1237.70	1230.31	1223.93
110 000	1328.11	1316.01	1305.60	1296.64	1288.90	1282.21
115 000	1388.48	1375.83	1364.95	1355.58	1347.49	1340.49
120 000	1448.85	1435.64	1424.29	1414.51	1406.07	1398.77
125 000	1509.22	1495.46	1483.64	1473.45	1464.66	1457.06
130 000	1569.59	1555.28	1542.98	1532.39	1523.25	1515.34
135 000	1629.96	1615.10	1602.33	1591.33	1581.83	1573.62
140 000	1690.32	1674.92	1661.67	1650.27	1640.42	1631.90
145 000	1750.69	1734.74	1721.02	1709.20	1699.00	1690.19
150 000	1811.06	1794.55	1780.37	1768.14	1757.59	1748.47
155 000	1871.43	1854.37	1839.71	1827.08	1816.18	1806.75
160 000	1931.80	1914.19	1899.06	1886.02	1874.76	1865.03
165 000	1992.17	1974.01	1958.40	1944.96	1933.35	1923.31
170 000	2052.54	2033.83	2017.75	2003.89	1991.94	1981.60
175 000	2112.91	2093.65	2077.09	2062.83	2050.52	2039.88
180 000	2173.27	2153.47	2136.44	2121.77	2109.11	2098.16
185 000	2233.64	2213.28	2195.78	2180.71	2167.70	2156.44
190 000	2294.01	2273.10	2255.13	2239.65	2226.28	2214.73
195 000	2354.38	2332.92	2314.48	2298.58	2284.87	2273.01
200 000	2414.75	2392.74	2373.82	2357.52	2343.45	2331.29
205 000	2475.12	2452.56	2433.17	2416.46	2402.04	2389.57
210 000	2535.49	2512.38	2492.51	2475.40	2460.63	2447.85
215 000	2595.86	2572.20	2551.86	2534.34	2519.21	2506.14
220 000	2656.22	2632.01	2611.20	2593.28	2577.80	2564.42
225 000	2716.59	2691.83	2670.55	2652.21	2636.39	2622.70
230 000	2776.96	2751.65	2729.89	2711.15	2694.97	2680.98
235 000	2837.33	2811.47	2789.24	2770.09	2753.56	2739.27
240 000	2897.70	2871.29	2848.59	2829.03	2812.14	2797.55
245 000	2958.07	2931.11	2907.93	2887.97	2870.73	2855.83
250 000	3018.44	2990.92	2967.28	2946.90	2929.32	2914.11
260 000	3139.17	3110.56	3085.97	3064.78	3046.49	3030.68
270 000	3259.91	3230.20	3204.66	3182.66	3163.66	3147.24
280 000	3380.65	3349.84	3323.35	3300.53	3280.84	3263.81
290 000	3501.39	3469.47	3442.04	3418.41	3398.01	3380.37
300 000	3622.12	3589.11	3560.73	3536.28	3515.18	3496.93
400 000	4829.50	4785.48	4747.64	4715.05	4686.91	4662.58
500 000	6036.87	5981.85	5934.55	5893.81	5858.64	5828.22

Term	26 Years	27 Years	28 Years	29 Years	30 Years	35 Years
AMOUNT						
30 000	348.11	346.74	345.55	344.52	343.62	340.60
40 000	464.15	462.32	460.74	459.36	458.16	454.14
50 000	580.19	577.91	575.92	574.20	572.71	567.67
55 000	638.21	635.70	633.52	631.62	629.98	624.44
60 000	696.23	693.49	691.11	689.04	687.25	681.20
65 000	754.25	751.28	748.70	746.46	744.52	737.97
70 000	812.26	809.07	806.29	803.88	801.79	794.74
75 000	870.28	866.86	863.89	861.30	859.06	851.51
80 000	928.30	924.65	921.48	918.72	916.33	908.27
85 000	986.32	982.44	979.07	976.15	973.60	965.04
90 000	1044.34	1040.23	1036.66	1033.57	1030.87	1021.81
95 000	1102.36	1098.02	1094.26	1090.99	1088.14	1078.57
100 000	1160.38	1155.81	1151.85	1148.41	1145.41	1135.34
105 000	1218.40	1213.60	1209.44	1205.83	1202.68	1192.11
110 000	1276.42	1271.39	1267.03	1263.25	1259.95	1248.87
115 000	1334.44	1329.18	1324.63	1320.67	1317.22	1305.64
120 000	1392.45	1386.97	1382.22	1378.09	1374.49	1362.41
125 000	1450.47	1444.77	1439.81	1435.51	1431.77	1419.18
130 000	1508.49	1502.56	1497.40	1492.93	1489.04	1475.94
135 000	1566.51	1560.35	1555.00	1550.35	1546.31	1532.71
140 000	1624.53	1618.14	1612.59	1607.77	1603.58	1589.48
145 000	1682.55	1675.93	1670.18	1665.19	1660.85	1646.24
150 000	1740.57	1733.72	1727.77	1722.61	1718.12	1703.01
155 000	1798.59	1791.51	1785.37	1780.03	1775.39	1759.78
160 000	1856.61	1849.30	1842.96	1837.45	1832.66	1816.54
165 000	1914.62	1907.09	1900.55	1894.87	1889.93	1873.31
170 000	1972.64	1964.88	1958.14	1952.29	1947.20	1930.08
175 000	2030.66	2022.67	2015.74	2009.71	2004.47	1986.85
180 000	2088.68	2080.46	2073.33	2067.13	2061.74	2043.61
185 000	2146.70	2138.25	2130.92	2124.55	2119.01	2100.38
190 000	2204.72	2196.04	2188.51	2181.97	2176.28	2157.15
195 000	2262.74	2253.83	2246.11	2239.39	2233.55	2213.91
200 000	2320.76	2311.62	2303.70	2296.81	2290.82	2270.68
205 000	2378.77	2369.41	2361.29	2354.23	2348.09	2327.45
210 000	2436.79	2427.21	2418.88	2411.65	2405.37	2384.22
215 000	2494.81	2485.00	2476.48	2469.07	2462.64	2440.98
220 000	2552.83	2542.79	2534.07	2526.49	2519.91	2497.75
225 000	2610.85	2600.58	2591.66	2583.91	2577.18	2554.52
230 000	2668.87	2658.37	2649.25	2641.33	2634.45	2611.28
235 000	2726.89	2716.16	2706.85	2698.75	2691.72	2668.05
240 000	2784.91	2773.95	2764.44	2756.17	2748.99	2724.82
245 000	2842.93	2831.74	2822.03	2813.59	2806.26	2781.58
250 000	2900.95	2889.53	2879.62	2871.01	2863.53	2838.35
260 000	3016.98	3005.11	2994.81	2985.86	2978.07	2951.89
270 000	3133.02	3120.69	3109.99	3100.70	3092.61	3065.42
280 000	3249.06	3236.27	3225.18	3215.54	3207.15	3178.95
290 000	3365.10	3351.86	3340.36	3330.38	3321.70	3292.49
300 000	3481.13	3467.44	3455.55	3445.22	3436.24	3406.02
400 000	4641.51	4623.25	4607.40	4593.62	4581.65	4541.36
500 000	5801.89	5779.06	5759.24	5742.03	5727.06	5676.70

MONTHLY PAYMENT
needed to pay back a mortgage

Term	1 Year	5 Years	10 Years	11 Years	12 Years	13 Years
AMOUNT						
30 000	2693.61	698.05	465.80	446.60	431.14	418.53
40 000	3591.48	930.73	621.07	595.47	574.85	558.04
50 000	4489.36	1163.41	776.33	744.33	718.56	697.55
55 000	4938.29	1279.75	853.97	818.77	790.42	767.31
60 000	5387.23	1396.10	931.60	893.20	862.28	837.06
65 000	5836.16	1512.44	1009.23	967.63	934.13	906.82
70 000	6285.10	1628.78	1086.87	1042.07	1005.99	976.57
75 000	6734.03	1745.12	1164.50	1116.50	1077.85	1046.33
80 000	7182.97	1861.46	1242.13	1190.93	1149.70	1116.08
85 000	7631.90	1977.80	1319.76	1265.37	1221.56	1185.84
90 000	8080.84	2094.14	1397.40	1339.80	1293.41	1255.59
95 000	8529.78	2210.48	1475.03	1414.23	1365.27	1325.35
100 000	8978.71	2326.83	1552.66	1488.67	1437.13	1395.10
105 000	9427.65	2443.17	1630.30	1563.10	1508.98	1464.86
110 000	9876.58	2559.51	1707.93	1637.53	1580.84	1534.61
115 000	10325.52	2675.85	1785.56	1711.97	1652.70	1604.37
120 000	10774.45	2792.19	1863.20	1786.40	1724.55	1674.12
125 000	11223.39	2908.53	1940.83	1860.83	1796.41	1743.88
130 000	11672.33	3024.87	2018.46	1935.27	1868.27	1813.63
135 000	12121.26	3141.21	2096.10	2009.70	1940.12	1883.39
140 000	12570.20	3257.56	2173.73	2084.13	2011.98	1953.14
145 000	13019.13	3373.90	2251.36	2158.57	2083.83	2022.90
150 000	13468.07	3490.24	2329.00	2233.00	2155.69	2092.65
155 000	13917.00	3606.58	2406.63	2307.43	2227.55	2162.41
160 000	14365.94	3722.92	2484.26	2381.87	2299.40	2232.17
165 000	14814.87	3839.26	2561.90	2456.30	2371.26	2301.92
170 000	15263.81	3955.60	2639.53	2530.73	2443.12	2371.68
175 000	15712.75	4071.94	2717.16	2605.17	2514.97	2441.43
180 000	16161.68	4188.29	2794.80	2679.60	2586.83	2511.19
185 000	16610.62	4304.63	2872.43	2754.03	2658.69	2580.94
190 000	17059.55	4420.97	2950.06	2828.47	2730.54	2650.70
195 000	17508.49	4537.31	3027.70	2902.90	2802.40	2720.45
200 000	17957.42	4653.65	3105.33	2977.33	2874.25	2790.21
205 000	18406.36	4769.99	3182.96	3051.77	2946.11	2859.96
210 000	18855.29	4886.33	3260.60	3126.20	3017.97	2929.72
215 000	19304.23	5002.67	3338.23	3200.63	3089.82	2999.47
220 000	19753.17	5119.02	3415.86	3275.07	3161.68	3069.23
225 000	20202.10	5235.36	3493.49	3349.50	3233.54	3138.98
230 000	20651.04	5351.70	3571.13	3423.93	3305.39	3208.74
235 000	21099.97	5468.04	3648.76	3498.37	3377.25	3278.49
240 000	21548.91	5584.38	3726.39	3572.80	3449.11	3348.25
245 000	21997.84	5700.72	3804.03	3647.23	3520.96	3418.00
250 000	22446.78	5817.06	3881.66	3721.67	3592.82	3487.76
260 000	23344.65	6049.75	4036.93	3870.53	3736.53	3627.27
270 000	24242.52	6282.43	4192.19	4019.40	3880.24	3766.78
280 000	25140.39	6515.11	4347.46	4168.27	4023.96	3906.29
290 000	26038.26	6747.79	4502.73	4317.13	4167.67	4045.80
300 000	26936.14	6980.48	4657.99	4466.00	4311.38	4185.31
400 000	35914.85	9307.30	6210.66	5954.66	5748.51	5580.41
500 000	44893.56	11634.13	7763.32	7443.33	7185.64	6975.52

Term	14 Years	15 Years	16 Years	17 Years	18 Years	19 Years
AMOUNT						
30 000	408.15	399.52	392.31	386.24	381.11	376.76
40 000	544.20	532.70	523.08	514.99	508.15	502.35
50 000	680.24	665.87	653.85	643.74	635.19	627.94
55 000	748.27	732.46	719.23	708.11	698.71	690.73
60 000	816.29	799.04	784.62	772.49	762.23	753.53
65 000	884.32	865.63	850.00	836.86	825.75	816.32
70 000	952.34	932.22	915.39	901.23	889.27	879.11
75 000	1020.37	998.81	980.77	965.61	952.79	941.91
80 000	1088.39	1065.39	1046.16	1029.98	1016.31	1004.70
85 000	1156.42	1131.98	1111.54	1094.35	1079.83	1067.49
90 000	1224.44	1198.57	1176.93	1158.73	1143.34	1130.29
95 000	1292.47	1265.15	1242.31	1223.10	1206.86	1193.08
100 000	1360.49	1331.74	1307.70	1287.48	1270.38	1255.88
105 000	1428.51	1398.33	1373.08	1351.85	1333.90	1318.67
110 000	1496.54	1464.92	1438.47	1416.22	1397.42	1381.46
115 000	1564.56	1531.50	1503.85	1480.60	1460.94	1444.26
120 000	1632.59	1598.09	1569.24	1544.97	1524.46	1507.05
125 000	1700.61	1664.68	1634.62	1609.35	1587.98	1569.84
130 000	1768.64	1731.26	1700.01	1673.72	1651.50	1632.64
135 000	1836.66	1797.85	1765.39	1738.09	1715.02	1695.43
140 000	1904.69	1864.44	1830.78	1802.47	1778.54	1758.23
145 000	1972.71	1931.03	1896.16	1866.84	1842.06	1821.02
150 000	2040.73	1997.61	1961.55	1931.21	1905.57	1883.81
155 000	2108.76	2064.20	2026.93	1995.59	1969.09	1946.61
160 000	2176.78	2130.79	2092.32	2059.96	2032.61	2009.40
165 000	2244.81	2197.37	2157.70	2124.34	2096.13	2072.20
170 000	2312.83	2263.96	2223.09	2188.71	2159.65	2134.99
175 000	2380.86	2330.55	2288.47	2253.08	2223.17	2197.78
180 000	2448.88	2397.13	2353.86	2317.46	2286.69	2260.58
185 000	2516.91	2463.72	2419.24	2381.83	2350.21	2323.37
190 000	2584.93	2530.31	2484.63	2446.20	2413.73	2386.16
195 000	2652.95	2596.90	2550.01	2510.58	2477.25	2448.96
200 000	2720.98	2663.48	2615.40	2574.95	2540.77	2511.75
205 000	2789.00	2730.07	2680.78	2639.33	2604.29	2574.55
210 000	2857.03	2796.66	2746.17	2703.70	2667.80	2637.34
215 000	2925.05	2863.24	2811.55	2768.07	2731.32	2700.13
220 000	2993.08	2929.83	2876.94	2832.45	2794.84	2762.93
225 000	3061.10	2996.42	2942.32	2896.82	2858.36	2825.72
230 000	3129.13	3063.01	3007.71	2961.20	2921.88	2888.51
235 000	3197.15	3129.59	3073.09	3025.57	2985.40	2951.31
240 000	3265.18	3196.18	3138.48	3089.94	3048.92	3014.10
245 000	3333.20	3262.77	3203.86	3154.32	3112.44	3076.90
250 000	3401.22	3329.35	3269.25	3218.69	3175.96	3139.69
260 000	3537.27	3462.53	3400.02	3347.44	3303.00	3265.28
270 000	3673.32	3595.70	3530.79	3476.19	3430.03	3390.87
280 000	3809.37	3728.88	3661.56	3604.93	3557.07	3516.45
290 000	3945.42	3862.05	3792.33	3733.68	3684.11	3642.04
300 000	4081.47	3995.22	3923.10	3862.43	3811.15	3767.63
400 000	5441.96	5326.97	5230.80	5149.90	5081.53	5023.50
500 000	6802.45	6658.71	6538.50	6437.38	6351.92	6279.38

14.00% INTEREST	MONTHLY PAYMENT needed to pay back a mortgage				
Term	20 Years	21 Years	22 Years	23 Years	24 Years	25 Years

Term	20 Years	21 Years	22 Years	23 Years	24 Years	25 Years
AMOUNT						
30 000	373.06	369.89	367.18	364.85	362.85	361.13
40 000	497.41	493.19	489.57	486.47	483.80	481.50
50 000	621.76	616.48	611.96	608.09	604.75	601.88
55 000	683.94	678.13	673.16	668.90	665.23	662.07
60 000	746.11	739.78	734.36	729.70	725.70	722.26
65 000	808.29	801.43	795.55	790.51	786.18	782.44
70 000	870.46	863.08	856.75	851.32	846.65	842.63
75 000	932.64	924.73	917.95	912.13	907.13	902.82
80 000	994.82	986.37	979.14	972.94	967.60	963.01
85 000	1056.99	1048.02	1040.34	1033.75	1028.08	1023.20
90 000	1119.17	1109.67	1101.54	1094.56	1088.55	1083.38
95 000	1181.34	1171.32	1162.73	1155.36	1149.03	1143.57
100 000	1243.52	1232.97	1223.93	1216.17	1209.50	1203.76
105 000	1305.70	1294.62	1285.13	1276.98	1269.98	1263.95
110 000	1367.87	1356.26	1346.32	1337.79	1330.45	1324.14
115 000	1430.05	1417.91	1407.52	1398.60	1390.93	1384.33
120 000	1492.22	1479.56	1468.72	1459.41	1451.41	1444.51
125 000	1554.40	1541.21	1529.91	1520.22	1511.88	1504.70
130 000	1616.58	1602.86	1591.11	1581.03	1572.36	1564.89
135 000	1678.75	1664.51	1652.30	1641.83	1632.83	1625.08
140 000	1740.93	1726.15	1713.50	1702.64	1693.31	1685.27
145 000	1803.11	1787.80	1774.70	1763.45	1753.78	1745.45
150 000	1865.28	1849.45	1835.89	1824.26	1814.26	1805.64
155 000	1927.46	1911.10	1897.09	1885.07	1874.73	1865.83
160 000	1989.63	1972.75	1958.29	1945.88	1935.21	1926.02
165 000	2051.81	2034.40	2019.48	2006.69	1995.68	1986.21
170 000	2113.99	2096.04	2080.68	2067.49	2056.16	2046.39
175 000	2176.16	2157.69	2141.88	2128.30	2116.63	2106.58
180 000	2238.34	2219.34	2203.07	2189.11	2177.11	2166.77
185 000	2300.51	2280.99	2264.27	2249.92	2237.58	2226.96
190 000	2362.69	2342.64	2325.47	2310.73	2298.06	2287.15
195 000	2424.87	2404.29	2386.66	2371.54	2358.53	2347.33
200 000	2487.04	2465.93	2447.86	2432.35	2419.01	2407.52
205 000	2549.22	2527.58	2509.06	2493.15	2479.48	2467.71
210 000	2611.39	2589.23	2570.25	2553.96	2539.96	2527.90
215 000	2673.57	2650.88	2631.45	2614.77	2600.43	2588.09
220 000	2735.75	2712.53	2692.64	2675.58	2660.91	2648.27
225 000	2797.92	2774.18	2753.84	2736.39	2721.38	2708.46
230 000	2860.10	2835.82	2815.04	2797.20	2781.86	2768.65
235 000	2922.27	2897.47	2876.23	2858.01	2842.33	2828.84
240 000	2984.45	2959.12	2937.43	2918.82	2902.81	2889.03
245 000	3046.63	3020.77	2998.63	2979.62	2963.29	2949.21
250 000	3108.80	3082.42	3059.82	3040.43	3023.76	3009.40
260 000	3233.15	3205.71	3182.22	3162.05	3144.71	3129.78
270 000	3357.51	3329.01	3304.61	3283.67	3265.66	3250.15
280 000	3481.86	3452.31	3427.00	3405.28	3386.61	3370.53
290 000	3606.21	3575.60	3549.40	3526.90	3507.56	3490.91
300 000	3730.56	3698.90	3671.79	3648.52	3628.51	3611.28
400 000	4974.08	4931.87	4895.72	4864.69	4838.02	4815.04
500 000	6217.60	6164.84	6119.65	6080.87	6047.52	6018.81

needed to pay back a mortgage

Term	26 Years	27 Years	28 Years	29 Years	30 Years	35 Years
AMOUNT						
30 000	359.64	358.36	357.25	356.29	355.46	352.70
40 000	479.52	477.81	476.33	475.06	473.95	470.27
50 000	599.40	597.27	595.42	593.82	592.44	587.84
55 000	659.34	656.99	654.96	653.20	651.68	646.62
60 000	719.28	716.72	714.50	712.58	710.92	705.40
65 000	779.23	776.45	774.04	771.97	770.17	764.19
70 000	839.17	836.17	833.59	831.35	829.41	822.97
75 000	899.11	895.90	893.13	890.73	888.65	881.75
80 000	959.05	955.63	952.67	950.11	947.90	940.54
85 000	1018.99	1015.35	1012.21	1009.49	1007.14	999.32
90 000	1078.93	1075.08	1071.75	1068.88	1066.38	1058.11
95 000	1138.87	1134.81	1131.29	1128.26	1125.63	1116.89
100 000	1198.81	1194.53	1190.84	1187.64	1184.87	1175.67
105 000	1258.75	1254.26	1250.38	1247.02	1244.12	1234.46
110 000	1318.69	1313.99	1309.92	1306.40	1303.36	1293.24
115 000	1378.63	1373.71	1369.46	1365.79	1362.60	1352.02
120 000	1438.57	1433.44	1429.00	1425.17	1421.85	1410.81
125 000	1498.51	1493.17	1488.55	1484.55	1481.09	1469.59
130 000	1558.45	1552.89	1548.09	1543.93	1540.33	1528.38
135 000	1618.39	1612.62	1607.63	1603.31	1599.58	1587.16
140 000	1678.33	1672.35	1667.17	1662.70	1658.82	1645.94
145 000	1738.27	1732.07	1726.71	1722.08	1718.06	1704.73
150 000	1798.21	1791.80	1786.25	1781.46	1777.31	1763.51
155 000	1858.15	1851.52	1845.80	1840.84	1836.55	1822.29
160 000	1918.09	1911.25	1905.34	1900.22	1895.79	1881.08
165 000	1978.03	1970.98	1964.88	1959.61	1955.04	1939.86
170 000	2037.97	2030.70	2024.42	2018.99	2014.28	1998.64
175 000	2097.91	2090.43	2083.96	2078.37	2073.53	2057.43
180 000	2157.85	2150.16	2143.51	2137.75	2132.77	2116.21
185 000	2217.80	2209.88	2203.05	2197.13	2192.01	2175.00
190 000	2277.74	2269.61	2262.59	2256.51	2251.26	2233.78
195 000	2337.68	2329.34	2322.13	2315.90	2310.50	2292.56
200 000	2397.62	2389.06	2381.67	2375.28	2369.74	2351.35
205 000	2457.56	2448.79	2441.21	2434.66	2428.99	2410.13
210 000	2517.50	2508.52	2500.76	2494.04	2488.23	2468.91
215 000	2577.44	2568.24	2560.30	2553.42	2547.47	2527.70
220 000	2637.38	2627.97	2619.84	2612.81	2606.72	2586.48
225 000	2697.32	2687.70	2679.38	2672.19	2665.96	2645.26
230 000	2757.26	2747.42	2738.92	2731.57	2725.21	2704.05
235 000	2817.20	2807.15	2798.47	2790.95	2784.45	2762.83
240 000	2877.14	2866.88	2858.01	2850.33	2843.69	2821.62
245 000	2937.08	2926.60	2917.55	2909.72	2902.94	2880.40
250 000	2997.02	2986.33	2977.09	2969.10	2962.18	2939.18
260 000	3116.90	3105.78	3096.17	3087.86	3080.67	3056.75
270 000	3236.78	3225.24	3215.26	3206.63	3199.15	3174.32
280 000	3356.66	3344.69	3334.34	3325.39	3317.64	3291.89
290 000	3476.54	3464.14	3453.43	3444.15	3436.13	3409.45
300 000	3596.42	3583.60	3572.51	3562.92	3554.62	3527.02
400 000	4795.23	4778.13	4763.35	4750.56	4739.49	4702.69
500 000	5994.04	5972.66	5954.18	5938.20	5924.36	5878.37

14.50% INTEREST	MONTHLY PAYMENT needed to pay back a mortgage				
Term	1 Year	5 Years	10 Years	11 Years	12 Years	13 Years

AMOUNT

	1 Year	5 Years	10 Years	11 Years	12 Years	13 Years
30 000	2700.68	705.85	474.86	455.89	440.65	428.26
40 000	3600.90	941.13	633.15	607.86	587.54	571.02
50 000	4501.13	1176.41	791.43	759.82	734.42	713.77
55 000	4951.24	1294.05	870.58	835.80	807.87	785.15
60 000	5401.35	1411.70	949.72	911.79	881.31	856.52
65 000	5851.47	1529.34	1028.86	987.77	954.75	927.90
70 000	6301.58	1646.98	1108.01	1063.75	1028.19	999.28
75 000	6751.69	1764.62	1187.15	1139.73	1101.64	1070.65
80 000	7201.80	1882.26	1266.29	1215.72	1175.08	1142.03
85 000	7651.92	1999.90	1345.44	1291.70	1248.52	1213.41
90 000	8102.03	2117.55	1424.58	1367.68	1321.96	1284.78
95 000	8552.14	2235.19	1503.72	1443.66	1395.41	1356.16
100 000	9002.25	2352.83	1582.87	1519.64	1468.85	1427.54
105 000	9452.37	2470.47	1662.01	1595.63	1542.29	1498.91
110 000	9902.48	2588.11	1741.15	1671.61	1615.73	1570.29
115 000	10352.59	2705.75	1820.30	1747.59	1689.18	1641.67
120 000	10802.71	2823.39	1899.44	1823.57	1762.62	1713.05
125 000	11252.82	2941.04	1978.58	1899.55	1836.06	1784.42
130 000	11702.93	3058.68	2057.73	1975.54	1909.50	1855.80
135 000	12153.04	3176.32	2136.87	2051.52	1982.95	1927.18
140 000	12603.16	3293.96	2216.02	2127.50	2056.39	1998.55
145 000	13053.27	3411.60	2295.16	2203.48	2129.83	2069.93
150 000	13503.38	3529.24	2374.30	2279.47	2203.27	2141.31
155 000	13953.49	3646.88	2453.45	2355.45	2276.72	2212.68
160 000	14403.61	3764.52	2532.59	2431.43	2350.16	2284.06
165 000	14853.72	3882.17	2611.73	2507.41	2423.60	2355.44
170 000	15303.83	3999.81	2690.88	2583.39	2497.04	2426.81
175 000	15753.95	4117.45	2770.02	2659.38	2570.49	2498.19
180 000	16204.06	4235.09	2849.16	2735.36	2643.93	2569.57
185 000	16654.17	4352.73	2928.31	2811.34	2717.37	2640.94
190 000	17104.28	4470.37	3007.45	2887.32	2790.81	2712.32
195 000	17554.40	4588.01	3086.59	2963.31	2864.26	2783.70
200 000	18004.51	4705.66	3165.74	3039.29	2937.70	2855.08
205 000	18454.62	4823.30	3244.88	3115.27	3011.14	2926.45
210 000	18904.73	4940.94	3324.02	3191.25	3084.58	2997.83
215 000	19354.85	5058.58	3403.17	3267.23	3158.03	3069.21
220 000	19804.96	5176.22	3482.31	3343.22	3231.47	3140.58
225 000	20255.07	5293.86	3561.45	3419.20	3304.91	3211.96
230 000	20705.19	5411.50	3640.60	3495.18	3378.35	3283.34
235 000	21155.30	5529.15	3719.74	3571.16	3451.80	3354.71
240 000	21605.41	5646.79	3798.88	3647.15	3525.24	3426.09
245 000	22055.52	5764.43	3878.03	3723.13	3598.68	3497.47
250 000	22505.64	5882.07	3957.17	3799.11	3672.12	3568.84
260 000	23405.86	6117.35	4115.46	3951.07	3819.01	3711.60
270 000	24306.09	6352.64	4273.74	4103.04	3965.89	3854.35
280 000	25206.31	6587.92	4432.03	4255.00	4112.78	3997.11
290 000	26106.54	6823.20	4590.32	4406.97	4259.66	4139.86
300 000	27006.76	7058.48	4748.60	4558.93	4406.55	4282.61
400 000	36009.02	9411.31	6331.47	6078.58	5875.40	5710.15
500 000	45011.27	11764.14	7914.34	7598.22	7344.24	7137.69

Term	14 Years	15 Years	16 Years	17 Years	18 Years	19 Years
AMOUNT						
30 000	418.08	409.65	402.62	396.73	391.76	387.56
40 000	557.44	546.20	536.83	528.97	522.35	516.75
50 000	696.80	682.75	671.04	661.21	652.94	645.94
55 000	766.48	751.03	738.14	727.33	718.23	710.53
60 000	836.16	819.30	805.24	793.45	783.52	775.13
65 000	905.84	887.58	872.35	859.58	848.82	839.72
70 000	975.52	955.85	939.45	925.70	914.11	904.31
75 000	1045.20	1024.13	1006.55	991.82	979.41	968.91
80 000	1114.88	1092.40	1073.66	1057.94	1044.70	1033.50
85 000	1184.56	1160.68	1140.76	1124.06	1109.99	1098.09
90 000	1254.24	1228.95	1207.86	1190.18	1175.29	1162.69
95 000	1323.92	1297.23	1274.97	1256.30	1240.58	1227.28
100 000	1393.60	1365.50	1342.07	1322.42	1305.87	1291.88
105 000	1463.28	1433.78	1409.17	1388.55	1371.17	1356.47
110 000	1532.96	1502.05	1476.28	1454.67	1436.46	1421.06
115 000	1602.64	1570.33	1543.38	1520.79	1501.76	1485.66
120 000	1672.32	1638.60	1610.48	1586.91	1567.05	1550.25
125 000	1742.00	1706.88	1677.59	1653.03	1632.34	1614.85
130 000	1811.68	1775.15	1744.69	1719.15	1697.64	1679.44
135 000	1881.36	1843.43	1811.79	1785.27	1762.93	1744.03
140 000	1951.04	1911.70	1878.90	1851.39	1828.22	1808.63
145 000	2020.72	1979.98	1946.00	1917.52	1893.52	1873.22
150 000	2090.41	2048.25	2013.11	1983.64	1958.81	1937.81
155 000	2160.09	2116.53	2080.21	2049.76	2024.10	2002.41
160 000	2229.77	2184.80	2147.31	2115.88	2089.40	2067.00
165 000	2299.45	2253.08	2214.42	2182.00	2154.69	2131.60
170 000	2369.13	2321.35	2281.52	2248.12	2219.99	2196.19
175 000	2438.81	2389.63	2348.62	2314.24	2285.28	2260.78
180 000	2508.49	2457.90	2415.73	2380.36	2350.57	2325.38
185 000	2578.17	2526.18	2482.83	2446.48	2415.87	2389.97
190 000	2647.85	2594.45	2549.93	2512.61	2481.16	2454.57
195 000	2717.53	2662.73	2617.04	2578.73	2546.45	2519.16
200 000	2787.21	2731.00	2684.14	2644.85	2611.75	2583.75
205 000	2856.89	2799.28	2751.24	2710.97	2677.04	2648.35
210 000	2926.57	2867.55	2818.35	2777.09	2742.34	2712.94
215 000	2996.25	2935.83	2885.45	2843.21	2807.63	2777.53
220 000	3065.93	3004.10	2952.55	2909.33	2872.92	2842.13
225 000	3135.61	3072.38	3019.66	2975.45	2938.22	2906.72
230 000	3205.29	3140.65	3086.76	3041.58	3003.51	2971.32
235 000	3274.97	3208.93	3153.86	3107.70	3068.80	3035.91
240 000	3344.65	3277.20	3220.97	3173.82	3134.10	3100.50
245 000	3414.33	3345.48	3288.07	3239.94	3199.39	3165.10
250 000	3484.01	3413.75	3355.18	3306.06	3264.69	3229.69
260 000	3623.37	3550.30	3489.38	3438.30	3395.27	3358.88
270 000	3762.73	3686.85	3623.59	3570.55	3525.86	3488.07
280 000	3902.09	3823.40	3757.80	3702.79	3656.45	3617.25
290 000	4041.45	3959.95	3892.00	3835.03	3787.03	3746.44
300 000	4180.81	4096.50	4026.21	3967.27	3917.62	3875.63
400 000	5574.41	5462.00	5368.28	5289.70	5223.50	5167.51
500 000	6968.02	6827.50	6710.35	6612.12	6529.37	6459.38

14.50% INTEREST	MONTHLY PAYMENT needed to pay back a mortgage					
Term	20 Years	21 Years	22 Years	23 Years	24 Years	25 Years
AMOUNT						
30 000	384.00	380.97	378.38	376.17	374.27	372.65
40 000	512.00	507.96	504.51	501.56	499.03	496.87
50 000	640.00	634.94	630.63	626.95	623.79	621.08
55 000	704.00	698.44	693.70	689.64	686.17	683.19
60 000	768.00	761.93	756.76	752.34	748.55	745.30
65 000	832.00	825.43	819.82	815.03	810.93	807.41
70 000	896.00	888.92	882.89	877.72	873.30	869.51
75 000	960.00	952.42	945.95	940.42	935.68	931.62
80 000	1024.00	1015.91	1009.01	1003.11	998.06	993.73
85 000	1088.00	1079.41	1072.07	1065.81	1060.44	1055.84
90 000	1152.00	1142.90	1135.14	1128.50	1122.82	1117.95
95 000	1216.00	1206.39	1198.20	1191.20	1185.20	1180.05
100 000	1280.00	1269.89	1261.26	1253.89	1247.58	1242.16
105 000	1344.00	1333.38	1324.33	1316.59	1309.96	1304.27
110 000	1408.00	1396.88	1387.39	1379.28	1372.34	1366.38
115 000	1472.00	1460.37	1450.45	1441.98	1434.71	1428.49
120 000	1536.00	1523.87	1513.52	1504.67	1497.09	1490.60
125 000	1600.00	1587.36	1576.58	1567.36	1559.47	1552.70
130 000	1664.00	1650.86	1639.64	1630.06	1621.85	1614.81
135 000	1728.00	1714.35	1702.71	1692.75	1684.23	1676.92
140 000	1792.00	1777.84	1765.77	1755.45	1746.61	1739.03
145 000	1856.00	1841.34	1828.83	1818.14	1808.99	1801.14
150 000	1920.00	1904.83	1891.90	1880.84	1871.37	1863.24
155 000	1984.00	1968.33	1954.96	1943.53	1933.75	1925.35
160 000	2048.00	2031.82	2018.02	2006.23	1996.12	1987.46
165 000	2112.00	2095.32	2081.09	2068.92	2058.50	2049.57
170 000	2176.00	2158.81	2144.15	2131.62	2120.88	2111.68
175 000	2240.00	2222.30	2207.21	2194.31	2183.26	2173.79
180 000	2304.00	2285.80	2270.28	2257.01	2245.64	2235.89
185 000	2368.00	2349.29	2333.34	2319.70	2308.02	2298.00
190 000	2432.00	2412.79	2396.40	2382.39	2370.40	2360.11
195 000	2496.00	2476.28	2459.47	2445.09	2432.78	2422.22
200 000	2560.00	2539.78	2522.53	2507.78	2495.16	2484.33
205 000	2624.00	2603.27	2585.59	2570.48	2557.53	2546.43
210 000	2688.00	2666.77	2648.66	2633.17	2619.91	2608.54
215 000	2752.00	2730.26	2711.72	2695.87	2682.29	2670.65
220 000	2816.00	2793.75	2774.78	2758.56	2744.67	2732.76
225 000	2879.99	2857.25	2837.84	2821.26	2807.05	2794.87
230 000	2943.99	2920.74	2900.91	2883.95	2869.43	2856.97
235 000	3007.99	2984.24	2963.97	2946.65	2931.81	2919.08
240 000	3071.99	3047.73	3027.03	3009.34	2994.19	2981.19
245 000	3135.99	3111.23	3090.10	3072.03	3056.57	3043.30
250 000	3199.99	3174.72	3153.16	3134.73	3118.95	3105.41
260 000	3327.99	3301.71	3279.29	3260.12	3243.70	3229.62
270 000	3455.99	3428.70	3405.41	3385.51	3368.46	3353.84
280 000	3583.99	3555.69	3531.54	3510.89	3493.22	3478.06
290 000	3711.99	3682.68	3657.67	3636.29	3617.98	3602.27
300 000	3839.99	3809.67	3783.79	3761.68	3742.73	3726.49
400 000	5119.99	5079.55	5045.06	5015.57	4990.31	4968.65
500 000	6399.99	6349.44	6306.32	6269.46	6237.89	6210.81

MONTHLY PAYMENT

14.50% INTEREST

needed to pay back a mortgage

Term	26 Years	27 Years	28 Years	29 Years	30 Years	35 Years
AMOUNT						
30 000	371.25	370.05	369.02	368.13	367.37	364.85
40 000	495.00	493.41	492.03	490.84	489.82	486.47
50 000	618.76	616.76	615.04	613.56	612.28	608.09
55 000	680.63	678.43	676.54	674.91	673.51	668.89
60 000	742.51	740.11	738.04	736.27	734.73	729.70
65 000	804.38	801.78	799.55	797.62	795.96	790.51
70 000	866.26	863.46	861.05	858.98	857.19	851.32
75 000	928.13	925.14	922.56	920.33	918.42	912.13
80 000	990.01	986.81	984.06	981.69	979.64	972.94
85 000	1051.89	1048.49	1045.56	1043.04	1040.87	1033.74
90 000	1113.76	1110.16	1107.07	1104.40	1102.10	1094.55
95 000	1175.64	1171.84	1168.57	1165.75	1163.33	1155.36
100 000	1237.51	1233.51	1230.07	1227.11	1224.56	1216.17
105 000	1299.39	1295.19	1291.58	1288.47	1285.78	1276.98
110 000	1361.26	1356.87	1353.08	1349.82	1347.01	1337.79
115 000	1423.14	1418.54	1414.58	1411.18	1408.24	1398.60
120 000	1485.01	1480.22	1476.09	1472.53	1469.47	1459.40
125 000	1546.89	1541.89	1537.59	1533.89	1530.69	1520.21
130 000	1608.77	1603.57	1599.10	1595.24	1591.92	1581.02
135 000	1670.64	1665.24	1660.60	1656.60	1653.15	1641.83
140 000	1732.52	1726.92	1722.10	1717.95	1714.38	1702.64
145 000	1794.39	1788.60	1783.61	1779.31	1775.61	1763.45
150 000	1856.27	1850.27	1845.11	1840.67	1836.83	1824.26
155 000	1918.14	1911.95	1906.61	1902.02	1898.06	1885.06
160 000	1980.02	1973.62	1968.12	1963.38	1959.29	1945.87
165 000	2041.90	2035.30	2029.62	2024.73	2020.52	2006.68
170 000	2103.77	2096.97	2091.12	2086.09	2081.75	2067.49
175 000	2165.65	2158.65	2152.63	2147.44	2142.97	2128.30
180 000	2227.52	2220.33	2214.13	2208.80	2204.20	2189.11
185 000	2289.40	2282.00	2275.64	2270.15	2265.43	2249.92
190 000	2351.27	2343.68	2337.14	2331.51	2326.66	2310.72
195 000	2413.15	2405.35	2398.64	2392.86	2387.88	2371.53
200 000	2475.02	2467.03	2460.15	2454.22	2449.11	2432.34
205 000	2536.90	2528.70	2521.65	2515.58	2510.34	2493.15
210 000	2598.78	2590.38	2583.15	2576.93	2571.57	2553.96
215 000	2660.65	2652.06	2644.66	2638.29	2632.80	2614.77
220 000	2722.53	2713.73	2706.16	2699.64	2694.02	2675.58
225 000	2784.40	2775.41	2767.67	2761.00	2755.25	2736.38
230 000	2846.28	2837.08	2829.17	2822.35	2816.48	2797.19
235 000	2908.15	2898.76	2890.67	2883.71	2877.71	2858.00
240 000	2970.03	2960.43	2952.18	2945.06	2938.93	2918.81
245 000	3031.91	3022.11	3013.68	3006.42	3000.16	2979.62
250 000	3093.78	3083.79	3075.18	3067.78	3061.39	3040.43
260 000	3217.53	3207.14	3198.19	3190.49	3183.85	3162.04
270 000	3341.28	3330.49	3321.20	3313.20	3306.30	3283.66
280 000	3465.03	3453.84	3444.21	3435.91	3428.76	3405.28
290 000	3588.79	3577.19	3567.21	3558.62	3551.21	3526.89
300 000	3712.54	3700.54	3690.22	3681.33	3673.67	3648.51
400 000	4950.05	4934.06	4920.29	4908.44	4898.22	4864.68
500 000	6187.56	6167.57	6150.37	6135.55	6122.78	6080.85

15.00% INTEREST	MONTHLY PAYMENT needed to pay back a mortgage				
Term	**1 Year**	**5 Years**	**10 Years**	**11 Years**	**12 Years**	**13 Years**

AMOUNT	1 Year	5 Years	10 Years	11 Years	12 Years	13 Years
30 000	2707.75	713.70	484.00	465.27	450.26	438.09
40 000	3610.33	951.60	645.34	620.37	600.35	584.11
50 000	4512.92	1189.50	806.67	775.46	750.44	730.14
55 000	4964.21	1308.45	887.34	853.00	825.48	803.16
60 000	5415.50	1427.40	968.01	930.55	900.53	876.17
65 000	5866.79	1546.35	1048.68	1008.09	975.57	949.19
70 000	6318.08	1665.30	1129.34	1085.64	1050.61	1022.20
75 000	6769.37	1784.24	1210.01	1163.19	1125.66	1095.22
80 000	7220.66	1903.19	1290.68	1240.73	1200.70	1168.23
85 000	7671.96	2022.14	1371.35	1318.28	1275.75	1241.24
90 000	8123.25	2141.09	1452.01	1395.82	1350.79	1314.26
95 000	8574.54	2260.04	1532.68	1473.37	1425.83	1387.27
100 000	9025.83	2378.99	1613.35	1550.91	1500.88	1460.29
105 000	9477.12	2497.94	1694.02	1628.46	1575.92	1533.30
110 000	9928.41	2616.89	1774.68	1706.01	1650.96	1606.32
115 000	10379.71	2735.84	1855.35	1783.55	1726.01	1679.33
120 000	10831.00	2854.79	1936.02	1861.10	1801.05	1752.34
125 000	11282.29	2973.74	2016.69	1938.64	1876.10	1825.36
130 000	11733.58	3092.69	2097.35	2016.19	1951.14	1898.37
135 000	12184.87	3211.64	2178.02	2093.74	2026.18	1971.39
140 000	12636.16	3330.59	2258.69	2171.28	2101.23	2044.40
145 000	13087.46	3449.54	2339.36	2248.83	2176.27	2117.42
150 000	13538.75	3568.49	2420.02	2326.37	2251.32	2190.43
155 000	13990.04	3687.44	2500.69	2403.92	2326.36	2263.45
160 000	14441.33	3806.39	2581.36	2481.46	2401.40	2336.46
165 000	14892.62	3925.34	2662.03	2559.01	2476.45	2409.47
170 000	15343.91	4044.29	2742.69	2636.56	2551.49	2482.49
175 000	15795.20	4163.24	2823.36	2714.10	2626.53	2555.50
180 000	16246.50	4282.19	2904.03	2791.65	2701.58	2628.52
185 000	16697.79	4401.14	2984.70	2869.19	2776.62	2701.53
190 000	17149.08	4520.09	3065.36	2946.74	2851.67	2774.55
195 000	17600.37	4639.04	3146.03	3024.28	2926.71	2847.56
200 000	18051.66	4757.99	3226.70	3101.83	3001.75	2920.57
205 000	18502.95	4876.94	3307.37	3179.38	3076.80	2993.59
210 000	18954.25	4995.89	3388.03	3256.92	3151.84	3066.60
215 000	19405.54	5114.83	3468.70	3334.47	3226.89	3139.62
220 000	19856.83	5233.78	3549.37	3412.01	3301.93	3212.63
225 000	20308.12	5352.73	3630.04	3489.56	3376.97	3285.65
230 000	20759.41	5471.68	3710.70	3567.10	3452.02	3358.66
235 000	21210.70	5590.63	3791.37	3644.65	3527.06	3431.68
240 000	21661.99	5709.58	3872.04	3722.20	3602.10	3504.69
245 000	22113.29	5828.53	3952.71	3799.74	3677.15	3577.70
250 000	22564.58	5947.48	4033.37	3877.29	3752.19	3650.72
260 000	23467.16	6185.38	4194.71	4032.38	3902.28	3796.75
270 000	24369.74	6423.28	4356.04	4187.47	4052.37	3942.78
280 000	25272.33	6661.18	4517.38	4342.56	4202.45	4088.80
290 000	26174.91	6899.08	4678.71	4497.65	4352.54	4234.83
300 000	27077.49	7136.98	4840.05	4652.74	4502.63	4380.86
400 000	36103.32	9515.97	6453.40	6203.66	6003.51	5841.15
500 000	45129.16	11894.97	8066.75	7754.57	7504.38	7301.44

Term	14 Years	15 Years	16 Years	17 Years	18 Years	19 Years
AMOUNT						
30 000	428.11	419.88	413.03	407.31	402.51	398.46
40 000	570.82	559.83	550.71	543.08	536.68	531.28
50 000	713.52	699.79	688.38	678.85	670.85	664.10
55 000	784.87	769.77	757.22	746.74	737.93	730.51
60 000	856.22	839.75	826.06	814.62	805.01	796.92
65 000	927.58	909.73	894.90	882.51	872.10	863.33
70 000	998.93	979.71	963.74	950.39	939.18	929.74
75 000	1070.28	1049.69	1032.58	1018.28	1006.27	996.15
80 000	1141.63	1119.67	1101.42	1086.16	1073.35	1062.56
85 000	1212.98	1189.65	1170.25	1154.05	1140.44	1128.97
90 000	1284.34	1259.63	1239.09	1221.93	1207.52	1195.38
95 000	1355.69	1329.61	1307.93	1289.82	1274.61	1261.79
100 000	1427.04	1399.59	1376.77	1357.70	1341.69	1328.20
105 000	1498.39	1469.57	1445.61	1425.59	1408.78	1394.61
110 000	1569.74	1539.55	1514.45	1493.47	1475.86	1461.02
115 000	1641.10	1609.53	1583.29	1561.36	1542.94	1527.43
120 000	1712.45	1679.50	1652.12	1629.24	1610.03	1593.84
125 000	1783.80	1749.48	1720.96	1697.13	1677.11	1660.25
130 000	1855.15	1819.46	1789.80	1765.01	1744.20	1726.66
135 000	1926.50	1889.44	1858.64	1832.90	1811.28	1793.07
140 000	1997.86	1959.42	1927.48	1900.78	1878.37	1859.48
145 000	2069.21	2029.40	1996.32	1968.67	1945.45	1925.89
150 000	2140.56	2099.38	2065.15	2036.55	2012.54	1992.30
155 000	2211.91	2169.36	2133.99	2104.44	2079.62	2058.71
160 000	2283.26	2239.34	2202.83	2172.32	2146.71	2125.12
165 000	2354.62	2309.32	2271.67	2240.21	2213.79	2191.53
170 000	2425.97	2379.30	2340.51	2308.09	2280.87	2257.94
175 000	2497.32	2449.28	2409.35	2375.98	2347.96	2324.35
180 000	2568.67	2519.26	2478.19	2443.86	2415.04	2390.76
185 000	2640.02	2589.24	2547.02	2511.75	2482.13	2457.17
190 000	2711.38	2659.22	2615.86	2579.63	2549.21	2523.58
195 000	2782.73	2729.19	2684.70	2647.52	2616.30	2589.99
200 000	2854.08	2799.17	2753.54	2715.40	2683.38	2656.40
205 000	2925.43	2869.15	2822.38	2783.29	2750.47	2722.81
210 000	2996.78	2939.13	2891.22	2851.17	2817.55	2789.22
215 000	3068.14	3009.11	2960.05	2919.06	2884.64	2855.63
220 000	3139.49	3079.09	3028.89	2986.94	2951.72	2922.04
225 000	3210.84	3149.07	3097.73	3054.83	3018.80	2988.45
230 000	3282.19	3219.05	3166.57	3122.71	3085.89	3054.86
235 000	3353.54	3289.03	3235.41	3190.60	3152.97	3121.27
240 000	3424.90	3359.01	3304.25	3258.48	3220.06	3187.68
245 000	3496.25	3428.99	3373.09	3326.37	3287.14	3254.09
250 000	3567.60	3498.97	3441.92	3394.25	3354.23	3320.49
260 000	3710.30	3638.93	3579.60	3530.02	3488.40	3453.31
270 000	3853.01	3778.89	3717.28	3665.79	3622.57	3586.13
280 000	3995.71	3918.84	3854.95	3801.56	3756.73	3718.95
290 000	4138.42	4058.80	3992.63	3937.33	3890.90	3851.77
300 000	4281.12	4198.76	4130.31	4073.10	4025.07	3984.59
400 000	5708.16	5598.35	5507.08	5430.80	5366.76	5312.79
500 000	7135.20	6997.94	6883.85	6788.50	6708.45	6640.99

MONTHLY PAYMENT
needed to pay back a mortgage

Term	20 Years	21 Years	22 Years	23 Years	24 Years	25 Years
AMOUNT						
30 000	395.04	392.14	389.67	387.57	385.78	384.25
40 000	526.72	522.85	519.56	516.76	514.37	512.33
50 000	658.39	653.56	649.45	645.95	642.96	640.42
55 000	724.23	718.91	714.39	710.54	707.26	704.46
60 000	790.07	784.27	779.34	775.14	771.56	768.50
65 000	855.91	849.63	844.28	839.73	835.85	832.54
70 000	921.75	914.98	909.23	904.33	900.15	896.58
75 000	987.59	980.34	974.17	968.92	964.45	960.62
80 000	1053.43	1045.69	1039.12	1033.52	1028.74	1024.66
85 000	1119.27	1111.05	1104.06	1098.11	1093.04	1088.71
90 000	1185.11	1176.41	1169.01	1162.71	1157.34	1152.75
95 000	1250.95	1241.76	1233.95	1227.30	1221.63	1216.79
100 000	1316.79	1307.12	1298.90	1291.90	1285.93	1280.83
105 000	1382.63	1372.47	1363.84	1356.49	1350.23	1344.87
110 000	1448.47	1437.83	1428.79	1421.09	1414.52	1408.91
115 000	1514.31	1503.18	1493.73	1485.68	1478.82	1472.96
120 000	1580.15	1568.54	1558.68	1550.28	1543.12	1537.00
125 000	1645.99	1633.90	1623.62	1614.87	1607.41	1601.04
130 000	1711.83	1699.25	1688.57	1679.47	1671.71	1665.08
135 000	1777.67	1764.61	1753.51	1744.06	1736.00	1729.12
140 000	1843.51	1829.96	1818.46	1808.66	1800.30	1793.16
145 000	1909.34	1895.32	1883.40	1873.25	1864.60	1857.20
150 000	1975.18	1960.68	1948.35	1937.85	1928.89	1921.25
155 000	2041.02	2026.03	2013.29	2002.44	1993.19	1985.29
160 000	2106.86	2091.39	2078.24	2067.04	2057.49	2049.33
165 000	2172.70	2156.74	2143.18	2131.63	2121.78	2113.37
170 000	2238.54	2222.10	2208.13	2196.23	2186.08	2177.41
175 000	2304.38	2287.46	2273.07	2260.82	2250.38	2241.45
180 000	2370.22	2352.81	2338.02	2325.42	2314.67	2305.50
185 000	2436.06	2418.17	2402.96	2390.01	2378.97	2369.54
190 000	2501.90	2483.52	2467.91	2454.61	2443.27	2433.58
195 000	2567.74	2548.88	2532.85	2519.20	2507.56	2497.62
200 000	2633.58	2614.23	2597.79	2583.80	2571.86	2561.66
205 000	2699.42	2679.59	2662.74	2648.39	2636.15	2625.70
210 000	2765.26	2744.95	2727.68	2712.99	2700.45	2689.74
215 000	2831.10	2810.30	2792.63	2777.58	2764.75	2753.79
220 000	2896.94	2875.66	2857.57	2842.18	2829.04	2817.83
225 000	2962.78	2941.01	2922.52	2906.77	2893.34	2881.87
230 000	3028.62	3006.37	2987.46	2971.37	2957.64	2945.91
235 000	3094.46	3071.73	3052.41	3035.96	3021.93	3009.95
240 000	3160.29	3137.08	3117.35	3100.56	3086.23	3073.99
245 000	3226.13	3202.44	3182.30	3165.15	3150.53	3138.03
250 000	3291.97	3267.79	3247.24	3229.75	3214.82	3202.08
260 000	3423.65	3398.50	3377.13	3358.94	3343.42	3330.16
270 000	3555.33	3529.22	3507.02	3488.13	3472.01	3458.24
280 000	3687.01	3659.93	3636.91	3617.32	3600.60	3586.33
290 000	3818.69	3790.64	3766.80	3746.51	3729.19	3714.41
300 000	3950.37	3921.35	3896.69	3875.70	3857.79	3842.49
400 000	5267.16	5228.47	5195.59	5167.59	5143.72	5123.32
500 000	6583.95	6535.59	6494.49	6459.49	6429.65	6404.15

Term	26 Years	27 Years	28 Years	29 Years	30 Years	35 Years
AMOUNT						
30 000	382.94	381.82	380.86	380.04	379.33	377.04
40 000	510.59	509.10	507.82	506.72	505.78	502.73
50 000	638.24	636.37	634.77	633.40	632.22	628.41
55 000	702.06	700.01	698.25	696.74	695.44	691.25
60 000	765.88	763.64	761.72	760.09	758.67	754.09
65 000	829.71	827.28	825.20	823.42	821.89	816.93
70 000	893.53	890.92	888.68	886.76	885.11	879.77
75 000	957.35	954.55	952.15	950.10	948.33	942.61
80 000	1021.18	1018.19	1015.63	1013.44	1011.56	1005.45
85 000	1085.00	1081.83	1079.11	1076.78	1074.78	1068.29
90 000	1148.82	1145.46	1142.59	1140.12	1138.00	1131.13
95 000	1212.65	1209.10	1206.06	1203.46	1201.22	1193.97
100 000	1276.47	1272.74	1269.54	1266.80	1264.44	1256.81
105 000	1340.29	1336.37	1333.02	1330.14	1327.67	1319.65
110 000	1404.12	1400.01	1396.49	1393.48	1390.89	1382.49
115 000	1467.94	1463.65	1459.97	1456.82	1454.11	1445.34
120 000	1531.76	1527.29	1523.45	1520.16	1517.33	1508.18
125 000	1595.59	1590.92	1586.92	1583.50	1580.56	1571.02
130 000	1659.41	1654.56	1650.40	1646.84	1643.78	1633.86
135 000	1723.24	1718.20	1713.88	1710.18	1707.00	1696.70
140 000	1787.06	1781.83	1777.36	1773.52	1770.22	1759.54
145 000	1850.88	1845.47	1840.83	1836.86	1833.44	1822.38
150 000	1914.71	1909.11	1904.31	1900.20	1896.67	1885.22
155 000	1978.53	1972.74	1967.79	1963.54	1959.89	1948.06
160 000	2042.35	2036.38	2031.26	2026.88	2023.11	2010.90
165 000	2106.18	2100.02	2094.74	2090.22	2086.33	2073.74
170 000	2170.00	2163.65	2158.22	2153.56	2149.55	2136.58
175 000	2233.82	2227.29	2221.69	2216.90	2212.78	2199.42
180 000	2297.65	2290.93	2285.17	2280.23	2276.00	2262.26
185 000	2361.47	2354.56	2348.65	2343.57	2339.22	2325.10
190 000	2425.29	2418.20	2412.13	2406.91	2402.44	2387.95
195 000	2489.12	2481.84	2475.60	2470.25	2465.67	2450.79
200 000	2552.94	2545.48	2539.08	2533.59	2528.89	2513.63
205 000	2616.76	2609.11	2602.56	2596.93	2592.11	2576.47
210 000	2680.59	2672.75	2666.03	2660.27	2655.33	2639.31
215 000	2744.41	2736.39	2729.51	2723.61	2718.55	2702.15
220 000	2808.23	2800.02	2792.99	2786.95	2781.78	2764.99
225 000	2872.06	2863.66	2856.46	2850.29	2845.00	2827.83
230 000	2935.88	2927.30	2919.94	2913.63	2908.22	2890.67
235 000	2999.71	2990.93	2983.42	2976.97	2971.44	2953.51
240 000	3063.53	3054.57	3046.90	3040.31	3034.67	3016.35
245 000	3127.35	3118.21	3110.37	3103.65	3097.89	3079.19
250 000	3191.18	3181.84	3173.85	3166.99	3161.11	3142.03
260 000	3318.82	3309.12	3300.80	3293.67	3287.55	3267.71
270 000	3446.47	3436.39	3427.76	3420.35	3414.00	3393.40
280 000	3574.12	3563.67	3554.71	3547.03	3540.44	3519.08
290 000	3701.76	3690.94	3681.66	3673.71	3666.89	3644.76
300 000	3829.41	3818.21	3808.62	3800.39	3793.33	3770.44
400 000	5105.88	5090.95	5078.16	5067.19	5057.78	5027.25
500 000	6382.35	6363.69	6347.70	6333.99	6322.22	6284.07

15.50% INTEREST	MONTHLY PAYMENT needed to pay back a mortgage				
Term	1 Year	5 Years	10 Years	11 Years	12 Years	13 Years

AMOUNT	1 Year	5 Years	10 Years	11 Years	12 Years	13 Years
30 000	2714.83	721.60	493.23	474.74	459.96	448.00
40 000	3619.78	962.13	657.64	632.99	613.28	597.34
50 000	4524.72	1202.66	822.05	791.24	766.60	746.67
55 000	4977.19	1322.93	904.26	870.36	843.26	821.34
60 000	5429.66	1443.19	986.46	949.48	919.92	896.01
65 000	5882.14	1563.46	1068.67	1028.61	996.58	970.67
70 000	6334.61	1683.72	1150.87	1107.73	1073.24	1045.34
75 000	6787.08	1803.99	1233.08	1186.86	1149.90	1120.01
80 000	7239.55	1924.26	1315.28	1265.98	1226.56	1194.68
85 000	7692.03	2044.52	1397.49	1345.10	1303.22	1269.34
90 000	8144.50	2164.79	1479.69	1424.23	1379.88	1344.01
95 000	8596.97	2285.05	1561.90	1503.35	1456.54	1418.68
100 000	9049.44	2405.32	1644.11	1582.47	1533.20	1493.35
105 000	9501.91	2525.59	1726.31	1661.60	1609.86	1568.01
110 000	9954.39	2645.85	1808.52	1740.72	1686.52	1642.68
115 000	10406.86	2766.12	1890.72	1819.85	1763.18	1717.35
120 000	10859.33	2886.38	1972.93	1898.97	1839.85	1792.01
125 000	11311.80	3006.65	2055.13	1978.09	1916.51	1866.68
130 000	11764.27	3126.91	2137.34	2057.22	1993.17	1941.35
135 000	12216.75	3247.18	2219.54	2136.34	2069.83	2016.02
140 000	12669.22	3367.45	2301.75	2215.46	2146.49	2090.68
145 000	13121.69	3487.71	2383.95	2294.59	2223.15	2165.35
150 000	13574.16	3607.98	2466.16	2373.71	2299.81	2240.02
155 000	14026.63	3728.24	2548.36	2452.84	2376.47	2314.69
160 000	14479.11	3848.51	2630.57	2531.96	2453.13	2389.35
165 000	14931.58	3968.78	2712.77	2611.08	2529.79	2464.02
170 000	15384.05	4089.04	2794.98	2690.21	2606.45	2538.69
175 000	15836.52	4209.31	2877.18	2769.33	2683.11	2613.35
180 000	16288.99	4329.57	2959.39	2848.45	2759.77	2688.02
185 000	16741.47	4449.84	3041.59	2927.58	2836.43	2762.69
190 000	17193.94	4570.11	3123.80	3006.70	2913.09	2837.36
195 000	17646.41	4690.37	3206.01	3085.83	2989.75	2912.02
200 000	18098.88	4810.64	3288.21	3164.95	3066.41	2986.69
205 000	18551.36	4930.90	3370.42	3244.07	3143.07	3061.36
210 000	19003.83	5051.17	3452.62	3323.20	3219.73	3136.03
215 000	19456.30	5171.44	3534.83	3402.32	3296.39	3210.69
220 000	19908.77	5291.70	3617.03	3481.44	3373.05	3285.36
225 000	20361.24	5411.97	3699.24	3560.57	3449.71	3360.03
230 000	20813.72	5532.23	3781.44	3639.69	3526.37	3434.69
235 000	21266.19	5652.50	3863.65	3718.81	3603.03	3509.36
240 000	21718.66	5772.77	3945.85	3797.94	3679.69	3584.03
245 000	22171.13	5893.03	4028.06	3877.06	3756.35	3658.70
250 000	22623.60	6013.30	4110.26	3956.19	3833.01	3733.36
260 000	23528.55	6253.83	4274.67	4114.43	3986.33	3882.70
270 000	24433.49	6494.36	4439.08	4272.68	4139.65	4032.03
280 000	25338.44	6734.89	4603.50	4430.93	4292.97	4181.37
290 000	26243.38	6975.43	4767.91	4589.18	4446.29	4330.70
300 000	27148.32	7215.96	4932.32	4747.42	4599.61	4480.04
400 000	36197.77	9621.28	6576.42	6329.90	6132.82	5973.38
500 000	45247.21	12026.60	8220.53	7912.37	7666.02	7466.73

68

Term	14 Years	15 Years	16 Years	17 Years	18 Years	19 Years
MONTHLY PAYMENT					**15.50%**	
needed to pay back a mortgage					INTEREST	

MONTHLY PAYMENT — 15.50% INTEREST
needed to pay back a mortgage

Term	14 Years	15 Years	16 Years	17 Years	18 Years	19 Years
AMOUNT						
30 000	438.24	430.20	423.54	417.99	413.35	409.45
40 000	584.32	573.60	564.71	557.32	551.13	545.93
50 000	730.39	717.00	705.89	696.65	688.91	682.41
55 000	803.43	788.69	776.48	766.31	757.80	750.65
60 000	876.47	860.39	847.07	835.98	826.69	818.90
65 000	949.51	932.09	917.66	905.64	895.58	887.14
70 000	1022.55	1003.79	988.25	975.30	964.47	955.38
75 000	1095.59	1075.49	1058.84	1044.97	1033.36	1023.62
80 000	1168.63	1147.19	1129.43	1114.63	1102.26	1091.86
85 000	1241.67	1218.89	1200.02	1184.30	1171.15	1160.10
90 000	1314.71	1290.59	1270.61	1253.96	1240.04	1228.34
95 000	1387.75	1362.29	1341.20	1323.63	1308.93	1296.58
100 000	1460.79	1433.99	1411.79	1393.29	1377.82	1364.83
105 000	1533.83	1505.69	1482.38	1462.96	1446.71	1433.07
110 000	1606.87	1577.39	1552.97	1532.62	1515.60	1501.31
115 000	1679.91	1649.09	1623.55	1602.29	1584.49	1569.55
120 000	1752.95	1720.79	1694.14	1671.95	1653.38	1637.79
125 000	1825.99	1792.49	1764.73	1741.62	1722.27	1706.03
130 000	1899.03	1864.19	1835.32	1811.28	1791.17	1774.27
135 000	1972.07	1935.89	1905.91	1880.94	1860.06	1842.52
140 000	2045.11	2007.59	1976.50	1950.61	1928.95	1910.76
145 000	2118.15	2079.29	2047.09	2020.27	1997.84	1979.00
150 000	2191.18	2150.99	2117.68	2089.94	2066.73	2047.24
155 000	2264.22	2222.69	2188.27	2159.60	2135.62	2115.48
160 000	2337.26	2294.38	2258.86	2229.27	2204.51	2183.72
165 000	2410.30	2366.08	2329.45	2298.93	2273.40	2251.96
170 000	2483.34	2437.78	2400.04	2368.60	2342.29	2320.20
175 000	2556.38	2509.48	2470.63	2438.26	2411.18	2388.45
180 000	2629.42	2581.18	2541.22	2507.93	2480.08	2456.69
185 000	2702.46	2652.88	2611.81	2577.59	2548.97	2524.93
190 000	2775.50	2724.58	2682.39	2647.26	2617.86	2593.17
195 000	2848.54	2796.28	2752.98	2716.92	2686.75	2661.41
200 000	2921.58	2867.98	2823.57	2786.58	2755.64	2729.65
205 000	2994.62	2939.68	2894.16	2856.25	2824.53	2797.89
210 000	3067.66	3011.38	2964.75	2925.91	2893.42	2866.13
215 000	3140.70	3083.08	3035.34	2995.58	2962.31	2934.38
220 000	3213.74	3154.78	3105.93	3065.24	3031.20	3002.62
225 000	3286.78	3226.48	3176.52	3134.91	3100.09	3070.86
230 000	3359.82	3298.18	3247.11	3204.57	3168.98	3139.10
235 000	3432.86	3369.88	3317.70	3274.24	3237.88	3207.34
240 000	3505.90	3441.58	3388.29	3343.90	3306.77	3275.58
245 000	3578.94	3513.28	3458.88	3413.57	3375.66	3343.82
250 000	3651.97	3584.98	3529.47	3483.23	3444.55	3412.07
260 000	3798.05	3728.37	3670.65	3622.56	3582.33	3548.55
270 000	3944.13	3871.77	3811.82	3761.89	3720.11	3685.03
280 000	4090.21	4015.17	3953.00	3901.22	3857.89	3821.51
290 000	4236.29	4158.57	4094.18	4040.55	3995.68	3958.00
300 000	4382.37	4301.97	4235.36	4179.88	4133.46	4094.48
400 000	5843.16	5735.96	5647.15	5573.17	5511.28	5459.30
500 000	7303.95	7169.95	7058.93	6966.46	6889.10	6824.13

MONTHLY PAYMENT
needed to pay back a mortgage

Term	20 Years	21 Years	22 Years	23 Years	24 Years	25 Years
AMOUNT						
30 000	406.16	403.39	401.04	399.05	397.36	395.92
40 000	541.55	537.85	534.72	532.07	529.82	527.90
50 000	676.94	672.32	668.41	665.09	662.27	659.87
55 000	744.63	739.55	735.25	731.60	728.50	725.86
60 000	812.33	806.78	802.09	798.11	794.72	791.85
65 000	880.02	874.01	868.93	864.61	860.95	857.83
70 000	947.72	941.25	935.77	931.12	927.18	923.82
75 000	1015.41	1008.48	1002.61	997.63	993.40	989.81
80 000	1083.10	1075.71	1069.45	1064.14	1059.63	1055.80
85 000	1150.80	1142.94	1136.29	1130.65	1125.86	1121.78
90 000	1218.49	1210.17	1203.13	1197.16	1192.09	1187.77
95 000	1286.19	1277.40	1269.97	1263.67	1258.31	1253.76
100 000	1353.88	1344.64	1336.81	1330.18	1324.54	1319.75
105 000	1421.57	1411.87	1403.65	1396.68	1390.77	1385.73
110 000	1489.27	1479.10	1470.49	1463.19	1456.99	1451.72
115 000	1556.96	1546.33	1537.33	1529.70	1523.22	1517.71
120 000	1624.66	1613.56	1604.17	1596.21	1589.45	1583.69
125 000	1692.35	1680.80	1671.01	1662.72	1655.67	1649.68
130 000	1760.04	1748.03	1737.86	1729.23	1721.90	1715.67
135 000	1827.74	1815.26	1804.70	1795.74	1788.13	1781.66
140 000	1895.43	1882.49	1871.54	1862.25	1854.36	1847.64
145 000	1963.13	1949.72	1938.38	1928.75	1920.58	1913.63
150 000	2030.82	2016.95	2005.22	1995.26	1986.81	1979.62
155 000	2098.52	2084.19	2072.06	2061.77	2053.04	2045.61
160 000	2166.21	2151.42	2138.90	2128.28	2119.26	2111.59
165 000	2233.90	2218.65	2205.74	2194.79	2185.49	2177.58
170 000	2301.60	2285.88	2272.58	2261.30	2251.72	2243.57
175 000	2369.29	2353.11	2339.42	2327.81	2317.94	2309.55
180 000	2436.99	2420.35	2406.26	2394.32	2384.17	2375.54
185 000	2504.68	2487.58	2473.10	2460.83	2450.40	2441.53
190 000	2572.37	2554.81	2539.94	2527.33	2516.62	2507.52
195 000	2640.07	2622.04	2606.78	2593.84	2582.85	2573.50
200 000	2707.76	2689.27	2673.62	2660.35	2649.08	2639.49
205 000	2775.46	2756.50	2740.46	2726.86	2715.31	2705.48
210 000	2843.15	2823.74	2807.30	2793.37	2781.53	2771.46
215 000	2910.84	2890.97	2874.14	2859.88	2847.76	2837.45
220 000	2978.54	2958.20	2940.99	2926.39	2913.99	2903.44
225 000	3046.23	3025.43	3007.83	2992.90	2980.21	2969.43
230 000	3113.93	3092.66	3074.67	3059.40	3046.44	3035.41
235 000	3181.62	3159.90	3141.51	3125.91	3112.67	3101.40
240 000	3249.31	3227.13	3208.35	3192.42	3178.89	3167.39
245 000	3317.01	3294.36	3275.19	3258.93	3245.12	3233.38
250 000	3384.70	3361.59	3342.03	3325.44	3311.35	3299.36
260 000	3520.09	3496.05	3475.71	3458.46	3443.80	3431.34
270 000	3655.48	3630.52	3609.39	3591.47	3576.26	3563.31
280 000	3790.87	3764.98	3743.07	3724.49	3708.71	3695.29
290 000	3926.25	3899.45	3876.75	3857.51	3841.16	3827.26
300 000	4061.64	4033.91	4010.43	3990.53	3973.62	3959.24
400 000	5415.52	5378.55	5347.25	5320.70	5298.16	5278.98
500 000	6769.40	6723.18	6684.06	6650.88	6622.70	6598.73

Term	26 Years	27 Years	28 Years	29 Years	30 Years	35 Years
AMOUNT						
30 000	394.70	393.66	392.76	392.00	391.36	389.28
40 000	526.27	524.87	523.69	522.67	521.81	519.03
50 000	657.83	656.09	654.61	653.34	652.26	648.79
55 000	723.61	721.70	720.07	718.67	717.48	713.67
60 000	789.40	787.31	785.53	784.01	782.71	778.55
65 000	855.18	852.92	850.99	849.34	847.94	843.43
70 000	920.96	918.53	916.45	914.68	913.16	908.31
75 000	986.75	984.14	981.91	980.01	978.39	973.19
80 000	1052.53	1049.75	1047.37	1045.35	1043.61	1038.07
85 000	1118.31	1115.36	1112.83	1110.68	1108.84	1102.95
90 000	1184.10	1180.97	1178.29	1176.01	1174.07	1167.83
95 000	1249.88	1246.57	1243.75	1241.35	1239.29	1232.71
100 000	1315.66	1312.18	1309.22	1306.68	1304.52	1297.58
105 000	1381.45	1377.79	1374.68	1372.02	1369.74	1362.46
110 000	1447.23	1443.40	1440.14	1437.35	1434.97	1427.34
115 000	1513.01	1509.01	1505.60	1502.68	1500.19	1492.22
120 000	1578.80	1574.62	1571.06	1568.02	1565.42	1557.10
125 000	1644.58	1640.23	1636.52	1633.35	1630.65	1621.98
130 000	1710.36	1705.84	1701.98	1698.69	1695.87	1686.86
135 000	1776.15	1771.45	1767.44	1764.02	1761.10	1751.74
140 000	1841.93	1837.06	1832.90	1829.35	1826.32	1816.62
145 000	1907.71	1902.67	1898.36	1894.69	1891.55	1881.50
150 000	1973.49	1968.28	1963.82	1960.02	1956.78	1946.38
155 000	2039.28	2033.88	2029.28	2025.36	2022.00	2011.26
160 000	2105.06	2099.49	2094.74	2090.69	2087.23	2076.14
165 000	2170.84	2165.10	2160.21	2156.02	2152.45	2141.01
170 000	2236.63	2230.71	2225.67	2221.36	2217.68	2205.89
175 000	2302.41	2296.32	2291.13	2286.69	2282.90	2270.77
180 000	2368.19	2361.93	2356.59	2352.03	2348.13	2335.65
185 000	2433.98	2427.54	2422.05	2417.36	2413.36	2400.53
190 000	2499.76	2493.15	2487.51	2482.69	2478.58	2465.41
195 000	2565.54	2558.76	2552.97	2548.03	2543.81	2530.29
200 000	2631.33	2624.37	2618.43	2613.36	2609.03	2595.17
205 000	2697.11	2689.98	2683.89	2678.70	2674.26	2660.05
210 000	2762.89	2755.59	2749.35	2744.03	2739.49	2724.93
215 000	2828.68	2821.19	2814.81	2809.36	2804.71	2789.81
220 000	2894.46	2886.80	2880.27	2874.70	2869.94	2854.69
225 000	2960.24	2952.41	2945.73	2940.03	2935.16	2919.57
230 000	3026.02	3018.02	3011.20	3005.37	3000.39	2984.44
235 000	3091.81	3083.63	3076.66	3070.70	3065.61	3049.32
240 000	3157.59	3149.24	3142.12	3136.04	3130.84	3114.20
245 000	3223.37	3214.85	3207.58	3201.37	3196.07	3179.08
250 000	3289.16	3280.46	3273.04	3266.70	3261.29	3243.96
260 000	3420.72	3411.68	3403.96	3397.37	3391.74	3373.72
270 000	3552.29	3542.90	3534.88	3528.04	3522.20	3503.48
280 000	3683.86	3674.11	3665.80	3658.71	3652.65	3633.24
290 000	3815.42	3805.33	3796.72	3789.38	3783.10	3763.00
300 000	3946.99	3936.55	3927.65	3920.04	3913.55	3892.75
400 000	5262.65	5248.73	5236.86	5226.73	5218.07	5190.34
500 000	6578.32	6560.92	6546.08	6533.41	6522.58	6487.92

Term	1 Year	5 Years	10 Years	11 Years	12 Years	13 Years
AMOUNT						
30 000	2721.93	729.54	502.54	484.30	469.75	458.01
40 000	3629.23	972.72	670.05	645.73	626.33	610.68
50 000	4536.54	1215.90	837.57	807.16	782.91	763.35
55 000	4990.20	1337.49	921.32	887.87	861.20	839.69
60 000	5443.85	1459.08	1005.08	968.59	939.50	916.02
65 000	5897.51	1580.67	1088.84	1049.31	1017.79	992.36
70 000	6351.16	1702.26	1172.59	1130.02	1096.08	1068.69
75 000	6804.81	1823.85	1256.35	1210.74	1174.37	1145.03
80 000	7258.47	1945.44	1340.10	1291.45	1252.66	1221.36
85 000	7712.12	2067.03	1423.86	1372.17	1330.95	1297.70
90 000	8165.78	2188.63	1507.62	1452.89	1409.24	1374.03
95 000	8619.43	2310.22	1591.37	1533.60	1487.53	1450.37
100 000	9073.09	2431.81	1675.13	1614.32	1565.83	1526.70
105 000	9526.74	2553.40	1758.89	1695.03	1644.12	1603.04
110 000	9980.39	2674.99	1842.64	1775.75	1722.41	1679.37
115 000	10434.05	2796.58	1926.40	1856.46	1800.70	1755.71
120 000	10887.70	2918.17	2010.16	1937.18	1878.99	1832.05
125 000	11341.36	3039.76	2093.91	2017.90	1957.28	1908.38
130 000	11795.01	3161.35	2177.67	2098.61	2035.57	1984.72
135 000	12248.67	3282.94	2261.43	2179.33	2113.86	2061.05
140 000	12702.32	3404.53	2345.18	2260.04	2192.16	2137.39
145 000	13155.97	3526.12	2428.94	2340.76	2270.45	2213.72
150 000	13609.63	3647.71	2512.70	2421.48	2348.74	2290.06
155 000	14063.28	3769.30	2596.45	2502.19	2427.03	2366.39
160 000	14516.94	3890.89	2680.21	2582.91	2505.32	2442.73
165 000	14970.59	4012.48	2763.97	2663.62	2583.61	2519.06
170 000	15424.25	4134.07	2847.72	2744.34	2661.90	2595.40
175 000	15877.90	4255.66	2931.48	2825.06	2740.19	2671.73
180 000	16331.55	4377.25	3015.24	2905.77	2818.49	2748.07
185 000	16785.21	4498.84	3098.99	2986.49	2896.78	2824.40
190 000	17238.86	4620.43	3182.75	3067.20	2975.07	2900.74
195 000	17692.52	4742.02	3266.51	3147.92	3053.36	2977.07
200 000	18146.17	4863.61	3350.26	3228.63	3131.65	3053.41
205 000	18599.83	4985.20	3434.02	3309.35	3209.94	3129.74
210 000	19053.48	5106.79	3517.78	3390.07	3288.23	3206.08
215 000	19507.13	5228.38	3601.53	3470.78	3366.52	3282.41
220 000	19960.79	5349.97	3685.29	3551.50	3444.82	3358.75
225 000	20414.44	5471.56	3769.05	3632.21	3523.11	3435.09
230 000	20868.10	5593.15	3852.80	3712.93	3601.40	3511.42
235 000	21321.75	5714.74	3936.56	3793.65	3679.69	3587.76
240 000	21775.41	5836.33	4020.31	3874.36	3757.98	3664.09
245 000	22229.06	5957.92	4104.07	3955.08	3836.27	3740.43
250 000	22682.71	6079.51	4187.83	4035.79	3914.56	3816.76
260 000	23590.02	6322.69	4355.34	4197.22	4071.15	3969.43
270 000	24497.33	6565.88	4522.85	4358.66	4227.73	4122.10
280 000	25404.64	6809.06	4690.37	4520.09	4384.31	4274.77
290 000	26311.95	7052.24	4857.88	4681.52	4540.89	4427.44
300 000	27219.26	7295.42	5025.39	4842.95	4697.48	4580.11
400 000	36292.34	9727.22	6700.52	6457.27	6263.30	6106.82
500 000	45365.43	12159.03	8375.66	8071.59	7829.13	7633.52

needed to pay back a mortgage

Term	14 Years	15 Years	16 Years	17 Years	18 Years	19 Years
AMOUNT						
30 000	448.45	440.61	434.13	428.76	424.27	420.52
40 000	597.94	587.48	578.84	571.68	565.70	560.70
50 000	747.42	734.35	723.56	714.59	707.12	700.87
55 000	822.16	807.79	795.91	786.05	777.84	770.96
60 000	896.91	881.22	868.27	857.51	848.55	841.05
65 000	971.65	954.66	940.62	928.97	919.26	911.14
70 000	1046.39	1028.09	1012.98	1000.43	989.97	981.22
75 000	1121.13	1101.53	1085.33	1071.89	1060.69	1051.31
80 000	1195.88	1174.96	1157.69	1143.35	1131.40	1121.40
85 000	1270.62	1248.40	1230.04	1214.81	1202.11	1191.48
90 000	1345.36	1321.83	1302.40	1286.27	1272.82	1261.57
95 000	1420.10	1395.27	1374.75	1357.73	1343.53	1331.66
100 000	1494.85	1468.70	1447.11	1429.19	1414.25	1401.75
105 000	1569.59	1542.14	1519.47	1500.65	1484.96	1471.83
110 000	1644.33	1615.57	1591.82	1572.11	1555.67	1541.92
115 000	1719.07	1689.01	1664.18	1643.57	1626.38	1612.01
120 000	1793.81	1762.44	1736.53	1715.03	1697.10	1682.10
125 000	1868.56	1835.88	1808.89	1786.49	1767.81	1752.18
130 000	1943.30	1909.31	1881.24	1857.94	1838.52	1822.27
135 000	2018.04	1982.75	1953.60	1929.40	1909.23	1892.36
140 000	2092.78	2056.18	2025.95	2000.86	1979.95	1962.44
145 000	2167.53	2129.62	2098.31	2072.32	2050.66	2032.53
150 000	2242.27	2203.05	2170.67	2143.78	2121.37	2102.62
155 000	2317.01	2276.49	2243.02	2215.24	2192.08	2172.71
160 000	2391.75	2349.92	2315.38	2286.70	2262.80	2242.79
165 000	2466.49	2423.36	2387.73	2358.16	2333.51	2312.88
170 000	2541.24	2496.79	2460.09	2429.62	2404.22	2382.97
175 000	2615.98	2570.23	2532.44	2501.08	2474.93	2453.06
180 000	2690.72	2643.66	2604.80	2572.54	2545.64	2523.14
185 000	2765.46	2717.10	2677.15	2644.00	2616.36	2593.23
190 000	2840.21	2790.53	2749.51	2715.46	2687.07	2663.32
195 000	2914.95	2863.97	2821.87	2786.92	2757.78	2733.41
200 000	2989.69	2937.40	2894.22	2858.38	2828.49	2803.49
205 000	3064.43	3010.84	2966.58	2929.84	2899.21	2873.58
210 000	3139.18	3084.27	3038.93	3001.30	2969.92	2943.67
215 000	3213.92	3157.71	3111.29	3072.75	3040.63	3013.75
220 000	3288.66	3231.14	3183.64	3144.21	3111.34	3083.84
225 000	3363.40	3304.58	3256.00	3215.67	3182.06	3153.93
230 000	3438.14	3378.01	3328.35	3287.13	3252.77	3224.02
235 000	3512.89	3451.45	3400.71	3358.59	3323.48	3294.10
240 000	3587.63	3524.88	3473.06	3430.05	3394.19	3364.19
245 000	3662.37	3598.32	3545.42	3501.51	3464.91	3434.28
250 000	3737.11	3671.75	3617.78	3572.97	3535.62	3504.37
260 000	3886.60	3818.62	3762.49	3715.89	3677.04	3644.54
270 000	4036.08	3965.49	3907.20	3858.81	3818.47	3784.72
280 000	4185.57	4112.36	4051.91	4001.73	3959.89	3924.89
290 000	4335.05	4259.23	4196.62	4144.65	4101.32	4065.06
300 000	4484.54	4406.10	4341.33	4287.56	4242.74	4205.24
400 000	5979.38	5874.80	5788.44	5716.75	5656.99	5606.99
500 000	7474.23	7343.50	7235.55	7145.94	7071.24	7008.73

MONTHLY PAYMENT

needed to pay back a mortgage

Term	20 Years	21 Years	22 Years	23 Years	24 Years	25 Years
AMOUNT						
30 000	417.38	414.73	412.50	410.61	409.02	407.67
40 000	556.50	552.97	550.00	547.48	545.36	543.56
50 000	695.63	691.22	687.50	684.35	681.70	679.44
55 000	765.19	760.34	756.24	752.79	749.86	747.39
60 000	834.75	829.46	824.99	821.22	818.03	815.33
65 000	904.32	898.58	893.74	889.66	886.20	883.28
70 000	973.88	967.70	962.49	958.09	954.37	951.22
75 000	1043.44	1036.82	1031.24	1026.53	1022.54	1019.17
80 000	1113.00	1105.94	1099.99	1094.96	1090.71	1087.11
85 000	1182.57	1175.07	1168.74	1163.40	1158.88	1155.06
90 000	1252.13	1244.19	1237.49	1231.84	1227.05	1223.00
95 000	1321.69	1313.31	1306.24	1300.27	1295.22	1290.94
100 000	1391.26	1382.43	1374.99	1368.71	1363.39	1358.89
105 000	1460.82	1451.55	1443.74	1437.14	1431.56	1426.83
110 000	1530.38	1520.67	1512.49	1505.58	1499.73	1494.78
115 000	1599.94	1589.80	1581.24	1574.01	1567.90	1562.72
120 000	1669.51	1658.92	1649.99	1642.45	1636.07	1630.67
125 000	1739.07	1728.04	1718.74	1710.88	1704.24	1698.61
130 000	1808.63	1797.16	1787.49	1779.32	1772.41	1766.56
135 000	1878.20	1866.28	1856.24	1847.75	1840.58	1834.50
140 000	1947.76	1935.40	1924.99	1916.19	1908.75	1902.44
145 000	2017.32	2004.52	1993.74	1984.62	1976.92	1970.39
150 000	2086.88	2073.65	2062.49	2053.06	2045.09	2038.33
155 000	2156.45	2142.77	2131.23	2121.49	2113.26	2106.28
160 000	2226.01	2211.89	2199.98	2189.93	2181.42	2174.22
165 000	2295.57	2281.01	2268.73	2258.36	2249.59	2242.17
170 000	2365.14	2350.13	2337.48	2326.80	2317.76	2310.11
175 000	2434.70	2419.25	2406.23	2395.24	2385.93	2378.06
180 000	2504.26	2488.37	2474.98	2463.67	2454.10	2446.00
185 000	2573.82	2557.50	2543.73	2532.11	2522.27	2513.94
190 000	2643.39	2626.62	2612.48	2600.54	2590.44	2581.89
195 000	2712.95	2695.74	2681.23	2668.98	2658.61	2649.83
200 000	2782.51	2764.86	2749.98	2737.41	2726.78	2717.78
205 000	2852.07	2833.98	2818.73	2805.85	2794.95	2785.72
210 000	2921.64	2903.10	2887.48	2874.28	2863.12	2853.67
215 000	2991.20	2972.23	2956.23	2942.72	2931.29	2921.61
220 000	3060.76	3041.35	3024.98	3011.15	2999.46	2989.56
225 000	3130.33	3110.47	3093.73	3079.59	3067.63	3057.50
230 000	3199.89	3179.59	3162.48	3148.02	3135.80	3125.44
235 000	3269.45	3248.71	3231.23	3216.46	3203.97	3193.39
240 000	3339.01	3317.83	3299.98	3284.89	3272.14	3261.33
245 000	3408.58	3386.95	3368.73	3353.33	3340.31	3329.28
250 000	3478.14	3456.08	3437.48	3421.76	3408.48	3397.22
260 000	3617.27	3594.32	3574.97	3558.64	3544.82	3533.11
270 000	3756.39	3732.56	3712.47	3695.51	3681.15	3669.00
280 000	3895.52	3870.81	3849.97	3832.38	3817.49	3804.89
290 000	4034.64	4009.05	3987.47	3969.25	3953.83	3940.78
300 000	4173.77	4147.29	4124.97	4106.12	4090.17	4076.67
400 000	5565.02	5529.72	5499.96	5474.82	5453.56	5435.56
500 000	6956.28	6912.15	6874.95	6843.53	6816.95	6794.44

Term	26 Years	27 Years	28 Years	29 Years	30 Years	35 Years
AMOUNT						
30 000	406.52	405.55	404.72	404.02	403.43	401.54
40 000	542.03	540.73	539.63	538.70	537.90	535.39
50 000	677.54	675.92	674.54	673.37	672.38	669.23
55 000	745.29	743.51	742.00	740.71	739.62	736.16
60 000	813.04	811.10	809.45	808.05	806.85	803.08
65 000	880.80	878.69	876.90	875.38	874.09	870.01
70 000	948.55	946.28	944.36	942.72	941.33	936.93
75 000	1016.30	1013.87	1011.81	1010.06	1008.57	1003.85
80 000	1084.06	1081.47	1079.27	1077.40	1075.81	1070.78
85 000	1151.81	1149.06	1146.72	1144.73	1143.04	1137.70
90 000	1219.56	1216.65	1214.17	1212.07	1210.28	1204.62
95 000	1287.32	1284.24	1281.63	1279.41	1277.52	1271.55
100 000	1355.07	1351.83	1349.08	1346.74	1344.76	1338.47
105 000	1422.83	1419.42	1416.54	1414.08	1411.99	1405.39
110 000	1490.58	1487.02	1483.99	1481.42	1479.23	1472.32
115 000	1558.33	1554.61	1551.44	1548.76	1546.47	1539.24
120 000	1626.09	1622.20	1618.90	1616.09	1613.71	1606.16
125 000	1693.84	1689.79	1686.35	1683.43	1680.95	1673.09
130 000	1761.59	1757.38	1753.81	1750.77	1748.18	1740.01
135 000	1829.35	1824.97	1821.26	1818.11	1815.42	1806.93
140 000	1897.10	1892.57	1888.72	1885.44	1882.66	1873.86
145 000	1964.85	1960.16	1956.17	1952.78	1949.90	1940.78
150 000	2032.61	2027.75	2023.62	2020.12	2017.14	2007.70
155 000	2100.36	2095.34	2091.08	2087.45	2084.37	2074.63
160 000	2168.12	2162.93	2158.53	2154.79	2151.61	2141.55
165 000	2235.87	2230.52	2225.99	2222.13	2218.85	2208.47
170 000	2303.62	2298.12	2293.44	2289.47	2286.09	2275.40
175 000	2371.38	2365.71	2360.89	2356.80	2353.32	2342.32
180 000	2439.13	2433.30	2428.35	2424.14	2420.56	2409.24
185 000	2506.88	2500.89	2495.80	2491.48	2487.80	2476.17
190 000	2574.64	2568.48	2563.26	2558.82	2555.04	2543.09
195 000	2642.39	2636.07	2630.71	2626.15	2622.28	2610.02
200 000	2710.14	2703.67	2698.16	2693.49	2689.51	2676.94
205 000	2777.90	2771.26	2765.62	2760.83	2756.75	2743.86
210 000	2845.65	2838.85	2833.07	2828.16	2823.99	2810.79
215 000	2913.41	2906.44	2900.53	2895.50	2891.23	2877.71
220 000	2981.16	2974.03	2967.98	2962.84	2958.47	2944.63
225 000	3048.91	3041.62	3035.44	3030.18	3025.70	3011.56
230 000	3116.67	3109.22	3102.89	3097.51	3092.94	3078.48
235 000	3184.42	3176.81	3170.34	3164.85	3160.18	3145.40
240 000	3252.17	3244.40	3237.80	3232.19	3227.42	3212.33
245 000	3319.93	3311.99	3305.25	3299.52	3294.65	3279.25
250 000	3387.68	3379.58	3372.71	3366.86	3361.89	3346.17
260 000	3523.19	3514.77	3507.61	3501.54	3496.37	3480.02
270 000	3658.69	3649.95	3642.52	3636.21	3630.84	3613.87
280 000	3794.20	3785.13	3777.43	3770.89	3765.32	3747.71
290 000	3929.71	3920.32	3912.34	3905.56	3899.80	3881.56
300 000	4065.22	4055.50	4047.25	4040.23	4034.27	4015.41
400 000	5420.29	5407.33	5396.33	5386.98	5379.03	5353.88
500 000	6775.36	6759.17	6745.41	6733.72	6723.78	6692.35

16.50% INTEREST	MONTHLY PAYMENT needed to pay back a mortgage				
Term	1 Year	5 Years	10 Years	11 Years	12 Years	13 Years

AMOUNT	1 Year	5 Years	10 Years	11 Years	12 Years	13 Years
30 000	2729.03	737.54	511.93	493.93	479.62	468.11
40 000	3638.71	983.38	682.57	658.58	639.49	624.14
50 000	4548.38	1229.23	853.21	823.22	799.37	780.18
55 000	5003.22	1352.15	938.53	905.54	879.30	858.20
60 000	5458.06	1475.07	1023.85	987.86	959.24	936.21
65 000	5912.90	1597.99	1109.17	1070.18	1039.18	1014.23
70 000	6367.73	1720.92	1194.50	1152.51	1119.11	1092.25
75 000	6822.57	1843.84	1279.82	1234.83	1199.05	1170.27
80 000	7277.41	1966.76	1365.14	1317.15	1278.99	1248.29
85 000	7732.25	2089.68	1450.46	1399.47	1358.92	1326.30
90 000	8187.09	2212.61	1535.78	1481.79	1438.86	1404.32
95 000	8641.93	2335.53	1621.10	1564.12	1518.80	1482.34
100 000	9096.76	2458.45	1706.42	1646.44	1598.73	1560.36
105 000	9551.60	2581.37	1791.74	1728.76	1678.67	1638.37
110 000	10006.44	2704.30	1877.07	1811.08	1758.61	1716.39
115 000	10461.28	2827.22	1962.39	1893.40	1838.54	1794.41
120 000	10916.12	2950.14	2047.71	1975.73	1918.48	1872.43
125 000	11370.95	3073.07	2133.03	2058.05	1998.42	1950.45
130 000	11825.79	3195.99	2218.35	2140.37	2078.35	2028.46
135 000	12280.63	3318.91	2303.67	2222.69	2158.29	2106.48
140 000	12735.47	3441.83	2388.99	2305.01	2238.23	2184.50
145 000	13190.31	3564.76	2474.31	2387.34	2318.16	2262.52
150 000	13645.15	3687.68	2559.63	2469.66	2398.10	2340.54
155 000	14099.98	3810.60	2644.96	2551.98	2478.04	2418.55
160 000	14554.82	3933.52	2730.28	2634.30	2557.97	2496.57
165 000	15009.66	4056.45	2815.60	2716.62	2637.91	2574.59
170 000	15464.50	4179.37	2900.92	2798.94	2717.85	2652.61
175 000	15919.34	4302.29	2986.24	2881.27	2797.78	2730.62
180 000	16374.17	4425.21	3071.56	2963.59	2877.72	2808.64
185 000	16829.01	4548.14	3156.88	3045.91	2957.66	2886.66
190 000	17283.85	4671.06	3242.20	3128.23	3037.59	2964.68
195 000	17738.69	4793.98	3327.52	3210.55	3117.53	3042.70
200 000	18193.53	4916.90	3412.85	3292.88	3197.47	3120.71
205 000	18648.37	5039.83	3498.17	3375.20	3277.40	3198.73
210 000	19103.20	5162.75	3583.49	3457.52	3357.34	3276.75
215 000	19558.04	5285.67	3668.81	3539.84	3437.28	3354.77
220 000	20012.88	5408.59	3754.13	3622.16	3517.21	3432.79
225 000	20467.72	5531.52	3839.45	3704.49	3597.15	3510.80
230 000	20922.56	5654.44	3924.77	3786.81	3677.09	3588.82
235 000	21377.39	5777.36	4010.09	3869.13	3757.02	3666.84
240 000	21832.23	5900.29	4095.42	3951.45	3836.96	3744.86
245 000	22287.07	6023.21	4180.74	4033.77	3916.90	3822.87
250 000	22741.91	6146.13	4266.06	4116.10	3996.83	3900.89
260 000	23651.59	6391.98	4436.70	4280.74	4156.71	4056.93
270 000	24561.26	6637.82	4607.34	4445.38	4316.58	4212.96
280 000	25470.94	6883.67	4777.98	4610.03	4476.45	4369.00
290 000	26380.61	7129.51	4948.63	4774.67	4636.33	4525.03
300 000	27290.29	7375.36	5119.27	4939.31	4796.20	4681.07
400 000	36387.05	9833.81	6825.69	6585.75	6394.93	6241.43
500 000	45483.82	12292.26	8532.11	8232.19	7993.67	7801.78

Term	14 Years	15 Years	16 Years	17 Years	18 Years	19 Years
AMOUNT						
30 000	458.76	451.11	444.82	439.61	435.29	431.68
40 000	611.68	601.48	593.09	586.15	580.38	575.58
50 000	764.60	751.85	741.36	732.69	725.48	719.47
55 000	841.06	827.04	815.50	805.96	798.03	791.42
60 000	917.52	902.23	889.64	879.23	870.58	863.37
65 000	993.98	977.41	963.77	952.49	943.12	935.31
70 000	1070.44	1052.60	1037.91	1025.76	1015.67	1007.26
75 000	1146.90	1127.78	1112.05	1099.03	1088.22	1079.21
80 000	1223.36	1202.97	1186.18	1172.30	1160.77	1151.16
85 000	1299.82	1278.15	1260.32	1245.57	1233.32	1223.10
90 000	1376.28	1353.34	1334.46	1318.84	1305.86	1295.05
95 000	1452.74	1428.52	1408.59	1392.11	1378.41	1367.00
100 000	1529.20	1503.71	1482.73	1465.38	1450.96	1438.94
105 000	1605.66	1578.89	1556.87	1538.64	1523.51	1510.89
110 000	1682.12	1654.08	1631.00	1611.91	1596.06	1582.84
115 000	1758.58	1729.26	1705.14	1685.18	1668.60	1654.79
120 000	1835.04	1804.45	1779.28	1758.45	1741.15	1726.73
125 000	1911.50	1879.64	1853.41	1831.72	1813.70	1798.68
130 000	1987.96	1954.82	1927.55	1904.99	1886.25	1870.63
135 000	2064.42	2030.01	2001.69	1978.26	1958.80	1942.58
140 000	2140.88	2105.19	2075.82	2051.53	2031.34	2014.52
145 000	2217.34	2180.38	2149.96	2124.79	2103.89	2086.47
150 000	2293.80	2255.56	2224.09	2198.06	2176.44	2158.42
155 000	2370.26	2330.75	2298.23	2271.33	2248.99	2230.36
160 000	2446.72	2405.93	2372.37	2344.60	2321.54	2302.31
165 000	2523.18	2481.12	2446.50	2417.87	2394.08	2374.26
170 000	2599.64	2556.30	2520.64	2491.14	2466.63	2446.21
175 000	2676.10	2631.49	2594.78	2564.41	2539.18	2518.15
180 000	2752.56	2706.68	2668.91	2637.68	2611.73	2590.10
185 000	2829.02	2781.86	2743.05	2710.95	2684.28	2662.05
190 000	2905.48	2857.05	2817.19	2784.21	2756.83	2734.00
195 000	2981.94	2932.23	2891.32	2857.48	2829.37	2805.94
200 000	3058.40	3007.42	2965.46	2930.75	2901.92	2877.89
205 000	3134.86	3082.60	3039.60	3004.02	2974.47	2949.84
210 000	3211.32	3157.79	3113.73	3077.29	3047.02	3021.78
215 000	3287.78	3232.97	3187.87	3150.56	3119.57	3093.73
220 000	3364.23	3308.16	3262.01	3223.83	3192.11	3165.68
225 000	3440.69	3383.34	3336.14	3297.10	3264.66	3237.63
230 000	3517.15	3458.53	3410.28	3370.36	3337.21	3309.57
235 000	3593.61	3533.72	3484.41	3443.63	3409.76	3381.52
240 000	3670.07	3608.90	3558.55	3516.90	3482.31	3453.47
245 000	3746.53	3684.09	3632.69	3590.17	3554.85	3525.42
250 000	3822.99	3759.27	3706.82	3663.44	3627.40	3597.36
260 000	3975.91	3909.64	3855.10	3809.98	3772.50	3741.26
270 000	4128.83	4060.01	4003.37	3956.51	3917.59	3885.15
280 000	4281.75	4210.38	4151.64	4103.05	4062.69	4029.05
290 000	4434.67	4360.75	4299.92	4249.59	4207.79	4172.94
300 000	4587.59	4511.13	4448.19	4396.13	4352.88	4316.83
400 000	6116.79	6014.83	5930.92	5861.50	5803.84	5755.78
500 000	7645.99	7518.54	7413.65	7326.88	7254.80	7194.72

Term	20 Years	21 Years	22 Years	23 Years	24 Years	25 Years
AMOUNT						
30 000	428.67	426.15	424.03	422.24	420.74	419.47
40 000	571.56	568.19	565.37	562.99	560.99	559.30
50 000	714.45	710.24	706.71	703.74	701.23	699.12
55 000	785.90	781.27	777.38	774.11	771.36	769.03
60 000	857.34	852.29	848.05	844.48	841.48	838.95
65 000	928.79	923.31	918.72	914.86	911.60	908.86
70 000	1000.23	994.34	989.39	985.23	981.73	978.77
75 000	1071.68	1065.36	1060.06	1055.60	1051.85	1048.68
80 000	1143.12	1136.39	1130.73	1125.98	1121.97	1118.60
85 000	1214.57	1207.41	1201.40	1196.35	1192.10	1188.51
90 000	1286.01	1278.44	1272.08	1266.73	1262.22	1258.42
95 000	1357.46	1349.46	1342.75	1337.10	1332.34	1328.33
100 000	1428.90	1420.48	1413.42	1407.47	1402.47	1398.24
105 000	1500.35	1491.51	1484.09	1477.85	1472.59	1468.16
110 000	1571.79	1562.53	1554.76	1548.22	1542.71	1538.07
115 000	1643.24	1633.56	1625.43	1618.59	1612.84	1607.98
120 000	1714.68	1704.58	1696.10	1688.97	1682.96	1677.89
125 000	1786.13	1775.60	1766.77	1759.34	1753.08	1747.81
130 000	1857.57	1846.63	1837.44	1829.71	1823.21	1817.72
135 000	1929.02	1917.65	1908.11	1900.09	1893.33	1887.63
140 000	2000.46	1988.68	1978.78	1970.46	1963.45	1957.54
145 000	2071.91	2059.70	2049.45	2040.84	2033.58	2027.45
150 000	2143.35	2130.73	2120.13	2111.21	2103.70	2097.37
155 000	2214.80	2201.75	2190.80	2181.58	2173.82	2167.28
160 000	2286.24	2272.77	2261.47	2251.96	2243.95	2237.19
165 000	2357.69	2343.80	2332.14	2322.33	2314.07	2307.10
170 000	2429.13	2414.82	2402.81	2392.70	2384.19	2377.02
175 000	2500.58	2485.85	2473.48	2463.08	2454.32	2446.93
180 000	2572.02	2556.87	2544.15	2533.45	2524.44	2516.84
185 000	2643.47	2627.90	2614.82	2603.82	2594.56	2586.75
190 000	2714.91	2698.92	2685.49	2674.20	2664.69	2656.66
195 000	2786.36	2769.94	2756.16	2744.57	2734.81	2726.58
200 000	2857.80	2840.97	2826.83	2814.95	2804.93	2796.49
205 000	2929.25	2911.99	2897.50	2885.32	2875.06	2866.40
210 000	3000.69	2983.02	2968.18	2955.69	2945.18	2936.31
215 000	3072.14	3054.04	3038.85	3026.07	3015.30	3006.23
220 000	3143.58	3125.06	3109.52	3096.44	3085.43	3076.14
225 000	3215.03	3196.09	3180.19	3166.81	3155.55	3146.05
230 000	3286.47	3267.11	3250.86	3237.19	3225.67	3215.96
235 000	3357.92	3338.14	3321.53	3307.56	3295.80	3285.87
240 000	3429.36	3409.16	3392.20	3377.93	3365.92	3355.79
245 000	3500.81	3480.19	3462.87	3448.31	3436.04	3425.70
250 000	3572.25	3551.21	3533.54	3518.68	3506.17	3495.61
260 000	3715.14	3693.26	3674.88	3659.43	3646.41	3635.44
270 000	3858.03	3835.31	3816.23	3800.18	3786.66	3775.26
280 000	4000.92	3977.35	3957.57	3940.92	3926.91	3915.09
290 000	4143.81	4119.40	4098.91	4081.67	4067.15	4054.91
300 000	4286.70	4261.45	4240.25	4222.42	4207.40	4194.73
400 000	5715.60	5681.94	5653.67	5629.89	5609.87	5592.98
500 000	7144.50	7102.42	7067.08	7037.36	7012.33	6991.22

			needed to pay back a mortgage		
Term	**26** Years	**27** Years	**28** Years	**29** Years	**30** Years	**35** Years

AMOUNT						
30 000	418.40	417.50	416.74	416.09	415.54	413.84
40 000	557.87	556.67	555.65	554.79	554.06	551.78
50 000	697.34	695.83	694.56	693.49	692.57	689.73
55 000	767.07	765.42	764.02	762.83	761.83	758.70
60 000	836.81	835.00	833.47	832.18	831.09	827.67
65 000	906.54	904.59	902.93	901.53	900.35	896.65
70 000	976.28	974.17	972.39	970.88	969.60	965.62
75 000	1046.01	1043.75	1041.84	1040.23	1038.86	1034.59
80 000	1115.74	1113.34	1111.30	1109.58	1108.12	1103.56
85 000	1185.48	1182.92	1180.76	1178.93	1177.38	1172.54
90 000	1255.21	1252.50	1250.21	1248.27	1246.63	1241.51
95 000	1324.95	1322.09	1319.67	1317.62	1315.89	1310.48
100 000	1394.68	1391.67	1389.12	1386.97	1385.15	1379.45
105 000	1464.41	1461.25	1458.58	1456.32	1454.41	1448.43
110 000	1534.15	1530.84	1528.04	1525.67	1523.66	1517.40
115 000	1603.88	1600.42	1597.49	1595.02	1592.92	1586.37
120 000	1673.62	1670.00	1666.95	1664.37	1662.18	1655.34
125 000	1743.35	1739.59	1736.41	1733.71	1731.44	1724.32
130 000	1813.09	1809.17	1805.86	1803.06	1800.69	1793.29
135 000	1882.82	1878.75	1875.32	1872.41	1869.95	1862.26
140 000	1952.55	1948.34	1944.77	1941.76	1939.21	1931.24
145 000	2022.29	2017.92	2014.23	2011.11	2008.46	2000.21
150 000	2092.02	2087.50	2083.69	2080.46	2077.72	2069.18
155 000	2161.76	2157.09	2153.14	2149.80	2146.98	2138.15
160 000	2231.49	2226.67	2222.60	2219.15	2216.24	2207.13
165 000	2301.22	2296.26	2292.06	2288.50	2285.49	2276.10
170 000	2370.96	2365.84	2361.51	2357.85	2354.75	2345.07
175 000	2440.69	2435.42	2430.97	2427.20	2424.01	2414.04
180 000	2510.43	2505.01	2500.42	2496.55	2493.27	2483.02
185 000	2580.16	2574.59	2569.88	2565.90	2562.52	2551.99
190 000	2649.89	2644.17	2639.34	2635.24	2631.78	2620.96
195 000	2719.63	2713.76	2708.79	2704.59	2701.04	2689.94
200 000	2789.36	2783.34	2778.25	2773.94	2770.30	2758.91
205 000	2859.10	2852.92	2847.71	2843.29	2839.55	2827.88
210 000	2928.83	2922.51	2917.16	2912.64	2908.81	2896.85
215 000	2998.56	2992.09	2986.62	2981.99	2978.07	2965.83
220 000	3068.30	3061.67	3056.07	3051.34	3047.33	3034.80
225 000	3138.03	3131.26	3125.53	3120.68	3116.58	3103.77
230 000	3207.77	3200.84	3194.99	3190.03	3185.84	3172.74
235 000	3277.50	3270.42	3264.44	3259.38	3255.10	3241.72
240 000	3347.23	3340.01	3333.90	3328.73	3324.36	3310.69
245 000	3416.97	3409.59	3403.35	3398.08	3393.61	3379.66
250 000	3486.70	3479.17	3472.81	3467.43	3462.87	3448.63
260 000	3626.17	3618.34	3611.72	3606.12	3601.39	3586.58
270 000	3765.64	3757.51	3750.64	3744.82	3739.90	3724.53
280 000	3905.11	3896.68	3889.55	3883.52	3878.41	3862.47
290 000	4044.57	4035.84	4028.46	4022.22	4016.93	4000.42
300 000	4184.04	4175.01	4167.37	4160.91	4155.44	4138.36
400 000	5578.72	5566.68	5556.50	5547.88	5540.59	5517.82
500 000	6973.40	6958.35	6945.62	6934.85	6925.74	6897.27

MONTHLY PAYMENT
needed to pay back a mortgage

Term	1 Year	5 Years	10 Years	11 Years	12 Years	13 Years
AMOUNT						
30 000	2736.14	745.58	521.39	503.65	489.58	478.29
40 000	3648.19	994.10	695.19	671.53	652.77	637.72
50 000	4560.24	1242.63	868.99	839.42	815.96	797.15
55 000	5016.26	1366.89	955.89	923.36	897.56	876.86
60 000	5472.29	1491.15	1042.79	1007.30	979.15	956.58
65 000	5928.31	1615.42	1129.68	1091.24	1060.75	1036.29
70 000	6384.33	1739.68	1216.58	1175.18	1142.35	1116.01
75 000	6840.36	1863.94	1303.48	1259.12	1223.94	1195.72
80 000	7296.38	1988.21	1390.38	1343.07	1305.54	1275.44
85 000	7752.40	2112.47	1477.28	1427.01	1387.13	1355.15
90 000	8208.43	2236.73	1564.18	1510.95	1468.73	1434.87
95 000	8664.45	2360.99	1651.08	1594.89	1550.33	1514.58
100 000	9120.48	2485.26	1737.98	1678.83	1631.92	1594.30
105 000	9576.50	2609.52	1824.88	1762.77	1713.52	1674.01
110 000	10032.52	2733.78	1911.77	1846.72	1795.12	1753.72
115 000	10488.55	2858.05	1998.67	1930.66	1876.71	1833.44
120 000	10944.57	2982.31	2085.57	2014.60	1958.31	1913.15
125 000	11400.59	3106.57	2172.47	2098.54	2039.90	1992.87
130 000	11856.62	3230.83	2259.37	2182.48	2121.50	2072.58
135 000	12312.64	3355.10	2346.27	2266.42	2203.10	2152.30
140 000	12768.67	3479.36	2433.17	2350.36	2284.69	2232.01
145 000	13224.69	3603.62	2520.07	2434.31	2366.29	2311.73
150 000	13680.71	3727.89	2606.96	2518.25	2447.88	2391.44
155 000	14136.74	3852.15	2693.86	2602.19	2529.48	2471.16
160 000	14592.76	3976.41	2780.76	2686.13	2611.08	2550.87
165 000	15048.78	4100.68	2867.66	2770.07	2692.67	2630.59
170 000	15504.81	4224.94	2954.56	2854.01	2774.27	2710.30
175 000	15960.83	4349.20	3041.46	2937.96	2855.87	2790.02
180 000	16416.86	4473.46	3128.36	3021.90	2937.46	2869.73
185 000	16872.88	4597.73	3215.26	3105.84	3019.06	2949.45
190 000	17328.90	4721.99	3302.16	3189.78	3100.65	3029.16
195 000	17784.93	4846.25	3389.05	3273.72	3182.25	3108.88
200 000	18240.95	4970.52	3475.95	3357.66	3263.85	3188.59
205 000	18696.97	5094.78	3562.85	3441.61	3345.44	3268.31
210 000	19153.00	5219.04	3649.75	3525.55	3427.04	3348.02
215 000	19609.02	5343.30	3736.65	3609.49	3508.63	3427.73
220 000	20065.05	5467.57	3823.55	3693.43	3590.23	3507.45
225 000	20521.07	5591.83	3910.45	3777.37	3671.83	3587.16
230 000	20977.09	5716.09	3997.35	3861.31	3753.42	3666.88
235 000	21433.12	5840.36	4084.24	3945.26	3835.02	3746.59
240 000	21889.14	5964.62	4171.14	4029.20	3916.62	3826.31
245 000	22345.16	6088.88	4258.04	4113.14	3998.21	3906.02
250 000	22801.19	6213.14	4344.94	4197.08	4079.81	3985.74
260 000	23713.24	6461.67	4518.74	4364.96	4243.00	4145.17
270 000	24625.28	6710.20	4692.54	4532.85	4406.19	4304.60
280 000	25537.33	6958.72	4866.33	4700.73	4569.38	4464.03
290 000	26449.38	7207.25	5040.13	4868.61	4732.58	4623.46
300 000	27361.43	7455.77	5213.93	5036.50	4895.77	4782.89
400 000	36481.90	9941.03	6951.91	6715.33	6527.69	6377.18
500 000	45602.38	12426.29	8689.88	8394.16	8159.61	7971.48

Term	14 Years	15 Years	16 Years	17 Years	18 Years	19 Years
AMOUNT						
30 000	469.15	461.70	455.59	450.55	446.38	442.92
40 000	625.54	615.60	607.45	600.74	595.18	590.56
50 000	781.92	769.50	759.32	750.92	743.97	738.20
55 000	860.11	846.45	835.25	826.01	818.37	812.02
60 000	938.30	923.40	911.18	901.11	892.77	885.85
65 000	1016.49	1000.35	987.11	976.20	967.17	959.67
70 000	1094.69	1077.30	1063.04	1051.29	1041.56	1033.49
75 000	1172.88	1154.25	1138.98	1126.38	1115.96	1107.31
80 000	1251.07	1231.20	1214.91	1201.47	1190.36	1181.13
85 000	1329.26	1308.15	1290.84	1276.57	1264.76	1254.95
90 000	1407.45	1385.10	1366.77	1351.66	1339.15	1328.77
95 000	1485.65	1462.05	1442.70	1426.75	1413.55	1402.59
100 000	1563.84	1539.00	1518.63	1501.84	1487.95	1476.41
105 000	1642.03	1615.95	1594.57	1576.94	1562.34	1550.23
110 000	1720.22	1692.90	1670.50	1652.03	1636.74	1624.05
115 000	1798.41	1769.85	1746.43	1727.12	1711.14	1697.87
120 000	1876.61	1846.81	1822.36	1802.21	1785.54	1771.69
125 000	1954.80	1923.76	1898.29	1877.30	1859.93	1845.51
130 000	2032.99	2000.71	1974.22	1952.40	1934.33	1919.33
135 000	2111.18	2077.66	2050.16	2027.49	2008.73	1993.15
140 000	2189.37	2154.61	2126.09	2102.58	2083.13	2066.97
145 000	2267.57	2231.56	2202.02	2177.67	2157.52	2140.79
150 000	2345.76	2308.51	2277.95	2252.77	2231.92	2214.61
155 000	2423.95	2385.46	2353.88	2327.86	2306.32	2288.43
160 000	2502.14	2462.41	2429.81	2402.95	2380.72	2362.25
165 000	2580.33	2539.36	2505.75	2478.04	2455.11	2436.07
170 000	2658.53	2616.31	2581.68	2553.13	2529.51	2509.89
175 000	2736.72	2693.26	2657.61	2628.23	2603.91	2583.71
180 000	2814.91	2770.21	2733.54	2703.32	2678.31	2657.54
185 000	2893.10	2847.16	2809.47	2778.41	2752.70	2731.36
190 000	2971.29	2924.11	2885.40	2853.50	2827.10	2805.18
195 000	3049.48	3001.06	2961.34	2928.59	2901.50	2879.00
200 000	3127.68	3078.01	3037.27	3003.69	2975.89	2952.82
205 000	3205.87	3154.96	3113.20	3078.78	3050.29	3026.64
210 000	3284.06	3231.91	3189.13	3153.87	3124.69	3100.46
215 000	3362.25	3308.86	3265.06	3228.96	3199.09	3174.28
220 000	3440.44	3385.81	3340.99	3304.06	3273.48	3248.10
225 000	3518.64	3462.76	3416.93	3379.15	3347.88	3321.92
230 000	3596.83	3539.71	3492.86	3454.24	3422.28	3395.74
235 000	3675.02	3616.66	3568.79	3529.33	3496.68	3469.56
240 000	3753.21	3693.61	3644.72	3604.42	3571.07	3543.38
245 000	3831.40	3770.56	3720.65	3679.52	3645.47	3617.20
250 000	3909.60	3847.51	3796.59	3754.61	3719.87	3691.02
260 000	4065.98	4001.41	3948.45	3904.79	3868.66	3838.66
270 000	4222.36	4155.31	4100.31	4054.98	4017.46	3986.30
280 000	4378.75	4309.21	4252.18	4205.16	4166.25	4133.94
290 000	4535.13	4463.11	4404.04	4355.35	4315.05	4281.58
300 000	4691.51	4617.01	4555.90	4505.53	4463.84	4429.23
400 000	6255.35	6156.02	6074.54	6007.37	5951.79	5905.63
500 000	7819.19	7695.02	7593.17	7509.22	7439.74	7382.04

17.00% INTEREST	MONTHLY PAYMENT needed to pay back a mortgage					
Term	20 Years	21 Years	22 Years	23 Years	24 Years	25 Years
AMOUNT						
30 000	440.04	437.63	435.62	433.94	432.53	431.34
40 000	586.72	583.51	580.83	578.58	576.70	575.12
50 000	733.40	729.39	726.04	723.23	720.88	718.90
55 000	806.74	802.33	798.64	795.55	792.96	790.79
60 000	880.08	875.27	871.25	867.88	865.05	862.68
65 000	953.42	948.21	943.85	940.20	937.14	934.57
70 000	1026.76	1021.15	1016.45	1012.52	1009.23	1006.46
75 000	1100.10	1094.09	1089.06	1084.85	1081.31	1078.35
80 000	1173.44	1167.03	1161.66	1157.17	1153.40	1150.24
85 000	1246.78	1239.96	1234.27	1229.49	1225.49	1222.13
90 000	1320.12	1312.90	1306.87	1301.81	1297.58	1294.02
95 000	1393.46	1385.84	1379.47	1374.14	1369.66	1365.91
100 000	1466.80	1458.78	1452.08	1446.46	1441.75	1437.80
105 000	1540.14	1531.72	1524.68	1518.78	1513.84	1509.69
110 000	1613.48	1604.66	1597.28	1591.11	1585.93	1581.58
115 000	1686.82	1677.60	1669.89	1663.43	1658.01	1653.47
120 000	1760.16	1750.54	1742.49	1735.75	1730.10	1725.36
125 000	1833.50	1823.48	1815.10	1808.08	1802.19	1797.25
130 000	1906.84	1896.42	1887.70	1880.40	1874.28	1869.14
135 000	1980.18	1969.36	1960.30	1952.72	1946.36	1941.03
140 000	2053.52	2042.29	2032.91	2025.05	2018.45	2012.92
145 000	2126.86	2115.23	2105.51	2097.37	2090.54	2084.81
150 000	2200.20	2188.17	2178.11	2169.69	2162.63	2156.69
155 000	2273.54	2261.11	2250.72	2242.01	2234.71	2228.58
160 000	2346.88	2334.05	2323.32	2314.34	2306.80	2300.47
165 000	2420.22	2406.99	2395.93	2386.66	2378.89	2372.36
170 000	2493.56	2479.93	2468.53	2458.98	2450.98	2444.25
175 000	2566.90	2552.87	2541.13	2531.31	2523.06	2516.14
180 000	2640.24	2625.81	2613.74	2603.63	2595.15	2588.03
185 000	2713.58	2698.75	2686.34	2675.95	2667.24	2659.92
190 000	2786.92	2771.69	2758.95	2748.28	2739.33	2731.81
195 000	2860.26	2844.62	2831.55	2820.60	2811.41	2803.70
200 000	2933.60	2917.56	2904.15	2892.92	2883.50	2875.59
205 000	3006.94	2990.50	2976.76	2965.24	2955.59	2947.48
210 000	3080.28	3063.44	3049.36	3037.57	3027.68	3019.37
215 000	3153.62	3136.38	3121.96	3109.89	3099.76	3091.26
220 000	3226.96	3209.32	3194.57	3182.21	3171.85	3163.15
225 000	3300.30	3282.26	3267.17	3254.54	3243.94	3235.04
230 000	3373.64	3355.20	3339.78	3326.86	3316.03	3306.93
235 000	3446.98	3428.14	3412.38	3399.18	3388.11	3378.82
240 000	3520.32	3501.08	3484.98	3471.51	3460.20	3450.71
245 000	3593.66	3574.02	3557.59	3543.83	3532.29	3522.60
250 000	3667.00	3646.95	3630.19	3616.15	3604.38	3594.49
260 000	3813.68	3792.83	3775.40	3760.80	3748.55	3738.27
270 000	3960.36	3938.71	3920.61	3905.44	3892.73	3882.05
280 000	4107.04	4084.59	4065.81	4050.09	4036.90	4025.83
290 000	4253.72	4230.47	4211.02	4194.74	4181.08	4169.61
300 000	4400.40	4376.35	4356.23	4339.38	4325.25	4313.39
400 000	5867.20	5835.13	5808.31	5785.84	5767.00	5751.19
500 000	7334.00	7293.91	7260.38	7232.30	7208.76	7188.98

needed to pay back a mortgage

Term	26 Years	27 Years	28 Years	29 Years	30 Years	35 Years
AMOUNT						
30 000	430.34	429.50	428.80	428.20	427.70	426.16
40 000	573.79	572.67	571.73	570.94	570.27	568.21
50 000	717.24	715.84	714.66	713.67	712.84	710.26
55 000	788.96	787.42	786.13	785.04	784.12	781.29
60 000	860.68	859.01	857.60	856.41	855.41	852.32
65 000	932.41	930.59	929.06	927.77	926.69	923.34
70 000	1004.13	1002.17	1000.53	999.14	997.97	994.37
75 000	1075.85	1073.76	1071.99	1070.51	1069.26	1065.39
80 000	1147.58	1145.34	1143.46	1141.88	1140.54	1136.42
85 000	1219.30	1216.93	1214.93	1213.24	1211.82	1207.45
90 000	1291.03	1288.51	1286.39	1284.61	1283.11	1278.47
95 000	1362.75	1360.09	1357.86	1355.98	1354.39	1349.50
100 000	1434.47	1431.68	1429.33	1427.34	1425.68	1420.53
105 000	1506.20	1503.26	1500.79	1498.71	1496.96	1491.55
110 000	1577.92	1574.85	1572.26	1570.08	1568.24	1562.58
115 000	1649.64	1646.43	1643.72	1641.45	1639.53	1633.61
120 000	1721.37	1718.01	1715.19	1712.81	1710.81	1704.63
125 000	1793.09	1789.60	1786.66	1784.18	1782.09	1775.66
130 000	1864.82	1861.18	1858.12	1855.55	1853.38	1846.68
135 000	1936.54	1932.77	1929.59	1926.92	1924.66	1917.71
140 000	2008.26	2004.35	2001.06	1998.28	1995.95	1988.74
145 000	2079.99	2075.93	2072.52	2069.65	2067.23	2059.76
150 000	2151.71	2147.52	2143.99	2141.02	2138.51	2130.79
155 000	2223.43	2219.10	2215.45	2212.38	2209.80	2201.82
160 000	2295.16	2290.68	2286.92	2283.75	2281.08	2272.84
165 000	2366.88	2362.27	2358.39	2355.12	2352.36	2343.87
170 000	2438.60	2433.85	2429.85	2426.49	2423.65	2414.89
175 000	2510.33	2505.44	2501.32	2497.85	2494.93	2485.92
180 000	2582.05	2577.02	2572.79	2569.22	2566.22	2556.95
185 000	2653.78	2648.60	2644.25	2640.59	2637.50	2627.97
190 000	2725.50	2720.19	2715.72	2711.95	2708.78	2699.00
195 000	2797.22	2791.77	2787.18	2783.32	2780.07	2770.03
200 000	2868.95	2863.36	2858.65	2854.69	2851.35	2841.05
205 000	2940.67	2934.94	2930.12	2926.06	2922.63	2912.08
210 000	3012.39	3006.52	3001.58	2997.42	2993.92	2983.10
215 000	3084.12	3078.11	3073.05	3068.79	3065.20	3054.13
220 000	3155.84	3149.69	3144.52	3140.16	3136.49	3125.16
225 000	3227.56	3221.28	3215.98	3211.53	3207.77	3196.18
230 000	3299.29	3292.86	3287.45	3282.89	3279.05	3267.21
235 000	3371.01	3364.44	3358.92	3354.26	3350.34	3338.24
240 000	3442.74	3436.03	3430.38	3425.63	3421.62	3409.26
245 000	3514.46	3507.61	3501.85	3496.99	3492.90	3480.29
250 000	3586.18	3579.20	3573.31	3568.36	3564.19	3551.32
260 000	3729.63	3722.36	3716.25	3711.10	3706.76	3693.37
270 000	3873.08	3865.53	3859.18	3853.83	3849.32	3835.42
280 000	4016.53	4008.70	4002.11	3996.56	3991.89	3977.47
290 000	4159.97	4151.87	4145.04	4139.30	4134.46	4119.53
300 000	4303.42	4295.03	4287.98	4282.03	4277.03	4261.58
400 000	5737.89	5726.71	5717.30	5709.38	5702.70	5682.10
500 000	7172.37	7158.39	7146.63	7136.72	7128.38	7102.63

17.50% INTEREST	MONTHLY PAYMENT needed to pay back a mortgage				
Term	**1 Year**	**5 Years**	**10 Years**	**11 Years**	**12 Years**	**13 Years**

AMOUNT	1 Year	5 Years	10 Years	11 Years	12 Years	13 Years
30 000	2743.27	753.67	530.94	513.45	499.62	488.55
40 000	3657.69	1004.89	707.92	684.60	666.15	651.40
50 000	4572.11	1256.11	884.89	855.75	832.69	814.26
55 000	5029.32	1381.72	973.38	941.32	915.96	895.68
60 000	5486.53	1507.33	1061.87	1026.90	999.23	977.11
65 000	5943.74	1632.94	1150.36	1112.47	1082.50	1058.53
70 000	6400.95	1758.55	1238.85	1198.05	1165.77	1139.96
75 000	6858.17	1884.17	1327.34	1283.62	1249.04	1221.38
80 000	7315.38	2009.78	1415.83	1369.19	1332.31	1302.81
85 000	7772.59	2135.39	1504.32	1454.77	1415.58	1384.24
90 000	8229.80	2261.00	1592.81	1540.34	1498.85	1465.66
95 000	8687.01	2386.61	1681.30	1625.92	1582.12	1547.09
100 000	9144.22	2512.22	1769.79	1711.49	1665.39	1628.51
105 000	9601.43	2637.83	1858.28	1797.07	1748.66	1709.94
110 000	10058.64	2763.44	1946.77	1882.64	1831.93	1791.36
115 000	10515.85	2889.05	2035.26	1968.22	1915.20	1872.79
120 000	10973.06	3014.67	2123.75	2053.79	1998.46	1954.21
125 000	11430.28	3140.28	2212.23	2139.37	2081.73	2035.64
130 000	11887.49	3265.89	2300.72	2224.94	2165.00	2117.07
135 000	12344.70	3391.50	2389.21	2310.52	2248.27	2198.49
140 000	12801.91	3517.11	2477.70	2396.09	2331.54	2279.92
145 000	13259.12	3642.72	2566.19	2481.67	2414.81	2361.34
150 000	13716.33	3768.33	2654.68	2567.24	2498.08	2442.77
155 000	14173.54	3893.94	2743.17	2652.82	2581.35	2524.19
160 000	14630.75	4019.56	2831.66	2738.39	2664.62	2605.62
165 000	15087.96	4145.17	2920.15	2823.96	2747.89	2687.05
170 000	15545.17	4270.78	3008.64	2909.54	2831.16	2768.47
175 000	16002.39	4396.39	3097.13	2995.11	2914.43	2849.90
180 000	16459.60	4522.00	3185.62	3080.69	2997.70	2931.32
185 000	16916.81	4647.61	3274.11	3166.26	3080.97	3012.75
190 000	17374.02	4773.22	3362.60	3251.84	3164.24	3094.17
195 000	17831.23	4898.83	3451.09	3337.41	3247.50	3175.60
200 000	18288.44	5024.44	3539.58	3422.99	3330.77	3257.02
205 000	18745.65	5150.05	3628.06	3508.56	3414.04	3338.45
210 000	19202.86	5275.66	3716.55	3594.14	3497.31	3419.88
215 000	19660.07	5401.28	3805.04	3679.71	3580.58	3501.30
220 000	20117.28	5526.89	3893.53	3765.29	3663.85	3582.73
225 000	20574.50	5652.50	3982.02	3850.86	3747.12	3664.15
230 000	21031.71	5778.11	4070.51	3936.44	3830.39	3745.58
235 000	21488.92	5903.72	4159.00	4022.01	3913.66	3827.00
240 000	21946.13	6029.33	4247.49	4107.58	3996.93	3908.43
245 000	22403.34	6154.94	4335.98	4193.16	4080.20	3989.86
250 000	22860.55	6280.55	4424.47	4278.73	4163.47	4071.28
260 000	23774.97	6531.78	4601.45	4449.88	4330.01	4234.13
270 000	24689.40	6783.00	4778.43	4621.03	4496.54	4396.98
280 000	25603.82	7034.22	4955.41	4792.18	4663.08	4559.83
290 000	26518.24	7285.44	5132.38	4963.33	4829.62	4722.69
300 000	27432.66	7536.66	5309.36	5134.48	4996.16	4885.54
400 000	36576.88	10048.89	7079.15	6845.97	6661.55	6514.05
500 000	45721.10	12561.11	8848.94	8557.47	8326.94	8142.56

Term	14 Years	15 Years	16 Years	17 Years	18 Years	19 Years
AMOUNT						
30 000	479.63	472.37	466.44	461.57	457.56	454.24
40 000	639.50	629.83	621.93	615.43	610.08	605.65
50 000	799.38	787.29	777.41	769.29	762.60	757.06
55 000	879.32	866.02	855.15	846.22	838.86	832.77
60 000	959.26	944.75	932.89	923.15	915.12	908.47
65 000	1039.19	1023.48	1010.63	1000.08	991.38	984.18
70 000	1119.13	1102.20	1088.37	1077.01	1067.64	1059.89
75 000	1199.07	1180.93	1166.11	1153.93	1143.90	1135.59
80 000	1279.01	1259.66	1243.85	1230.86	1220.16	1211.30
85 000	1358.94	1338.39	1321.59	1307.79	1296.42	1287.01
90 000	1438.88	1417.12	1399.33	1384.72	1372.68	1362.71
95 000	1518.82	1495.85	1477.07	1461.65	1448.94	1438.42
100 000	1598.76	1574.58	1554.81	1538.58	1525.19	1514.12
105 000	1678.70	1653.31	1632.55	1615.51	1601.45	1589.83
110 000	1758.63	1732.04	1710.29	1692.44	1677.71	1665.54
115 000	1838.57	1810.76	1788.03	1769.37	1753.97	1741.24
120 000	1918.51	1889.49	1865.78	1846.30	1830.23	1816.95
125 000	1998.45	1968.22	1943.52	1923.22	1906.49	1892.65
130 000	2078.39	2046.95	2021.26	2000.15	1982.75	1968.36
135 000	2158.32	2125.68	2099.00	2077.08	2059.01	2044.07
140 000	2238.26	2204.41	2176.74	2154.01	2135.27	2119.77
145 000	2318.20	2283.14	2254.48	2230.94	2211.53	2195.48
150 000	2398.14	2361.87	2332.22	2307.87	2287.79	2271.19
155 000	2478.08	2440.60	2409.96	2384.80	2364.05	2346.89
160 000	2558.01	2519.33	2487.70	2461.73	2440.31	2422.60
165 000	2637.95	2598.05	2565.44	2538.66	2516.57	2498.30
170 000	2717.89	2676.78	2643.18	2615.59	2592.83	2574.01
175 000	2797.83	2755.51	2720.92	2692.51	2669.09	2649.72
180 000	2877.77	2834.24	2798.66	2769.44	2745.35	2725.42
185 000	2957.70	2912.97	2876.40	2846.37	2821.61	2801.13
190 000	3037.64	2991.70	2954.14	2923.30	2897.87	2876.84
195 000	3117.58	3070.43	3031.89	3000.23	2974.13	2952.54
200 000	3197.52	3149.16	3109.63	3077.16	3050.39	3028.25
205 000	3277.46	3227.89	3187.37	3154.09	3126.65	3103.95
210 000	3357.39	3306.61	3265.11	3231.02	3202.91	3179.66
215 000	3437.33	3385.34	3342.85	3307.95	3279.17	3255.37
220 000	3517.27	3464.07	3420.59	3384.87	3355.43	3331.07
225 000	3597.21	3542.80	3498.33	3461.80	3431.69	3406.78
230 000	3677.14	3621.53	3576.07	3538.73	3507.95	3482.48
235 000	3757.08	3700.26	3653.81	3615.66	3584.21	3558.19
240 000	3837.02	3778.99	3731.55	3692.59	3660.47	3633.90
245 000	3916.96	3857.72	3809.29	3769.52	3736.73	3709.60
250 000	3996.90	3936.45	3887.03	3846.45	3812.99	3785.31
260 000	4156.77	4093.90	4042.51	4000.31	3965.51	3936.72
270 000	4316.65	4251.36	4197.99	4154.16	4118.03	4088.13
280 000	4476.52	4408.82	4353.48	4308.02	4270.55	4239.55
290 000	4636.40	4566.28	4508.96	4461.88	4423.07	4390.96
300 000	4796.28	4723.73	4664.44	4615.74	4575.58	4542.37
400 000	6395.03	6298.31	6219.25	6154.32	6100.78	6056.50
500 000	7993.79	7872.89	7774.06	7692.90	7625.97	7570.62

17.50% INTEREST	**MONTHLY PAYMENT** needed to pay back a mortgage				
Term	20 Years	21 Years	22 Years	23 Years	24 Years	25 Years
AMOUNT						
30 000	451.48	449.19	447.29	445.70	444.37	443.26
40 000	601.98	598.92	596.38	594.26	592.49	591.01
50 000	752.47	748.66	745.48	742.83	740.61	738.76
55 000	827.72	823.52	820.03	817.11	814.68	812.64
60 000	902.97	898.39	894.57	891.39	888.74	886.52
65 000	978.21	973.25	969.12	965.68	962.80	960.39
70 000	1053.46	1048.12	1043.67	1039.96	1036.86	1034.27
75 000	1128.71	1122.98	1118.22	1114.24	1110.92	1108.15
80 000	1203.95	1197.85	1192.76	1188.52	1184.98	1182.02
85 000	1279.20	1272.71	1267.31	1262.81	1259.04	1255.90
90 000	1354.45	1347.58	1341.86	1337.09	1333.11	1329.78
95 000	1429.69	1422.44	1416.41	1411.37	1407.17	1403.65
100 000	1504.94	1497.31	1490.95	1485.65	1481.23	1477.53
105 000	1580.19	1572.18	1565.50	1559.94	1555.29	1551.41
110 000	1655.44	1647.04	1640.05	1634.22	1629.35	1625.28
115 000	1730.68	1721.91	1714.60	1708.50	1703.41	1699.16
120 000	1805.93	1796.77	1789.15	1782.79	1777.48	1773.04
125 000	1881.18	1871.64	1863.69	1857.07	1851.54	1846.91
130 000	1956.42	1946.50	1938.24	1931.35	1925.60	1920.79
135 000	2031.67	2021.37	2012.79	2005.63	1999.66	1994.67
140 000	2106.92	2096.23	2087.34	2079.92	2073.72	2068.54
145 000	2182.17	2171.10	2161.88	2154.20	2147.78	2142.42
150 000	2257.41	2245.97	2236.43	2228.48	2221.84	2216.29
155 000	2332.66	2320.83	2310.98	2302.77	2295.91	2290.17
160 000	2407.91	2395.70	2385.53	2377.05	2369.97	2364.05
165 000	2483.15	2470.56	2460.08	2451.33	2444.03	2437.92
170 000	2558.40	2545.43	2534.62	2525.61	2518.09	2511.80
175 000	2633.65	2620.29	2609.17	2599.90	2592.15	2585.68
180 000	2708.90	2695.16	2683.72	2674.18	2666.21	2659.55
185 000	2784.14	2770.02	2758.27	2748.46	2740.27	2733.43
190 000	2859.39	2844.89	2832.81	2822.74	2814.34	2807.31
195 000	2934.64	2919.75	2907.36	2897.03	2888.40	2881.18
200 000	3009.88	2994.62	2981.91	2971.31	2962.46	2955.06
205 000	3085.13	3069.49	3056.46	3045.59	3036.52	3028.94
210 000	3160.38	3144.35	3131.01	3119.88	3110.58	3102.81
215 000	3235.63	3219.22	3205.55	3194.16	3184.64	3176.69
220 000	3310.87	3294.08	3280.10	3268.44	3258.70	3250.57
225 000	3386.12	3368.95	3354.65	3342.72	3332.77	3324.44
230 000	3461.37	3443.81	3429.20	3417.01	3406.83	3398.32
235 000	3536.61	3518.68	3503.74	3491.29	3480.89	3472.19
240 000	3611.86	3593.54	3578.29	3565.57	3554.95	3546.07
245 000	3687.11	3668.41	3652.84	3639.85	3629.01	3619.95
250 000	3762.35	3743.28	3727.39	3714.14	3703.07	3693.82
260 000	3912.85	3893.01	3876.48	3862.70	3851.20	3841.58
270 000	4063.34	4042.74	4025.58	4011.27	3999.32	3989.33
280 000	4213.84	4192.47	4174.67	4159.83	4147.44	4137.08
290 000	4364.33	4342.20	4323.77	4308.40	4295.56	4284.84
300 000	4514.83	4491.93	4472.86	4456.96	4443.69	4432.59
400 000	6019.77	5989.24	5963.82	5942.62	5924.92	5910.12
500 000	7524.71	7486.55	7454.77	7428.27	7406.15	7387.65

MONTHLY PAYMENT

17.50% INTEREST

needed to pay back a mortgage

Term	26 Years	27 Years	28 Years	29 Years	30 Years	35 Years
AMOUNT						
30 000	442.33	441.55	440.90	440.36	439.90	438.50
40 000	589.77	588.74	587.87	587.14	586.53	584.67
50 000	737.22	735.92	734.84	733.93	733.16	730.84
55 000	810.94	809.51	808.32	807.32	806.48	803.92
60 000	884.66	883.11	881.80	880.71	879.80	877.01
65 000	958.38	956.70	955.29	954.10	953.11	950.09
70 000	1032.10	1030.29	1028.77	1027.50	1026.43	1023.17
75 000	1105.83	1103.88	1102.25	1100.89	1099.74	1096.26
80 000	1179.55	1177.47	1175.74	1174.28	1173.06	1169.34
85 000	1253.27	1251.07	1249.22	1247.67	1246.38	1242.42
90 000	1326.99	1324.66	1322.70	1321.07	1319.69	1315.51
95 000	1400.71	1398.25	1396.19	1394.46	1393.01	1388.59
100 000	1474.43	1471.84	1469.67	1467.85	1466.33	1461.68
105 000	1548.16	1545.43	1543.16	1541.24	1539.64	1534.76
110 000	1621.88	1619.03	1616.64	1614.64	1612.96	1607.84
115 000	1695.60	1692.62	1690.12	1688.03	1686.27	1680.93
120 000	1769.32	1766.21	1763.61	1761.42	1759.59	1754.01
125 000	1843.04	1839.80	1837.09	1834.81	1832.91	1827.09
130 000	1916.76	1913.40	1910.57	1908.21	1906.22	1900.18
135 000	1990.49	1986.99	1984.06	1981.60	1979.54	1973.26
140 000	2064.21	2060.58	2057.54	2054.99	2052.86	2046.35
145 000	2137.93	2134.17	2131.02	2128.38	2126.17	2119.43
150 000	2211.65	2207.76	2204.51	2201.78	2199.49	2192.51
155 000	2285.37	2281.36	2277.99	2275.17	2272.80	2265.60
160 000	2359.10	2354.95	2351.47	2348.56	2346.12	2338.68
165 000	2432.82	2428.54	2424.96	2421.96	2419.44	2411.76
170 000	2506.54	2502.13	2498.44	2495.35	2492.75	2484.85
175 000	2580.26	2575.72	2571.93	2568.74	2566.07	2557.93
180 000	2653.98	2649.32	2645.41	2642.13	2639.39	2631.02
185 000	2727.70	2722.91	2718.89	2715.53	2712.70	2704.10
190 000	2801.43	2796.50	2792.38	2788.92	2786.02	2777.18
195 000	2875.15	2870.09	2865.86	2862.31	2859.33	2850.27
200 000	2948.87	2943.69	2939.34	2935.70	2932.65	2923.35
205 000	3022.59	3017.28	3012.83	3009.10	3005.97	2996.43
210 000	3096.31	3090.87	3086.31	3082.49	3079.28	3069.52
215 000	3170.03	3164.46	3159.79	3155.88	3152.60	3142.60
220 000	3243.76	3238.05	3233.28	3229.27	3225.92	3215.69
225 000	3317.48	3311.65	3306.76	3302.67	3299.23	3288.77
230 000	3391.20	3385.24	3380.24	3376.06	3372.55	3361.85
235 000	3464.92	3458.83	3453.73	3449.45	3445.86	3434.94
240 000	3538.64	3532.42	3527.21	3522.84	3519.18	3508.02
245 000	3612.36	3606.01	3600.70	3596.24	3592.50	3581.10
250 000	3686.09	3679.61	3674.18	3669.63	3665.81	3654.19
260 000	3833.53	3826.79	3821.15	3816.41	3812.45	3800.36
270 000	3980.97	3973.98	3968.11	3963.20	3959.08	3946.52
280 000	4128.42	4121.16	4115.08	4109.98	4105.71	4092.69
290 000	4275.86	4268.34	4262.05	4256.77	4252.34	4238.86
300 000	4423.30	4415.53	4409.01	4403.55	4398.98	4385.03
400 000	5897.74	5887.37	5878.69	5871.41	5865.30	5846.70
500 000	7372.17	7359.21	7348.36	7339.26	7331.63	7308.38

18.00% INTEREST	MONTHLY PAYMENT needed to pay back a mortgage				
Term	**1** Year	**5** Years	**10** Years	**11** Years	**12** Years	**13** Years

AMOUNT	1 Year	5 Years	10 Years	11 Years	12 Years	13 Years
30 000	2750.40	761.80	540.56	523.33	509.74	498.90
40 000	3667.20	1015.74	720.74	697.77	679.65	665.20
50 000	4584.00	1269.67	900.93	872.21	849.56	831.50
55 000	5042.40	1396.64	991.02	959.43	934.52	914.65
60 000	5500.80	1523.61	1081.11	1046.65	1019.47	997.80
65 000	5959.20	1650.57	1171.20	1133.87	1104.43	1080.95
70 000	6417.60	1777.54	1261.30	1221.09	1189.38	1164.10
75 000	6876.00	1904.51	1351.39	1308.31	1274.34	1247.25
80 000	7334.40	2031.47	1441.48	1395.53	1359.30	1330.40
85 000	7792.80	2158.44	1531.57	1482.76	1444.25	1413.55
90 000	8251.20	2285.41	1621.67	1569.98	1529.21	1496.70
95 000	8709.60	2412.38	1711.76	1657.20	1614.16	1579.85
100 000	9168.00	2539.34	1801.85	1744.42	1699.12	1663.00
105 000	9626.40	2666.31	1891.94	1831.64	1784.08	1746.15
110 000	10084.80	2793.28	1982.04	1918.86	1869.03	1829.30
115 000	10543.20	2920.24	2072.13	2006.08	1953.99	1912.45
120 000	11001.60	3047.21	2162.22	2093.30	2038.94	1995.60
125 000	11460.00	3174.18	2252.31	2180.52	2123.90	2078.75
130 000	11918.40	3301.15	2342.41	2267.74	2208.86	2161.90
135 000	12376.80	3428.11	2432.50	2354.96	2293.81	2245.05
140 000	12835.20	3555.08	2522.59	2442.19	2378.77	2328.20
145 000	13293.60	3682.05	2612.69	2529.41	2463.72	2411.35
150 000	13752.00	3809.01	2702.78	2616.63	2548.68	2494.50
155 000	14210.40	3935.98	2792.87	2703.85	2633.64	2577.65
160 000	14668.80	4062.95	2882.96	2791.07	2718.59	2660.80
165 000	15127.20	4189.92	2973.06	2878.29	2803.55	2743.95
170 000	15585.60	4316.88	3063.15	2965.51	2888.50	2827.10
175 000	16044.00	4443.85	3153.24	3052.73	2973.46	2910.25
180 000	16502.40	4570.82	3243.33	3139.95	3058.42	2993.40
185 000	16960.80	4697.78	3333.43	3227.17	3143.37	3076.55
190 000	17419.20	4824.75	3423.52	3314.39	3228.33	3159.70
195 000	17877.60	4951.72	3513.61	3401.61	3313.28	3242.85
200 000	18336.00	5078.69	3603.70	3488.84	3398.24	3326.00
205 000	18794.40	5205.65	3693.80	3576.06	3483.20	3409.15
210 000	19252.80	5332.62	3783.89	3663.28	3568.15	3492.30
215 000	19711.20	5459.59	3873.98	3750.50	3653.11	3575.45
220 000	20169.60	5586.55	3964.07	3837.72	3738.06	3658.60
225 000	20628.00	5713.52	4054.17	3924.94	3823.02	3741.75
230 000	21086.40	5840.49	4144.26	4012.16	3907.97	3824.90
235 000	21544.80	5967.46	4234.35	4099.38	3992.93	3908.05
240 000	22003.20	6094.42	4324.44	4186.60	4077.89	3991.20
245 000	22461.60	6221.39	4414.54	4273.82	4162.84	4074.35
250 000	22920.00	6348.36	4504.63	4361.04	4247.80	4157.50
260 000	23836.80	6602.29	4684.82	4535.49	4417.71	4323.80
270 000	24753.60	6856.23	4865.00	4709.93	4587.62	4490.10
280 000	25670.40	7110.16	5045.19	4884.37	4757.53	4656.40
290 000	26587.20	7364.09	5225.37	5058.81	4927.45	4822.70
300 000	27504.00	7618.03	5405.56	5233.25	5097.36	4989.00
400 000	36672.00	10157.37	7207.41	6977.67	6796.48	6652.00
500 000	45840.00	12696.71	9009.26	8722.09	8495.60	8315.00

Term	14 Years	15 Years	16 Years	17 Years	18 Years	19 Years
AMOUNT						
30 000	490.19	483.13	477.38	472.67	468.81	465.62
40 000	653.58	644.17	636.50	630.23	625.08	620.83
50 000	816.98	805.21	795.63	787.79	781.35	776.04
55 000	898.67	885.73	875.19	866.57	859.48	853.64
60 000	980.37	966.25	954.75	945.34	937.61	931.25
65 000	1062.07	1046.77	1034.32	1024.12	1015.75	1008.85
70 000	1143.77	1127.29	1113.88	1102.90	1093.88	1086.45
75 000	1225.46	1207.82	1193.44	1181.68	1172.02	1164.06
80 000	1307.16	1288.34	1273.00	1260.46	1250.15	1241.66
85 000	1388.86	1368.86	1352.57	1339.24	1328.29	1319.27
90 000	1470.56	1449.38	1432.13	1418.02	1406.42	1396.87
95 000	1552.25	1529.90	1511.69	1496.79	1484.56	1474.47
100 000	1633.95	1610.42	1591.26	1575.57	1562.69	1552.08
105 000	1715.65	1690.94	1670.82	1654.35	1640.83	1629.68
110 000	1797.35	1771.46	1750.38	1733.13	1718.96	1707.29
115 000	1879.04	1851.98	1829.94	1811.91	1797.10	1784.89
120 000	1960.74	1932.51	1909.51	1890.69	1875.23	1862.49
125 000	2042.44	2013.03	1989.07	1969.47	1953.36	1940.10
130 000	2124.14	2093.55	2068.63	2048.24	2031.50	2017.70
135 000	2205.83	2174.07	2148.20	2127.02	2109.63	2095.31
140 000	2287.53	2254.59	2227.76	2205.80	2187.77	2172.91
145 000	2369.23	2335.11	2307.32	2284.58	2265.90	2250.51
150 000	2450.93	2415.63	2386.88	2363.36	2344.04	2328.12
155 000	2532.62	2496.15	2466.45	2442.14	2422.17	2405.72
160 000	2614.32	2576.67	2546.01	2520.92	2500.31	2483.33
165 000	2696.02	2657.19	2625.57	2599.70	2578.44	2560.93
170 000	2777.72	2737.72	2705.13	2678.47	2656.58	2638.53
175 000	2859.41	2818.24	2784.70	2757.25	2734.71	2716.14
180 000	2941.11	2898.76	2864.26	2836.03	2812.84	2793.74
185 000	3022.81	2979.28	2943.82	2914.81	2890.98	2871.34
190 000	3104.51	3059.80	3023.39	2993.59	2969.11	2948.95
195 000	3186.20	3140.32	3102.95	3072.37	3047.25	3026.55
200 000	3267.90	3220.84	3182.51	3151.15	3125.38	3104.16
205 000	3349.60	3301.36	3262.07	3229.92	3203.52	3181.76
210 000	3431.30	3381.88	3341.64	3308.70	3281.65	3259.36
215 000	3512.99	3462.41	3421.20	3387.48	3359.79	3336.97
220 000	3594.69	3542.93	3500.76	3466.26	3437.92	3414.57
225 000	3676.39	3623.45	3580.33	3545.04	3516.06	3492.18
230 000	3758.09	3703.97	3659.89	3623.82	3594.19	3569.78
235 000	3839.78	3784.49	3739.45	3702.60	3672.32	3647.38
240 000	3921.48	3865.01	3819.01	3781.37	3750.46	3724.99
245 000	4003.18	3945.53	3898.58	3860.15	3828.59	3802.59
250 000	4084.88	4026.05	3978.14	3938.93	3906.73	3880.20
260 000	4248.27	4187.09	4137.26	4096.49	4063.00	4035.40
270 000	4411.67	4348.14	4296.39	4254.05	4219.27	4190.61
280 000	4575.06	4509.18	4455.52	4411.60	4375.54	4345.82
290 000	4738.46	4670.22	4614.64	4569.16	4531.81	4501.03
300 000	4901.85	4831.26	4773.77	4726.72	4688.07	4656.23
400 000	6535.80	6441.68	6365.02	6302.29	6250.77	6208.31
500 000	8169.75	8052.11	7956.28	7877.86	7813.46	7760.39

18.00% INTEREST	**MONTHLY PAYMENT** needed to pay back a mortgage					
Term	20 Years	21 Years	22 Years	23 Years	24 Years	25 Years
AMOUNT						
30 000	462.99	460.82	459.01	457.51	456.27	455.23
40 000	617.32	614.42	612.02	610.02	608.35	606.97
50 000	771.66	768.03	765.02	762.52	760.44	758.71
55 000	848.82	844.83	841.52	838.77	836.49	834.59
60 000	925.99	921.63	918.02	915.02	912.53	910.46
65 000	1003.15	998.44	994.52	991.28	988.58	986.33
70 000	1080.32	1075.24	1071.03	1067.53	1064.62	1062.20
75 000	1157.48	1152.04	1147.53	1143.78	1140.67	1138.07
80 000	1234.65	1228.84	1224.03	1220.03	1216.71	1213.94
85 000	1311.81	1305.65	1300.53	1296.28	1292.75	1289.82
90 000	1388.98	1382.45	1377.03	1372.54	1368.80	1365.69
95 000	1466.15	1459.25	1453.54	1448.79	1444.84	1441.56
100 000	1543.31	1536.05	1530.04	1525.04	1520.89	1517.43
105 000	1620.48	1612.86	1606.54	1601.29	1596.93	1593.30
110 000	1697.64	1689.66	1683.04	1677.55	1672.98	1669.17
115 000	1774.81	1766.46	1759.54	1753.80	1749.02	1745.04
120 000	1851.97	1843.27	1836.05	1830.05	1825.06	1820.92
125 000	1929.14	1920.07	1912.55	1906.30	1901.11	1896.79
130 000	2006.30	1996.87	1989.05	1982.55	1977.15	1972.66
135 000	2083.47	2073.67	2065.55	2058.81	2053.20	2048.53
140 000	2160.64	2150.48	2142.05	2135.06	2129.24	2124.40
145 000	2237.80	2227.28	2218.55	2211.31	2205.29	2200.27
150 000	2314.97	2304.08	2295.06	2287.56	2281.33	2276.14
155 000	2392.13	2380.89	2371.56	2363.81	2357.37	2352.02
160 000	2469.30	2457.69	2448.06	2440.07	2433.42	2427.89
165 000	2546.46	2534.49	2524.56	2516.32	2509.46	2503.76
170 000	2623.63	2611.29	2601.06	2592.57	2585.51	2579.63
175 000	2700.80	2688.10	2677.57	2668.82	2661.55	2655.50
180 000	2777.96	2764.90	2754.07	2745.07	2737.60	2731.37
185 000	2855.13	2841.70	2830.57	2821.33	2813.64	2807.25
190 000	2932.29	2918.50	2907.07	2897.58	2889.69	2883.12
195 000	3009.46	2995.31	2983.57	2973.83	2965.73	2958.99
200 000	3086.62	3072.11	3060.08	3050.08	3041.77	3034.86
205 000	3163.79	3148.91	3136.58	3126.33	3117.82	3110.73
210 000	3240.95	3225.72	3213.08	3202.59	3193.86	3186.60
215 000	3318.12	3302.52	3289.58	3278.84	3269.91	3262.47
220 000	3395.29	3379.32	3366.08	3355.09	3345.95	3338.35
225 000	3472.45	3456.12	3442.58	3431.34	3422.00	3414.22
230 000	3549.62	3532.93	3519.09	3507.59	3498.04	3490.09
235 000	3626.78	3609.73	3595.59	3583.85	3574.08	3565.96
240 000	3703.95	3686.53	3672.09	3660.10	3650.13	3641.83
245 000	3781.11	3763.33	3748.59	3736.35	3726.17	3717.70
250 000	3858.28	3840.14	3825.09	3812.60	3802.22	3793.57
260 000	4012.61	3993.74	3978.10	3965.11	3954.31	3945.32
270 000	4166.94	4147.35	4131.10	4117.61	4106.39	4097.06
280 000	4321.27	4300.95	4284.11	4270.12	4258.48	4248.80
290 000	4475.60	4454.56	4437.11	4422.62	4410.57	4400.55
300 000	4629.93	4608.16	4590.11	4575.12	4562.66	4552.29
400 000	6173.25	6144.22	6120.15	6100.16	6083.55	6069.72
500 000	7716.56	7680.27	7650.19	7625.21	7604.44	7587.15

MONTHLY PAYMENT

18.00% INTEREST

needed to pay back a mortgage

Term	26 Years	27 Years	28 Years	29 Years	30 Years	35 Years
AMOUNT						
30 000	454.37	453.65	453.04	452.54	452.13	450.87
40 000	605.82	604.86	604.06	603.39	602.83	601.16
50 000	757.28	756.08	755.07	754.24	753.54	751.45
55 000	833.00	831.68	830.58	829.66	828.90	826.59
60 000	908.73	907.29	906.09	905.09	904.25	901.74
65 000	984.46	982.90	981.60	980.51	979.61	976.88
70 000	1060.19	1058.51	1057.10	1055.94	1054.96	1052.02
75 000	1135.91	1134.11	1132.61	1131.36	1130.31	1127.17
80 000	1211.64	1209.72	1208.12	1206.78	1205.67	1202.31
85 000	1287.37	1285.33	1283.63	1282.21	1281.02	1277.46
90 000	1363.10	1360.94	1359.13	1357.63	1356.38	1352.60
95 000	1438.82	1436.54	1434.64	1433.06	1431.73	1427.75
100 000	1514.55	1512.15	1510.15	1508.48	1507.09	1502.89
105 000	1590.28	1587.76	1585.66	1583.90	1582.44	1578.04
110 000	1666.01	1663.37	1661.16	1659.33	1657.79	1653.18
115 000	1741.73	1738.97	1736.67	1734.75	1733.15	1728.33
120 000	1817.46	1814.58	1812.18	1810.18	1808.50	1803.47
125 000	1893.19	1890.19	1887.69	1885.60	1883.86	1878.61
130 000	1968.92	1965.80	1963.19	1961.02	1959.21	1953.76
135 000	2044.64	2041.40	2038.70	2036.45	2034.57	2028.90
140 000	2120.37	2117.01	2114.21	2111.87	2109.92	2104.05
145 000	2196.10	2192.62	2189.72	2187.29	2185.27	2179.19
150 000	2271.83	2268.23	2265.22	2262.72	2260.63	2254.34
155 000	2347.55	2343.83	2340.73	2338.14	2335.98	2329.48
160 000	2423.28	2419.44	2416.24	2413.57	2411.34	2404.63
165 000	2499.01	2495.05	2491.75	2488.99	2486.69	2479.77
170 000	2574.74	2570.66	2567.25	2564.41	2562.05	2554.92
175 000	2650.46	2646.26	2642.76	2639.84	2637.40	2630.06
180 000	2726.19	2721.87	2718.27	2715.26	2712.75	2705.21
185 000	2801.92	2797.48	2793.78	2790.69	2788.11	2780.35
190 000	2877.65	2873.09	2869.28	2866.11	2863.46	2855.49
195 000	2953.37	2948.69	2944.79	2941.53	2938.82	2930.64
200 000	3029.10	3024.30	3020.30	3016.96	3014.17	3005.78
205 000	3104.83	3099.91	3095.81	3092.38	3089.53	3080.93
210 000	3180.56	3175.52	3171.31	3167.81	3164.88	3156.07
215 000	3256.28	3251.12	3246.82	3243.23	3240.23	3231.22
220 000	3332.01	3326.73	3322.33	3318.65	3315.59	3306.36
225 000	3407.74	3402.34	3397.84	3394.08	3390.94	3381.51
230 000	3483.47	3477.95	3473.34	3469.50	3466.30	3456.65
235 000	3559.19	3553.55	3548.85	3544.93	3541.65	3531.80
240 000	3634.92	3629.16	3624.36	3620.35	3617.00	3606.94
245 000	3710.65	3704.77	3699.87	3695.77	3692.36	3682.09
250 000	3786.38	3780.38	3775.37	3771.20	3767.71	3757.23
260 000	3937.83	3931.59	3926.39	3922.05	3918.42	3907.52
270 000	4089.29	4082.81	4077.40	4072.89	4069.13	4057.81
280 000	4240.74	4234.02	4228.42	4223.74	4219.84	4208.10
290 000	4392.20	4385.24	4379.43	4374.59	4370.55	4358.39
300 000	4543.65	4536.45	4530.45	4525.44	4521.26	4508.68
400 000	6058.20	6048.60	6040.60	6033.92	6028.34	6011.57
500 000	7572.75	7560.75	7550.75	7542.40	7535.43	7514.46

Annual
Mortgage
Payment
Schedules &
Tax-Savings
Tables

PART II

Annual
Mortgage
Payment
Checklists &
Tax-Savings
Tables

ANNUAL MORTGAGE PAYMENT SCHEDULES AND TAX-SAVINGS TABLES

Borrowers are usually shocked to learn in the early years of their loan that they have paid significant, often burdensome monthly payments, but they have repaid only a tiny fraction of the amount they originally borrowed. Although you make equal monthly payments over the term of your mortgage, the allocation of interest payment and principal repayment varies. The interest portion of the payment remains large for several years. This is so since more of the principal remains outstanding in the early years of a loan. Correspondingly, interest charges on the large balance of principal are high. More of the fixed-mortgage payment must go toward paying the lender interest, and so less is applied against the principal of the loan.

The allocation of interest and principal gradually shifts over the term of the loan as the cumulative amount of principal repayments increases. Less of the monthly payment is needed to pay interest, and more is available for principal repayment. Just how gradual the shift is depends upon the terms of your loan. The higher the interest rate on the loan, the greater is the amount of early payments that goes toward interest and, accordingly, the less is available to repay the loan. In contrast, the shorter the loan-repayment term, the larger is the amount allocated to principal. Therefore the proportion of the monthly payment that goes toward interest drops at a faster rate.

The Annual Mortgage Payment Schedules reflect the allocation of yearly mortgage loan payments to principal and interest for each year throughout the term of a loan of $1,000. The tables are arranged according to the applicable interest rate and are presented for both fifteen and thirty year loans. To apply the information in the tables to your own loan, you must multiply the data in the table by the number of thousands that you borrowed.

How Much Do You Save Through Tax Deductions?

One of the cherished benefits of home ownership is the tax deductibility of mortgage interest and real estate taxes. Renters indirectly pay the interest and taxes of their landlord, but the tax laws deny tenants any tax deductions. Homeowners, on the other hand, are permitted to claim very valuable deductions for mortgage interest and real estate taxes on their personal income-tax returns.

The tax deduction serves as a subsidy to homeowners, typically allowing them to afford larger monthly payments for mortgage and real estate taxes than they can afford to pay as rent. Moreover, the disparity between affordable mortgage payments and rental payments expands as the applicable tax rate increases; a higher tax rate increases the value of your tax deduction. To arrive at the true net out-of-pocket cost of home ownership and to compare your net monthly cost to an equivalent nondeductible rent payment, you must subtract the tax savings from your total monthly payment for mortgage and taxes.

Since the relative allocation of your payments to interest and principal varies over the term of your mortgage loan, your tax savings will vary accordingly.

The Tax-Savings Tables in Part II set forth the tax savings and resulting net cost of the annual payments for each of the years throughout the term of a $1,000 mortgage loan. The tax savings reflected in the Tax-Savings Table are computed for the three federal tax rates that currently apply. Under each rate, you will find the value of the tax deduction of the interest expense reflected in the corresponding Annual Mortgage Payment Schedule. The net-cost column appearing next to each tax-rate column reflects the after tax cost of the yearly payment after subtracting the value of the tax deduction.

Of course, if you live in a state or city that has income-tax laws permitting the deduction of home-ownership costs, you should also take your state and local tax rates into account in determining which tax rate column to select. See Appendix A for a selected list of state and local tax rates, and for an explanation of how to use them to calculate the total net out-of-pocket cost of your mortgage.

Note that since local real estate taxes vary widely, it is not possible to include the value of real estate tax deductions in the tables appearing in this book. However, it is important to take the value of these deductions into account when figuring the net out-of-pocket cost of home ownership. To do so, merely multiply your property-tax bill by your own overall income tax rate, and subtract this deduction from the yearly cost.

Some final words of caution are in order here. Although it is correct to compare your after-tax mortgage payment to a comparable rent payment when measuring your monthly cash flow, remember that your monthly mortgage payment includes the repayment of nondeductible loan principal. Paying a mortgage builds equity in your home. Once paid, rental payments provide you with no continuing economic value.

Finally, it is always important to consult with an experienced tax adviser to help you make the decision that is compatible with your own tax circumstances.

HOW TO USE THE TABLES

10.75% INTEREST	ANNUAL MORTGAGE PAYMENT SCHEDULE

For a mortgage of $1,000.00

	MORTGAGE TERM:	**30 years**
	Monthly payment:	**$9.33**
	Annual payment:	**$112.02**

Year	Balance of Loan	Principal Paid	Interest Paid	Yearly Payment
1	$995.25	$4.75	$107.27	$112.02
2	989.97	5.28	106.73	112.02
3	984.09	5.88	106.14	112.02
4	977.54	6.54	105.47	112.02
5	970.26	7.28	104.73	112.02
6	962.15	8.11	103.91	112.02
7	953.13	9.02	103.00	112.02
8	943.09	10.04	101.98	112.02
9	931.92	11.18	100.84	112.02
10	919.48	12.44	99.58	112.02

Amount owed after 5 years

Interest paid in year 5

USING THE ANNUAL MORTGAGE PAYMENT SCHEDULES

Example 1: Finding Your Current Loan Balance

Suppose you want to know how much of your loan balance remains unpaid after making payments for five years on a loan of $160,000 at 10.75 percent interest over thirty years. Your first step is to turn to

10.75%
INTEREST

Multiply all figures by the number of thousands in your loan.
Net cost equals yearly payment minus tax savings.

	Federal Tax Bracket					
	15.0%		28.0%		33.0%	
Year	Tax Savings	Net Cost	Tax Savings	Net Cost	Tax Savings	Net Cost
1	$16.09	$95.93	$30.04	$81.98	$35.40	$76.62
2	16.01	96.01	29.89	82.13	35.22	76.80
3	15.92	96.10	29.72	82.30	35.03	76.99
4	15.82	96.20	29.53	82.49	34.81	77.21
5	15.71	96.31	29.33	82.69	34.56	77.46
6	15.59	96.43	29.10	82.92	34.29	77.73
7	15.45	96.57	28.84	83.18	33.99	78.03
8	15.30	96.72	28.55	83.46	33.65	78.37
9	15.13	96.89	28.24	83.78	33.28	78.74
10	14.94	97.08	27.88	84.14	32.86	79.16

**Value of tax
deduction in
year 5**

**Net mortgage
cost in year 5**

the Annual Mortgage Payment Schedule covering
10.75 percent thirty-year loans. Scan down the year
column until you get to year 5. Skim across the horizontal row until you find the balance-of-loan column.
As you can see, the remaining balance on a $1,000
loan is $970.26. Multiplying $970.26 by 160, the
number of thousands in the original $160,000 loan,
produces an outstanding balance after five years of
$155,241.60.

Example 2: Finding Your Annual Interest Cost

Suppose you are preparing your income-tax return and you want to know how much interest expense you paid in year 5 of the loan in Example 1. Once again, turn to the Annual Mortgage Payment Schedule covering 10.75 percent thirty-year loans, scan down the year column until you get to year 5. Skim across the horizontal row until you get to the interest column. As you can see, the interest in year 5 on a $1,000 loan is $104.73. Multiplying $104.73 by 160, the number of thousands in the original $160,000 loan, produces your interest expense in year 5 of $16,760.80.

Example 3: The Principal/Interest Tip-off Point

Suppose you want to determine the tip-off point when principal repayments are larger than interest payments for the loan in Examples 1 and 2. To find out, turn to the table that covers 10.75 percent thirty-year loans. Scan the principal-paid and interest-paid columns simultaneously until you find the point where the amount in the principal-paid column equals or exceeds the amount in the interest-paid column. In this case, you'll note that the tip-off occurs before the end of the twenty-fifth year and you've barely paid off half of your original loan. Hard to believe!

USING THE TAX-SAVINGS TABLES

Example 4: Tax Savings and Monthly Cost After Federal Taxes

This example demonstrates how to use the Tax-Savings Tables. Suppose you are subject to a 28 percent Federal income-tax bracket. You would like to know the tax savings and the after-tax cost in the fifth year of a loan for $160,000 at 10.75 percent interest over thirty years. After turning to the table covering 10.75 percent thirty-year loans and scanning down the year column to year 5, scan across the row until you find the Tax Savings and Net Cost columns that correspond to the 28 percent federal tax rate. As you can see, the tax savings for a $1,000 loan for the fifth year is $29.33, and the net cost is $82.69. This is the annual payment of $112.02 minus the value of the tax deduction amounting to $29.33. Multiplying both figures by 160, the number of thousands in the original loan, produces an annual tax savings of $4,692.80 and a total annual cost of $13,230.40. Dividing the total annual cost by twelve months produces an average net cost of $1,102.53 for each of the months in the fifth year. You can compare this amount to your current rent payment.

Example 5: Finding Tax Savings and Monthly Cost After Federal, State, and Local Taxes

The income-tax laws of some states and localities allow deduction of home-mortgage interest expense. Using the same $160,000 loan in the fifth year of the mortgage as in the previous examples, suppose your federal tax rate is 28 percent and your state tax rate is 8 percent. We'll assume your state tax payment is fully deductible on your federal tax return.

From Example 2 above, you know the interest expense in year 5 is $16,760.80. Now, you need to know your combined effective federal, state, and local tax rate; that is, your net tax rate after taking into account the federal deduction of your state and local taxes. The tables in Appendix A, present a selection of combined federal, state, and local tax rates. Under the 28 percent federal tax rate, the entry corresponding to a state or local rate of 8 percent presents an effective tax rate of 33.76 percent. Multiply the effective tax rate of 33.76 percent times the interest expense of $16,760.80 to get your total tax savings of $5,658.45 or $471.54 per month.

The net cost of the mortgage equals the gross loan payment less your tax savings. The monthly payment for a $160,000, 10.75 percent loan amounts to $1,493.58, as reflected in the Monthly Payment Table in Part I. Subtracting your total monthly tax savings of $471.54 produces a net monthly cost of $1,022.04 for each month in the fifth year—quite a bit less than your monthly payment. So you see, the combined federal and state tax breaks make a real difference.

Example 6: Finding Your Revised Monthly Payment On An Adjustable Rate Mortgage

Suppose you have a thirty-year ARM for $160,000 with initial interest rate of 10.75 percent, with adjustments made every five years. After five years, or with twenty-five years remaining, your interest rate changes to 11 percent. What will your new monthly payment be?

First, find the outstanding loan balance in the Annual Mortgage Payment Schedule for 10.75 percent loans, following Example 1 above. The balance for a $1,000 loan after five years is $970.26. Multiplying by 160, the number of thousands in your loan, you find your balance is $155,241.60. Now, turn to the Mortgage Payment Table in Part I for 11 percent loans to find your adjusted payment. Find the nearest mortgage amount, which in this case is $155,000. Then scan across the row until you find the figure corresponding

to the number of years remaining on your loan. In
this example, the remaining term is twenty-five years
and the monthly payment for a $155,000 loan is
$1,498.77. This is your approximate adjusted
monthly payment.

ANNUAL MORTGAGE PAYMENT SCHEDULE

For a mortgage of $1,000.00

	MORTGAGE TERM:	**15 years**
	Monthly payment:	**$9.56**
	Annual payment:	**$114.68**

Year	Balance of Loan	Principal Paid	Interest Paid	Yearly Payment
1	$964.02	$35.98	$78.70	$114.68
2	925.06	38.96	75.71	114.68
3	882.86	42.20	72.48	114.68
4	837.16	45.70	68.98	114.68
5	787.66	49.49	65.18	114.68
6	734.06	53.60	61.08	114.68
7	676.01	58.05	56.63	114.68
8	613.14	62.87	51.81	114.68
9	545.05	68.09	46.59	114.68
10	471.31	73.74	40.94	114.68
11	391.45	79.86	34.82	114.68
12	304.97	86.49	28.19	114.68
13	211.30	93.67	21.01	114.68
14	109.86	101.44	13.24	114.68
15	.00	109.86	4.76	114.61
Totals:		**$1000.00**	**$720.11**	**$1720.11**

TAX-SAVINGS TABLE

8.00% INTEREST

Multiply all figures by the number of thousands in your loan.
Net cost equals yearly payment minus tax savings.

Federal Tax Bracket					
15.0%		28.0%		33.0%	
Tax Savings	Net Cost	Tax Savings	Net Cost	Tax Savings	Net Cost
$11.80	$102.87	$22.04	$92.64	$25.97	$88.71
11.36	103.32	21.20	93.48	24.99	89.69
10.87	103.81	20.29	94.38	23.92	90.76
10.35	104.33	19.31	95.36	22.76	91.92
9.78	104.90	18.25	96.43	21.51	93.17
9.16	105.52	17.10	97.58	20.16	94.52
8.49	106.18	15.86	98.82	18.69	95.99
7.77	106.91	14.51	100.17	17.10	97.58
6.99	107.69	13.05	101.63	15.37	99.30
6.14	108.54	11.46	103.22	13.51	101.17
5.22	109.46	9.75	104.93	11.49	103.19
4.23	110.45	7.89	106.78	9.30	105.38
3.15	111.53	5.88	108.79	6.93	107.74
1.99	112.69	3.71	110.97	4.37	110.31
.71	113.90	1.33	113.28	1.57	113.05
Totals:					
$108.02	**$1612.09**	**$201.63**	**$1518.48**	**$237.64**	**$1482.47**

	8.00% INTEREST	**ANNUAL MORTGAGE** **PAYMENT SCHEDULE**

For a mortgage of $1,000.00

		MORTGAGE TERM:	**30 years**
		Monthly payment:	**$7.34**
		Annual payment:	**$88.05**

Year	Balance of Loan	Principal Paid	Interest Paid	Yearly Payment
1	$991.65	$8.35	$79.70	$88.05
2	982.60	9.05	79.00	88.05
3	972.80	9.80	78.25	88.05
4	962.19	10.61	77.44	88.05
5	950.70	11.49	76.56	88.05
6	938.25	12.45	75.61	88.05
7	924.77	13.48	74.57	88.05
8	910.18	14.60	73.45	88.05
9	894.37	15.81	72.24	88.05
10	877.25	17.12	70.93	88.05
11	858.70	18.54	69.51	88.05
12	838.62	20.08	67.97	88.05
13	816.88	21.75	66.30	88.05
14	793.32	23.55	64.50	88.05
15	767.82	25.51	62.54	88.05
16	740.19	27.62	60.43	88.05
17	710.27	29.92	58.13	88.05
18	677.87	32.40	55.65	88.05
19	642.78	35.09	52.96	88.05
20	604.78	38.00	50.05	88.05
21	563.62	41.16	46.90	88.05
22	519.05	44.57	43.48	88.05
23	470.78	48.27	39.78	88.05
24	418.50	52.28	35.77	88.05
25	361.88	56.62	31.43	88.05
26	300.56	61.32	26.73	88.05
27	234.16	66.41	21.65	88.05
28	162.24	71.92	16.13	88.05
29	84.35	77.89	10.16	88.05
30	.00	84.35	3.65	88.00
Totals:		**$1000.00**	**$1641.50**	**$2641.50**

TAX-SAVINGS TABLE

8.00%
INTEREST

Multiply all figures by the number of thousands in your loan.
Net cost equals yearly payment minus tax savings.

| Federal Tax Bracket | | | | | |
| 15.0% | | 28.0% | | 33.0% | |
Tax Savings	Net Cost	Tax Savings	Net Cost	Tax Savings	Net Cost
$11.95	$76.10	$22.32	$65.74	$26.30	$61.75
11.85	76.20	22.12	65.93	26.07	61.98
11.74	76.31	21.91	66.14	25.82	62.23
11.62	76.44	21.68	66.37	25.56	62.50
11.48	76.57	21.44	66.61	25.26	62.79
11.34	76.71	21.17	66.88	24.95	63.10
11.19	76.87	20.88	67.17	24.61	63.44
11.02	77.03	20.57	67.48	24.24	63.81
10.84	77.22	20.23	67.82	23.84	64.21
10.64	77.41	19.86	68.19	23.41	64.64
10.43	77.63	19.46	68.59	22.94	65.11
10.20	77.86	19.03	69.02	22.43	65.62
9.95	78.11	18.57	69.49	21.88	66.17
9.67	78.38	18.06	69.99	21.28	66.77
9.38	78.67	17.51	70.54	20.64	67.41
9.06	78.99	16.92	71.13	19.94	68.11
8.72	79.33	16.28	71.77	19.18	68.87
8.35	79.70	15.58	72.47	18.36	69.69
7.94	80.11	14.83	73.22	17.48	70.57
7.51	80.54	14.01	74.04	16.52	71.54
7.03	81.02	13.13	74.92	15.48	72.58
6.52	81.53	12.17	75.88	14.35	73.70
5.97	82.08	11.14	76.91	13.13	74.92
5.37	82.69	10.02	78.04	11.81	76.25
4.72	83.34	8.80	79.25	10.37	77.68
4.01	84.04	7.49	80.57	8.82	79.23
3.25	84.80	6.06	81.99	7.14	80.91
2.42	85.63	4.52	83.53	5.32	82.73
1.52	86.53	2.85	85.21	3.35	84.70
.55	87.46	1.02	86.98	1.20	86.80
Totals:					
$246.23	**$2395.28**	**$459.62**	**$2181.88**	**$541.70**	**$2099.81**

8.25% INTEREST	**ANNUAL MORTGAGE PAYMENT SCHEDULE**

For a mortgage of $1,000.00

MORTGAGE TERM: **15 years**
Monthly payment: **$9.70**
Annual payment: **$116.42**

Year	Balance of Loan	Principal Paid	Interest Paid	Yearly Payment
1	$964.77	$35.23	$81.19	$116.42
2	926.52	38.25	78.17	116.42
3	885.00	41.53	74.89	116.42
4	839.91	45.08	71.33	116.42
5	790.97	48.95	67.47	116.42
6	737.82	53.14	63.28	116.42
7	680.13	57.70	58.72	116.42
8	617.49	62.64	53.78	116.42
9	549.48	68.01	48.41	116.42
10	475.65	73.84	42.58	116.42
11	395.48	80.16	36.25	116.42
12	308.45	87.03	29.39	116.42
13	213.96	94.49	21.93	116.42
14	111.38	102.59	13.83	116.42
15	.00	111.38	4.97	116.35
Totals:		**$1000.00**	**$746.19**	**$1746.19**

TAX-SAVINGS TABLE

8.25% INTEREST

Multiply all figures by the number of thousands in your loan.
Net cost equals yearly payment minus tax savings.

Federal Tax Bracket					
15.0%		28.0%		33.0%	
Tax Savings	Net Cost	Tax Savings	Net Cost	Tax Savings	Net Cost
$12.18	$104.24	$22.73	$93.68	$26.79	$89.62
11.73	104.69	21.89	94.53	25.80	90.62
11.23	105.18	20.97	95.45	24.71	91.70
10.70	105.72	19.97	96.44	23.54	92.88
10.12	106.30	18.89	97.53	22.26	94.15
9.49	106.93	17.72	98.70	20.88	95.54
8.81	107.61	16.44	99.97	19.38	97.04
8.07	108.35	15.06	101.36	17.75	98.67
7.26	109.16	13.55	102.86	15.98	100.44
6.39	110.03	11.92	104.49	14.05	102.36
5.44	110.98	10.15	106.27	11.96	104.45
4.41	112.01	8.23	108.19	9.70	106.72
3.29	113.13	6.14	110.28	7.24	109.18
2.07	114.34	3.87	112.54	4.56	111.85
.75	115.60	1.39	114.96	1.64	114.71
Totals:					
$111.93	**$1634.26**	**$208.93**	**$1537.25**	**$246.24**	**$1499.94**

<table>
<tr><td colspan="2">8.25% INTEREST</td><td colspan="3">ANNUAL MORTGAGE PAYMENT SCHEDULE</td></tr>
</table>

8.25% INTEREST	**ANNUAL MORTGAGE PAYMENT SCHEDULE**

For a mortgage of $1,000.00

MORTGAGE TERM: **30 years**
Monthly payment: **$7.51**
Annual payment: **$90.15**

Year	Balance of Loan	Principal Paid	Interest Paid	Yearly Payment
1	$992.05	$7.95	$82.20	$90.15
2	983.42	8.63	81.52	90.15
3	974.05	9.37	80.78	90.15
4	963.88	10.17	79.98	90.15
5	952.84	11.04	79.11	90.15
6	940.85	11.99	78.16	90.15
7	927.83	13.02	77.14	90.15
8	913.70	14.13	76.02	90.15
9	898.36	15.34	74.81	90.15
10	881.70	16.66	73.49	90.15
11	863.61	18.09	72.07	90.15
12	843.98	19.64	70.52	90.15
13	822.66	21.32	68.83	90.15
14	799.52	23.14	67.01	90.15
15	774.39	25.13	65.02	90.15
16	747.11	27.28	62.87	90.15
17	717.49	29.62	60.53	90.15
18	685.33	32.16	58.00	90.15
19	650.42	34.91	55.24	90.15
20	612.52	37.90	52.25	90.15
21	571.36	41.15	49.00	90.15
22	526.68	44.68	45.47	90.15
23	478.18	48.51	41.64	90.15
24	425.51	52.66	37.49	90.15
25	368.34	57.18	32.97	90.15
26	306.26	62.08	28.08	90.15
27	238.86	67.40	22.76	90.15
28	165.69	73.17	16.98	90.15
29	86.25	79.44	10.71	90.15
30	.00	86.25	3.85	90.10
Totals:		**$1000.00**	**$1704.51**	**$2704.51**

TAX-SAVINGS TABLE

8.25% INTEREST

Multiply all figures by the number of thousands in your loan.
Net cost equals yearly payment minus tax savings.

Federal Tax Bracket					
15.0%		**28.0%**		**33.0%**	
Tax Savings	Net Cost	Tax Savings	Net Cost	Tax Savings	Net Cost
$12.33	$77.82	$23.02	$67.13	$27.13	$63.02
12.23	77.92	22.83	67.33	26.90	63.25
12.12	78.03	22.62	67.53	26.66	63.49
12.00	78.15	22.39	67.76	26.39	63.76
11.87	78.29	22.15	68.00	26.11	64.05
11.72	78.43	21.89	68.27	25.79	64.36
11.57	78.58	21.60	68.55	25.45	64.70
11.40	78.75	21.29	68.87	25.09	65.07
11.22	78.93	20.95	69.21	24.69	65.47
11.02	79.13	20.58	69.57	24.25	65.90
10.81	79.34	20.18	69.97	23.78	66.37
10.58	79.57	19.74	70.41	23.27	66.88
10.33	79.83	19.27	70.88	22.72	67.44
10.05	80.10	18.76	71.39	22.11	68.04
9.75	80.40	18.21	71.95	21.46	68.69
9.43	80.72	17.60	72.55	20.75	69.40
9.08	81.07	16.95	73.20	19.98	70.18
8.70	81.45	16.24	73.91	19.14	71.01
8.29	81.87	15.47	74.68	18.23	71.92
7.84	82.31	14.63	75.52	17.24	72.91
7.35	82.80	13.72	76.43	16.17	73.98
6.82	83.33	12.73	77.42	15.01	75.15
6.25	83.91	11.66	78.49	13.74	76.41
5.62	84.53	10.50	79.66	12.37	77.78
4.95	85.21	9.23	80.92	10.88	79.27
4.21	85.94	7.86	82.29	9.26	80.89
3.41	86.74	6.37	83.78	7.51	82.64
2.55	87.60	4.75	85.40	5.60	84.55
1.61	88.55	3.00	87.15	3.53	86.62
.58	89.52	1.08	89.02	1.27	88.83
Totals:					
$255.68	**$2448.83**	**$477.26**	**$2227.25**	**$562.49**	**$2142.02**

For a mortgage of $1,000.00

	MORTGAGE TERM:	**15 years**
	Monthly payment:	**$9.85**
	Annual payment:	**$118.17**

Year	Balance of Loan	Principal Paid	Interest Paid	Yearly Payment
1	$965.51	$34.49	$83.68	$118.17
2	927.97	37.54	80.63	118.17
3	887.11	40.86	77.31	118.17
4	842.64	44.47	73.70	118.17
5	794.24	48.40	69.77	118.17
6	741.56	52.68	65.49	118.17
7	684.22	57.34	60.83	118.17
8	621.82	62.40	55.76	118.17
9	553.90	67.92	50.25	118.17
10	479.97	73.92	44.25	118.17
11	399.52	80.46	37.71	118.17
12	311.95	87.57	30.60	118.17
13	216.64	95.31	22.86	118.17
14	112.90	103.73	14.43	118.17
15	.00	112.90	5.20	118.10
Totals:		**$1000.00**	**$772.46**	**$1772.46**

TAX-SAVINGS TABLE

8.50% INTEREST

Multiply all figures by the number of thousands in your loan.
Net cost equals yearly payment minus tax savings.

| Federal Tax Bracket | | | | | |
| 15.0% | | 28.0% | | 33.0% | |
Tax Savings	Net Cost	Tax Savings	Net Cost	Tax Savings	Net Cost
$12.55	$105.62	$23.43	$94.74	$27.61	$90.56
12.09	106.07	22.58	95.59	26.61	91.56
11.60	106.57	21.65	96.52	25.51	92.66
11.05	107.11	20.64	97.53	24.32	93.85
10.47	107.70	19.53	98.63	23.02	95.15
9.82	108.35	18.34	99.83	21.61	96.56
9.12	109.04	17.03	101.14	20.07	98.09
8.36	109.80	15.61	102.55	18.40	99.77
7.54	110.63	14.07	104.10	16.58	101.59
6.64	111.53	12.39	105.78	14.60	103.57
5.66	112.51	10.56	107.61	12.44	105.72
4.59	113.58	8.57	109.60	10.10	108.07
3.43	114.74	6.40	111.77	7.54	110.63
2.17	116.00	4.04	114.13	4.76	113.41
.78	117.32	1.45	116.64	1.71	116.38
Totals:					
$115.87	**$1656.59**	**$216.29**	**$1556.17**	**$254.91**	**$1517.55**

8.50% INTEREST	**ANNUAL MORTGAGE PAYMENT SCHEDULE**

For a mortgage of $1,000.00

MORTGAGE TERM: **30 years**
Monthly payment: **$7.69**
Annual payment: **$92.27**

Year	Balance of Loan	Principal Paid	Interest Paid	Yearly Payment
1	$992.44	$7.56	$84.71	$92.27
2	984.21	8.23	84.04	92.27
3	975.26	8.96	83.31	92.27
4	965.51	9.75	82.52	92.27
5	954.90	10.61	81.66	92.27
6	943.36	11.55	80.72	92.27
7	930.79	12.57	79.70	92.27
8	917.11	13.68	78.59	92.27
9	902.23	14.89	77.38	92.27
10	886.03	16.20	76.07	92.27
11	868.39	17.63	74.64	92.27
12	849.20	19.19	73.08	92.27
13	828.31	20.89	71.38	92.27
14	805.57	22.74	69.53	92.27
15	780.83	24.75	67.52	92.27
16	753.90	26.93	65.34	92.27
17	724.58	29.31	62.96	92.27
18	692.68	31.90	60.37	92.27
19	657.96	34.72	57.55	92.27
20	620.16	37.79	54.48	92.27
21	579.03	41.13	51.14	92.27
22	534.26	44.77	47.50	92.27
23	485.53	48.73	43.54	92.27
24	432.50	53.03	39.24	92.27
25	374.78	57.72	34.55	92.27
26	311.95	62.82	29.45	92.27
27	243.58	68.38	23.89	92.27
28	169.16	74.42	17.85	92.27
29	88.16	81.00	11.27	92.27
30	.00	88.16	4.06	92.22
Totals:		$1000.00	$1768.03	$2768.03

TAX-SAVINGS TABLE

8.50% INTEREST

Multiply all figures by the number of thousands in your loan.
Net cost equals yearly payment minus tax savings.

Federal Tax Bracket					
15.0%		28.0%		33.0%	
Tax Savings	Net Cost	Tax Savings	Net Cost	Tax Savings	Net Cost
$12.71	$79.56	$23.72	$68.55	$27.95	$64.32
12.61	79.66	23.53	68.74	27.73	64.54
12.50	79.77	23.33	68.94	27.49	64.78
12.38	79.89	23.11	69.16	27.23	65.04
12.25	80.02	22.87	69.40	26.95	65.32
12.11	80.16	22.60	69.67	26.64	65.63
11.96	80.31	22.32	69.95	26.30	65.97
11.79	80.48	22.01	70.26	25.94	66.33
11.61	80.66	21.67	70.60	25.54	66.73
11.41	80.86	21.30	70.97	25.10	67.17
11.20	81.07	20.90	71.37	24.63	67.64
10.96	81.31	20.46	71.81	24.12	68.15
10.71	81.56	19.99	72.28	23.56	68.71
10.43	81.84	19.47	72.80	22.95	69.32
10.13	82.14	18.91	73.36	22.28	69.99
9.80	82.47	18.29	73.98	21.56	70.71
9.44	82.83	17.63	74.64	20.78	71.49
9.05	83.21	16.90	75.37	19.92	72.35
8.63	83.64	16.11	76.16	18.99	73.28
8.17	84.10	15.25	77.02	17.98	74.29
7.67	84.60	14.32	77.95	16.87	75.39
7.13	85.14	13.30	78.97	15.68	76.59
6.53	85.74	12.19	80.08	14.37	77.90
5.89	86.38	10.99	81.28	12.95	79.32
5.18	87.09	9.67	82.60	11.40	80.87
4.42	87.85	8.24	84.02	9.72	82.55
3.58	88.69	6.69	85.58	7.88	84.38
2.68	89.59	5.00	87.27	5.89	86.38
1.69	90.58	3.16	89.11	3.72	88.55
.61	91.61	1.14	91.08	1.34	90.88
Totals:					
$265.21	**$2502.83**	**$495.05**	**$2272.98**	**$583.45**	**$2184.58**

117

8.75% INTEREST	**ANNUAL MORTGAGE PAYMENT SCHEDULE**

For a mortgage of $1,000.00

MORTGAGE TERM: **15 years**
Monthly payment: **$9.99**
Annual payment: **$119.93**

Year	Balance of Loan	Principal Paid	Interest Paid	Yearly Payment
1	$966.23	$33.77	$86.17	$119.93
2	929.39	36.84	83.09	119.93
3	889.19	40.20	79.73	119.93
4	845.33	43.86	76.07	119.93
5	797.47	47.86	72.08	119.93
6	745.26	52.22	67.72	119.93
7	688.29	56.97	62.96	119.93
8	626.12	62.16	57.77	119.93
9	558.30	67.83	52.11	119.93
10	484.29	74.00	45.93	119.93
11	403.55	80.75	39.19	119.93
12	315.45	88.10	31.83	119.93
13	219.32	96.13	23.81	119.93
14	114.44	104.88	15.05	119.93
15	.00	114.44	5.42	119.86
Totals:		**$1000.00**	**$798.94**	**$1798.94**

TAX-SAVINGS TABLE

8.75% INTEREST

Multiply all figures by the number of thousands in your loan.
Net cost equals yearly payment minus tax savings.

| Federal Tax Bracket | | | | | |
| 15.0% | | 28.0% | | 33.0% | |
Tax Savings	Net Cost	Tax Savings	Net Cost	Tax Savings	Net Cost
$12.93	$107.01	$24.13	$95.81	$28.44	$91.50
12.46	107.47	23.27	96.67	27.42	92.51
11.96	107.97	22.33	97.61	26.31	93.62
11.41	108.52	21.30	98.63	25.10	94.83
10.81	109.12	20.18	99.75	23.79	96.15
10.16	109.78	18.96	100.97	22.35	97.59
9.44	110.49	17.63	102.30	20.78	99.16
8.67	111.27	16.18	103.76	19.06	100.87
7.82	112.12	14.59	105.34	17.20	102.74
6.89	113.04	12.86	107.07	15.16	104.78
5.88	114.06	10.97	108.96	12.93	107.00
4.77	115.16	8.91	111.02	10.50	109.43
3.57	116.36	6.67	113.27	7.86	112.08
2.26	117.68	4.21	115.72	4.97	114.97
.81	119.05	1.52	118.34	1.79	118.07
Totals:					
$119.84	**$1679.09**	**$223.70**	**$1575.23**	**$263.65**	**$1535.29**

ANNUAL MORTGAGE PAYMENT SCHEDULE

For a mortgage of $1,000.00

	MORTGAGE TERM:	30 years
	Monthly payment:	$7.87
	Annual payment:	$94.40

Year	Balance of Loan	Principal Paid	Interest Paid	Yearly Payment
1	$992.81	$7.19	$87.22	$94.40
2	984.97	7.84	86.56	94.40
3	976.41	8.56	85.85	94.40
4	967.08	9.34	85.07	94.40
5	956.89	10.19	84.22	94.40
6	945.77	11.11	83.29	94.40
7	933.65	12.13	82.28	94.40
8	920.41	13.23	81.17	94.40
9	905.98	14.44	79.97	94.40
10	890.22	15.75	78.65	94.40
11	873.04	17.19	77.22	94.40
12	854.28	18.75	75.65	94.40
13	833.82	20.46	73.94	94.40
14	811.49	22.33	72.08	94.40
15	787.13	24.36	70.04	94.40
16	760.56	26.58	67.83	94.40
17	731.56	29.00	65.40	94.40
18	699.91	31.64	62.76	94.40
19	665.39	34.52	59.88	94.40
20	627.72	37.67	56.73	94.40
21	586.62	41.10	53.30	94.40
22	541.77	44.85	49.56	94.40
23	492.84	48.93	45.47	94.40
24	439.46	53.39	41.02	94.40
25	381.20	58.25	36.15	94.40
26	317.65	63.56	30.85	94.40
27	248.30	69.35	25.06	94.40
28	172.64	75.66	18.74	94.40
29	90.08	82.56	11.85	94.40
30	.00	90.08	4.27	94.35
Totals:		$1000.00	$1832.06	$2832.06

| 8.75% |
| INTEREST |

Multiply all figures by the number of thousands in your loan.
Net cost equals yearly payment minus tax savings.

| Federal Tax Bracket | | | | | |
| 15.0% | | 28.0% | | 33.0% | |
Tax Savings	Net Cost	Tax Savings	Net Cost	Tax Savings	Net Cost
$13.08	$81.32	$24.42	$69.98	$28.78	$65.62
12.98	81.42	24.24	70.17	28.57	65.84
12.88	81.53	24.04	70.37	28.33	66.07
12.76	81.64	23.82	70.59	28.07	66.33
12.63	81.77	23.58	70.82	27.79	66.61
12.49	81.91	23.32	71.08	27.49	66.92
12.34	82.06	23.04	71.37	27.15	67.25
12.18	82.23	22.73	71.68	26.79	67.62
11.99	82.41	22.39	72.01	26.39	68.02
11.80	82.61	22.02	72.38	25.95	68.45
11.58	82.82	21.62	72.78	25.48	68.92
11.35	83.06	21.18	73.22	24.96	69.44
11.09	83.31	20.70	73.70	24.40	70.00
10.81	83.59	20.18	74.22	23.79	70.62
10.51	83.90	19.61	74.79	23.11	71.29
10.17	84.23	18.99	75.41	22.38	72.02
9.81	84.59	18.31	76.09	21.58	72.82
9.41	84.99	17.57	76.83	20.71	73.69
8.98	85.42	16.77	77.64	19.76	74.64
8.51	85.89	15.89	78.52	18.72	75.68
8.00	86.41	14.92	79.48	17.59	76.81
7.43	86.97	13.88	80.53	16.35	78.05
6.82	87.58	12.73	81.67	15.01	79.40
6.15	88.25	11.48	82.92	13.54	80.87
5.42	88.98	10.12	84.28	11.93	82.47
4.63	89.78	8.64	85.77	10.18	84.22
3.76	90.65	7.02	87.39	8.27	86.14
2.81	91.59	5.25	89.16	6.18	88.22
1.78	92.63	3.32	91.09	3.91	90.49
.64	93.71	1.20	93.15	1.41	92.94
Totals:					
$274.81	**$2557.25**	**$512.98**	**$2319.09**	**$604.58**	**$2227.48**

9.00% INTEREST	ANNUAL MORTGAGE PAYMENT SCHEDULE

For a mortgage of $1,000.00

MORTGAGE TERM: **15 years**
Monthly payment: **$10.14**
Annual payment: **$121.71**

Year	Balance of Loan	Principal Paid	Interest Paid	Yearly Payment
1	$966.95	$33.05	$88.66	$121.71
2	930.79	36.15	85.56	121.71
3	891.25	39.55	82.17	121.71
4	847.99	43.26	78.46	121.71
5	800.68	47.31	74.40	121.71
6	748.93	51.75	69.96	121.71
7	692.32	56.61	65.11	121.71
8	630.41	61.92	59.80	121.71
9	562.68	67.72	53.99	121.71
10	488.61	74.08	47.64	121.71
11	407.58	81.03	40.69	121.71
12	318.95	88.63	33.09	121.71
13	222.01	96.94	24.77	121.71
14	115.98	106.03	15.68	121.71
15	.00	115.98	5.66	121.64
Totals:		$1000.00	$825.60	$1825.60

TAX-SAVINGS TABLE

9.00% INTEREST

Multiply all figures by the number of thousands in your loan.
Net cost equals yearly payment minus tax savings.

Federal Tax Bracket					
15.0%		28.0%		33.0%	
Tax Savings	Net Cost	Tax Savings	Net Cost	Tax Savings	Net Cost
$13.30	$108.41	$24.82	$96.89	$29.26	$92.45
12.83	108.88	23.96	97.76	28.23	93.48
12.32	109.39	23.01	98.71	27.11	94.60
11.77	109.94	21.97	99.74	25.89	95.82
11.16	110.55	20.83	100.88	24.55	97.16
10.49	111.22	19.59	102.12	23.09	98.62
9.77	111.95	18.23	103.48	21.49	100.23
8.97	112.74	16.74	104.97	19.73	101.98
8.10	113.61	15.12	106.60	17.82	103.90
7.15	114.57	13.34	108.37	15.72	105.99
6.10	115.61	11.39	110.32	13.43	108.29
4.96	116.75	9.26	112.45	10.92	110.79
3.72	118.00	6.94	114.78	8.17	113.54
2.35	119.36	4.39	117.32	5.17	116.54
.85	120.79	1.58	120.05	1.87	119.77
Totals:					
$123.84	**$1701.76**	**$231.17**	**$1594.44**	**$272.45**	**$1553.15**

9.00% INTEREST	ANNUAL MORTGAGE PAYMENT SCHEDULE

For a mortgage of $1,000.00

MORTGAGE TERM: **30 years**
Monthly payment: **$8.05**
Annual payment: **$96.55**

Year	Balance of Loan	Principal Paid	Interest Paid	Yearly Payment
1	$993.17	$6.83	$89.72	$96.55
2	985.70	7.47	89.08	96.55
3	977.52	8.17	88.38	96.55
4	968.58	8.94	87.61	96.55
5	958.80	9.78	86.78	96.55
6	948.10	10.70	85.86	96.55
7	936.40	11.70	84.85	96.55
8	923.61	12.80	83.76	96.55
9	909.61	14.00	82.56	96.55
10	894.30	15.31	81.24	96.55
11	877.55	16.75	79.81	96.55
12	859.23	18.32	78.24	96.55
13	839.19	20.04	76.52	96.55
14	817.28	21.92	74.64	96.55
15	793.30	23.97	72.58	96.55
16	767.08	26.22	70.33	96.55
17	738.40	28.68	67.87	96.55
18	707.03	31.37	65.18	96.55
19	672.72	34.31	62.24	96.55
20	635.18	37.53	59.02	96.55
21	594.13	41.05	55.50	96.55
22	549.22	44.91	51.65	96.55
23	500.10	49.12	47.44	96.55
24	446.38	53.73	42.83	96.55
25	387.61	58.77	37.79	96.55
26	323.34	64.28	32.28	96.55
27	253.03	70.31	26.25	96.55
28	176.13	76.90	19.65	96.55
29	92.01	84.12	12.44	96.55
30	.00	92.01	4.49	96.49
Totals:		**$1000.00**	**$1896.58**	**$2896.58**

TAX-SAVINGS TABLE

9.00%
INTEREST

Multiply all figures by the number of thousands in your loan.
Net cost equals yearly payment minus tax savings.

Federal Tax Bracket					
15.0%		28.0%		33.0%	
Tax Savings	Net Cost	Tax Savings	Net Cost	Tax Savings	Net Cost
$13.46	$83.10	$25.12	$71.43	$29.61	$66.95
13.36	83.19	24.94	71.61	29.40	67.16
13.26	83.30	24.75	71.81	29.17	67.39
13.14	83.41	24.53	72.02	28.91	67.64
13.02	83.54	24.30	72.26	28.64	67.92
12.88	83.68	24.04	72.51	28.33	68.22
12.73	83.83	23.76	72.80	28.00	68.55
12.56	83.99	23.45	73.10	27.64	68.91
12.38	84.17	23.12	73.44	27.24	69.31
12.19	84.37	22.75	73.81	26.81	69.74
11.97	84.58	22.35	74.21	26.34	70.22
11.74	84.82	21.91	74.65	25.82	70.74
11.48	85.08	21.42	75.13	25.25	71.30
11.20	85.36	20.90	75.66	24.63	71.92
10.89	85.67	20.32	76.23	23.95	72.60
10.55	86.00	19.69	76.86	23.21	73.34
10.18	86.37	19.00	77.55	22.40	74.16
9.78	86.78	18.25	78.30	21.51	75.04
9.34	87.22	17.43	79.13	20.54	76.02
8.85	87.70	16.53	80.03	19.48	77.08
8.33	88.23	15.54	81.01	18.32	78.24
7.75	88.81	14.46	82.09	17.04	79.51
7.12	89.44	13.28	83.27	15.65	80.90
6.42	90.13	11.99	84.56	14.13	82.42
5.67	90.89	10.58	85.97	12.47	84.08
4.84	91.71	9.04	87.52	10.65	85.90
3.94	92.62	7.35	89.21	8.66	87.89
2.95	93.61	5.50	91.05	6.49	90.07
1.87	94.69	3.48	93.07	4.10	92.45
.67	95.82	1.26	95.24	1.48	95.01
Totals:					
$284.49	**$2612.09**	**$531.04**	**$2365.54**	**$625.87**	**$2270.71**

| | 9.25% INTEREST | ANNUAL MORTGAGE PAYMENT SCHEDULE |

9.25% INTEREST

ANNUAL MORTGAGE PAYMENT SCHEDULE

For a mortgage of $1,000.00

MORTGAGE TERM: **15 years**
Monthly payment: **$10.29**
Annual payment: **$123.50**

Year	Balance of Loan	Principal Paid	Interest Paid	Yearly Payment
1	$967.65	$32.35	$91.15	$123.50
2	932.17	35.47	88.03	123.50
3	893.27	38.90	84.60	123.50
4	850.62	42.65	80.85	123.50
5	803.85	46.77	76.73	123.50
6	752.57	51.28	72.22	123.50
7	696.33	56.24	67.27	123.50
8	634.67	61.66	61.84	123.50
9	567.05	67.62	55.89	123.50
10	492.91	74.14	49.36	123.50
11	411.61	81.30	42.20	123.50
12	322.47	89.15	34.36	123.50
13	224.72	97.75	25.75	123.50
14	117.53	107.19	16.32	123.50
15	.00	117.53	5.89	123.42
Totals:		**$1000.00**	**$852.47**	**$1852.47**

TAX-SAVINGS TABLE

9.25%
INTEREST

Multiply all figures by the number of thousands in your loan.
Net cost equals yearly payment minus tax savings.

Federal Tax Bracket					
15.0%		28.0%		33.0%	
Tax Savings	Net Cost	Tax Savings	Net Cost	Tax Savings	Net Cost
$13.67	$109.83	$25.52	$97.98	$30.08	$93.42
13.20	110.30	24.65	98.86	29.05	94.45
12.69	110.81	23.69	99.81	27.92	95.58
12.13	111.38	22.64	100.87	26.68	96.82
11.51	111.99	21.49	102.02	25.32	98.18
10.83	112.67	20.22	103.28	23.83	99.67
10.09	113.41	18.84	104.67	22.20	101.30
9.28	114.23	17.32	106.19	20.41	103.10
8.38	115.12	15.65	107.85	18.44	105.06
7.40	116.10	13.82	109.68	16.29	107.21
6.33	117.17	11.82	111.69	13.93	109.58
5.15	118.35	9.62	113.88	11.34	112.17
3.86	119.64	7.21	116.29	8.50	115.00
2.45	121.06	4.57	118.93	5.38	118.12
.88	122.54	1.65	121.77	1.94	121.48
Totals:					
$127.87	**$1724.60**	**$238.69**	**$1613.78**	**$281.31**	**$1571.15**

ANNUAL MORTGAGE PAYMENT SCHEDULE

For a mortgage of $1,000.00

MORTGAGE TERM: **30 years**
Monthly payment: **$8.23**
Annual payment: **$98.72**

Year	Balance of Loan	Principal Paid	Interest Paid	Yearly Payment
1	$993.51	$6.49	$92.23	$98.72
2	986.39	7.12	91.60	98.72
3	978.58	7.81	90.92	98.72
4	970.03	8.56	90.16	98.72
5	960.64	9.38	89.34	98.72
6	950.35	10.29	88.43	98.72
7	939.07	11.28	87.44	98.72
8	926.69	12.37	86.35	98.72
9	913.13	13.57	85.15	98.72
10	898.25	14.88	83.84	98.72
11	881.93	16.31	82.41	98.72
12	864.05	17.89	80.83	98.72
13	844.43	19.61	79.11	98.72
14	822.92	21.51	77.21	98.72
15	799.34	23.58	75.14	98.72
16	773.48	25.86	72.86	98.72
17	745.12	28.36	70.36	98.72
18	714.03	31.09	67.63	98.72
19	679.94	34.09	64.63	98.72
20	642.55	37.39	61.34	98.72
21	601.56	40.99	57.73	98.72
22	556.61	44.95	53.77	98.72
23	507.32	49.29	49.43	98.72
24	453.27	54.05	44.67	98.72
25	394.00	59.26	39.46	98.72
26	329.02	64.98	33.74	98.72
27	257.76	71.26	27.46	98.72
28	179.63	78.14	20.59	98.72
29	93.95	85.68	13.04	98.72
30	.00	93.95	4.71	98.66
Totals:		**$1000.00**	**$1961.57**	**$2961.57**

TAX-SAVINGS TABLE

	9.25%
	INTEREST

Multiply all figures by the number of thousands in your loan.
Net cost equals yearly payment minus tax savings.

Federal Tax Bracket					
15.0%		28.0%		33.0%	
Tax Savings	Net Cost	Tax Savings	Net Cost	Tax Savings	Net Cost
$13.83	$84.89	$25.82	$72.90	$30.44	$68.29
13.74	84.98	25.65	73.07	30.23	68.49
13.64	85.08	25.46	73.26	30.00	68.72
13.52	85.20	25.25	73.48	29.75	68.97
13.40	85.32	25.01	73.71	29.48	69.24
13.26	85.46	24.76	73.96	29.18	69.54
13.12	85.61	24.48	74.24	28.85	69.87
12.95	85.77	24.18	74.54	28.49	70.23
12.77	85.95	23.84	74.88	28.10	70.62
12.58	86.14	23.48	75.24	27.67	71.05
12.36	86.36	23.07	75.65	27.19	71.53
12.12	86.60	22.63	76.09	26.67	72.05
11.87	86.86	22.15	76.57	26.11	72.62
11.58	87.14	21.62	77.10	25.48	73.24
11.27	87.45	21.04	77.68	24.80	73.93
10.93	87.79	20.40	78.32	24.04	74.68
10.55	88.17	19.70	79.02	23.22	75.50
10.14	88.58	18.94	79.79	22.32	76.40
9.69	89.03	18.10	80.63	21.33	77.39
9.20	89.52	17.17	81.55	20.24	78.48
8.66	90.06	16.16	82.56	19.05	79.67
8.07	90.66	15.06	83.67	17.74	80.98
7.41	91.31	13.84	84.88	16.31	82.41
6.70	92.02	12.51	86.21	14.74	83.98
5.92	92.80	11.05	87.67	13.02	85.70
5.06	93.66	9.45	89.27	11.13	87.59
4.12	94.60	7.69	91.03	9.06	89.66
3.09	95.63	5.76	92.96	6.79	91.93
1.96	96.76	3.65	95.07	4.30	94.42
.71	97.95	1.32	97.34	1.55	97.10
Totals:					
$294.24	$2667.33	$549.24	$2412.33	$647.32	$2314.25

	9.50% INTEREST	**ANNUAL MORTGAGE PAYMENT SCHEDULE**

For a mortgage of $1,000.00

	MORTGAGE TERM:	**15 years**
	Monthly payment:	**$10.44**
	Annual payment:	**$125.31**

Year	Balance of Loan	Principal Paid	Interest Paid	Yearly Payment
1	$968.34	$31.66	$93.64	$125.31
2	933.53	34.80	90.50	125.31
3	895.27	38.26	87.05	125.31
4	853.22	42.06	83.25	125.31
5	806.99	46.23	79.08	125.31
6	756.17	50.82	74.49	125.31
7	700.31	55.86	69.45	125.31
8	638.90	61.41	63.90	125.31
9	571.40	67.50	57.81	125.31
10	497.21	74.20	51.11	125.31
11	415.64	81.56	43.74	125.31
12	325.98	89.66	35.65	125.31
13	227.43	98.56	26.75	125.31
14	119.09	108.34	16.97	125.31
15	.00	119.09	6.13	125.22
Totals:		**$1000.00**	**$879.52**	**$1879.52**

TAX-SAVINGS TABLE

9.50%
INTEREST

Multiply all figures by the number of thousands in your loan.
Net cost equals yearly payment minus tax savings.

| Federal Tax Bracket | | | | | |
| 15.0% | | 28.0% | | 33.0% | |
Tax Savings	Net Cost	Tax Savings	Net Cost	Tax Savings	Net Cost
$14.05	$111.26	$26.22	$99.09	$30.90	$94.40
13.58	111.73	25.34	99.97	29.87	95.44
13.06	112.25	24.37	100.93	28.73	96.58
12.49	112.82	23.31	102.00	27.47	97.83
11.86	113.45	22.14	103.17	26.10	99.21
11.17	114.13	20.86	104.45	24.58	100.73
10.42	114.89	19.44	105.86	22.92	102.39
9.59	115.72	17.89	107.41	21.09	104.22
8.67	116.64	16.19	109.12	19.08	106.23
7.67	117.64	14.31	111.00	16.87	108.44
6.56	118.75	12.25	113.06	14.44	110.87
5.35	119.96	9.98	115.33	11.76	113.54
4.01	121.29	7.49	117.82	8.83	116.48
2.55	122.76	4.75	120.56	5.60	119.71
.92	124.30	1.72	123.51	2.02	123.20
Totals:					
$131.93	**$1747.59**	**$246.27**	**$1633.26**	**$290.24**	**$1589.28**

	9.50% INTEREST	**ANNUAL MORTGAGE PAYMENT SCHEDULE**

For a mortgage of $1,000.00

MORTGAGE TERM: **30 years**
Monthly payment: **$8.41**
Annual payment: **$100.90**

Year	Balance of Loan	Principal Paid	Interest Paid	Yearly Payment
1	$993.83	$6.17	$94.74	$100.90
2	987.06	6.78	94.12	100.90
3	979.60	7.45	93.45	100.90
4	971.41	8.19	92.71	100.90
5	962.41	9.00	91.90	100.90
6	952.51	9.90	91.01	100.90
7	941.63	10.88	90.02	100.90
8	929.67	11.96	88.94	100.90
9	916.53	13.15	87.76	100.90
10	902.08	14.45	86.45	100.90
11	886.19	15.89	85.02	100.90
12	868.73	17.46	83.44	100.90
13	849.54	19.19	81.71	100.90
14	828.44	21.10	79.80	100.90
15	805.24	23.19	77.71	100.90
16	779.75	25.50	75.41	100.90
17	751.72	28.03	72.88	100.90
18	720.91	30.81	70.09	100.90
19	687.05	33.87	67.04	100.90
20	649.82	37.23	63.68	100.90
21	608.90	40.92	59.98	100.90
22	563.92	44.98	55.92	100.90
23	514.47	49.45	51.46	100.90
24	460.12	54.35	46.55	100.90
25	400.37	59.75	41.15	100.90
26	334.69	65.68	35.22	100.90
27	262.50	72.20	28.71	100.90
28	183.13	79.36	21.54	100.90
29	95.90	87.24	13.66	100.90
30	.00	95.90	4.94	100.84
Totals:		**$1000.00**	**$2027.01**	**$3027.01**

132

TAX-SAVINGS TABLE

9.50%
INTEREST

Multiply all figures by the number of thousands in your loan.
Net cost equals yearly payment minus tax savings.

Federal Tax Bracket					
15.0%		28.0%		33.0%	
Tax Savings	Net Cost	Tax Savings	Net Cost	Tax Savings	Net Cost
$14.21	$86.69	$26.53	$74.38	$31.26	$69.64
14.12	86.78	26.35	74.55	31.06	69.84
14.02	86.88	26.17	74.74	30.84	70.06
13.91	87.00	25.96	74.94	30.59	70.31
13.78	87.12	25.73	75.17	30.33	70.58
13.65	87.25	25.48	75.42	30.03	70.87
13.50	87.40	25.21	75.70	29.71	71.19
13.34	87.56	24.90	76.00	29.35	71.55
13.16	87.74	24.57	76.33	28.96	71.94
12.97	87.93	24.21	76.70	28.53	72.37
12.75	88.15	23.80	77.10	28.06	72.85
12.52	88.39	23.36	77.54	27.54	73.37
12.26	88.65	22.88	78.02	26.96	73.94
11.97	88.93	22.34	78.56	26.33	74.57
11.66	89.25	21.76	79.14	25.64	75.26
11.31	89.59	21.11	79.79	24.88	76.02
10.93	89.97	20.41	80.50	24.05	76.85
10.51	90.39	19.63	81.28	23.13	77.77
10.06	90.85	18.77	82.13	22.12	78.78
9.55	91.35	17.83	83.07	21.01	79.89
9.00	91.91	16.79	84.11	19.79	81.11
8.39	92.51	15.66	85.24	18.45	82.45
7.72	93.18	14.41	86.49	16.98	83.92
6.98	93.92	13.03	87.87	15.36	85.54
6.17	94.73	11.52	89.38	13.58	87.32
5.28	95.62	9.86	91.04	11.62	89.28
4.31	96.60	8.04	92.86	9.47	91.43
3.23	97.67	6.03	94.87	7.11	93.79
2.05	98.85	3.83	97.08	4.51	96.39
.74	100.10	1.38	99.45	1.63	99.21
Totals:					
$304.05	**$2722.96**	**$567.56**	**$2459.45**	**$668.91**	**$2358.10**

	9.75% INTEREST	**ANNUAL MORTGAGE PAYMENT SCHEDULE**

For a mortgage of $1,000.00

MORTGAGE TERM: **15 years**
Monthly payment: **$10.59**
Annual payment: **$127.12**

Year	Balance of Loan	Principal Paid	Interest Paid	Yearly Payment
1	$969.02	$30.98	$96.14	$127.12
2	934.87	34.14	92.98	127.12
3	897.25	37.63	89.50	127.12
4	855.79	41.46	85.66	127.12
5	810.09	45.69	81.43	127.12
6	759.74	50.35	76.77	127.12
7	704.26	55.48	71.64	127.12
8	643.12	61.14	65.98	127.12
9	575.74	67.38	59.75	127.12
10	501.49	74.25	52.87	127.12
11	419.67	81.82	45.30	127.12
12	329.51	90.16	36.96	127.12
13	230.15	99.36	27.76	127.12
14	120.66	109.49	17.63	127.12
15	.00	120.66	6.38	127.04
Totals:		**$1000.00**	**$906.77**	**$1906.77**

TAX-SAVINGS TABLE

9.75%
INTEREST

Multiply all figures by the number of thousands in your loan.
Net cost equals yearly payment minus tax savings.

Federal Tax Bracket					
15.0%		28.0%		33.0%	
Tax Savings	Net Cost	Tax Savings	Net Cost	Tax Savings	Net Cost
$14.42	$112.70	$26.92	$100.20	$31.73	$95.40
13.95	113.18	26.03	101.09	30.68	96.44
13.42	113.70	25.06	102.06	29.53	97.59
12.85	114.27	23.99	103.14	28.27	98.86
12.21	114.91	22.80	104.32	26.87	100.25
11.52	115.61	21.50	105.63	25.34	101.79
10.75	116.38	20.06	107.06	23.64	103.48
9.90	117.23	18.47	108.65	21.77	105.35
8.96	118.16	16.73	110.39	19.72	107.41
7.93	119.19	14.80	112.32	17.45	109.67
6.80	120.33	12.68	114.44	14.95	112.17
5.54	121.58	10.35	116.77	12.20	114.93
4.16	122.96	7.77	119.35	9.16	117.96
2.64	124.48	4.94	122.19	5.82	121.30
.96	126.08	1.79	125.25	2.11	124.93
Totals:					
$136.02	**$1770.75**	**$253.89**	**$1652.87**	**$299.23**	**$1607.53**

9.75% INTEREST	**ANNUAL MORTGAGE PAYMENT SCHEDULE**

For a mortgage of $1,000.00

MORTGAGE TERM:	30 years
Monthly payment:	$8.59
Annual payment:	$103.10

Year	Balance of Loan	Principal Paid	Interest Paid	Yearly Payment
1	$994.14	$5.86	$97.24	$103.10
2	987.69	6.45	96.65	103.10
3	980.58	7.11	95.99	103.10
4	972.74	7.84	95.26	103.10
5	964.11	8.64	94.46	103.10
6	954.59	9.52	93.58	103.10
7	944.11	10.49	92.61	103.10
8	932.55	11.56	91.54	103.10
9	919.82	12.73	90.36	103.10
10	905.79	14.03	89.07	103.10
11	890.32	15.46	87.64	103.10
12	873.28	17.04	86.06	103.10
13	854.51	18.78	84.32	103.10
14	833.81	20.69	82.41	103.10
15	811.01	22.80	80.30	103.10
16	785.88	25.13	77.97	103.10
17	758.19	27.69	75.41	103.10
18	727.68	30.51	72.58	103.10
19	694.05	33.63	69.47	103.10
20	657.00	37.06	66.04	103.10
21	616.16	40.83	62.26	103.10
22	571.16	45.00	58.10	103.10
23	521.58	49.59	53.51	103.10
24	466.93	54.64	48.45	103.10
25	406.71	60.22	42.88	103.10
26	340.36	66.36	36.74	103.10
27	267.23	73.12	29.97	103.10
28	186.65	80.58	22.52	103.10
29	97.85	88.80	14.30	103.10
30	.00	97.85	5.18	103.03
Totals:		**$1000.00**	**$2092.89**	**$3092.89**

Multiply all figures by the number of thousands in your loan.
Net cost equals yearly payment minus tax savings.

| Federal Tax Bracket | | | | | |
| 15.0% | | 28.0% | | 33.0% | |
Tax Savings	Net Cost	Tax Savings	Net Cost	Tax Savings	Net Cost
$14.59	$88.51	$27.23	$75.87	$32.09	$71.01
14.50	88.60	27.06	76.04	31.89	71.21
14.40	88.70	26.88	76.22	31.68	71.42
14.29	88.81	26.67	76.43	31.44	71.66
14.17	88.93	26.45	76.65	31.17	71.93
14.04	89.06	26.20	76.90	30.88	72.22
13.89	89.21	25.93	77.17	30.56	72.54
13.73	89.37	25.63	77.47	30.21	72.89
13.55	89.54	25.30	77.80	29.82	73.28
13.36	89.74	24.94	78.16	29.39	73.71
13.15	89.95	24.54	78.56	28.92	74.18
12.91	90.19	24.10	79.00	28.40	74.70
12.65	90.45	23.61	79.49	27.83	75.27
12.36	90.74	23.07	80.02	27.19	75.90
12.04	91.05	22.48	80.62	26.50	76.60
11.70	91.40	21.83	81.27	25.73	77.37
11.31	91.79	21.11	81.98	24.88	78.21
10.89	92.21	20.32	82.78	23.95	79.15
10.42	92.68	19.45	83.65	22.93	80.17
9.91	93.19	18.49	84.61	21.79	81.30
9.34	93.76	17.43	85.66	20.55	82.55
8.72	94.38	16.27	86.83	19.17	83.93
8.03	95.07	14.98	88.12	17.66	85.44
7.27	95.83	13.57	89.53	15.99	87.11
6.43	96.67	12.01	91.09	14.15	88.95
5.51	97.59	10.29	92.81	12.12	90.97
4.50	98.60	8.39	94.71	9.89	93.21
3.38	99.72	6.30	96.79	7.43	95.67
2.14	100.95	4.00	99.09	4.72	98.38
.78	102.25	1.45	101.58	1.71	101.32
Totals:					
$313.93	$2778.95	$586.01	$2506.88	$690.65	$2402.23

10.00% INTEREST	ANNUAL MORTGAGE PAYMENT SCHEDULE

For a mortgage of $1,000.00

MORTGAGE TERM: **15 years**
Monthly payment: **$10.75**
Annual payment: **$128.95**

Year	Balance of Loan	Principal Paid	Interest Paid	Yearly Payment
1	$969.68	$30.32	$98.64	$128.95
2	936.19	33.49	95.46	128.95
3	899.19	37.00	91.95	128.95
4	858.32	40.87	88.08	128.95
5	813.17	45.15	83.80	128.95
6	763.29	49.88	79.07	128.95
7	708.18	55.10	73.85	128.95
8	647.31	60.87	68.08	128.95
9	580.06	67.25	61.70	128.95
10	505.77	74.29	54.66	128.95
11	423.70	82.07	46.88	128.95
12	333.03	90.66	38.29	128.95
13	232.88	100.16	28.80	128.95
14	122.23	110.65	18.31	128.95
15	.00	122.23	6.63	128.86
Totals:		**$1000.00**	**$934.20**	**$1934.20**

TAX-SAVINGS TABLE

10.00%
INTEREST

Multiply all figures by the number of thousands in your loan.
Net cost equals yearly payment minus tax savings.

Federal Tax Bracket					
15.0%		28.0%		33.0%	
Tax Savings	Net Cost	Tax Savings	Net Cost	Tax Savings	Net Cost
$14.80	$114.16	$27.62	$101.33	$32.55	$96.40
14.32	114.63	26.73	102.22	31.50	97.45
13.79	115.16	25.75	103.21	30.34	98.61
13.21	115.74	24.66	104.29	29.07	99.89
12.57	116.38	23.46	105.49	27.65	101.30
11.86	117.09	22.14	106.81	26.09	102.86
11.08	117.88	20.68	108.28	24.37	104.58
10.21	118.74	19.06	109.89	22.47	106.49
9.26	119.70	17.28	111.68	20.36	108.59
8.20	120.75	15.31	113.65	18.04	110.91
7.03	121.92	13.13	115.83	15.47	113.48
5.74	123.21	10.72	118.23	12.64	116.32
4.32	124.63	8.06	120.89	9.50	119.45
2.75	126.21	5.13	123.83	6.04	122.91
.99	127.87	1.86	127.01	2.19	126.67
Totals:					
$140.13	**$1794.07**	**$261.58**	**$1672.62**	**$308.29**	**$1625.91**

| | 10.00% INTEREST | **ANNUAL MORTGAGE PAYMENT SCHEDULE** |

10.00% INTEREST

ANNUAL MORTGAGE PAYMENT SCHEDULE

For a mortgage of $1,000.00

MORTGAGE TERM: **30 years**
Monthly payment: **$8.78**
Annual payment: **$105.31**

Year	Balance of Loan	Principal Paid	Interest Paid	Yearly Payment
1	$994.44	$5.56	$99.75	$105.31
2	988.30	6.14	99.17	105.31
3	981.52	6.78	98.52	105.31
4	974.02	7.49	97.81	105.31
5	965.74	8.28	97.03	105.31
6	956.60	9.15	96.16	105.31
7	946.49	10.10	95.20	105.31
8	935.33	11.16	94.15	105.31
9	923.00	12.33	92.98	105.31
10	909.38	13.62	91.69	105.31
11	894.33	15.05	90.26	105.31
12	877.71	16.62	88.69	105.31
13	859.34	18.36	86.94	105.31
14	839.06	20.29	85.02	105.31
15	816.65	22.41	82.90	105.31
16	791.89	24.76	80.55	105.31
17	764.54	27.35	77.96	105.31
18	734.32	30.21	75.09	105.31
19	700.94	33.38	71.93	105.31
20	664.07	36.87	68.43	105.31
21	623.33	40.74	64.57	105.31
22	578.33	45.00	60.31	105.31
23	528.62	49.71	55.60	105.31
24	473.70	54.92	50.39	105.31
25	413.03	60.67	44.64	105.31
26	346.01	67.02	38.29	105.31
27	271.97	74.04	31.27	105.31
28	190.18	81.79	23.52	105.31
29	99.82	90.36	14.95	105.31
30	.00	99.82	5.42	105.24
Totals:		**$1000.00**	**$2159.19**	**$3159.19**

TAX-SAVINGS TABLE

10.00% INTEREST

Multiply all figures by the number of thousands in your loan.
Net cost equals yearly payment minus tax savings.

Federal Tax Bracket					
15.0%		**28.0%**		**33.0%**	
Tax Savings	**Net Cost**	**Tax Savings**	**Net Cost**	**Tax Savings**	**Net Cost**
$14.96	$90.35	$27.93	$77.38	$32.92	$72.39
14.88	90.43	27.77	77.54	32.73	72.58
14.78	90.53	27.59	77.72	32.51	72.80
14.67	90.64	27.39	77.92	32.28	73.03
14.55	90.75	27.17	78.14	32.02	73.29
14.42	90.88	26.93	78.38	31.73	73.57
14.28	91.03	26.66	78.65	31.42	73.89
14.12	91.19	26.36	78.95	31.07	74.24
13.95	91.36	26.03	79.27	30.68	74.63
13.75	91.56	25.67	79.64	30.26	75.05
13.54	91.77	25.27	80.04	29.79	75.52
13.30	92.01	24.83	80.48	29.27	76.04
13.04	92.27	24.34	80.96	28.69	76.62
12.75	92.56	23.81	81.50	28.06	77.25
12.43	92.87	23.21	82.10	27.36	77.95
12.08	93.23	22.55	82.75	26.58	78.73
11.69	93.61	21.83	83.48	25.73	79.58
11.26	94.04	21.03	84.28	24.78	80.53
10.79	94.52	20.14	85.17	23.74	81.57
10.27	95.04	19.16	86.15	22.58	82.73
9.69	95.62	18.08	87.23	21.31	84.00
9.05	96.26	16.89	88.42	19.90	85.41
8.34	96.97	15.57	89.74	18.35	86.96
7.56	97.75	14.11	91.20	16.63	88.68
6.70	98.61	12.50	92.81	14.73	90.58
5.74	99.57	10.72	94.59	12.63	92.67
4.69	100.62	8.76	96.55	10.32	94.99
3.53	101.78	6.58	98.72	7.76	97.55
2.24	103.07	4.19	101.12	4.93	100.37
.81	104.42	1.52	103.72	1.79	103.45
Totals:					
$323.88	**$2835.31**	**$604.57**	**$2554.61**	**$712.53**	**$2446.65**

| | 10.25% INTEREST | **ANNUAL MORTGAGE PAYMENT SCHEDULE** |

10.25% INTEREST

ANNUAL MORTGAGE PAYMENT SCHEDULE

For a mortgage of $1,000.00

MORTGAGE TERM: **15 years**
Monthly payment: **$10.90**
Annual payment: **$130.79**

Year	Balance of Loan	Principal Paid	Interest Paid	Yearly Payment
1	$970.34	$29.66	$101.13	$130.79
2	937.49	32.85	97.94	130.79
3	901.11	36.38	94.42	130.79
4	860.82	40.29	90.51	130.79
5	816.20	44.62	86.18	130.79
6	766.79	49.41	81.38	130.79
7	712.07	54.72	76.07	130.79
8	651.47	60.60	70.19	130.79
9	584.36	67.11	63.68	130.79
10	510.03	74.32	56.47	130.79
11	427.72	82.31	48.48	130.79
12	336.56	91.16	39.64	130.79
13	235.61	100.95	29.84	130.79
14	123.81	111.80	18.99	130.79
15	.00	123.81	6.89	130.70
Totals:		**$1000.00**	**$961.82**	**$1961.82**

TAX-SAVINGS TABLE

10.25%
INTEREST

Multiply all figures by the number of thousands in your loan.
Net cost equals yearly payment minus tax savings.

| Federal Tax Bracket | | | | | |
| 15.0% | | 28.0% | | 33.0% | |
Tax Savings	Net Cost	Tax Savings	Net Cost	Tax Savings	Net Cost
$15.17	$115.62	$28.32	$102.48	$33.37	$97.42
14.69	116.10	27.42	103.37	32.32	98.47
14.16	116.63	26.44	104.36	31.16	99.64
13.58	117.22	25.34	105.45	29.87	100.93
12.93	117.87	24.13	106.66	28.44	102.36
12.21	118.59	22.79	108.01	26.86	103.94
11.41	119.38	21.30	109.49	25.10	105.69
10.53	120.27	19.65	111.14	23.16	107.63
9.55	121.24	17.83	112.96	21.01	109.78
8.47	122.32	15.81	114.98	18.63	112.16
7.27	123.52	13.58	117.22	16.00	114.79
5.95	124.85	11.10	119.70	13.08	117.71
4.48	126.32	8.36	122.44	9.85	120.95
2.85	127.94	5.32	125.48	6.27	124.53
1.03	129.67	1.93	128.77	2.27	128.43
Totals:					
$144.27	**$1817.55**	**$269.31**	**$1692.51**	**$317.40**	**$1644.42**

10.25% INTEREST	**ANNUAL MORTGAGE PAYMENT SCHEDULE**

For a mortgage of $1,000.00

MORTGAGE TERM: **30 years**
Monthly payment: **$8.96**
Annual payment: **$107.53**

Year	Balance of Loan	Principal Paid	Interest Paid	Yearly Payment
1	$994.72	$5.28	$102.26	$107.53
2	988.88	5.84	101.69	107.53
3	982.41	6.47	101.06	107.53
4	975.25	7.17	100.37	107.53
5	967.31	7.94	99.60	107.53
6	958.52	8.79	98.74	107.53
7	948.79	9.73	97.80	107.53
8	938.01	10.78	96.75	107.53
9	926.08	11.94	95.60	107.53
10	912.86	13.22	94.31	107.53
11	898.22	14.64	92.89	107.53
12	882.01	16.21	91.32	107.53
13	864.05	17.95	89.58	107.53
14	844.17	19.88	87.65	107.53
15	822.15	22.02	85.51	107.53
16	797.76	24.39	83.15	107.53
17	770.75	27.01	80.53	107.53
18	740.85	29.91	77.62	107.53
19	707.72	33.12	74.41	107.53
20	671.04	36.68	70.85	107.53
21	630.42	40.62	66.91	107.53
22	585.43	44.99	62.54	107.53
23	535.60	49.82	57.71	107.53
24	480.43	55.18	52.36	107.53
25	419.32	61.11	46.43	107.53
26	351.65	67.67	39.86	107.53
27	276.71	74.94	32.59	107.53
28	193.71	83.00	24.53	107.53
29	101.79	91.92	15.62	107.53
30	.00	101.79	5.66	107.46
Totals:		**$1000.00**	**$2225.89**	**$3225.89**

TAX-SAVINGS TABLE

10.25% INTEREST

Multiply all figures by the number of thousands in your loan.
Net cost equals yearly payment minus tax savings.

Federal Tax Bracket					
15.0%		28.0%		33.0%	
Tax Savings	Net Cost	Tax Savings	Net Cost	Tax Savings	Net Cost
$15.34	$92.19	$28.63	$78.90	$33.74	$73.79
15.25	92.28	28.47	79.06	33.56	73.97
15.16	92.37	28.30	79.23	33.35	74.18
15.06	92.48	28.10	79.43	33.12	74.41
14.94	92.59	27.89	79.65	32.87	74.67
14.81	92.72	27.65	79.88	32.59	74.95
14.67	92.86	27.38	80.15	32.27	75.26
14.51	93.02	27.09	80.44	31.93	75.60
14.34	93.19	26.77	80.77	31.55	75.99
14.15	93.39	26.41	81.12	31.12	76.41
13.93	93.60	26.01	81.52	30.65	76.88
13.70	93.83	25.57	81.96	30.14	77.40
13.44	94.10	25.08	82.45	29.56	77.97
13.15	94.38	24.54	82.99	28.92	78.61
12.83	94.71	23.94	83.59	28.22	79.31
12.47	95.06	23.28	84.25	27.44	80.09
12.08	95.45	22.55	84.99	26.57	80.96
11.64	95.89	21.73	85.80	25.62	81.92
11.16	96.37	20.83	86.70	24.56	82.98
10.63	96.90	19.84	87.69	23.38	84.15
10.04	97.50	18.73	88.80	22.08	85.45
9.38	98.15	17.51	90.02	20.64	86.89
8.66	98.88	16.16	91.37	19.04	88.49
7.85	99.68	14.66	92.87	17.28	90.25
6.96	100.57	13.00	94.53	15.32	92.21
5.98	101.55	11.16	96.37	13.15	94.38
4.89	102.64	9.12	98.41	10.75	96.78
3.68	103.85	6.87	100.66	8.10	99.44
2.34	105.19	4.37	103.16	5.15	102.38
.85	106.61	1.59	105.87	1.87	105.59
Totals:					
$333.88	**$2892.01**	**$623.25**	**$2602.64**	**$734.54**	**$2491.35**

For a mortgage of $1,000.00

MORTGAGE TERM:	**15 years**
Monthly payment:	**$11.05**
Annual payment:	**$132.65**

Year	Balance of Loan	Principal Paid	Interest Paid	Yearly Payment
1	$970.98	$29.02	$103.63	$132.65
2	938.77	32.22	100.43	132.65
3	903.00	35.77	96.88	132.65
4	863.29	39.71	92.94	132.65
5	819.21	44.08	88.56	132.65
6	770.27	48.94	83.71	132.65
7	715.93	54.34	78.31	132.65
8	655.61	60.32	72.32	132.65
9	588.64	66.97	65.68	132.65
10	514.28	74.35	58.30	132.65
11	431.74	82.55	50.10	132.65
12	340.10	91.64	41.01	132.65
13	238.36	101.74	30.91	132.65
14	125.40	112.95	19.69	132.65
15	.00	125.40	7.15	132.55
Totals:		**$1000.00**	**$989.62**	**$1989.62**

TAX-SAVINGS TABLE

10.50% INTEREST

Multiply all figures by the number of thousands in your loan.
Net cost equals yearly payment minus tax savings.

Federal Tax Bracket					
15.0%		28.0%		33.0%	
Tax Savings	Net Cost	Tax Savings	Net Cost	Tax Savings	Net Cost
$15.54	$117.10	$29.02	$103.63	$34.20	$98.45
15.06	117.58	28.12	104.53	33.14	99.51
14.53	118.12	27.13	105.52	31.97	100.68
13.94	118.71	26.02	106.62	30.67	101.98
13.28	119.36	24.80	107.85	29.23	103.42
12.56	120.09	23.44	109.21	27.62	105.02
11.75	120.90	21.93	110.72	25.84	106.80
10.85	121.80	20.25	112.40	23.87	108.78
9.85	122.80	18.39	114.26	21.67	110.97
8.74	123.90	16.32	116.32	19.24	113.41
7.52	125.13	14.03	118.62	16.53	116.11
6.15	126.50	11.48	121.17	13.53	119.12
4.64	128.01	8.65	123.99	10.20	122.45
2.95	129.69	5.51	127.13	6.50	126.15
1.07	131.48	2.00	130.55	2.36	130.19
Totals:					
$148.44	**$1841.18**	**$277.09**	**$1712.53**	**$326.58**	**$1663.05**

<table>
<tr><th colspan="2">10.50% INTEREST</th><th colspan="3">ANNUAL MORTGAGE
PAYMENT SCHEDULE</th></tr>
</table>

For a mortgage of $1,000.00

	MORTGAGE TERM:	**30 years**	
	Monthly payment:	**$9.15**	
	Annual payment:	**$109.77**	

Year	Balance of Loan	Principal Paid	Interest Paid	Yearly Payment
1	$994.99	$5.01	$104.76	$109.77
2	989.44	5.56	104.21	109.77
3	983.27	6.17	103.60	109.77
4	976.42	6.85	102.92	109.77
5	968.82	7.60	102.17	109.77
6	960.38	8.44	101.33	109.77
7	951.00	9.37	100.40	109.77
8	940.60	10.40	99.36	109.77
9	929.05	11.55	98.22	109.77
10	916.22	12.82	96.94	109.77
11	901.99	14.24	95.53	109.77
12	886.18	15.81	93.96	109.77
13	868.63	17.55	92.22	109.77
14	849.15	19.48	90.29	109.77
15	827.52	21.63	88.14	109.77
16	803.51	24.01	85.76	109.77
17	776.85	26.66	83.11	109.77
18	747.25	29.60	80.17	109.77
19	714.39	32.86	76.91	109.77
20	677.91	36.48	73.29	109.77
21	637.41	40.50	69.27	109.77
22	592.45	44.96	64.81	109.77
23	542.53	49.92	59.85	109.77
24	487.11	55.42	54.35	109.77
25	425.58	61.53	48.24	109.77
26	357.27	68.31	41.46	109.77
27	281.44	75.84	33.93	109.77
28	197.24	84.19	25.58	109.77
29	103.77	93.47	16.30	109.77
30	.00	103.77	5.92	109.69
Totals:		$1000.00	$2292.98	$3292.98

TAX-SAVINGS TABLE

10.50% INTEREST

Multiply all figures by the number of thousands in your loan.
Net cost equals yearly payment minus tax savings.

Federal Tax Bracket					
15.0%		28.0%		33.0%	
Tax Savings	Net Cost	Tax Savings	Net Cost	Tax Savings	Net Cost
$15.71	$94.05	$29.33	$80.43	$34.57	$75.20
15.63	94.14	29.18	80.59	34.39	75.38
15.54	94.23	29.01	80.76	34.19	75.58
15.44	94.33	28.82	80.95	33.96	75.81
15.32	94.44	28.61	81.16	33.71	76.05
15.20	94.57	28.37	81.40	33.44	76.33
15.06	94.71	28.11	81.66	33.13	76.64
14.90	94.86	27.82	81.95	32.79	76.98
14.73	95.04	27.50	82.27	32.41	77.36
14.54	95.23	27.14	82.62	31.99	77.78
14.33	95.44	26.75	83.02	31.53	78.24
14.09	95.67	26.31	83.46	31.01	78.76
13.83	95.94	25.82	83.95	30.43	79.34
13.54	96.23	25.28	84.49	29.79	79.97
13.22	96.55	24.68	85.09	29.09	80.68
12.86	96.91	24.01	85.76	28.30	81.47
12.47	97.30	23.27	86.50	27.43	82.34
12.03	97.74	22.45	87.32	26.46	83.31
11.54	98.23	21.53	88.23	25.38	84.39
10.99	98.78	20.52	89.25	24.19	85.58
10.39	99.38	19.40	90.37	22.86	86.91
9.72	100.05	18.15	91.62	21.39	88.38
8.98	100.79	16.76	93.01	19.75	90.02
8.15	101.62	15.22	94.55	17.94	91.83
7.24	102.53	13.51	96.26	15.92	93.85
6.22	103.55	11.61	98.16	13.68	96.09
5.09	104.68	9.50	100.27	11.20	98.57
3.84	105.93	7.16	102.61	8.44	101.33
2.44	107.32	4.56	105.21	5.38	104.39
.89	108.80	1.66	108.03	1.95	107.74
Totals:					
$343.95	$2949.03	$642.03	$2650.95	$756.68	$2536.30

	10.75% INTEREST	**ANNUAL MORTGAGE PAYMENT SCHEDULE**

For a mortgage of $1,000.00

MORTGAGE TERM: **15 years**
Monthly payment: **$11.21**
Annual payment: **$134.51**

Year	Balance of Loan	Principal Paid	Interest Paid	Yearly Payment
1	$971.61	$28.39	$106.13	$134.51
2	940.02	31.59	102.92	134.51
3	904.86	35.16	99.35	134.51
4	865.73	39.13	95.38	134.51
5	822.18	43.55	90.96	134.51
6	773.71	48.47	86.04	134.51
7	719.76	53.95	80.57	134.51
8	659.72	60.04	74.47	134.51
9	592.90	66.82	67.69	134.51
10	518.53	74.37	60.14	134.51
11	435.75	82.77	51.74	134.51
12	343.63	92.12	42.39	134.51
13	241.11	102.53	31.99	134.51
14	127.00	114.11	20.41	134.51
15	.00	127.00	7.42	134.41
Totals:		**$1000.00**	**$1017.61**	**$2017.61**

TAX-SAVINGS TABLE

10.75%
INTEREST

Multiply all figures by the number of thousands in your loan.
Net cost equals yearly payment minus tax savings.

Federal Tax Bracket					
15.0%		28.0%		33.0%	
Tax Savings	Net Cost	Tax Savings	Net Cost	Tax Savings	Net Cost
$15.92	$118.59	$29.72	$104.80	$35.02	$99.49
15.44	119.08	28.82	105.70	33.96	100.55
14.90	119.61	27.82	106.69	32.79	101.73
14.31	120.21	26.71	107.81	31.48	103.04
13.64	120.87	25.47	109.04	30.02	104.50
12.91	121.61	24.09	110.42	28.39	106.12
12.09	122.43	22.56	111.96	26.59	107.93
11.17	123.34	20.85	113.66	24.58	109.94
10.15	124.36	18.95	115.56	22.34	112.18
9.02	125.49	16.84	117.67	19.85	114.67
7.76	126.75	14.49	120.03	17.07	117.44
6.36	128.15	11.87	122.64	13.99	120.52
4.80	129.72	8.96	125.56	10.56	123.96
3.06	131.45	5.71	128.80	6.73	127.78
1.11	133.30	2.08	132.34	2.45	131.97
Totals:					
$152.64	**$1864.97**	**$284.93**	**$1732.68**	**$335.81**	**$1681.80**

| | 10.75% INTEREST | **ANNUAL MORTGAGE PAYMENT SCHEDULE** |

10.75% INTEREST — ANNUAL MORTGAGE PAYMENT SCHEDULE

For a mortgage of $1,000.00

MORTGAGE TERM: **30 years**
Monthly payment: **$9.33**
Annual payment: **$112.02**

Year	Balance of Loan	Principal Paid	Interest Paid	Yearly Payment
1	$995.25	$4.75	$107.27	$112.02
2	989.97	5.28	106.73	112.02
3	984.09	5.88	106.14	112.02
4	977.54	6.54	105.47	112.02
5	970.26	7.28	104.73	112.02
6	962.15	8.11	103.91	112.02
7	953.13	9.02	103.00	112.02
8	943.09	10.04	101.98	112.02
9	931.92	11.18	100.84	112.02
10	919.48	12.44	99.58	112.02
11	905.64	13.84	98.18	112.02
12	890.23	15.41	96.61	112.02
13	873.08	17.15	94.87	112.02
14	854.00	19.08	92.93	112.02
15	832.76	21.24	90.78	112.02
16	809.12	23.64	88.38	112.02
17	782.81	26.31	85.71	112.02
18	753.53	29.28	82.74	112.02
19	720.95	32.59	79.43	112.02
20	684.68	36.27	75.75	112.02
21	644.31	40.37	71.65	112.02
22	599.39	44.92	67.09	112.02
23	549.39	50.00	62.02	112.02
24	493.74	55.65	56.37	112.02
25	431.81	61.93	50.08	112.02
26	362.88	68.93	43.09	112.02
27	286.16	76.72	35.30	112.02
28	200.78	85.38	26.64	112.02
29	105.76	95.03	16.99	112.02
30	.00	105.76	6.18	111.93
Totals:		**$1000.00**	**$2360.45**	**$3360.45**

TAX-SAVINGS TABLE

	10.75%
	INTEREST

Multiply all figures by the number of thousands in your loan.
Net cost equals yearly payment minus tax savings.

Federal Tax Bracket					
15.0%		28.0%		33.0%	
Tax Savings	Net Cost	Tax Savings	Net Cost	Tax Savings	Net Cost
$16.09	$95.93	$30.04	$81.98	$35.40	$76.62
16.01	96.01	29.89	82.13	35.22	76.80
15.92	96.10	29.72	82.30	35.03	76.99
15.82	96.20	29.53	82.49	34.81	77.21
15.71	96.31	29.33	82.69	34.56	77.46
15.59	96.43	29.10	82.92	34.29	77.73
15.45	96.57	28.84	83.18	33.99	78.03
15.30	96.72	28.55	83.46	33.65	78.37
15.13	96.89	28.24	83.78	33.28	78.74
14.94	97.08	27.88	84.14	32.86	79.16
14.73	97.29	27.49	84.53	32.40	79.62
14.49	97.53	27.05	84.97	31.88	80.14
14.23	97.79	26.56	85.45	31.31	80.71
13.94	98.08	26.02	86.00	30.67	81.35
13.62	98.40	25.42	86.60	29.96	82.06
13.26	98.76	24.75	87.27	29.17	82.85
12.86	99.16	24.00	88.02	28.28	83.73
12.41	99.61	23.17	88.85	27.30	84.71
11.91	100.10	22.24	89.78	26.21	85.81
11.36	100.66	21.21	90.81	25.00	87.02
10.75	101.27	20.06	91.96	23.65	88.37
10.06	101.95	18.79	93.23	22.14	89.88
9.30	102.72	17.37	94.65	20.47	91.55
8.46	103.56	15.78	96.23	18.60	93.42
7.51	104.51	14.02	97.99	16.53	95.49
6.46	105.55	12.06	99.95	14.22	97.80
5.30	106.72	9.88	102.13	11.65	100.37
4.00	108.02	7.46	104.56	8.79	103.23
2.55	109.47	4.76	107.26	5.61	106.41
.93	111.01	1.73	110.21	2.04	109.90
Totals:					
$354.07	$3006.38	$660.93	$2699.52	$778.95	$2581.50

ANNUAL MORTGAGE PAYMENT SCHEDULE

For a mortgage of $1,000.00

MORTGAGE TERM: **15 years**
Monthly payment: **$11.37**
Annual payment: **$136.39**

Year	Balance of Loan	Principal Paid	Interest Paid	Yearly Payment
1	$972.24	$27.76	$108.63	$136.39
2	941.26	30.98	105.42	136.39
3	906.70	34.56	101.83	136.39
4	868.14	38.56	97.83	136.39
5	825.12	43.02	93.37	136.39
6	777.11	48.00	88.39	136.39
7	723.56	53.56	82.84	136.39
8	663.81	59.75	76.64	136.39
9	597.14	66.67	69.72	136.39
10	522.76	74.38	62.01	136.39
11	439.77	82.99	53.40	136.39
12	347.17	92.59	43.80	136.39
13	243.86	103.31	33.08	136.39
14	128.60	115.26	21.13	136.39
15	.00	128.60	7.69	136.29
Totals:		**$1000.00**	**$1045.77**	**$2045.77**

TAX-SAVINGS TABLE

11.00%
INTEREST

Multiply all figures by the number of thousands in your loan.
Net cost equals yearly payment minus tax savings.

Federal Tax Bracket					
15.0%		28.0%		33.0%	
Tax Savings	Net Cost	Tax Savings	Net Cost	Tax Savings	Net Cost
$16.29	$120.10	$30.42	$105.98	$35.85	$100.54
15.81	120.58	29.52	106.88	34.79	101.60
15.27	121.12	28.51	107.88	33.60	102.79
14.67	121.72	27.39	109.00	32.28	104.11
14.01	122.39	26.14	110.25	30.81	105.58
13.26	123.13	24.75	111.64	29.17	107.22
12.43	123.97	23.19	113.20	27.34	109.06
11.50	124.90	21.46	114.93	25.29	111.10
10.46	125.93	19.52	116.87	23.01	113.38
9.30	127.09	17.36	119.03	20.46	115.93
8.01	128.38	14.95	121.44	17.62	118.77
6.57	129.82	12.26	124.13	14.45	121.94
4.96	131.43	9.26	127.13	10.92	125.47
3.17	133.22	5.92	130.48	6.97	129.42
1.15	135.14	2.15	134.14	2.54	133.75
Totals:					
$156.87	**$1888.91**	**$292.82**	**$1752.96**	**$345.10**	**$1700.67**

11.00% INTEREST	**ANNUAL MORTGAGE PAYMENT SCHEDULE**

For a mortgage of $1,000.00

MORTGAGE TERM: **30 years**
Monthly payment: **$9.52**
Annual payment: **$114.28**

Year	Balance of Loan	Principal Paid	Interest Paid	Yearly Payment
1	$995.50	$4.50	$109.78	$114.28
2	990.48	5.02	109.26	114.28
3	984.87	5.60	108.68	114.28
4	978.62	6.25	108.03	114.28
5	971.65	6.98	107.30	114.28
6	963.86	7.78	106.50	114.28
7	955.18	8.68	105.60	114.28
8	945.49	9.69	104.59	114.28
9	934.68	10.81	103.47	114.28
10	922.63	12.06	102.22	114.28
11	909.17	13.45	100.82	114.28
12	894.16	15.01	99.27	114.28
13	877.41	16.75	97.53	114.28
14	858.72	18.69	95.59	114.28
15	837.87	20.85	93.43	114.28
16	814.61	23.26	91.02	114.28
17	788.66	25.95	88.32	114.28
18	759.70	28.96	85.32	114.28
19	727.39	32.31	81.97	114.28
20	691.34	36.05	78.23	114.28
21	651.12	40.22	74.06	114.28
22	606.25	44.87	69.41	114.28
23	556.18	50.07	64.21	114.28
24	500.33	55.86	58.42	114.28
25	438.00	62.32	51.96	114.28
26	368.47	69.53	44.74	114.28
27	290.89	77.58	36.70	114.28
28	204.33	86.56	27.72	114.28
29	107.75	96.58	17.70	114.28
30	.00	107.75	6.44	114.19
Totals:		**$1000.00**	**$2428.28**	**$3428.28**

TAX-SAVINGS TABLE

11.00% INTEREST

Multiply all figures by the number of thousands in your loan.
Net cost equals yearly payment minus tax savings.

| Federal Tax Bracket | | | | | |
| 15.0% | | 28.0% | | 33.0% | |
Tax Savings	Net Cost	Tax Savings	Net Cost	Tax Savings	Net Cost
$16.47	$97.81	$30.74	$83.54	$36.23	$78.05
16.39	97.89	30.59	83.69	36.05	78.22
16.30	97.98	30.43	83.85	35.86	78.42
16.20	98.07	30.25	84.03	35.65	78.63
16.10	98.18	30.05	84.23	35.41	78.87
15.97	98.30	29.82	84.46	35.14	79.13
15.84	98.44	29.57	84.71	34.85	79.43
15.69	98.59	29.29	84.99	34.52	79.76
15.52	98.76	28.97	85.31	34.15	80.13
15.33	98.95	28.62	85.66	33.73	80.55
15.12	99.16	28.23	86.05	33.27	81.01
14.89	99.39	27.79	86.48	32.76	81.52
14.63	99.65	27.31	86.97	32.18	82.09
14.34	99.94	26.77	87.51	31.55	82.73
14.01	100.26	26.16	88.12	30.83	83.45
13.65	100.63	25.48	88.79	30.04	84.24
13.25	101.03	24.73	89.55	29.15	85.13
12.80	101.48	23.89	90.39	28.16	86.12
12.30	101.98	22.95	91.33	27.05	87.23
11.73	102.54	21.90	92.37	25.82	88.46
11.11	103.17	20.74	93.54	24.44	89.84
10.41	103.87	19.43	94.85	22.90	91.37
9.63	104.65	17.98	96.30	21.19	93.09
8.76	105.52	16.36	97.92	19.28	95.00
7.79	106.49	14.55	99.73	17.15	97.13
6.71	107.57	12.53	101.75	14.77	99.51
5.50	108.77	10.28	104.00	12.11	102.17
4.16	110.12	7.76	106.52	9.15	105.13
2.66	111.62	4.96	109.32	5.84	108.44
.97	113.23	1.80	112.39	2.13	112.07
Totals:					
$364.24	**$3064.04**	**$679.92**	**$2748.36**	**$801.33**	**$2626.95**

11.25% INTEREST	**ANNUAL MORTGAGE PAYMENT SCHEDULE**

For a mortgage of $1,000.00

MORTGAGE TERM: **15 years**
Monthly payment: **$11.52**
Annual payment: **$138.28**

Year	Balance of Loan	Principal Paid	Interest Paid	Yearly Payment
1	$972.85	$27.15	$111.13	$138.28
2	942.48	30.37	107.91	138.28
3	908.51	33.97	104.31	138.28
4	870.51	37.99	100.29	138.28
5	828.02	42.50	95.79	138.28
6	780.49	47.53	90.75	138.28
7	727.33	53.16	85.12	138.28
8	667.86	59.46	78.82	138.28
9	601.36	66.51	71.77	138.28
10	526.97	74.39	63.89	138.28
11	443.77	83.20	55.08	138.28
12	350.71	93.06	45.22	138.28
13	246.63	104.08	34.20	138.28
14	130.21	116.42	21.86	138.28
15	.00	130.21	7.96	138.17
Totals:		**$1000.00**	**$1074.11**	**$2074.11**

TAX-SAVINGS TABLE

Multiply all figures by the number of thousands in your loan.
Net cost equals yearly payment minus tax savings.

Federal Tax Bracket					
15.0%		28.0%		33.0%	
Tax Savings	Net Cost	Tax Savings	Net Cost	Tax Savings	Net Cost
$16.67	$121.61	$31.12	$107.17	$36.67	$101.61
16.19	122.09	30.22	108.07	35.61	102.67
15.65	122.63	29.21	109.07	34.42	103.86
15.04	123.24	28.08	110.20	33.09	105.19
14.37	123.91	26.82	111.46	31.61	106.67
13.61	124.67	25.41	112.87	29.95	108.33
12.77	125.51	23.83	114.45	28.09	110.19
11.82	126.46	22.07	116.21	26.01	112.27
10.77	127.52	20.10	118.18	23.69	114.60
9.58	128.70	17.89	120.39	21.09	117.20
8.26	130.02	15.42	122.86	18.18	120.10
6.78	131.50	12.66	125.62	14.92	123.36
5.13	133.15	9.58	128.71	11.28	127.00
3.28	135.00	6.12	132.16	7.22	131.07
1.19	136.98	2.23	135.94	2.63	135.55
Totals:					
$161.12	**$1913.00**	**$300.75**	**$1773.36**	**$354.46**	**$1719.66**

ANNUAL MORTGAGE PAYMENT SCHEDULE

For a mortgage of $1,000.00

	MORTGAGE TERM:	30 years
	Monthly payment:	$9.71
	Annual payment:	$116.55

Year	Balance of Loan	Principal Paid	Interest Paid	Yearly Payment
1	$995.73	$4.27	$112.28	$116.55
2	990.96	4.77	111.78	116.55
3	985.62	5.34	111.21	116.55
4	979.65	5.97	110.58	116.55
5	972.97	6.68	109.87	116.55
6	965.51	7.47	109.08	116.55
7	957.15	8.35	108.20	116.55
8	947.81	9.34	107.21	116.55
9	937.36	10.45	106.10	116.55
10	925.67	11.69	104.86	116.55
11	912.59	13.07	103.48	116.55
12	897.97	14.62	101.93	116.55
13	881.61	16.36	100.20	116.55
14	863.32	18.29	98.26	116.55
15	842.86	20.46	96.09	116.55
16	819.97	22.89	93.67	116.55
17	794.37	25.60	90.95	116.55
18	765.74	28.63	87.92	116.55
19	733.72	32.02	84.53	116.55
20	697.90	35.82	80.73	116.55
21	657.84	40.06	76.49	116.55
22	613.03	44.81	71.74	116.55
23	562.91	50.12	66.43	116.55
24	506.86	56.06	60.50	116.55
25	444.16	62.70	53.85	116.55
26	374.04	70.13	46.43	116.55
27	295.60	78.43	38.12	116.55
28	207.87	87.73	28.82	116.55
29	109.75	98.12	18.43	116.55
30	.00	109.75	6.71	116.46
Totals:		**$1000.00**	**$2496.45**	**$3496.45**

TAX-SAVINGS TABLE

11.25% INTEREST

Multiply all figures by the number of thousands in your loan.
Net cost equals yearly payment minus tax savings.

| Federal Tax Bracket | | | | | |
| 15.0% | | 28.0% | | 33.0% | |
Tax Savings	Net Cost	Tax Savings	Net Cost	Tax Savings	Net Cost
$16.84	$99.71	$31.44	$85.11	$37.05	$79.50
16.77	99.78	31.30	85.25	36.89	79.66
16.68	99.87	31.14	85.41	36.70	79.85
16.59	99.96	30.96	85.59	36.49	80.06
16.48	100.07	30.76	85.79	36.26	80.29
16.36	100.19	30.54	86.01	36.00	80.55
16.23	100.32	30.30	86.26	35.71	80.85
16.08	100.47	30.02	86.53	35.38	81.17
15.92	100.64	29.71	86.84	35.01	81.54
15.73	100.82	29.36	87.19	34.60	81.95
15.52	101.03	28.97	87.58	34.15	82.40
15.29	101.26	28.54	88.01	33.64	82.92
15.03	101.52	28.05	88.50	33.06	83.49
14.74	101.81	27.51	89.04	32.42	84.13
14.41	102.14	26.91	89.65	31.71	84.84
14.05	102.50	26.23	90.33	30.91	85.64
13.64	102.91	25.47	91.08	30.01	86.54
13.19	103.36	24.62	91.93	29.01	87.54
12.68	103.87	23.67	92.88	27.89	88.66
12.11	104.44	22.61	93.95	26.64	89.91
11.47	105.08	21.42	95.13	25.24	91.31
10.76	105.79	20.09	96.46	23.68	92.88
9.97	106.59	18.60	97.95	21.92	94.63
9.07	107.48	16.94	99.61	19.96	96.59
8.08	108.47	15.08	101.47	17.77	98.78
6.96	109.59	13.00	103.55	15.32	101.23
5.72	110.83	10.67	105.88	12.58	103.97
4.32	112.23	8.07	108.48	9.51	107.04
2.76	113.79	5.16	111.39	6.08	110.47
1.01	115.45	1.88	114.58	2.21	114.25
Totals:					
$374.47	**$3121.98**	**$699.01**	**$2797.44**	**$823.83**	**$2672.62**

11.50% INTEREST	**ANNUAL MORTGAGE PAYMENT SCHEDULE**

For a mortgage of $1,000.00

MORTGAGE TERM: **15 years**
Monthly payment: **$11.68**
Annual payment: **$140.18**

Year	Balance of Loan	Principal Paid	Interest Paid	Yearly Payment
1	$973.45	$26.55	$113.63	$140.18
2	943.67	29.77	110.41	140.18
3	910.29	33.38	106.80	140.18
4	872.86	37.43	102.75	140.18
5	830.89	41.97	98.21	140.18
6	783.83	47.06	93.12	140.18
7	731.06	52.77	87.42	140.18
8	671.90	59.16	81.02	140.18
9	605.56	66.34	73.84	140.18
10	531.17	74.38	65.80	140.18
11	447.77	83.40	56.78	140.18
12	354.25	93.52	46.67	140.18
13	249.40	104.86	35.33	140.18
14	131.83	117.57	22.61	140.18
15	.00	131.83	8.24	140.07
Totals:		**$1000.00**	**$1102.63**	**$2102.63**

TAX-SAVINGS TABLE

11.50% INTEREST

Multiply all figures by the number of thousands in your loan.
Net cost equals yearly payment minus tax savings.

Federal Tax Bracket					
15.0%		28.0%		33.0%	
Tax Savings	Net Cost	Tax Savings	Net Cost	Tax Savings	Net Cost
$17.04	$123.14	$31.82	$108.37	$37.50	$102.69
16.56	123.62	30.91	109.27	36.44	103.75
16.02	124.16	29.90	110.28	35.24	104.94
15.41	124.77	28.77	111.41	33.91	106.27
14.73	125.45	27.50	112.68	32.41	107.77
13.97	126.21	26.07	114.11	30.73	109.45
13.11	127.07	24.48	115.71	28.85	111.34
12.15	128.03	22.69	117.50	26.74	113.45
11.08	129.11	20.68	119.51	24.37	115.81
9.87	130.31	18.42	121.76	21.71	118.47
8.52	131.67	15.90	124.28	18.74	121.45
7.00	133.18	13.07	127.12	15.40	124.78
5.30	134.88	9.89	130.29	11.66	128.52
3.39	136.79	6.33	133.85	7.46	132.72
1.24	138.84	2.31	137.76	2.72	137.35
Totals:					
$165.39	**$1937.24**	**$308.74**	**$1793.89**	**$363.87**	**$1738.76**

| | 11.50% INTEREST | **ANNUAL MORTGAGE PAYMENT SCHEDULE** |

ANNUAL MORTGAGE PAYMENT SCHEDULE

For a mortgage of $1,000.00

MORTGAGE TERM: 30 years
Monthly payment: $9.90
Annual payment: $118.83

Year	Balance of Loan	Principal Paid	Interest Paid	Yearly Payment
1	$995.96	$4.04	$114.79	$118.83
2	991.42	4.53	114.30	118.83
3	986.34	5.08	113.75	118.83
4	980.64	5.70	113.13	118.83
5	974.25	6.39	112.44	118.83
6	967.08	7.17	111.67	118.83
7	959.04	8.04	110.80	118.83
8	950.03	9.01	109.83	118.83
9	939.93	10.10	108.73	118.83
10	928.60	11.33	107.51	118.83
11	915.90	12.70	106.13	118.83
12	901.66	14.24	104.59	118.83
13	885.69	15.97	102.87	118.83
14	867.79	17.90	100.93	118.83
15	847.71	20.08	98.76	118.83
16	825.20	22.51	96.33	118.83
17	799.97	25.24	93.60	118.83
18	771.67	28.30	90.54	118.83
19	739.93	31.73	87.10	118.83
20	704.36	35.58	83.26	118.83
21	664.46	39.89	78.94	118.83
22	619.73	44.73	74.10	118.83
23	569.58	50.15	68.68	118.83
24	513.34	56.24	62.60	118.83
25	450.28	63.06	55.78	118.83
26	379.58	70.70	48.13	118.83
27	300.31	79.28	39.56	118.83
28	211.42	88.89	29.95	118.83
29	111.75	99.67	19.17	118.83
30	.00	111.75	6.99	118.74
Totals:		**$1000.00**	**$2564.96**	**$3564.96**

TAX-SAVINGS TABLE

11.50% INTEREST

Multiply all figures by the number of thousands in your loan.
Net cost equals yearly payment minus tax savings.

Federal Tax Bracket					
15.0%		28.0%		33.0%	
Tax Savings	Net Cost	Tax Savings	Net Cost	Tax Savings	Net Cost
$17.22	$101.62	$32.14	$86.69	$37.88	$80.95
17.15	101.69	32.00	86.83	37.72	81.12
17.06	101.77	31.85	86.98	37.54	81.30
16.97	101.86	31.68	87.16	37.33	81.50
16.87	101.97	31.48	87.35	37.11	81.73
16.75	102.08	31.27	87.57	36.85	81.98
16.62	102.22	31.02	87.81	36.56	82.27
16.47	102.36	30.75	88.08	36.24	82.59
16.31	102.53	30.45	88.39	35.88	82.95
16.13	102.71	30.10	88.73	35.48	83.36
15.92	102.91	29.72	89.12	35.02	83.81
15.69	103.15	29.29	89.55	34.52	84.32
15.43	103.40	28.80	90.03	33.95	84.89
15.14	103.70	28.26	90.57	33.31	85.53
14.81	104.02	27.65	91.18	32.59	86.24
14.45	104.39	26.97	91.86	31.79	87.05
14.04	104.80	26.21	92.63	30.89	87.95
13.58	105.25	25.35	93.49	29.88	88.96
13.07	105.77	24.39	94.45	28.74	90.09
12.49	106.35	23.31	95.52	27.47	91.36
11.84	106.99	22.10	96.73	26.05	92.78
11.12	107.72	20.75	98.09	24.45	94.38
10.30	108.53	19.23	99.60	22.66	96.17
9.39	109.45	17.53	101.31	20.66	98.18
8.37	110.47	15.62	103.22	18.41	100.43
7.22	111.62	13.48	105.36	15.88	102.95
5.93	112.90	11.08	107.76	13.05	105.78
4.49	114.34	8.39	110.45	9.88	108.95
2.88	115.96	5.37	113.47	6.33	112.51
1.05	117.69	1.96	116.78	2.31	116.43
Totals:					
$384.74	**$3180.21**	**$718.19**	**$2846.77**	**$846.44**	**$2718.52**

11.75% INTEREST	ANNUAL MORTGAGE PAYMENT SCHEDULE

For a mortgage of $1,000.00

MORTGAGE TERM: 15 years
Monthly payment: $11.84
Annual payment: $142.10

Year	Balance of Loan	Principal Paid	Interest Paid	Yearly Payment
1	$974.04	$25.96	$116.13	$142.10
2	944.85	29.19	112.91	142.10
3	912.05	32.81	109.29	142.10
4	875.17	36.87	105.22	142.10
5	833.72	41.45	100.65	142.10
6	787.13	46.59	95.51	142.10
7	734.76	52.37	89.73	142.10
8	675.90	58.86	83.23	142.10
9	609.73	66.17	75.93	142.10
10	535.36	74.37	67.72	142.10
11	451.76	83.60	58.50	142.10
12	357.80	93.97	48.13	142.10
13	252.17	105.62	36.47	142.10
14	133.45	118.72	23.37	142.10
15	.00	133.45	8.53	141.98
Totals:		$1000.00	$1131.32	$2131.32

TAX-SAVINGS TABLE

11.75% INTEREST

Multiply all figures by the number of thousands in your loan.
Net cost equals yearly payment minus tax savings.

| Federal Tax Bracket | | | | | |
| 15.0% | | 28.0% | | 33.0% | |
Tax Savings	Net Cost	Tax Savings	Net Cost	Tax Savings	Net Cost
$17.42	$124.68	$32.52	$109.58	$38.32	$103.77
16.94	125.16	31.61	110.48	37.26	104.84
16.39	125.70	30.60	111.49	36.07	106.03
15.78	126.31	29.46	112.63	34.72	107.37
15.10	127.00	28.18	113.91	33.21	108.88
14.33	127.77	26.74	115.35	31.52	110.58
13.46	128.64	25.12	116.97	29.61	112.49
12.48	129.61	23.30	118.79	27.47	114.63
11.39	130.71	21.26	120.84	25.06	117.04
10.16	131.94	18.96	123.13	22.35	119.75
8.77	133.32	16.38	125.72	19.30	122.79
7.22	134.88	13.48	128.62	15.88	126.21
5.47	136.62	10.21	131.88	12.04	130.06
3.51	138.59	6.54	135.55	7.71	134.38
1.28	140.70	2.39	139.59	2.82	139.17
Totals:					
$169.70	**$1961.62**	**$316.77**	**$1814.55**	**$373.34**	**$1757.99**

11.75% INTEREST	ANNUAL MORTGAGE PAYMENT SCHEDULE

For a mortgage of $1,000.00

MORTGAGE TERM: 30 years
Monthly payment: $10.09
Annual payment: $121.13

Year	Balance of Loan	Principal Paid	Interest Paid	Yearly Payment
1	$996.17	$3.83	$117.30	$121.13
2	991.86	4.31	116.82	121.13
3	987.02	4.84	116.29	121.13
4	981.58	5.44	115.69	121.13
5	975.47	6.12	115.01	121.13
6	968.59	6.87	114.25	121.13
7	960.86	7.73	113.40	121.13
8	952.18	8.69	112.44	121.13
9	942.42	9.76	111.37	121.13
10	931.44	10.97	110.16	121.13
11	919.11	12.34	108.79	121.13
12	905.24	13.87	107.26	121.13
13	889.66	15.58	105.54	121.13
14	872.14	17.52	103.61	121.13
15	852.45	19.69	101.44	121.13
16	830.31	22.13	99.00	121.13
17	805.44	24.88	96.25	121.13
18	777.47	27.96	93.16	121.13
19	746.04	31.43	89.70	121.13
20	710.70	35.33	85.80	121.13
21	670.99	39.72	81.41	121.13
22	626.35	44.64	76.49	121.13
23	576.17	50.18	70.95	121.13
24	519.77	56.40	64.73	121.13
25	456.37	63.40	57.73	121.13
26	385.11	71.26	49.87	121.13
27	305.00	80.10	41.03	121.13
28	214.97	90.04	31.09	121.13
29	113.76	101.21	19.92	121.13
30	.00	113.76	7.27	121.03
Totals:		$1000.00	$2633.78	$3633.78

TAX-SAVINGS TABLE

11.75%
INTEREST

Multiply all figures by the number of thousands in your loan.
Net cost equals yearly payment minus tax savings.

Federal Tax Bracket					
15.0%		28.0%		33.0%	
Tax Savings	Net Cost	Tax Savings	Net Cost	Tax Savings	Net Cost
$17.59	$103.53	$32.84	$88.29	$38.71	$82.42
17.52	103.61	32.71	88.42	38.55	82.58
17.44	103.69	32.56	88.57	38.38	82.75
17.35	103.78	32.39	88.74	38.18	82.95
17.25	103.88	32.20	88.93	37.95	83.17
17.14	103.99	31.99	89.14	37.70	83.43
17.01	104.12	31.75	89.38	37.42	83.71
16.87	104.26	31.48	89.64	37.11	84.02
16.70	104.42	31.18	89.95	36.75	84.38
16.52	104.61	30.84	90.29	36.35	84.78
16.32	104.81	30.46	90.67	35.90	85.23
16.09	105.04	30.03	91.10	35.40	85.73
15.83	105.30	29.55	91.58	34.83	86.30
15.54	105.59	29.01	92.12	34.19	86.94
15.22	105.91	28.40	92.73	33.47	87.65
14.85	106.28	27.72	93.41	32.67	88.46
14.44	106.69	26.95	94.18	31.76	89.37
13.97	107.15	26.09	95.04	30.74	90.38
13.45	107.67	25.11	96.01	29.60	91.53
12.87	108.26	24.02	97.11	28.31	92.82
12.21	108.92	22.80	98.33	26.87	94.26
11.47	109.66	21.42	99.71	25.24	95.89
10.64	110.49	19.87	101.26	23.41	97.72
9.71	111.42	18.12	103.01	21.36	99.77
8.66	112.47	16.16	104.96	19.05	102.08
7.48	113.65	13.96	107.17	16.46	104.67
6.15	114.98	11.49	109.64	13.54	107.59
4.66	116.47	8.71	112.42	10.26	110.87
2.99	118.14	5.58	115.55	6.57	114.55
1.09	119.94	2.04	119.00	2.40	118.63
Totals:					
$395.07	**$3238.71**	**$737.46**	**$2896.32**	**$869.15**	**$2764.63**

12.00% INTEREST	ANNUAL MORTGAGE PAYMENT SCHEDULE

For a mortgage of $1,000.00

MORTGAGE TERM: 15 years
Monthly payment: $12.00
Annual payment: $144.02

Year	Balance of Loan	Principal Paid	Interest Paid	Yearly Payment
1	$974.61	$25.39	$118.63	$144.02
2	946.01	28.61	115.41	144.02
3	913.77	32.23	111.79	144.02
4	877.45	36.32	107.70	144.02
5	836.52	40.93	103.09	144.02
6	790.40	46.12	97.90	144.02
7	738.44	51.97	92.05	144.02
8	679.88	58.56	85.46	144.02
9	613.89	65.99	78.03	144.02
10	539.54	74.35	69.67	144.02
11	455.75	83.78	60.24	144.02
12	361.34	94.41	49.61	144.02
13	254.96	106.38	37.64	144.02
14	135.08	119.88	24.14	144.02
15	.00	135.08	8.82	143.90
Totals:		$1000.00	$1160.18	$2160.18

TAX-SAVINGS TABLE

12.00%
INTEREST

Multiply all figures by the number of thousands in your loan.
Net cost equals yearly payment minus tax savings.

| Federal Tax Bracket | | | | | |
| 15.0% | | 28.0% | | 33.0% | |
Tax Savings	Net Cost	Tax Savings	Net Cost	Tax Savings	Net Cost
$17.80	$126.23	$33.22	$110.80	$39.15	$104.87
17.31	126.71	32.32	111.70	38.09	105.93
16.77	127.25	31.30	112.72	36.89	107.13
16.15	127.87	30.16	113.86	35.54	108.48
15.46	128.56	28.87	115.15	34.02	110.00
14.69	129.34	27.41	116.61	32.31	111.71
13.81	130.21	25.77	118.25	30.38	113.64
12.82	131.20	23.93	120.09	28.20	115.82
11.71	132.32	21.85	122.17	25.75	118.27
10.45	133.57	19.51	124.51	22.99	121.03
9.04	134.98	16.87	127.15	19.88	124.14
7.44	136.58	13.89	130.13	16.37	127.65
5.65	138.37	10.54	133.48	12.42	131.60
3.62	140.40	6.76	137.26	7.97	136.05
1.32	142.58	2.47	141.43	2.91	140.99
Totals:					
$174.03	**$1986.16**	**$324.85**	**$1835.33**	**$382.86**	**$1777.32**

<table>
<tr><td colspan="2">**12.00%** INTEREST</td><td colspan="3">**ANNUAL MORTGAGE PAYMENT SCHEDULE**</td></tr>
</table>

12.00% INTEREST

ANNUAL MORTGAGE PAYMENT SCHEDULE

For a mortgage of $1,000.00

MORTGAGE TERM: **30 years**
Monthly payment: **$10.29**
Annual payment: **$123.43**

Year	Balance of Loan	Principal Paid	Interest Paid	Yearly Payment
1	$996.37	$3.63	$119.80	$123.43
2	992.28	4.09	119.34	123.43
3	987.67	4.61	118.83	123.43
4	982.48	5.19	118.24	123.43
5	976.63	5.85	117.58	123.43
6	970.04	6.59	116.84	123.43
7	962.61	7.43	116.01	123.43
8	954.24	8.37	115.06	123.43
9	944.81	9.43	114.00	123.43
10	934.18	10.63	112.81	123.43
11	922.20	11.98	111.46	123.43
12	908.71	13.50	109.94	123.43
13	893.50	15.21	108.23	123.43
14	876.37	17.14	106.30	123.43
15	857.06	19.31	104.12	123.43
16	835.30	21.76	101.68	123.43
17	810.78	24.52	98.92	123.43
18	783.16	27.63	95.81	123.43
19	752.03	31.13	92.30	123.43
20	716.95	35.08	88.36	123.43
21	677.42	39.53	83.91	123.43
22	632.88	44.54	78.89	123.43
23	582.69	50.19	73.24	123.43
24	526.14	56.55	66.88	123.43
25	462.41	63.73	59.71	123.43
26	390.60	71.81	51.63	123.43
27	309.69	80.92	42.52	123.43
28	218.51	91.18	32.26	123.43
29	115.77	102.74	20.69	123.43
30	.00	115.77	7.56	123.33
Totals:		**$1000.00**	**$2702.90**	**$3702.90**

TAX-SAVINGS TABLE

12.00% INTEREST

Multiply all figures by the number of thousands in your loan.
Net cost equals yearly payment minus tax savings.

| Federal Tax Bracket | | | | | |
| 15.0% | | 28.0% | | 33.0% | |
Tax Savings	Net Cost	Tax Savings	Net Cost	Tax Savings	Net Cost
$17.97	$105.46	$33.55	$89.89	$39.54	$83.90
17.90	105.53	33.42	90.02	39.38	84.05
17.82	105.61	33.27	90.16	39.21	84.22
17.74	105.70	33.11	90.33	39.02	84.41
17.64	105.80	32.92	90.51	38.80	84.63
17.53	105.91	32.72	90.72	38.56	84.88
17.40	106.03	32.48	90.95	38.28	85.15
17.26	106.17	32.22	91.22	37.97	85.46
17.10	106.33	31.92	91.51	37.62	85.81
16.92	106.51	31.59	91.85	37.23	86.21
16.72	106.71	31.21	92.23	36.78	86.65
16.49	106.94	30.78	92.65	36.28	87.15
16.23	107.20	30.30	93.13	35.71	87.72
15.94	107.49	29.76	93.67	35.08	88.36
15.62	107.81	29.15	94.28	34.36	89.07
15.25	108.18	28.47	94.96	33.55	89.88
14.84	108.60	27.70	95.74	32.64	90.79
14.37	109.06	26.83	96.61	31.62	91.82
13.85	109.59	25.84	97.59	30.46	92.97
13.25	110.18	24.74	98.69	29.16	94.28
12.59	110.85	23.49	99.94	27.69	95.74
11.83	111.60	22.09	101.34	26.03	97.40
10.99	112.45	20.51	102.92	24.17	99.26
10.03	113.40	18.73	104.71	22.07	101.36
8.96	114.48	16.72	106.72	19.70	103.73
7.74	115.69	14.46	108.98	17.04	106.40
6.38	117.06	11.91	111.53	14.03	109.40
4.84	118.60	9.03	114.40	10.64	112.79
3.10	120.33	5.79	117.64	6.83	116.60
1.13	122.20	2.12	121.21	2.49	120.84
Totals:					
$405.44	**$3297.47**	**$756.81**	**$2946.09**	**$891.96**	**$2810.95**

| | 12.25% INTEREST | **ANNUAL MORTGAGE PAYMENT SCHEDULE** |

12.25% INTEREST

ANNUAL MORTGAGE PAYMENT SCHEDULE

For a mortgage of $1,000.00

MORTGAGE TERM: **15 years**
Monthly payment: **$12.16**
Annual payment: **$145.96**

Year	Balance of Loan	Principal Paid	Interest Paid	Yearly Payment
1	$975.18	$24.82	$121.14	$145.96
2	947.15	28.04	117.92	145.96
3	915.48	31.67	114.29	145.96
4	879.70	35.77	110.18	145.96
5	839.29	40.41	105.54	145.96
6	793.64	45.65	100.31	145.96
7	742.07	51.57	94.39	145.96
8	683.82	58.25	87.71	145.96
9	618.02	65.80	80.16	145.96
10	543.69	74.33	71.63	145.96
11	459.73	83.96	61.99	145.96
12	364.88	94.85	51.11	145.96
13	257.74	107.14	38.82	145.96
14	136.72	121.03	24.93	145.96
15	.00	136.72	9.12	145.83
Totals:		**$1000.00**	**$1189.21**	**$2189.21**

TAX-SAVINGS TABLE

12.25% INTEREST

Multiply all figures by the number of thousands in your loan.
Net cost equals yearly payment minus tax savings.

Federal Tax Bracket					
15.0%		28.0%		33.0%	
Tax Savings	Net Cost	Tax Savings	Net Cost	Tax Savings	Net Cost
$18.17	$127.79	$33.92	$112.04	$39.98	$105.98
17.69	128.27	33.02	112.94	38.91	107.04
17.14	128.81	32.00	113.96	37.71	108.24
16.53	129.43	30.85	115.11	36.36	109.60
15.83	130.12	29.55	116.40	34.83	111.13
15.05	130.91	28.09	117.87	33.10	112.85
14.16	131.80	26.43	119.53	31.15	114.81
13.16	132.80	24.56	121.40	28.94	117.01
12.02	133.93	22.44	123.51	26.45	119.50
10.74	135.21	20.06	125.90	23.64	122.32
9.30	136.66	17.36	128.60	20.46	125.50
7.67	138.29	14.31	131.65	16.87	129.09
5.82	140.13	10.87	135.09	12.81	133.15
3.74	142.22	6.98	138.98	8.23	137.73
1.37	144.47	2.55	143.28	3.01	142.82
Totals:					
$178.38	**$2010.83**	**$332.98**	**$1856.23**	**$392.44**	**$1796.77**

ANNUAL MORTGAGE PAYMENT SCHEDULE

For a mortgage of $1,000.00

MORTGAGE TERM:	30 years
Monthly payment:	$10.48
Annual payment:	$125.75

Year	Balance of Loan	Principal Paid	Interest Paid	Yearly Payment
1	$996.56	$3.44	$122.31	$125.75
2	992.68	3.88	121.87	125.75
3	988.30	4.38	121.36	125.75
4	983.34	4.95	120.79	125.75
5	977.75	5.60	120.15	125.75
6	971.43	6.32	119.43	125.75
7	964.29	7.14	118.61	125.75
8	956.22	8.07	117.68	125.75
9	947.11	9.11	116.64	125.75
10	936.82	10.29	115.46	125.75
11	925.20	11.63	114.12	125.75
12	912.07	13.13	112.62	125.75
13	897.23	14.83	110.91	125.75
14	880.47	16.76	108.99	125.75
15	861.55	18.93	106.82	125.75
16	840.16	21.38	104.37	125.75
17	816.01	24.15	101.59	125.75
18	788.72	27.28	98.46	125.75
19	757.90	30.82	94.93	125.75
20	723.09	34.82	90.93	125.75
21	683.76	39.33	86.42	125.75
22	639.33	44.43	81.32	125.75
23	589.15	50.19	75.56	125.75
24	532.46	56.69	69.06	125.75
25	468.42	64.04	61.71	125.75
26	396.08	72.34	53.41	125.75
27	314.36	81.71	44.03	125.75
28	222.06	92.31	33.44	125.75
29	117.79	104.27	21.48	125.75
30	.00	117.79	7.86	125.64
Totals:		**$1000.00**	**$2772.32**	**$3772.32**

TAX-SAVINGS TABLE

12.25% INTEREST

Multiply all figures by the number of thousands in your loan.
Net cost equals yearly payment minus tax savings.

Federal Tax Bracket					
15.0%		28.0%		33.0%	
Tax Savings	Net Cost	Tax Savings	Net Cost	Tax Savings	Net Cost
$18.35	$107.40	$34.25	$91.50	$40.36	$85.38
18.28	107.47	34.12	91.63	40.22	85.53
18.20	107.54	33.98	91.77	40.05	85.70
18.12	107.63	33.82	91.93	39.86	85.89
18.02	107.72	33.64	92.10	39.65	86.10
17.91	107.83	33.44	92.31	39.41	86.34
17.79	107.96	33.21	92.54	39.14	86.61
17.65	108.10	32.95	92.80	38.84	86.91
17.50	108.25	32.66	93.09	38.49	87.26
17.32	108.43	32.33	93.42	38.10	87.65
17.12	108.63	31.95	93.79	37.66	88.09
16.89	108.86	31.53	94.22	37.16	88.58
16.64	109.11	31.06	94.69	36.60	89.15
16.35	109.40	30.52	95.23	35.97	89.78
16.02	109.72	29.91	95.84	35.25	90.50
15.65	110.09	29.22	96.53	34.44	91.31
15.24	110.51	28.45	97.30	33.53	92.22
14.77	110.98	27.57	98.18	32.49	93.25
14.24	111.51	26.58	99.17	31.33	94.42
13.64	112.11	25.46	100.29	30.01	95.74
12.96	112.78	24.20	101.55	28.52	97.23
12.20	113.55	22.77	102.98	26.84	98.91
11.33	114.41	21.16	104.59	24.94	100.81
10.36	115.39	19.34	106.41	22.79	102.96
9.26	116.49	17.28	108.47	20.36	105.38
8.01	117.74	14.95	110.79	17.62	108.12
6.60	119.14	12.33	113.42	14.53	111.22
5.02	120.73	9.36	116.38	11.04	114.71
3.22	122.53	6.01	119.73	7.09	118.66
1.18	124.46	2.20	123.44	2.59	123.05
Totals:					
$415.85	**$3356.47**	**$776.25**	**$2996.07**	**$914.87**	**$2857.46**

12.50% INTEREST	**ANNUAL MORTGAGE PAYMENT SCHEDULE**

For a mortgage of $1,000.00

MORTGAGE TERM: **15 years**
Monthly payment: **$12.33**
Annual payment: **$147.90**

Year	Balance of Loan	Principal Paid	Interest Paid	Yearly Payment
1	$975.74	$24.26	$123.64	$147.90
2	948.26	27.47	120.43	147.90
3	917.15	31.11	116.79	147.90
4	881.92	35.23	112.67	147.90
5	842.02	39.90	108.01	147.90
6	796.84	45.18	102.72	147.90
7	745.68	51.16	96.74	147.90
8	687.74	57.94	89.97	147.90
9	622.13	65.61	82.29	147.90
10	547.84	74.30	73.61	147.90
11	463.70	84.13	63.77	147.90
12	368.43	95.28	52.63	147.90
13	260.54	107.89	40.01	147.90
14	138.36	122.18	25.72	147.90
15	.00	138.36	9.42	147.78
Totals:		**$1000.00**	**$1218.41**	**$2218.41**

TAX-SAVINGS TABLE

12.50% INTEREST

Multiply all figures by the number of thousands in your loan.
Net cost equals yearly payment minus tax savings.

Federal Tax Bracket					
15.0%		28.0%		33.0%	
Tax Savings	Net Cost	Tax Savings	Net Cost	Tax Savings	Net Cost
$18.55	$129.36	$34.62	$113.28	$40.80	$107.10
18.06	129.84	33.72	114.18	39.74	108.16
17.52	130.38	32.70	115.20	38.54	109.36
16.90	131.00	31.55	116.35	37.18	110.72
16.20	131.70	30.24	117.66	35.64	112.26
15.41	132.49	28.76	119.14	33.90	114.00
14.51	133.39	27.09	120.82	31.92	115.98
13.49	134.41	25.19	122.71	29.69	118.21
12.34	135.56	23.04	124.86	27.16	120.75
11.04	136.86	20.61	127.29	24.29	123.61
9.57	138.34	17.85	130.05	21.04	126.86
7.89	140.01	14.74	133.17	17.37	130.54
6.00	141.90	11.20	136.70	13.20	134.70
3.86	144.04	7.20	140.70	8.49	139.41
1.41	146.36	2.64	145.14	3.11	144.67
Totals:					
$182.76	**$2035.65**	**$341.16**	**$1877.26**	**$402.08**	**$1816.34**

12.50% INTEREST	**ANNUAL MORTGAGE PAYMENT SCHEDULE**

For a mortgage of $1,000.00

MORTGAGE TERM: **30 years**
Monthly payment: **$10.67**
Annual payment: **$128.07**

Year	Balance of Loan	Principal Paid	Interest Paid	Yearly Payment
1	$996.75	$3.25	$124.82	$128.07
2	993.06	3.68	124.39	128.07
3	988.89	4.17	123.90	128.07
4	984.17	4.72	123.35	128.07
5	978.82	5.35	122.72	128.07
6	972.76	6.06	122.01	128.07
7	965.90	6.86	121.21	128.07
8	958.13	7.77	120.30	128.07
9	949.33	8.80	119.27	128.07
10	939.37	9.96	118.11	128.07
11	928.09	11.28	116.79	128.07
12	915.31	12.78	115.30	128.07
13	900.85	14.47	113.60	128.07
14	884.47	16.38	111.69	128.07
15	865.91	18.55	109.52	128.07
16	844.91	21.01	107.06	128.07
17	821.12	23.79	104.28	128.07
18	794.17	26.94	101.13	128.07
19	763.67	30.51	97.56	128.07
20	729.12	34.55	93.52	128.07
21	690.00	39.12	88.95	128.07
22	645.70	44.30	83.77	128.07
23	595.53	50.17	77.90	128.07
24	538.71	56.81	71.26	128.07
25	474.38	64.33	63.74	128.07
26	401.53	72.85	55.22	128.07
27	319.03	82.50	45.57	128.07
28	225.60	93.43	34.65	128.07
29	119.81	105.80	22.27	128.07
30	.00	119.81	8.16	127.96
Totals:		$1000.00	$2842.02	$3842.02

TAX-SAVINGS TABLE

12.50% INTEREST

Multiply all figures by the number of thousands in your loan.
Net cost equals yearly payment minus tax savings.

Federal Tax Bracket					
15.0%		28.0%		33.0%	
Tax Savings	Net Cost	Tax Savings	Net Cost	Tax Savings	Net Cost
$18.72	$109.35	$34.95	$93.12	$41.19	$86.88
18.66	109.41	34.83	93.24	41.05	87.02
18.58	109.49	34.69	93.38	40.89	87.18
18.50	109.57	34.54	93.53	40.70	87.37
18.41	109.66	34.36	93.71	40.50	87.57
18.30	109.77	34.16	93.91	40.26	87.81
18.18	109.89	33.94	94.13	40.00	88.07
18.05	110.03	33.68	94.39	39.70	88.37
17.89	110.18	33.40	94.67	39.36	88.71
17.72	110.35	33.07	95.00	38.98	89.10
17.52	110.55	32.70	95.37	38.54	89.53
17.29	110.78	32.28	95.79	38.05	90.02
17.04	111.03	31.81	96.26	37.49	90.58
16.75	111.32	31.27	96.80	36.86	91.21
16.43	111.64	30.67	97.41	36.14	91.93
16.06	112.01	29.98	98.09	35.33	92.74
15.64	112.43	29.20	98.87	34.41	93.66
15.17	112.90	28.32	99.75	33.37	94.70
14.63	113.44	27.32	100.75	32.20	95.88
14.03	114.04	26.19	101.88	30.86	97.21
13.34	114.73	24.91	103.17	29.35	98.72
12.57	115.51	23.46	104.62	27.64	100.43
11.69	116.39	21.81	106.26	25.71	102.36
10.69	117.38	19.95	108.12	23.52	104.56
9.56	118.51	17.85	110.22	21.03	107.04
8.28	119.79	15.46	112.61	18.22	109.85
6.84	121.24	12.76	115.31	15.04	113.03
5.20	122.87	9.70	118.37	11.43	116.64
3.34	124.73	6.24	121.83	7.35	120.72
1.22	126.74	2.28	125.68	2.69	125.27
Totals:					
$426.30	**$3415.72**	**$795.77**	**$3046.25**	**$937.87**	**$2904.15**

12.75% INTEREST	ANNUAL MORTGAGE PAYMENT SCHEDULE

For a mortgage of $1,000.00

	MORTGAGE TERM:	15 years
	Monthly payment:	$12.49
	Annual payment:	$149.86

Year	Balance of Loan	Principal Paid	Interest Paid	Yearly Payment
1	$976.29	$23.71	$126.15	$149.86
2	949.36	26.92	122.94	149.86
3	918.80	30.56	119.30	149.86
4	884.11	34.69	115.17	149.86
5	844.72	39.39	110.47	149.86
6	800.01	44.71	105.15	149.86
7	749.25	50.76	99.10	149.86
8	691.63	57.62	92.24	149.86
9	626.22	65.41	84.45	149.86
10	551.96	74.26	75.60	149.86
11	467.67	84.30	65.56	149.86
12	371.97	95.70	54.16	149.86
13	263.33	108.64	41.22	149.86
14	140.00	123.33	26.53	149.86
15	.00	140.00	9.73	149.73
Totals:		**$1000.00**	**$1247.78**	**$2247.78**

TAX-SAVINGS TABLE

12.75% INTEREST

Multiply all figures by the number of thousands in your loan.
Net cost equals yearly payment minus tax savings.

Federal Tax Bracket					
15.0%		28.0%		33.0%	
Tax Savings	Net Cost	Tax Savings	Net Cost	Tax Savings	Net Cost
$18.92	$130.94	$35.32	$114.54	$41.63	$108.23
18.44	131.42	34.42	115.44	40.57	109.29
17.89	131.97	33.40	116.46	39.37	110.49
17.27	132.59	32.25	117.61	38.00	111.86
16.57	133.29	30.93	118.93	36.46	113.40
15.77	134.09	29.44	120.42	34.70	115.16
14.87	134.99	27.75	122.11	32.70	117.16
13.84	136.02	25.83	124.03	30.44	119.42
12.67	137.19	23.65	126.21	27.87	121.99
11.34	138.52	21.17	128.69	24.95	124.91
9.83	140.03	18.36	131.50	21.64	128.22
8.12	141.74	15.17	134.69	17.87	131.99
6.18	143.68	11.54	138.32	13.60	136.26
3.98	145.88	7.43	142.43	8.76	141.10
1.46	148.27	2.72	147.01	3.21	146.52
Totals:					
$187.17	**$2060.61**	**$349.38**	**$1898.40**	**$411.77**	**$1836.01**

12.75% INTEREST	ANNUAL MORTGAGE PAYMENT SCHEDULE

For a mortgage of $1,000.00

MORTGAGE TERM: **30 years**
Monthly payment: **$10.87**
Annual payment: **$130.40**

Year	Balance of Loan	Principal Paid	Interest Paid	Yearly Payment
1	$996.92	$3.08	$127.32	$130.40
2	993.43	3.50	126.91	130.40
3	989.46	3.97	126.44	130.40
4	984.95	4.50	125.90	130.40
5	979.84	5.11	125.29	130.40
6	974.03	5.81	124.60	130.40
7	967.44	6.59	123.81	130.40
8	959.96	7.48	122.92	130.40
9	951.47	8.49	121.91	130.40
10	941.83	9.64	120.76	130.40
11	930.88	10.94	119.46	130.40
12	918.46	12.42	117.98	130.40
13	904.35	14.11	116.30	130.40
14	888.34	16.01	114.39	130.40
15	870.16	18.18	112.23	130.40
16	849.53	20.64	109.77	130.40
17	826.10	23.43	106.98	130.40
18	799.51	26.59	103.81	130.40
19	769.32	30.19	100.21	130.40
20	735.05	34.27	96.13	130.40
21	696.14	38.91	91.50	130.40
22	651.97	44.17	86.24	130.40
23	601.84	50.14	80.26	130.40
24	544.92	56.92	73.48	130.40
25	480.30	64.62	65.79	130.40
26	406.95	73.35	57.05	130.40
27	323.67	83.27	47.13	130.40
28	229.14	94.53	35.87	130.40
29	121.83	107.32	23.09	130.40
30	.00	121.83	8.46	130.29
Totals:		$1000.00	$2911.98	$3911.98

TAX-SAVINGS TABLE

12.75% INTEREST

Multiply all figures by the number of thousands in your loan.
Net cost equals yearly payment minus tax savings.

Federal Tax Bracket					
15.0%		**28.0%**		**33.0%**	
Tax Savings	Net Cost	Tax Savings	Net Cost	Tax Savings	Net Cost
$19.10	$111.30	$35.65	$94.75	$42.02	$88.39
19.04	111.37	35.53	94.87	41.88	88.52
18.97	111.44	35.40	95.00	41.72	88.68
18.88	111.52	35.25	95.15	41.55	88.86
18.79	111.61	35.08	95.32	41.35	89.06
18.69	111.71	34.89	95.52	41.12	89.29
18.57	111.83	34.67	95.74	40.86	89.54
18.44	111.96	34.42	95.99	40.56	89.84
18.29	112.12	34.13	96.27	40.23	90.17
18.11	112.29	33.81	96.59	39.85	90.55
17.92	112.48	33.45	96.95	39.42	90.98
17.70	112.71	33.03	97.37	38.93	91.47
17.44	112.96	32.56	97.84	38.38	92.02
17.16	113.24	32.03	98.37	37.75	92.65
16.83	113.57	31.42	98.98	37.03	93.37
16.47	113.94	30.73	99.67	36.22	94.18
16.05	114.36	29.95	100.45	35.30	95.10
15.57	114.83	29.07	101.34	34.26	96.15
15.03	115.37	28.06	102.34	33.07	97.33
14.42	115.98	26.92	103.49	31 72	98.68
13.72	116.68	25.62	104.78	30 19	100.21
12.94	117.47	24.15	106.26	28;46	101.95
12.04	118.36	22.47	107.93	26.49	103.92
11.02	119.38	20.58	109.83	24.25	106.15
9.87	120.54	18.42	111.98	21.71	108.69
8.56	121.85	15.97	114.43	18.83	111.58
7.07	123.33	13.20	117.21	15.55	114.85
5.38	125.02	10.04	120.36	11.84	118.57
3.46	126.94	6.46	123.94	7.62	122.78
1.27	129.02	2.37	127.92	2.79	127.50
Totals:					
$436.80	**$3475.18**	**$815.35**	**$3096.63**	**$960.95**	**$2951.03**

ANNUAL MORTGAGE PAYMENT SCHEDULE

For a mortgage of $1,000.00

	MORTGAGE TERM:	**15 years**
	Monthly payment:	**$12.65**
	Annual payment:	**$151.83**

Year	Balance of Loan	Principal Paid	Interest Paid	Yearly Payment
1	$976.82	$23.18	$128.65	$151.83
2	950.45	26.38	125.45	151.83
3	920.43	30.02	121.81	151.83
4	886.27	34.16	117.67	151.83
5	847.39	38.88	112.95	151.83
6	803.15	44.24	107.59	151.83
7	752.80	50.35	101.48	151.83
8	695.50	57.30	94.53	151.83
9	630.29	65.21	86.62	151.83
10	556.08	74.21	77.62	151.83
11	471.62	84.45	67.38	151.83
12	375.51	96.11	55.72	151.83
13	266.13	109.38	42.45	151.83
14	141.66	124.48	27.35	151.83
15	.00	141.66	10.04	151.69
Totals:		**$1000.00**	**$1277.30**	**$2277.30**

Multiply all figures by the number of thousands in your loan.
Net cost equals yearly payment minus tax savings.

Federal Tax Bracket					
15.0%		28.0%		33.0%	
Tax Savings	Net Cost	Tax Savings	Net Cost	Tax Savings	Net Cost
$19.30	$132.53	$36.02	$115.81	$42.45	$109.37
18.82	133.01	35.13	116.70	41.40	110.43
18.27	133.56	34.11	117.72	40.20	111.63
17.65	134.18	32.95	118.88	38.83	113.00
16.94	134.89	31.63	120.20	37.27	114.55
16.14	135.69	30.12	121.71	35.50	116.33
15.22	136.61	28.41	123.41	33.49	118.34
14.18	137.65	26.47	125.36	31.19	120.63
12.99	138.84	24.25	127.58	28.58	123.24
11.64	140.19	21.73	130.10	25.61	126.21
10.11	141.72	18.87	132.96	22.23	129.60
8.36	143.47	15.60	136.23	18.39	133.44
6.37	145.46	11.89	139.94	14.01	137.82
4.10	147.73	7.66	144.17	9.03	142.80
1.51	150.19	2.81	148.88	3.31	148.38
Totals:					
$191.60	**$2085.71**	**$357.64**	**$1919.66**	**$421.51**	**$1855.79**

13.00% INTEREST	**ANNUAL MORTGAGE PAYMENT SCHEDULE**

For a mortgage of $1,000.00

MORTGAGE TERM: **30 years**
Monthly payment: **$11.06**
Annual payment: **$132.74**

Year	Balance of Loan	Principal Paid	Interest Paid	Yearly Payment
1	$997.09	$2.91	$129.83	$132.74
2	993.77	3.32	129.43	132.74
3	990.00	3.77	128.97	132.74
4	985.70	4.29	128.45	132.74
5	980.82	4.89	127.86	132.74
6	975.26	5.56	127.18	132.74
7	968.93	6.33	126.41	132.74
8	961.72	7.20	125.54	132.74
9	953.53	8.20	124.55	132.74
10	944.20	9.33	123.42	132.74
11	933.58	10.62	122.13	132.74
12	921.50	12.08	120.66	132.74
13	907.75	13.75	119.00	132.74
14	892.11	15.65	117.10	132.74
15	874.30	17.81	114.94	132.74
16	854.03	20.26	112.48	132.74
17	830.97	23.06	109.68	132.74
18	804.73	26.24	106.50	132.74
19	774.86	29.87	102.88	132.74
20	740.87	33.99	98.75	132.74
21	702.19	38.68	94.06	132.74
22	658.17	44.02	88.72	132.74
23	608.07	50.10	82.65	132.74
24	551.06	57.01	75.73	132.74
25	486.18	64.88	67.86	132.74
26	412.34	73.84	58.91	132.74
27	328.31	84.03	48.71	132.74
28	232.68	95.63	37.12	132.74
29	123.85	108.83	23.92	132.74
30	.00	123.85	8.77	132.63
Totals:		**$1000.00**	**$2982.20**	**$3982.20**

TAX-SAVINGS TABLE

13.00% INTEREST

Multiply all figures by the number of thousands in your loan.
Net cost equals yearly payment minus tax savings.

Federal Tax Bracket					
15.0%		28.0%		33.0%	
Tax Savings	Net Cost	Tax Savings	Net Cost	Tax Savings	Net Cost
$19.47	$113.27	$36.35	$96.39	$42.84	$89.90
19.41	113.33	36.24	96.50	42.71	90.03
19.35	113.40	36.11	96.63	42.56	90.18
19.27	113.48	35.97	96.78	42.39	90.36
19.18	113.57	35.80	96.94	42.19	90.55
19.08	113.67	35.61	97.13	41.97	90.77
18.96	113.78	35.40	97.35	41.72	91.03
18.83	113.91	35.15	97.59	41.43	91.32
18.68	114.06	34.87	97.87	41.10	91.64
18.51	114.23	34.56	98.19	40.73	92.02
18.32	114.42	34.20	98.55	40.30	92.44
18.10	114.64	33.79	98.96	39.82	92.93
17.85	114.89	33.32	99.43	39.27	93.48
17.56	115.18	32.79	99.96	38.64	94.10
17.24	115.50	32.18	100.56	37.93	94.81
16.87	115.87	31.49	101.25	37.12	95.63
16.45	116.29	30.71	102.03	36.20	96.55
15.97	116.77	29.82	102.92	35.14	97.60
15.43	117.31	28.81	103.94	33.95	98.79
14.81	117.93	27.65	105.09	32.59	100.16
14.11	118.63	26.34	106.41	31.04	101.70
13.31	119.44	24.84	107.90	29.28	103.47
12.40	120.35	23.14	109.60	27.27	105.47
11.36	121.38	21.20	111.54	24.99	107.75
10.18	122.56	19.00	113.74	22.39	110.35
8.84	123.91	16.49	116.25	19.44	113.30
7.31	125.44	13.64	119.10	16.08	116.67
5.57	127.18	10.39	122.35	12.25	120.50
3.59	129.16	6.70	126.05	7.89	124.85
1.32	131.31	2.46	130.17	2.90	129.73
Totals:					
$447.33	$3534.87	$835.02	$3147.18	$984.13	$2998.07

ANNUAL MORTGAGE PAYMENT SCHEDULE

For a mortgage of $1,000.00

MORTGAGE TERM: **15 years**
Monthly payment: **$12.82**
Annual payment: **$153.81**

Year	Balance of Loan	Principal Paid	Interest Paid	Yearly Payment
1	$977.35	$22.65	$131.16	$153.81
2	951.51	25.84	127.97	153.81
3	922.03	29.48	124.33	153.81
4	888.39	33.63	120.17	153.81
5	850.02	38.37	115.44	153.81
6	806.24	43.78	110.03	153.81
7	756.30	49.94	103.87	153.81
8	699.33	56.98	96.83	153.81
9	634.33	65.00	88.81	153.81
10	560.17	74.16	79.65	153.81
11	475.57	84.60	69.21	153.81
12	379.05	96.52	57.29	153.81
13	268.94	110.11	43.70	153.81
14	143.32	125.62	28.19	153.81
15	.00	143.32	10.35	153.67
Totals:		**$1000.00**	**$1306.99**	**$2306.99**

TAX-SAVINGS TABLE

13.25%
INTEREST

Multiply all figures by the number of thousands in your loan.
Net cost equals yearly payment minus tax savings.

| Federal Tax Bracket | | | | | |
| 15.0% | | 28.0% | | 33.0% | |
Tax Savings	Net Cost	Tax Savings	Net Cost	Tax Savings	Net Cost
$19.67	$134.13	$36.72	$117.08	$43.28	$110.53
19.20	134.61	35.83	117.98	42.23	111.58
18.65	135.16	34.81	119.00	41.03	112.78
18.03	135.78	33.65	120.16	39.66	114.15
17.32	136.49	32.32	121.49	38.09	115.71
16.50	137.30	30.81	123.00	36.31	117.50
15.58	138.23	29.08	124.73	34.28	119.53
14.52	139.28	27.11	126.70	31.95	121.85
13.32	140.49	24.87	128.94	29.31	124.50
11.95	141.86	22.30	131.51	26.29	127.52
10.38	143.43	19.38	134.43	22.84	130.97
8.59	145.21	16.04	137.77	18.91	134.90
6.55	147.25	12.23	141.57	14.42	139.39
4.23	149.58	7.89	145.92	9.30	144.51
1.55	152.12	2.90	150.77	3.42	150.25
Totals:					
$196.05	$2110.94	$365.96	$1941.03	$431.31	$1875.68

		ANNUAL MORTGAGE		
13.25% INTEREST		**PAYMENT SCHEDULE**		
		For a mortgage of $1,000.00		

MORTGAGE TERM: **30 years**
Monthly payment: **$11.26**
Annual payment: **$135.09**

Year	Balance of Loan	Principal Paid	Interest Paid	Yearly Payment
1	$997.24	$2.76	$132.34	$135.09
2	994.10	3.14	131.95	135.09
3	990.51	3.59	131.51	135.09
4	986.42	4.09	131.00	135.09
5	981.75	4.67	130.42	135.09
6	976.42	5.33	129.77	135.09
7	970.35	6.08	129.02	135.09
8	963.41	6.93	128.16	135.09
9	955.50	7.91	127.18	135.09
10	946.48	9.02	126.07	135.09
11	936.19	10.29	124.80	135.09
12	924.44	11.74	123.35	135.09
13	911.04	13.40	121.69	135.09
14	895.76	15.29	119.81	135.09
15	878.32	17.44	117.65	135.09
16	858.42	19.90	115.20	135.09
17	835.73	22.70	112.40	135.09
18	809.83	25.89	109.20	135.09
19	780.29	29.54	105.55	135.09
20	746.59	33.70	101.39	135.09
21	708.14	38.45	96.64	135.09
22	664.28	43.86	91.23	135.09
23	614.23	50.04	85.05	135.09
24	557.14	57.09	78.00	135.09
25	492.01	65.13	69.96	135.09
26	417.70	74.31	60.79	135.09
27	332.93	84.77	50.32	135.09
28	236.21	96.71	38.38	135.09
29	125.88	110.34	24.76	135.09
30	.00	125.88	9.09	134.97
Totals:		**$1000.00**	**$3052.66**	**$4052.66**

TAX-SAVINGS TABLE

13.25%	INTEREST

Multiply all figures by the number of thousands in your loan.
Net cost equals yearly payment minus tax savings.

Federal Tax Bracket					
15.0%		28.0%		33.0%	
Tax Savings	Net Cost	Tax Savings	Net Cost	Tax Savings	Net Cost
$19.85	$115.24	$37.05	$98.04	$43.67	$91.42
19.79	115.30	36.95	98.15	43.54	91.55
19.73	115.37	36.82	98.27	43.40	91.70
19.65	115.44	36.68	98.41	43.23	91.86
19.56	115.53	36.52	98.57	43.04	92.05
19.46	115.63	36.33	98.76	42.82	92.27
19.35	115.74	36.12	98.97	42.58	92.52
19.22	115.87	35.88	99.21	42.29	92.80
19.08	116.02	35.61	99.48	41.97	93.12
18.91	116.18	35.30	99.79	41.60	93.49
18.72	116.37	34.94	100.15	41.18	93.91
18.50	116.59	34.54	100.56	40.70	94.39
18.25	116.84	34.07	101.02	40.16	94.93
17.97	117.12	33.55	101.55	39.54	95.56
17.65	117.44	32.94	102.15	38.83	96.27
17.28	117.81	32.26	102.84	38.02	97.08
16.86	118.23	31.47	103.62	37.09	98.00
16.38	118.71	30.58	104.52	36.04	99.06
15.83	119.26	29.55	105.54	34.83	100.26
15.21	119.88	28.39	106.70	33.46	101.63
14.50	120.60	27.06	108.03	31.89	103.20
13.68	121.41	25.54	109.55	30.11	104.99
12.76	122.34	23.81	111.28	28.07	107.03
11.70	123.39	21.84	113.25	25.74	109.35
10.49	124.60	19.59	115.50	23.09	112.01
9.12	125.97	17.02	118.07	20.06	115.03
7.55	127.54	14.09	121.00	16.61	118.49
5.76	129.34	10.75	124.35	12.67	122.43
3.71	131.38	6.93	128.16	8.17	126.92
1.36	133.61	2.55	132.42	3.00	131.97
Totals:					
$457.90	**$3594.76**	**$854.75**	**$3197.92**	**$1007.38**	**$3045.28**

| | 13.50% INTEREST | **ANNUAL MORTGAGE PAYMENT SCHEDULE** |

For a mortgage of $1,000.00

		MORTGAGE TERM:	**15 years**
		Monthly payment:	**$12.98**
		Annual payment:	**$155.80**

Year	Balance of Loan	Principal Paid	Interest Paid	Yearly Payment
1	$977.87	$22.13	$133.66	$155.80
2	952.55	25.31	130.48	155.80
3	923.60	28.95	126.85	155.80
4	890.49	33.11	122.69	155.80
5	852.62	37.87	117.93	155.80
6	809.31	43.31	112.49	155.80
7	759.78	49.53	106.27	155.80
8	703.13	56.65	99.15	155.80
9	638.34	64.79	91.01	155.80
10	564.24	74.10	81.70	155.80
11	479.50	84.74	71.06	155.80
12	382.59	96.92	58.88	155.80
13	271.75	110.84	44.96	155.80
14	144.98	126.77	29.03	155.80
15	.00	144.98	10.67	155.65
Totals:		**$1000.00**	**$1336.83**	**$2336.83**

TAX-SAVINGS TABLE

13.50%
INTEREST

Multiply all figures by the number of thousands in your loan.
Net cost equals yearly payment minus tax savings.

Federal Tax Bracket					
15.0%		**28.0%**		**33.0%**	
Tax Savings	Net Cost	Tax Savings	Net Cost	Tax Savings	Net Cost
$20.05	$135.75	$37.43	$118.37	$44.11	$111.69
19.57	136.23	36.54	119.26	43.06	112.74
19.03	136.77	35.52	120.28	41.86	113.94
18.40	137.40	34.35	121.45	40.49	115.31
17.69	138.11	33.02	122.78	38.92	116.88
16.87	138.92	31.50	124.30	37.12	118.68
15.94	139.86	29.75	126.04	35.07	120.73
14.87	140.93	27.76	128.04	32.72	123.08
13.65	142.15	25.48	130.32	30.03	125.76
12.26	143.54	22.88	132.92	26.96	128.84
10.66	145.14	19.90	135.90	23.45	132.35
8.83	146.97	16.49	139.31	19.43	136.37
6.74	149.05	12.59	143.21	14.84	140.96
4.35	151.44	8.13	147.67	9.58	146.22
1.60	154.05	2.99	152.66	3.52	152.13
Totals:					
$200.52	**$2136.30**	**$374.31**	**$1962.52**	**$441.15**	**$1895.68**

| | 13.50% INTEREST | **ANNUAL MORTGAGE PAYMENT SCHEDULE** |

For a mortgage of $1,000.00

MORTGAGE TERM: **30 years**
Monthly payment: **$11.45**
Annual payment: **$137.45**

Year	Balance of Loan	Principal Paid	Interest Paid	Yearly Payment
1	$997.39	$2.61	$134.84	$137.45
2	994.41	2.98	134.47	137.45
3	991.00	3.41	134.04	137.45
4	987.10	3.90	133.55	137.45
5	982.64	4.46	132.99	137.45
6	977.54	5.10	132.35	137.45
7	971.71	5.83	131.62	137.45
8	965.04	6.67	130.78	137.45
9	957.41	7.63	129.82	137.45
10	948.68	8.73	128.72	137.45
11	938.70	9.98	127.47	137.45
12	927.29	11.41	126.04	137.45
13	914.23	13.05	124.40	137.45
14	899.30	14.93	122.52	137.45
15	882.23	17.07	120.37	137.45
16	862.70	19.53	117.92	137.45
17	840.37	22.33	115.12	137.45
18	814.82	25.54	111.91	137.45
19	785.61	29.21	108.24	137.45
20	752.20	33.41	104.04	137.45
21	713.99	38.21	99.24	137.45
22	670.30	43.70	93.75	137.45
23	620.32	49.98	87.47	137.45
24	563.16	57.16	80.29	137.45
25	497.79	65.37	72.08	137.45
26	423.03	74.76	62.69	137.45
27	337.53	85.50	51.95	137.45
28	239.74	97.79	39.66	137.45
29	127.90	111.84	25.61	137.45
30	.00	127.90	9.42	137.32
Totals:		**$1000.00**	**$3123.36**	**$4123.36**

TAX-SAVINGS TABLE

13.50% INTEREST

Multiply all figures by the number of thousands in your loan.
Net cost equals yearly payment minus tax savings.

Federal Tax Bracket					
15.0%		28.0%		33.0%	
Tax Savings	Net Cost	Tax Savings	Net Cost	Tax Savings	Net Cost
$20.23	$117.22	$37.76	$99.69	$44.50	$92.95
20.17	117.28	37.65	99.80	44.37	93.07
20.11	117.34	37.53	99.92	44.23	93.22
20.03	117.42	37.39	100.06	44.07	93.38
19.95	117.50	37.24	100.21	43.89	93.56
19.85	117.60	37.06	100.39	43.68	93.77
19.74	117.71	36.85	100.60	43.43	94.02
19.62	117.83	36.62	100.83	43.16	94.29
19.47	117.98	36.35	101.10	42.84	94.61
19.31	118.14	36.04	101.41	42.48	94.97
19.12	118.33	35.69	101.76	42.06	95.38
18.91	118.54	35.29	102.16	41.59	95.86
18.66	118.79	34.83	102.62	41.05	96.40
18.38	119.07	34.31	103.14	40.43	97.02
18.06	119.39	33.70	103.74	39.72	97.73
17.69	119.76	33.02	104.43	38.91	98.54
17.27	120.18	32.23	105.22	37.99	99.46
16.79	120.66	31.33	106.12	36.93	100.52
16.24	121.21	30.31	107.14	35.72	101.73
15.61	121.84	29.13	108.32	34.33	103.12
14.89	122.56	27.79	109.66	32.75	104.70
14.06	123.39	26.25	111.20	30.94	106.51
13.12	124.33	24.49	112.96	28.87	108.58
12.04	125.41	22.48	114.97	26.50	110.95
10.81	126.64	20.18	117.27	23.79	113.66
9.40	128.05	17.55	119.90	20.69	116.76
7.79	129.66	14.55	122.90	17.14	120.31
5.95	131.50	11.11	126.34	13.09	124.36
3.84	133.61	7.17	130.28	8.45	129.00
1.41	135.91	2.64	134.69	3.11	134.21
Totals:					
$468.50	**$3654.85**	**$874.54**	**$3248.82**	**$1030.71**	**$3092.65**

	13.75% INTEREST	**ANNUAL MORTGAGE PAYMENT SCHEDULE**

ANNUAL MORTGAGE PAYMENT SCHEDULE

For a mortgage of $1,000.00

MORTGAGE TERM: **15 years**
Monthly payment: **$13.15**
Annual payment: **$157.80**

Year	Balance of Loan	Principal Paid	Interest Paid	Yearly Payment
1	$978.37	$21.63	$136.17	$157.80
2	953.58	24.80	133.00	157.80
3	925.15	28.43	129.37	157.80
4	892.55	32.59	125.20	157.80
5	855.18	37.37	120.43	157.80
6	812.34	42.84	114.95	157.80
7	763.22	49.12	108.68	157.80
8	706.90	56.32	101.48	157.80
9	642.33	64.57	93.23	157.80
10	568.30	74.03	83.77	157.80
11	483.43	84.87	72.92	157.80
12	386.12	97.31	60.49	157.80
13	274.56	111.56	46.23	157.80
14	146.65	127.91	29.89	157.80
15	.00	146.65	11.00	157.65
Totals:		**$1000.00**	**$1366.83**	**$2366.83**

TAX-SAVINGS TABLE

13.75%
INTEREST

Multiply all figures by the number of thousands in your loan.
Net cost equals yearly payment minus tax savings.

Federal Tax Bracket					
15.0%		28.0%		33.0%	
Tax Savings	Net Cost	Tax Savings	Net Cost	Tax Savings	Net Cost
$20.43	$137.37	$38.13	$119.67	$44.94	$112.86
19.95	137.85	37.24	120.56	43.89	113.91
19.41	138.39	36.22	121.58	42.69	115.11
18.78	139.02	35.06	122.74	41.32	116.48
18.06	139.73	33.72	124.08	39.74	118.06
17.24	140.56	32.19	125.61	37.93	119.86
16.30	141.50	30.43	127.37	35.86	121.93
15.22	142.58	28.41	129.38	33.49	124.31
13.98	143.81	26.10	131.69	30.77	127.03
12.57	145.23	23.46	134.34	27.64	130.15
10.94	146.86	20.42	137.38	24.07	133.73
9.07	148.72	16.94	140.86	19.96	137.84
6.94	150.86	12.95	144.85	15.26	142.54
4.48	153.32	8.37	149.43	9.86	147.93
1.65	156.00	3.08	154.57	3.63	154.02
Totals:					
$205.02	**$2161.80**	**$382.71**	**$1984.12**	**$451.05**	**$1915.77**

13.75% INTEREST	**ANNUAL MORTGAGE PAYMENT SCHEDULE**

For a mortgage of $1,000.00

MORTGAGE TERM: **30 years**
Monthly payment: **$11.65**
Annual payment: **$139.81**

Year	Balance of Loan	Principal Paid	Interest Paid	Yearly Payment
1	$997.53	$2.47	$137.35	$139.81
2	994.71	2.83	136.99	139.81
3	991.47	3.24	136.57	139.81
4	987.75	3.71	136.10	139.81
5	983.49	4.26	135.55	139.81
6	978.61	4.88	134.93	139.81
7	973.01	5.60	134.21	139.81
8	966.59	6.42	133.39	139.81
9	959.23	7.36	132.45	139.81
10	950.80	8.44	131.38	139.81
11	941.12	9.67	130.14	139.81
12	930.03	11.09	128.72	139.81
13	917.32	12.72	127.10	139.81
14	902.74	14.58	125.24	139.81
15	886.03	16.71	123.10	139.81
16	866.86	19.16	120.65	139.81
17	844.89	21.97	117.84	139.81
18	819.70	25.19	114.62	139.81
19	790.82	28.88	110.93	139.81
20	757.71	33.11	106.70	139.81
21	719.75	37.96	101.85	139.81
22	676.23	43.52	96.29	139.81
23	626.33	49.90	89.91	139.81
24	569.12	57.21	82.60	139.81
25	503.53	65.59	74.22	139.81
26	428.33	75.20	64.61	139.81
27	342.11	86.22	53.60	139.81
28	243.26	98.85	40.96	139.81
29	129.93	113.33	26.48	139.81
30	.00	129.93	9.75	139.68
Totals:		**$1000.00**	**$3194.27**	**$4194.27**

TAX-SAVINGS TABLE

13.75% INTEREST

Multiply all figures by the number of thousands in your loan.
Net cost equals yearly payment minus tax savings.

Federal Tax Bracket					
15.0%		28.0%		33.0%	
Tax Savings	Net Cost	Tax Savings	Net Cost	Tax Savings	Net Cost
$20.60	$119.21	$38.46	$101.36	$45.33	$94.49
20.55	119.27	38.36	101.46	45.21	94.61
20.49	119.33	38.24	101.57	45.07	94.74
20.41	119.40	38.11	101.71	44.91	94.90
20.33	119.48	37.96	101.86	44.73	95.08
20.24	119.57	37.78	102.03	44.53	95.29
20.13	119.68	37.58	102.23	44.29	95.52
20.01	119.80	37.35	102.46	44.02	95.79
19.87	119.95	37.09	102.73	43.71	96.10
19.71	120.11	36.79	103.03	43.35	96.46
19.52	120.29	36.44	103.37	42.95	96.87
19.31	120.51	36.04	103.77	42.48	97.33
19.06	120.75	35.59	104.23	41.94	97.87
18.79	121.03	35.07	104.75	41.33	98.49
18.46	121.35	34.47	105.35	40.62	99.19
18.10	121.72	33.78	106.03	39.81	100.00
17.68	122.14	33.00	106.82	38.89	100.93
17.19	122.62	32.09	107.72	37.83	101.99
16.64	123.17	31.06	108.75	36.61	103.21
16.01	123.81	29.88	109.94	35.21	104.60
15.28	124.54	28.52	111.29	33.61	106.20
14.44	125.37	26.96	112.85	31.78	108.04
13.49	126.33	25.18	114.64	29.67	110.14
12.39	127.42	23.13	116.68	27.26	112.55
11.13	128.68	20.78	119.03	24.49	115.32
9.69	130.12	18.09	121.72	21.32	118.49
8.04	131.77	15.01	124.81	17.69	122.13
6.14	133.67	11.47	128.34	13.52	126.30
3.97	135.84	7.42	132.40	8.74	131.07
1.46	138.22	2.73	136.95	3.22	136.46
Totals:					
$479.14	**$3715.13**	**$894.40**	**$3299.88**	**$1054.11**	**$3140.16**

		ANNUAL MORTGAGE PAYMENT SCHEDULE		
14.00% INTEREST				

ANNUAL MORTGAGE PAYMENT SCHEDULE

For a mortgage of $1,000.00

MORTGAGE TERM: **15 years**
Monthly payment: **$13.32**
Annual payment: **$159.81**

Year	Balance of Loan	Principal Paid	Interest Paid	Yearly Payment
1	$978.87	$21.13	$138.68	$159.81
2	954.58	24.29	135.52	159.81
3	926.67	27.91	131.90	159.81
4	894.59	32.08	127.73	159.81
5	857.71	36.87	122.94	159.81
6	815.33	42.38	117.43	159.81
7	766.62	48.71	111.10	159.81
8	710.64	55.98	103.83	159.81
9	646.30	64.34	95.46	159.81
10	572.34	73.95	85.86	159.81
11	487.34	85.00	74.81	159.81
12	389.65	97.69	62.12	159.81
13	277.37	112.28	47.53	159.81
14	148.32	129.05	30.76	159.81
15	.00	148.32	11.33	159.66
Totals:		**$1000.00**	**$1396.98**	**$2396.98**

14.00%
INTEREST

Multiply all figures by the number of thousands in your loan.
Net cost equals yearly payment minus tax savings.

Federal Tax Bracket					
15.0%		28.0%		33.0%	
Tax Savings	Net Cost	Tax Savings	Net Cost	Tax Savings	Net Cost
$20.80	$139.01	$38.83	$120.98	$45.76	$114.05
20.33	139.48	37.95	121.86	44.72	115.09
19.78	140.02	36.93	122.88	43.53	116.28
19.16	140.65	35.76	124.05	42.15	117.66
18.44	141.37	34.42	125.39	40.57	119.24
17.61	142.19	32.88	126.93	38.75	121.06
16.66	143.14	31.11	128.70	36.66	123.15
15.57	144.24	29.07	130.74	34.26	125.55
14.32	145.49	26.73	133.08	31.50	128.31
12.88	146.93	24.04	135.77	28.33	131.48
11.22	148.59	20.95	138.86	24.69	135.12
9.32	150.49	17.39	142.42	20.50	139.31
7.13	152.68	13.31	146.50	15.68	144.12
4.61	155.20	8.61	151.20	10.15	149.66
1.70	157.96	3.17	156.48	3.74	155.92
Totals:					
$209.55	**$2187.43**	**$391.15**	**$2005.83**	**$461.00**	**$1935.98**

14.00% INTEREST	**ANNUAL MORTGAGE PAYMENT SCHEDULE**

For a mortgage of $1,000.00

	MORTGAGE TERM:	**30 years**
	Monthly payment:	**$11.85**
	Annual payment:	**$142.18**

Year	Balance of Loan	Principal Paid	Interest Paid	Yearly Payment
1	$997.67	$2.33	$139.85	$142.18
2	994.99	2.68	139.51	142.18
3	991.91	3.08	139.11	142.18
4	988.37	3.54	138.65	142.18
5	984.31	4.07	138.12	142.18
6	979.63	4.67	137.51	142.18
7	974.26	5.37	136.81	142.18
8	968.09	6.17	136.01	142.18
9	960.99	7.10	135.09	142.18
10	952.84	8.16	134.03	142.18
11	943.46	9.37	132.81	142.18
12	932.69	10.77	131.41	142.18
13	920.31	12.38	129.80	142.18
14	906.07	14.23	127.95	142.18
15	889.72	16.36	125.83	142.18
16	870.92	18.80	123.38	142.18
17	849.31	21.61	120.58	142.18
18	824.47	24.84	117.35	142.18
19	795.93	28.54	113.64	142.18
20	763.12	32.81	109.38	142.18
21	725.42	37.71	104.48	142.18
22	682.08	43.34	98.85	142.18
23	632.27	49.81	92.38	142.18
24	575.02	57.25	84.94	142.18
25	509.22	65.80	76.39	142.18
26	433.60	75.62	66.56	142.18
27	346.68	86.92	55.27	142.18
28	246.78	99.90	42.29	142.18
29	131.96	114.82	27.37	142.18
30	.00	131.96	10.08	142.05
Totals:		**$1000.00**	**$3265.40**	**$4265.40**

TAX-SAVINGS TABLE

14.00%
INTEREST

Multiply all figures by the number of thousands in your loan.
Net cost equals yearly payment minus tax savings.

Federal Tax Bracket					
15.0%		28.0%		33.0%	
Tax Savings	Net Cost	Tax Savings	Net Cost	Tax Savings	Net Cost
$20.98	$121.21	$39.16	$103.03	$46.15	$96.03
20.93	121.26	39.06	103.12	46.04	96.15
20.87	121.32	38.95	103.23	45.91	96.28
20.80	121.39	38.82	103.36	45.75	96.43
20.72	121.47	38.67	103.51	45.58	96.61
20.63	121.56	38.50	103.68	45.38	96.81
20.52	121.66	38.31	103.88	45.15	97.04
20.40	121.78	38.08	104.10	44.88	97.30
20.26	121.92	37.82	104.36	44.58	97.61
20.10	122.08	37.53	104.66	44.23	97.96
19.92	122.26	37.19	105.00	43.83	98.36
19.71	122.47	36.80	105.39	43.37	98.82
19.47	122.71	36.34	105.84	42.83	99.35
19.19	122.99	35.83	106.36	42.22	99.96
18.87	123.31	35.23	106.95	41.52	100.66
18.51	123.68	34.55	107.64	40.72	101.47
18.09	124.10	33.76	108.42	39.79	102.39
17.60	124.58	32.86	109.33	38.73	103.46
17.05	125.14	31.82	110.37	37.50	104.68
16.41	125.78	30.63	111.56	36.09	106.09
15.67	126.51	29.25	112.93	34.48	107.71
14.83	127.36	27.68	114.51	32.62	109.57
13.86	128.33	25.87	116.32	30.48	111.70
12.74	129.44	23.78	118.40	28.03	114.16
11.46	130.73	21.39	120.80	25.21	116.98
9.98	132.20	18.64	123.55	21.96	120.22
8.29	133.89	15.47	126.71	18.24	123.95
6.34	135.84	11.84	130.34	13.95	128.23
4.11	138.08	7.66	134.52	9.03	133.15
1.51	140.54	2.82	139.22	3.33	138.72
Totals:					
$489.81	**$3775.59**	**$914.31**	**$3351.09**	**$1077.58**	**$3187.82**

ANNUAL MORTGAGE PAYMENT SCHEDULE

For a mortgage of $1,000.00

MORTGAGE TERM: **15 years**
Monthly payment: **$13.49**
Annual payment: **$161.83**

Year	Balance of Loan	Principal Paid	Interest Paid	Yearly Payment
1	$979.36	$20.64	$141.19	$161.83
2	955.57	23.78	138.04	161.83
3	928.17	27.40	134.42	161.83
4	896.59	31.58	130.25	161.83
5	860.21	36.38	125.45	161.83
6	818.29	41.92	119.91	161.83
7	770.00	48.30	113.53	161.83
8	714.35	55.65	106.18	161.83
9	650.24	64.11	97.71	161.83
10	576.36	73.87	87.96	161.83
11	491.25	85.11	76.71	161.83
12	393.18	98.07	63.76	161.83
13	280.19	112.99	48.84	161.83
14	150.00	130.19	31.64	161.83
15	.00	150.00	11.67	161.67
Totals:		**$1000.00**	**$1427.29**	**$2427.29**

TAX-SAVINGS TABLE

14.25%
INTEREST

Multiply all figures by the number of thousands in your loan.
Net cost equals yearly payment minus tax savings.

Federal Tax Bracket					
15.0%		28.0%		33.0%	
Tax Savings	Net Cost	Tax Savings	Net Cost	Tax Savings	Net Cost
$21.18	$140.65	$39.53	$122.30	$46.59	$115.24
20.71	141.12	38.65	123.18	45.55	116.27
20.16	141.67	37.64	124.19	44.36	117.47
19.54	142.29	36.47	125.36	42.98	118.85
18.82	143.01	35.13	126.70	41.40	120.43
17.99	143.84	33.58	128.25	39.57	122.26
17.03	144.80	31.79	130.04	37.47	124.36
15.93	145.90	29.73	132.10	35.04	126.79
14.66	147.17	27.36	134.47	32.25	129.58
13.19	148.64	24.63	137.20	29.03	132.80
11.51	150.32	21.48	140.35	25.32	136.51
9.56	152.27	17.85	143.98	21.04	140.79
7.33	154.50	13.67	148.16	16.12	145.71
4.75	157.08	8.86	152.97	10.44	151.39
1.75	159.92	3.27	158.40	3.85	157.82
Totals:					
$214.09	**$2213.19**	**$399.64**	**$2027.65**	**$471.00**	**$1956.28**

| | 14.25% INTEREST | **ANNUAL MORTGAGE PAYMENT SCHEDULE** |

14.25% INTEREST

ANNUAL MORTGAGE PAYMENT SCHEDULE

For a mortgage of $1,000.00

MORTGAGE TERM: **30 years**
Monthly payment: **$12.05**
Annual payment: **$144.56**

Year	Balance of Loan	Principal Paid	Interest Paid	Yearly Payment
1	$997.80	$2.20	$142.36	$144.56
2	995.26	2.54	142.02	144.56
3	992.34	2.92	141.64	144.56
4	988.97	3.37	141.19	144.56
5	985.08	3.88	140.68	144.56
6	980.61	4.47	140.09	144.56
7	975.46	5.15	139.41	144.56
8	969.52	5.94	138.63	144.56
9	962.68	6.84	137.72	144.56
10	954.80	7.88	136.68	144.56
11	945.72	9.08	135.48	144.56
12	935.25	10.46	134.10	144.56
13	923.20	12.06	132.51	144.56
14	909.31	13.89	130.67	144.56
15	893.30	16.00	128.56	144.56
16	874.86	18.44	126.12	144.56
17	853.61	21.25	123.32	144.56
18	829.13	24.48	120.08	144.56
19	800.93	28.21	116.36	144.56
20	768.43	32.50	112.06	144.56
21	730.98	37.44	107.12	144.56
22	687.84	43.14	101.42	144.56
23	638.13	49.71	94.85	144.56
24	580.86	57.27	87.29	144.56
25	514.87	65.99	78.57	144.56
26	438.83	76.03	68.53	144.56
27	351.23	87.60	56.96	144.56
28	250.29	100.94	43.63	144.56
29	134.00	116.30	28.27	144.56
30	.00	134.00	10.43	144.42
Totals:		**$1000.00**	**$3336.73**	**$4336.73**

TAX-SAVINGS TABLE

14.25%
INTEREST

Multiply all figures by the number of thousands in your loan.
Net cost equals yearly payment minus tax savings.

| Federal Tax Bracket | | | | | |
| 15.0% | | 28.0% | | 33.0% | |
Tax Savings	Net Cost	Tax Savings	Net Cost	Tax Savings	Net Cost
$21.35	$123.21	$39.86	$104.70	$46.98	$97.58
21.30	123.26	39.77	104.80	46.87	97.69
21.25	123.32	39.66	104.90	46.74	97.82
21.18	123.38	39.53	105.03	46.59	97.97
21.10	123.46	39.39	105.17	46.42	98.14
21.01	123.55	39.23	105.34	46.23	98.33
20.91	123.65	39.03	105.53	46.01	98.56
20.79	123.77	38.82	105.75	45.75	98.82
20.66	123.90	38.56	106.00	45.45	99.11
20.50	124.06	38.27	106.29	45.10	99.46
20.32	124.24	37.93	106.63	44.71	99.85
20.11	124.45	37.55	107.01	44.25	100.31
19.88	124.69	37.10	107.46	43.73	100.84
19.60	124.96	36.59	107.97	43.12	101.44
19.28	125.28	36.00	108.57	42.42	102.14
18.92	125.64	35.31	109.25	41.62	102.94
18.50	126.07	34.53	110.03	40.69	103.87
18.01	126.55	33.62	110.94	39.63	104.94
17.45	127.11	32.58	111.98	38.40	106.16
16.81	127.75	31.38	113.18	36.98	107.58
16.07	128.49	29.99	114.57	35.35	109.21
15.21	129.35	28.40	116.17	33.47	111.09
14.23	130.33	26.56	118.00	31.30	113.26
13.09	131.47	24.44	120.12	28.81	115.76
11.79	132.78	22.00	122.56	25.93	118.63
10.28	134.28	19.19	125.37	22.61	121.95
8.54	136.02	15.95	128.61	18.80	125.77
6.54	138.02	12.22	132.35	14.40	130.17
4.24	140.32	7.91	136.65	9.33	135.23
1.56	142.86	2.92	141.50	3.44	140.98
Totals:					
$500.51	**$3836.22**	**$934.29**	**$3402.45**	**$1101.12**	**$3235.61**

For a mortgage of $1,000.00

	MORTGAGE TERM:	**15 years**
	Monthly payment:	**$13.66**
	Annual payment:	**$163.86**

Year	Balance of Loan	Principal Paid	Interest Paid	Yearly Payment
1	$979.83	$20.17	$143.69	$163.86
2	956.54	23.29	140.57	163.86
3	929.64	26.90	136.96	163.86
4	898.57	31.07	132.79	163.86
5	862.68	35.89	127.97	163.86
6	821.22	41.46	122.40	163.86
7	773.34	47.88	115.98	163.86
8	718.03	55.31	108.55	163.86
9	654.15	63.88	99.98	163.86
10	580.37	73.78	90.08	163.86
11	495.14	85.22	78.64	163.86
12	396.71	98.44	65.42	163.86
13	283.01	113.70	50.16	163.86
14	151.68	131.32	32.54	163.86
15	.00	151.68	12.01	163.70
Totals:		**$1000.00**	**$1457.74**	**$2457.74**

TAX-SAVINGS TABLE

14.50% INTEREST

Multiply all figures by the number of thousands in your loan.
Net cost equals yearly payment minus tax savings.

Federal Tax Bracket					
15.0%		28.0%		33.0%	
Tax Savings	Net Cost	Tax Savings	Net Cost	Tax Savings	Net Cost
$21.55	$142.31	$40.23	$123.63	$47.42	$116.44
21.09	142.77	39.36	124.50	46.39	117.47
20.54	143.32	38.35	125.51	45.20	118.66
19.92	143.94	37.18	126.68	43.82	120.04
19.20	144.66	35.83	128.03	42.23	121.63
18.36	145.50	34.27	129.59	40.39	123.47
17.40	146.46	32.47	131.39	38.27	125.59
16.28	147.58	30.40	133.47	35.82	128.04
15.00	148.86	27.99	135.87	32.99	130.87
13.51	150.35	25.22	138.64	29.72	134.14
11.80	152.06	22.02	141.84	25.95	137.91
9.81	154.05	18.32	145.54	21.59	142.27
7.52	156.34	14.05	149.81	16.55	147.31
4.88	158.98	9.11	154.75	10.74	153.12
1.80	161.90	3.36	160.33	3.96	159.73
Totals:					
$218.66	**$2239.08**	**$408.17**	**$2049.57**	**$481.05**	**$1976.68**

14.50% INTEREST	ANNUAL MORTGAGE PAYMENT SCHEDULE

For a mortgage of $1,000.00

MORTGAGE TERM: **30 years**
Monthly payment: **$12.25**
Annual payment: **$146.95**

Year	Balance of Loan	Principal Paid	Interest Paid	Yearly Payment
1	$997.92	$2.08	$144.87	$146.95
2	995.51	2.40	144.54	146.95
3	992.74	2.78	144.17	146.95
4	989.53	3.21	143.74	146.95
5	985.83	3.70	143.24	146.95
6	981.55	4.28	142.67	146.95
7	976.60	4.94	142.00	146.95
8	970.90	5.71	141.24	146.95
9	964.30	6.59	140.35	146.95
10	956.69	7.62	139.33	146.95
11	947.89	8.80	138.15	146.95
12	937.73	10.16	136.79	146.95
13	925.99	11.74	135.21	146.95
14	912.44	13.56	133.39	146.95
15	896.78	15.66	131.29	146.95
16	878.70	18.08	128.86	146.95
17	857.81	20.89	126.06	146.95
18	833.68	24.13	122.82	146.95
19	805.82	27.87	119.08	146.95
20	773.63	32.19	114.76	146.95
21	736.45	37.18	109.77	146.95
22	693.51	42.94	104.01	146.95
23	643.92	49.60	97.35	146.95
24	586.63	57.29	89.66	146.95
25	520.46	66.17	80.78	146.95
26	444.03	76.43	70.52	146.95
27	355.76	88.28	58.67	146.95
28	253.80	101.96	44.99	146.95
29	136.03	117.77	29.18	146.95
30	.00	136.03	10.77	146.80
Totals:		**$1000.00**	**$3408.26**	**$4408.26**

TAX-SAVINGS TABLE

14.50%
INTEREST

Multiply all figures by the number of thousands in your loan.
Net cost equals yearly payment minus tax savings.

Federal Tax Bracket					
15.0%		28.0%		33.0%	
Tax Savings	Net Cost	Tax Savings	Net Cost	Tax Savings	Net Cost
$21.73	$125.22	$40.56	$106.38	$47.81	$99.14
21.68	125.27	40.47	106.47	47.70	99.25
21.63	125.32	40.37	106.58	47.58	99.37
21.56	125.39	40.25	106.70	47.43	99.51
21.49	125.46	40.11	106.84	47.27	99.68
21.40	125.55	39.95	107.00	47.08	99.87
21.30	125.65	39.76	107.19	46.86	100.09
21.19	125.76	39.55	107.40	46.61	100.34
21.05	125.89	39.30	107.65	46.32	100.63
20.90	126.05	39.01	107.93	45.98	100.97
20.72	126.22	38.68	108.26	45.59	101.36
20.52	126.43	38.30	108.65	45.14	101.81
20.28	126.67	37.86	109.09	44.62	102.33
20.01	126.94	37.35	109.60	44.02	102.93
19.69	127.25	36.76	110.19	43.33	103.62
19.33	127.62	36.08	110.87	42.52	104.42
18.91	128.04	35.30	111.65	41.60	105.35
18.42	128.52	34.39	112.56	40.53	106.42
17.86	129.08	33.34	113.60	39.30	107.65
17.21	129.73	32.13	114.81	37.87	109.08
16.47	130.48	30.74	116.21	36.22	110.72
15.60	131.35	29.12	117.82	34.32	112.62
14.60	132.34	27.26	119.69	32.13	114.82
13.45	133.50	25.10	121.84	29.59	117.36
12.12	134.83	22.62	124.33	26.66	120.29
10.58	136.37	19.75	127.20	23.27	123.68
8.80	138.15	16.43	130.52	19.36	127.59
6.75	140.20	12.60	134.35	14.85	132.10
4.38	142.57	8.17	138.78	9.63	137.32
1.62	145.18	3.02	143.78	3.56	143.25
Totals:					
$511.24	**$3897.02**	**$954.31**	**$3453.94**	**$1124.72**	**$3283.53**

	14.75% INTEREST	**ANNUAL MORTGAGE PAYMENT SCHEDULE**

For a mortgage of $1,000.00

MORTGAGE TERM: **15 years**
Monthly payment: **$13.83**
Annual payment: **$165.90**

Year	Balance of Loan	Principal Paid	Interest Paid	Yearly Payment
1	$980.30	$19.70	$146.20	$165.90
2	957.50	22.81	143.09	165.90
3	931.09	26.41	139.49	165.90
4	900.51	30.58	135.32	165.90
5	865.11	35.41	130.50	165.90
6	824.11	41.00	124.91	165.90
7	776.64	47.47	118.43	165.90
8	721.68	54.96	110.94	165.90
9	658.04	63.64	102.26	165.90
10	584.35	73.69	92.21	165.90
11	499.02	85.32	80.58	165.90
12	400.23	98.80	67.10	165.90
13	285.83	114.40	51.50	165.90
14	153.37	132.46	33.44	165.90
15	.00	153.37	12.36	165.73
Totals:		**$1000.00**	**$1488.34**	**$2488.34**

TAX-SAVINGS TABLE

14.75%
INTEREST

Multiply all figures by the number of thousands in your loan.
Net cost equals yearly payment minus tax savings.

Federal Tax Bracket					
15.0%		28.0%		33.0%	
Tax Savings	Net Cost	Tax Savings	Net Cost	Tax Savings	Net Cost
$21.93	$143.97	$40.94	$124.96	$48.25	$117.65
21.46	144.44	40.07	125.83	47.22	118.68
20.92	144.98	39.06	126.84	46.03	119.87
20.30	145.60	37.89	128.01	44.66	121.24
19.57	146.33	36.54	129.36	43.06	122.84
18.74	147.16	34.97	130.93	41.22	124.68
17.76	148.14	33.16	132.74	39.08	126.82
16.64	149.26	31.06	134.84	36.61	129.29
15.34	150.56	28.63	137.27	33.75	132.15
13.83	152.07	25.82	140.08	30.43	135.47
12.09	153.81	22.56	143.34	26.59	139.31
10.07	155.83	18.79	147.11	22.14	143.76
7.73	158.17	14.42	151.48	17.00	148.90
5.02	160.88	9.36	156.54	11.04	154.86
1.85	163.88	3.46	162.27	4.08	161.65
Totals:					
$223.25	**$2265.09**	**$416.73**	**$2071.60**	**$491.15**	**$1997.19**

<table>
<tr><td colspan="2">**14.75%** INTEREST</td><td colspan="3">**ANNUAL MORTGAGE PAYMENT SCHEDULE**</td></tr>
</table>

14.75% INTEREST	**ANNUAL MORTGAGE PAYMENT SCHEDULE**

For a mortgage of $1,000.00

	MORTGAGE TERM:	**30 years**
	Monthly payment:	**$12.44**
	Annual payment:	**$149.34**

Year	Balance of Loan	Principal Paid	Interest Paid	Yearly Payment
1	$998.03	$1.97	$147.37	$149.34
2	995.76	2.28	147.06	149.34
3	993.12	2.64	146.70	149.34
4	990.07	3.05	146.28	149.34
5	986.53	3.53	145.80	149.34
6	982.44	4.09	145.24	149.34
7	977.70	4.74	144.60	149.34
8	972.21	5.49	143.85	149.34
9	965.86	6.35	142.98	149.34
10	958.50	7.36	141.98	149.34
11	949.98	8.52	140.82	149.34
12	940.12	9.86	139.47	149.34
13	928.70	11.42	137.92	149.34
14	915.47	13.22	136.11	149.34
15	900.16	15.31	134.02	149.34
16	882.43	17.73	131.61	149.34
17	861.90	20.53	128.81	149.34
18	838.13	23.77	125.57	149.34
19	810.61	27.52	121.81	149.34
20	778.73	31.87	117.47	149.34
21	741.83	36.90	112.43	149.34
22	699.10	42.73	106.61	149.34
23	649.63	49.48	99.86	149.34
24	592.34	57.29	92.05	149.34
25	526.01	66.33	83.00	149.34
26	449.20	76.81	72.53	149.34
27	360.27	88.93	60.40	149.34
28	257.29	102.97	46.36	149.34
29	138.06	119.23	30.10	149.34
30	.00	138.06	11.13	149.19
Totals:		**$1000.00**	**$3479.96**	**$4479.96**

TAX-SAVINGS TABLE

14.75% INTEREST

Multiply all figures by the number of thousands in your loan.
Net cost equals yearly payment minus tax savings.

Federal Tax Bracket					
15.0%		28.0%		33.0%	
Tax Savings	Net Cost	Tax Savings	Net Cost	Tax Savings	Net Cost
$22.11	$127.23	$41.26	$108.07	$48.63	$100.70
22.06	127.28	41.18	108.16	48.53	100.81
22.01	127.33	41.08	108.26	48.41	100.93
21.94	127.39	40.96	108.38	48.27	101.06
21.87	127.47	40.82	108.51	48.11	101.22
21.79	127.55	40.67	108.67	47.93	101.41
21.69	127.65	40.49	108.85	47.72	101.62
21.58	127.76	40.28	109.06	47.47	101.87
21.45	127.89	40.04	109.30	47.18	102.15
21.30	128.04	39.75	109.58	46.85	102.48
21.12	128.21	39.43	109.91	46.47	102.87
20.92	128.42	39.05	110.28	46.03	103.31
20.69	128.65	38.62	110.72	45.51	103.82
20.42	128.92	38.11	111.23	44.92	104.42
20.10	129.23	37.53	111.81	44.23	105.11
19.74	129.60	36.85	112.49	43.43	105.91
19.32	130.02	36.07	113.27	42.51	106.83
18.83	130.50	35.16	114.18	41.44	107.90
18.27	131.07	34.11	115.23	40.20	109.14
17.62	131 72	32.89	116.45	38.76	110.57
16.87	132.47	31.48	117.86	37.10	112.23
15.99	133.35	29.85	119.49	35.18	114.16
14.98	134.36	27.96	121.38	32.95	116.38
13.81	135.53	25.77	123.56	30.38	118.96
12.45	136.89	23.24	126.10	27 39	121.95
10.88	138.46	20.31	129.03	23.94	125.40
9.06	140.28	16.91	132.42	19.93	129.40
6.95	142.38	12.98	136.36	15.30	134.04
4.52	144.82	8.43	140.91	9.93	139.40
1.67	147.52	3.12	146.07	3.67	145.51
Totals:					
$521.99	**$3957.97**	**$974.39**	**$3505.57**	**$1148.39**	**$3331.57**

| 15.00% INTEREST | **ANNUAL MORTGAGE PAYMENT SCHEDULE** |

For a mortgage of $1,000.00

MORTGAGE TERM: **15 years**
Monthly payment: **$14.00**
Annual payment: **$167.95**

Year	Balance of Loan	Principal Paid	Interest Paid	Yearly Payment
1	$980.76	$19.24	$148.71	$167.95
2	958.43	22.33	145.62	167.95
3	932.51	25.92	142.03	167.95
4	902.43	30.09	137.86	167.95
5	867.50	34.92	133.03	167.95
6	826.97	40.54	127.41	167.95
7	779.91	47.05	120.90	167.95
8	725.30	54.62	113.33	167.95
9	661.90	63.40	104.55	167.95
10	588.31	73.59	94.36	167.95
11	502.89	85.42	82.53	167.95
12	403.74	99.15	68.80	167.95
13	288.65	115.09	52.86	167.95
14	155.06	133.59	34.36	167.95
15	.00	155.06	12.71	167.78
Totals:		$1000.00	$1519.08	$2519.08

TAX-SAVINGS TABLE

15.00%
INTEREST

Multiply all figures by the number of thousands in your loan.
Net cost equals yearly payment minus tax savings.

Federal Tax Bracket					
15.0%		28.0%		33.0%	
Tax Savings	Net Cost	Tax Savings	Net Cost	Tax Savings	Net Cost
$22.31	$145.64	$41.64	$126.31	$49.08	$118.88
21.84	146.11	40.77	127.18	48.05	119.90
21.30	146.65	39.77	128.18	46.87	121.08
20.68	147.27	38.60	129.35	45.50	122.46
19.95	148.00	37.25	130.70	43.90	124.05
19.11	148.84	35.68	132.27	42.05	125.90
18.13	149.82	33.85	134.10	39.90	128.05
17.00	150.95	31.73	136.22	37.40	130.55
15.68	152.27	29.27	138.68	34.50	133.45
14.15	153.80	26.42	141.53	31.14	136.81
12.38	155.57	23.11	144.84	27.24	140.71
10.32	157.63	19.26	148.69	22.70	145.25
7.93	160.02	14.80	153.15	17.44	150.51
5.15	162.80	9.62	158.33	11.34	156.61
1.91	165.87	3.56	164.22	4.20	163.58
Totals:					
$227.86	**$2291.22**	**$425.34**	**$2093.74**	**$501.30**	**$2017.79**

<table>
<tr><td colspan="2">15.00%
INTEREST</td><td colspan="3">ANNUAL MORTGAGE PAYMENT SCHEDULE</td></tr>
</table>

15.00% INTEREST

ANNUAL MORTGAGE PAYMENT SCHEDULE

For a mortgage of $1,000.00

MORTGAGE TERM: **30 years**
Monthly payment: **$12.64**
Annual payment: **$151.73**

Year	Balance of Loan	Principal Paid	Interest Paid	Yearly Payment
1	$998.14	$1.86	$149.88	$151.73
2	995.99	2.16	149.58	151.73
3	993.48	2.50	149.23	151.73
4	990.58	2.91	148.83	151.73
5	987.21	3.37	148.36	151.73
6	983.29	3.91	147.82	151.73
7	978.75	4.54	147.19	151.73
8	973.47	5.27	146.46	151.73
9	967.35	6.12	145.61	151.73
10	960.25	7.11	144.63	151.73
11	952.00	8.25	143.49	151.73
12	942.43	9.57	142.16	151.73
13	931.31	11.11	140.62	151.73
14	918.41	12.90	138.83	151.73
15	903.44	14.97	136.76	151.73
16	886.06	17.38	134.35	151.73
17	865.89	20.17	131.56	151.73
18	842.47	23.42	128.32	151.73
19	815.29	27.18	124.55	151.73
20	783.74	31.55	120.18	151.73
21	747.12	36.62	115.11	151.73
22	704.61	42.51	109.22	151.73
23	655.26	49.34	102.39	151.73
24	597.99	57.28	94.46	151.73
25	531.50	66.48	85.25	151.73
26	454.33	77.17	74.56	151.73
27	364.76	89.58	62.16	151.73
28	260.78	103.98	47.76	151.73
29	140.09	120.69	31.04	151.73
30	.00	140.09	11.49	151.58
Totals:		**$1000.00**	**$3551.84**	**$4551.84**

TAX-SAVINGS TABLE

15.00%
INTEREST

Multiply all figures by the number of thousands in your loan.
Net cost equals yearly payment minus tax savings.

Federal Tax Bracket					
15.0%		28.0%		33.0%	
Tax Savings	Net Cost	Tax Savings	Net Cost	Tax Savings	Net Cost
$22.48	$129.25	$41.97	$109.77	$49.46	$102.27
22.44	129.30	41.88	109.85	49.36	102.37
22.38	129.35	41.78	109.95	49.25	102.49
22.32	129.41	41.67	110.06	49.11	102.62
22.25	129.48	41.54	110.19	48.96	102.77
22.17	129.56	41.39	110.34	48.78	102.95
22.08	129.65	41.21	110.52	48.57	103.16
21.97	129.76	41.01	110.72	48.33	103.40
21.84	129.89	40.77	110.96	48.05	103.68
21.69	130.04	40.50	111.24	47.73	104.01
21.52	130.21	40.18	111.56	47.35	104.38
21.32	130.41	39.80	111.93	46.91	104.82
21.09	130.64	39.37	112.36	46.40	105.33
20.83	130.91	38.87	112.86	45.82	105.92
20.51	131.22	38.29	113.44	45.13	106.60
20.15	131.58	37.62	114.11	44.34	107.40
19.73	132.00	36.84	114.90	43.41	108.32
19.25	132.49	35.93	115.80	42.34	109.39
18.68	133.05	34.87	116.86	41.10	110.63
18.03	133.71	33.65	118.08	39.66	112.07
17.27	134.47	32.23	119.50	37.99	113.75
16.38	135.35	30.58	121.15	36.04	115.69
15.36	136.37	28.67	123.06	33.79	117.94
14.17	137.56	26.45	125.29	31.17	120.56
12.79	138.95	23.87	127.86	28.13	123.60
11.18	140.55	20.88	130.86	24.61	127.13
9.32	142.41	17.40	134.33	20.51	131.22
7.16	144.57	13.37	138.36	15.76	135.97
4.66	147.08	8.69	143.04	10.24	141.49
1.72	149.85	3.22	148.36	3.79	147.79
Totals:					
$532.78	**$4019.07**	**$994.52**	**$3557.33**	**$1172.11**	**$3379.73**

ANNUAL MORTGAGE PAYMENT SCHEDULE

For a mortgage of $1,000.00

	MORTGAGE TERM:	15 years
	Monthly payment:	$14.17
	Annual payment:	$170.01

Year	Balance of Loan	Principal Paid	Interest Paid	Yearly Payment
1	$981.21	$18.79	$151.22	$170.01
2	959.35	21.86	148.15	170.01
3	933.91	25.44	144.57	170.01
4	904.31	29.60	140.41	170.01
5	869.87	34.44	135.57	170.01
6	829.79	40.08	129.93	170.01
7	783.15	46.64	123.37	170.01
8	728.88	54.27	115.74	170.01
9	665.73	63.15	106.86	170.01
10	592.25	73.48	96.53	170.01
11	506.75	85.50	84.51	170.01
12	407.25	99.49	70.52	170.01
13	291.48	115.77	54.24	170.01
14	156.76	134.72	35.29	170.01
15	.00	156.76	13.07	169.83
Totals:		$1000.00	$1549.97	$2549.97

15.25%
INTEREST

Multiply all figures by the number of thousands in your loan.
Net cost equals yearly payment minus tax savings.

Federal Tax Bracket					
15.0%		28.0%		33.0%	
Tax Savings	Net Cost	Tax Savings	Net Cost	Tax Savings	Net Cost
$22.68	$147.33	$42.34	$127.67	$49.90	$120.11
22.22	147.79	41.48	128.53	48.89	121.12
21.69	148.32	40.48	129.53	47.71	122.30
21.06	148.95	39.31	130.70	46.34	123.67
20.33	149.68	37.96	132.05	44.74	125.27
19.49	150.52	36.38	133.63	42.88	127.13
18.51	151.50	34.54	135.47	40.71	129.30
17.36	152.65	32.41	137.60	38.19	131.82
16.03	153.98	29.92	140.09	35.26	134.75
14.48	155.53	27.03	142.98	31.85	138.16
12.68	157.33	23.66	146.35	27.89	142.12
10.58	159.43	19.74	150.27	23.27	146.74
8.14	161.87	15.19	154.82	17.90	152.11
5.29	164.72	9.88	160.13	11.65	158.36
1.96	167.87	3.66	166.17	4.31	165.52
Totals:					
$232.50	$2317.48	$433.99	$2115.98	$511.49	$2038.48

| | 15.25% INTEREST | **ANNUAL MORTGAGE PAYMENT SCHEDULE** |

For a mortgage of $1,000.00

MORTGAGE TERM: **30 years**
Monthly payment: **$12.84**
Annual payment: **$154.14**

Year	Balance of Loan	Principal Paid	Interest Paid	Yearly Payment
1	$998.25	$1.75	$152.38	$154.14
2	996.20	2.04	152.09	154.14
3	993.83	2.38	151.76	154.14
4	991.07	2.76	151.37	154.14
5	987.85	3.22	150.92	154.14
6	984.11	3.74	150.39	154.14
7	979.75	4.35	149.78	154.14
8	974.68	5.07	149.07	154.14
9	968.79	5.90	148.24	154.14
10	961.93	6.86	147.27	154.14
11	953.94	7.98	146.15	154.14
12	944.65	9.29	144.84	154.14
13	933.84	10.81	143.32	154.14
14	921.26	12.58	141.56	154.14
15	906.62	14.64	139.50	154.14
16	889.59	17.03	137.10	154.14
17	869.77	19.82	134.32	154.14
18	846.71	23.06	131.07	154.14
19	819.87	26.84	127.30	154.14
20	788.64	31.23	122.91	154.14
21	752.31	36.34	117.80	154.14
22	710.02	42.28	111.85	154.14
23	660.82	49.20	104.93	154.14
24	603.57	57.25	96.88	154.14
25	536.95	66.62	87.52	154.14
26	459.43	77.52	76.61	154.14
27	369.23	90.20	63.93	154.14
28	264.26	104.96	49.17	154.14
29	142.12	122.14	32.00	154.14
30	.00	142.12	11.85	153.97
Totals:		**$1000.00**	**$3623.89**	**$4623.89**

TAX-SAVINGS TABLE

15.25%
INTEREST

Multiply all figures by the number of thousands in your loan.
Net cost equals yearly payment minus tax savings.

Federal Tax Bracket					
15.0%		28.0%		33.0%	
Tax Savings	Net Cost	Tax Savings	Net Cost	Tax Savings	Net Cost
$22.86	$131.28	$42.67	$111.47	$50.29	$103.85
22.81	131.32	42.59	111.55	50.19	103.94
22.76	131.37	42.49	111.64	50.08	104.05
22.71	131.43	42.38	111.75	49.95	104.18
22.64	131.50	42.26	111.88	49.80	104.33
22.56	131.58	42.11	112.03	49.63	104.51
22.47	131.67	41.94	112.20	49.43	104.71
22.36	131.77	41.74	112.40	49.19	104.94
22.24	131.90	41.51	112.63	48.92	105.22
22.09	132.04	41.24	112.90	48.60	105.53
21.92	132.21	40.92	113.21	48.23	105.91
21.73	132.41	40.56	113.58	47.80	106.34
21.50	132.64	40.13	114.00	47.30	106.84
21.23	132.90	39.64	114.50	46.71	107.42
20.92	133.21	39.06	115.08	46.03	108.10
20.57	133.57	38.39	115.75	45.24	108.89
20.15	133.99	37.61	116.53	44.32	109.81
19.66	134.47	36.70	117.43	43.25	110.88
19.09	135.04	35.64	118.49	42.01	112.13
18.44	135.70	34.41	119.72	40.56	113.58
17.67	136.47	32.98	121.15	38.87	115.26
16.78	137.36	31.32	122.82	36.91	117.22
15.74	138.39	29.38	124.75	34.63	119.51
14.53	139.60	27.13	127.01	31.97	122.16
13.13	141.01	24.50	129.63	28.88	125.25
11.49	142.64	21.45	132.68	25.28	128.85
9.59	144.55	17.90	136.23	21.10	133.04
7.38	146.76	13.77	140.37	16.23	137.91
4.80	149.34	8.96	145.18	10.56	143.58
1.78	152.20	3.32	150.66	3.91	150.06
Totals:					
$543.58	$4080.31	$1014.69	$3609.20	$1195.88	$3428.01

ANNUAL MORTGAGE PAYMENT SCHEDULE

For a mortgage of $1,000.00

	MORTGAGE TERM:	**15 years**
	Monthly payment:	**$14.34**
	Annual payment:	**$172.08**

Year	Balance of Loan	Principal Paid	Interest Paid	Yearly Payment
1	$981.65	$18.35	$153.73	$172.08
2	960.25	21.40	150.68	172.08
3	935.29	24.96	147.12	172.08
4	906.17	29.12	142.96	172.08
5	872.20	33.97	138.11	172.08
6	832.58	39.62	132.45	172.08
7	786.35	46.22	125.86	172.08
8	732.44	53.92	118.16	172.08
9	669.54	62.90	109.18	172.08
10	596.17	73.37	98.71	172.08
11	510.59	85.58	86.50	172.08
12	410.76	99.83	72.25	172.08
13	294.31	116.45	55.62	172.08
14	158.46	135.84	36.24	172.08
15	.00	158.46	13.43	171.90
Totals:		**$1000.00**	**$1581.00**	**$2581.00**

TAX-SAVINGS TABLE

15.50% INTEREST

Multiply all figures by the number of thousands in your loan.
Net cost equals yearly payment minus tax savings.

Federal Tax Bracket					
15.0%		28.0%		33.0%	
Tax Savings	Net Cost	Tax Savings	Net Cost	Tax Savings	Net Cost
$23.06	$149.02	$43.05	$129.03	$50.73	$121.35
22.60	149.48	42.19	129.89	49.72	122.35
22.07	150.01	41.19	130.89	48.55	123.53
21.44	150.64	40.03	132.05	47.18	124.90
20.72	151.36	38.67	133.41	45.58	126.50
19.87	152.21	37.09	134.99	43.71	128.37
18.88	153.20	35.24	136.84	41.53	130.55
17.72	154.35	33.09	138.99	38.99	133.09
16.38	155.70	30.57	141.51	36.03	136.05
14.81	157.27	27.64	144.44	32.57	139.50
12.97	159.10	24.22	147.86	28.54	143.54
10.84	161.24	20.23	151.85	23.84	148.24
8.34	163.74	15.57	156.50	18.36	153.72
5.44	166.64	10.15	161.93	11.96	160.12
2.02	169.88	3.76	168.13	4.43	167.46
Totals:					
$237.15	**$2343.85**	**$442.68**	**$2138.32**	**$521.73**	**$2059.27**

ANNUAL MORTGAGE PAYMENT SCHEDULE

For a mortgage of $1,000.00

MORTGAGE TERM: **30 years**
Monthly payment: **$13.05**
Annual payment: **$156.54**

Year	Balance of Loan	Principal Paid	Interest Paid	Yearly Payment
1	$998.34	$1.66	$154.89	$156.54
2	996.41	1.93	154.61	156.54
3	994.16	2.25	154.29	156.54
4	991.53	2.63	153.91	156.54
5	988.46	3.07	153.48	156.54
6	984.88	3.58	152.96	156.54
7	980.71	4.17	152.37	156.54
8	975.84	4.87	151.67	156.54
9	970.16	5.68	150.86	156.54
10	963.54	6.62	149.92	156.54
11	955.81	7.73	148.81	156.54
12	946.80	9.01	147.53	156.54
13	936.28	10.51	146.03	156.54
14	924.02	12.27	144.28	156.54
15	909.71	14.31	142.23	156.54
16	893.02	16.69	139.85	156.54
17	873.55	19.47	137.07	156.54
18	850.84	22.71	133.83	156.54
19	824.35	26.49	130.05	156.54
20	793.45	30.90	125.64	156.54
21	757.40	36.05	120.50	156.54
22	715.36	42.05	114.49	156.54
23	666.31	49.05	107.49	156.54
24	609.09	57.22	99.33	156.54
25	542.35	66.74	89.80	156.54
26	464.49	77.86	78.69	156.54
27	373.67	90.82	65.72	156.54
28	267.73	105.94	50.60	156.54
29	144.15	123.58	32.96	156.54
30	.00	144.15	12.22	156.38
Totals:		**$1000.00**	**$3696.09**	**$4696.09**

TAX-SAVINGS TABLE

	15.50%
	INTEREST

Multiply all figures by the number of thousands in your loan.
Net cost equals yearly payment minus tax savings.

Federal Tax Bracket					
15.0%		28.0%		33.0%	
Tax Savings	Net Cost	Tax Savings	Net Cost	Tax Savings	Net Cost
$23.23	$133.31	$43.37	$113.17	$51.11	$105.43
23.19	133.35	43.29	113.25	51.02	105.52
23.14	133.40	43.20	113.34	50.92	105.63
23.09	133.46	43.10	113.45	50.79	105.75
23.02	133.52	42.97	113.57	50.65	105.90
22.94	133.60	42.83	113.71	50.48	106.06
22.86	133.69	42.66	113.88	50.28	106.26
22.75	133.79	42.47	114.07	50.05	106.49
22.63	133.91	42.24	114.30	49.78	106.76
22.49	134.05	41.98	114.57	49.47	107.07
22.32	134.22	41.67	114.87	49.11	107.43
22.13	134.41	41.31	115.23	48.68	107.86
21.90	134.64	40.89	115.65	48.19	108.35
21.64	134.90	40.40	116.14	47.61	108.93
21.34	135.21	39.83	116.72	46.94	109.60
20.98	135.56	39.16	117.38	46.15	110.39
20.56	135.98	38.38	118.16	45.23	111.31
20.07	136.47	37.47	119.07	44.16	112.38
19.51	137.03	36.41	120.13	42.92	113.63
18.85	137.70	35.18	121.36	41.46	115.08
18.07	138.47	33.74	122.80	39.76	116.78
17.17	139.37	32.06	124.48	37.78	118.76
16.12	140.42	30.10	126.44	35.47	121.07
14.90	141.64	27.81	128.73	32.78	123.76
13.47	143.07	25.14	131.40	29.63	126.91
11.80	144.74	22.03	134.51	25.97	130.58
9.86	146.68	18.40	138.14	21.69	134.85
7.59	148.95	14.17	142.37	16.70	139.84
4.94	151.60	9.23	147.31	10.88	145.66
1.83	154.54	3.42	152.95	4.03	152.34
Totals:					
$554.41	$4141.68	$1034.91	$3661.19	$1219.71	$3476.38

<table>
<tr><td>**15.75%** INTEREST</td><td colspan="3">**ANNUAL MORTGAGE PAYMENT SCHEDULE**</td></tr>
</table>

	ANNUAL MORTGAGE PAYMENT SCHEDULE
15.75% INTEREST	

For a mortgage of $1,000.00

MORTGAGE TERM: **15 years**
Monthly payment: **$14.51**
Annual payment: **$174.16**

Year	Balance of Loan	Principal Paid	Interest Paid	Yearly Payment
1	$982.09	$17.91	$156.24	$174.16
2	961.14	20.95	153.21	174.16
3	936.64	24.50	149.66	174.16
4	908.00	28.65	145.51	174.16
5	874.50	33.50	140.66	174.16
6	835.33	39.17	134.99	174.16
7	789.52	45.81	128.35	174.16
8	735.96	53.56	120.59	174.16
9	673.32	62.64	111.52	174.16
10	600.08	73.25	100.91	174.16
11	514.42	85.65	88.50	174.16
12	414.26	100.16	74.00	174.16
13	297.13	117.13	57.03	174.16
14	160.17	136.97	37.19	174.16
15	.00	160.17	13.80	173.97
Totals:		**$1000.00**	**$1612.17**	**$2612.17**

TAX-SAVINGS TABLE

15.75%
INTEREST

Multiply all figures by the number of thousands in your loan.
Net cost equals yearly payment minus tax savings.

| Federal Tax Bracket | | | | | |
| 15.0% | | 28.0% | | 33.0% | |
Tax Savings	Net Cost	Tax Savings	Net Cost	Tax Savings	Net Cost
$23.44	$150.72	$43.75	$130.41	$51.56	$122.60
22.98	151.18	42.90	131.26	50.56	123.60
22.45	151.71	41.91	132.25	49.39	124.77
21.83	152.33	40.74	133.41	48.02	126.14
21.10	153.06	39.38	134.77	46.42	127.74
20.25	153.91	37.80	136.36	44.55	129.61
19.25	154.90	35.94	138.22	42.36	131.80
18.09	156.07	33.77	140.39	39.80	134.36
16.73	157.43	31.23	142.93	36.80	137.36
15.14	159.02	28.25	145.90	33.30	140.86
13.28	160.88	24.78	149.38	29.21	144.95
11.10	163.06	20.72	153.44	24.42	149.74
8.55	165.60	15.97	158.19	18.82	155.34
5.58	168.58	10.41	163.74	12.27	161.88
2.07	171.90	3.86	170.10	4.55	169.41
Totals:					
$241.82	**$2370.34**	**$451.41**	**$2160.76**	**$532.01**	**$2080.15**

15.75% INTEREST	**ANNUAL MORTGAGE PAYMENT SCHEDULE**

For a mortgage of $1,000.00

	MORTGAGE TERM:	**30 years**
	Monthly payment:	**$13.25**
	Annual payment:	**$158.95**

Year	Balance of Loan	Principal Paid	Interest Paid	Yearly Payment
1	$998.44	$1.56	$157.39	$158.95
2	996.61	1.83	157.13	158.95
3	994.47	2.14	156.82	158.95
4	991.97	2.50	156.45	158.95
5	989.04	2.92	156.03	158.95
6	985.63	3.42	155.53	158.95
7	981.63	4.00	154.96	158.95
8	976.95	4.68	154.28	158.95
9	971.48	5.47	153.49	158.95
10	965.09	6.39	152.56	158.95
11	957.61	7.48	151.48	158.95
12	948.87	8.74	150.21	158.95
13	938.64	10.22	148.73	158.95
14	926.69	11.96	147.00	158.95
15	912.71	13.98	144.97	158.95
16	896.36	16.35	142.60	158.95
17	877.24	19.12	139.83	158.95
18	854.88	22.36	136.60	158.95
19	828.73	26.14	132.81	158.95
20	798.16	30.57	128.38	158.95
21	762.41	35.75	123.20	158.95
22	720.60	41.81	117.15	158.95
23	671.71	48.89	110.07	158.95
24	614.55	57.17	101.78	158.95
25	547.69	66.85	92.10	158.95
26	469.52	78.18	80.78	158.95
27	378.10	91.42	67.54	158.95
28	271.19	106.90	52.05	158.95
29	146.18	125.01	33.94	158.95
30	.00	146.18	12.60	158.78
Totals:		**$1000.00**	**$3768.45**	**$4768.45**

TAX-SAVINGS TABLE

15.75% INTEREST

Multiply all figures by the number of thousands in your loan.
Net cost equals yearly payment minus tax savings.

| Federal Tax Bracket | | | | | |
| 15.0% | | 28.0% | | 33.0% | |
Tax Savings	Net Cost	Tax Savings	Net Cost	Tax Savings	Net Cost
$23.61	$135.35	$44.07	$114.88	$51.94	$107.02
23.57	135.39	44.00	114.96	51.85	107.10
23.52	135.43	43.91	115.05	51.75	107.20
23.47	135.49	43.81	115.15	51.63	107.32
23.40	135.55	43.69	115.27	51.49	107.46
23.33	135.62	43.55	115.40	51.33	107.63
23.24	135.71	43.39	115.57	51.14	107.82
23.14	135.81	43.20	115.76	50.91	108.04
23.02	135.93	42.98	115.98	50.65	108.30
22.88	136.07	42.72	116.24	50.34	108.61
22.72	136.23	42.41	116.54	49.99	108.97
22.53	136.42	42.06	116.90	49.57	109.38
22.31	136.64	41.64	117.31	49.08	109.87
22.05	136.90	41.16	117.79	48.51	110.44
21.75	137.21	40.59	118.36	47.84	111.11
21.39	137.56	39.93	119.02	47.06	111.89
20.98	137.98	39.15	119.80	46.15	112.81
20.49	138.46	38.25	120.71	45.08	113.88
19.92	139.03	37.19	121.77	43.83	115.13
19.26	139.70	35.95	123.01	42.37	116.59
18.48	140.47	34.50	124.46	40.66	118.30
17.57	141.38	32.80	126.15	38.66	120.30
16.51	142.44	30.82	128.14	36.32	122.63
15.27	143.69	28.50	130.45	33.59	125.37
13.82	145.14	25.79	133.17	30.39	128.56
12.12	146.84	22.62	136.34	26.66	132.30
10.13	148.82	18.91	140.04	22.29	136.67
7.81	151.15	14.57	144.38	17.18	141.78
5.09	153.86	9.50	149.45	11.20	147.75
1.89	156.89	3.53	155.26	4.16	154.63
Totals:					
$565.27	**$4203.18**	**$1055.17**	**$3713.28**	**$1243.59**	**$3524.86**

For a mortgage of $1,000.00

	MORTGAGE TERM:	**15 years**
	Monthly payment:	**$14.69**
	Annual payment:	**$176.24**

Year	Balance of Loan	Principal Paid	Interest Paid	Yearly Payment
1	$982.51	$17.49	$158.75	$176.24
2	962.01	20.50	155.74	176.24
3	937.97	24.03	152.21	176.24
4	909.80	28.18	148.07	176.24
5	876.77	33.03	143.21	176.24
6	838.05	38.72	137.52	176.24
7	792.66	45.39	130.85	176.24
8	739.45	53.21	123.04	176.24
9	677.08	62.38	113.87	176.24
10	603.95	73.12	103.12	176.24
11	518.24	85.72	90.53	176.24
12	417.75	100.48	75.76	176.24
13	299.96	117.79	58.45	176.24
14	161.87	138.09	38.16	176.24
15	.00	161.87	14.18	176.05
Totals:		**$1000.00**	**$1643.47**	**$2643.47**

TAX-SAVINGS TABLE

16.00%
INTEREST

Multiply all figures by the number of thousands in your loan.
Net cost equals yearly payment minus tax savings.

Federal Tax Bracket					
15.0%		28.0%		33.0%	
Tax Savings	Net Cost	Tax Savings	Net Cost	Tax Savings	Net Cost
$23.81	$152.43	$44.45	$131.79	$52.39	$123.86
23.36	152.88	43.61	132.64	51.39	124.85
22.83	153.41	42.62	133.63	50.23	126.02
22.21	154.03	41.46	134.78	48.86	127.38
21.48	154.76	40.10	136.14	47.26	128.98
20.63	155.62	38.51	137.74	45.38	130.86
19.63	156.62	36.64	139.60	43.18	133.06
18.46	157.79	34.45	141.79	40.60	135.64
17.08	159.16	31.88	144.36	37.58	138.67
15.47	160.78	28.87	147.37	34.03	142.21
13.58	162.67	25.35	150.90	29.87	146.37
11.36	164.88	21.21	155.03	25.00	151.24
8.77	167.48	16.37	159.88	19.29	156.96
5.72	170.52	10.68	165.56	12.59	163.65
2.13	173.92	3.97	172.08	4.68	171.37
Totals:					
$246.52	**$2396.95**	**$460.17**	**$2183.30**	**$542.34**	**$2101.12**

For a mortgage of $1,000.00

	MORTGAGE TERM:	**30 years**
	Monthly payment:	**$13.45**
	Annual payment:	**$161.37**

Year	Balance of Loan	Principal Paid	Interest Paid	Yearly Payment
1	$998.52	$1.48	$159.89	$161.37
2	996.79	1.73	159.64	161.37
3	994.77	2.03	159.34	161.37
4	992.39	2.38	158.99	161.37
5	989.60	2.79	158.58	161.37
6	986.33	3.27	158.10	161.37
7	982.50	3.83	157.54	161.37
8	978.01	4.49	156.88	161.37
9	972.75	5.26	156.11	161.37
10	966.58	6.17	155.20	161.37
11	959.34	7.23	154.14	161.37
12	950.86	8.48	152.89	161.37
13	940.92	9.94	151.43	161.37
14	929.27	11.65	149.72	161.37
15	915.61	13.66	147.71	161.37
16	899.60	16.01	145.36	161.37
17	880.82	18.77	142.60	161.37
18	858.82	22.01	139.36	161.37
19	833.02	25.80	135.57	161.37
20	802.78	30.24	131.13	161.37
21	767.33	35.45	125.92	161.37
22	725.77	41.56	119.81	161.37
23	677.05	48.72	112.65	161.37
24	619.94	57.11	104.26	161.37
25	552.99	66.95	94.42	161.37
26	474.50	78.48	82.89	161.37
27	382.50	92.00	69.37	161.37
28	274.65	107.85	53.52	161.37
29	148.21	126.43	34.94	161.37
30	.00	148.21	12.98	161.19
Totals:		**$1000.00**	**$3840.95**	**$4840.95**

TAX-SAVINGS TABLE

16.00%
INTEREST

Multiply all figures by the number of thousands in your loan.
Net cost equals yearly payment minus tax savings.

Federal Tax Bracket					
15.0%		28.0%		33.0%	
Tax Savings	Net Cost	Tax Savings	Net Cost	Tax Savings	Net Cost
$23.98	$137.39	$44.77	$116.60	$52.77	$108.61
23.95	137.42	44.70	116.67	52.68	108.69
23.90	137.47	44.62	116.75	52.58	108.79
23.85	137.52	44.52	116.85	52.47	108.90
23.79	137.58	44.40	116.97	52.33	109.04
23.72	137.66	44.27	117.10	52.17	109.20
23.63	137.74	44.11	117.26	51.99	109.38
23.53	137.84	43.93	117.44	51.77	109.60
23.42	137.95	43.71	117.66	51.52	109.86
23.28	138.09	43.46	117.91	51.22	110.15
23.12	138.25	43.16	118.21	50.87	110.51
22.93	138.44	42.81	118.56	50.45	110.92
22.71	138.66	42.40	118.97	49.97	111.40
22.46	138.91	41.92	119.45	49.41	111.96
22.16	139.21	41.36	120.01	48.74	112.63
21.80	139.57	40.70	120.67	47.97	113.40
21.39	139.98	39.93	121.44	47.06	114.31
20.90	140.47	39.02	122.35	45.99	115.38
20.34	141.03	37.96	123.41	44.74	116.63
19.67	141.70	36.72	124.65	43.27	118.10
18.89	142.48	35.26	126.11	41.55	119.82
17.97	143.40	33.55	127.82	39.54	121.83
16.90	144.47	31.54	129.83	37.18	124.20
15.64	145.73	29.19	132.18	34.41	126.97
14.16	147.21	26.44	134.93	31.16	130.21
12.43	148.94	23.21	138.16	27.35	134.02
10.41	150.97	19.42	141.95	22.89	138.48
8.03	153.34	14.98	146.39	17.66	143.71
5.24	156.13	9.78	151.59	11.53	149.84
1.95	159.25	3.63	157.56	4.28	156.91
Totals:					
$576.14	**$4264.81**	**$1075.47**	**$3765.48**	**$1267.51**	**$3573.44**

ANNUAL MORTGAGE PAYMENT SCHEDULE

For a mortgage of $1,000.00

MORTGAGE TERM: **15 years**
Monthly payment: **$14.86**
Annual payment: **$178.34**

Year	Balance of Loan	Principal Paid	Interest Paid	Yearly Payment
1	$982.93	$17.07	$161.27	$178.34
2	962.86	20.07	158.27	178.34
3	939.28	23.58	154.76	178.34
4	911.57	27.71	150.63	178.34
5	879.00	32.57	145.77	178.34
6	840.73	38.27	140.07	178.34
7	795.76	44.97	133.37	178.34
8	742.91	52.85	125.49	178.34
9	680.80	62.11	116.23	178.34
10	607.81	72.99	105.35	178.34
11	522.04	85.77	92.57	178.34
12	421.24	100.80	77.54	178.34
13	302.79	118.45	59.89	178.34
14	163.59	139.20	39.14	178.34
15	.00	163.59	14.56	178.14
Totals:		**$1000.00**	**$1674.90**	**$2674.90**

TAX-SAVINGS TABLE

16.25%
INTEREST

Multiply all figures by the number of thousands in your loan.
Net cost equals yearly payment minus tax savings.

Federal Tax Bracket					
15.0%		28.0%		33.0%	
Tax Savings	Net Cost	Tax Savings	Net Cost	Tax Savings	Net Cost
$24.19	$154.15	$45.15	$133.19	$53.22	$125.12
23.74	154.60	44.32	134.02	52.23	126.11
23.21	155.13	43.33	135.01	51.07	127.27
22.59	155.75	42.18	136.16	49.71	128.63
21.87	156.47	40.82	137.52	48.11	130.23
21.01	157.33	39.22	139.12	46.22	132.12
20.01	158.34	37.34	141.00	44.01	134.33
18.82	159.52	35.14	143.20	41.41	136.93
17.43	160.91	32.54	145.80	38.36	139.98
15.80	162.54	29.50	148.84	34.77	143.57
13.89	164.46	25.92	152.42	30.55	147.79
11.63	166.71	21.71	156.63	25.59	152.75
8.98	169.36	16.77	161.57	19.76	158.58
5.87	172.47	10.96	167.38	12.92	165.42
2.18	175.96	4.08	174.07	4.80	173.34
Totals:					
$251.24	**$2423.67**	**$468.97**	**$2205.93**	**$552.72**	**$2122.19**

<table>
<tr><td></td><td colspan="4">

16.25% INTEREST   **ANNUAL MORTGAGE PAYMENT SCHEDULE**

</td></tr>
</table>

16.25%
INTEREST

ANNUAL MORTGAGE PAYMENT SCHEDULE

For a mortgage of $1,000.00

	MORTGAGE TERM:	**30 years**
	Monthly payment:	**$13.65**
	Annual payment:	**$163.79**

Year	Balance of Loan	Principal Paid	Interest Paid	Yearly Payment
1	$998.61	$1.39	$162.40	$163.79
2	996.97	1.64	162.16	163.79
3	995.05	1.92	161.87	163.79
4	992.79	2.26	161.53	163.79
5	990.13	2.66	161.14	163.79
6	987.01	3.12	160.67	163.79
7	983.34	3.67	160.12	163.79
8	979.03	4.31	159.48	163.79
9	973.96	5.07	158.73	163.79
10	968.01	5.95	157.84	163.79
11	961.01	7.00	156.80	163.79
12	952.79	8.22	155.57	163.79
13	943.13	9.66	154.13	163.79
14	931.77	11.36	152.44	163.79
15	918.43	13.34	150.45	163.79
16	902.74	15.68	148.11	163.79
17	884.31	18.43	145.36	163.79
18	862.66	21.66	142.14	163.79
19	837.21	25.45	138.34	163.79
20	807.30	29.91	133.88	163.79
21	772.15	35.15	128.64	163.79
22	730.85	41.30	122.49	163.79
23	682.31	48.54	115.25	163.79
24	625.26	57.04	106.75	163.79
25	558.23	67.03	96.76	163.79
26	479.45	78.78	85.02	163.79
27	386.88	92.57	71.22	163.79
28	278.09	108.79	55.00	163.79
29	150.24	127.85	35.94	163.79
30	.00	150.24	13.37	163.61
Totals:		**$1000.00**	**$3913.58**	**$4913.58**

TAX-SAVINGS TABLE

16.25%
INTEREST

Multiply all figures by the number of thousands in your loan.
Net cost equals yearly payment minus tax savings.

Federal Tax Bracket					
15.0%		28.0%		33.0%	
Tax Savings	Net Cost	Tax Savings	Net Cost	Tax Savings	Net Cost
$24.36	$139.43	$45.47	$118.32	$53.59	$110.20
24.32	139.47	45.40	118.39	53.51	110.28
24.28	139.51	45.32	118.47	53.42	110.38
24.23	139.56	45.23	118.56	53.31	110.49
24.17	139.62	45.12	118.67	53.17	110.62
24.10	139.69	44.99	118.80	53.02	110.77
24.02	139.77	44.83	118.96	52.84	110.95
23.92	139.87	44.65	119.14	52.63	111.16
23.81	139.98	44.44	119.35	52.38	111.41
23.68	140.12	44.19	119.60	52.09	111.71
23.52	140.27	43.90	119.89	51.74	112.05
23.34	140.46	43.56	120.23	51.34	112.45
23.12	140.67	43.16	120.64	50.86	112.93
22.87	140.93	42.68	121.11	50.30	113.49
22.57	141.23	42.13	121.67	49.65	114.14
22.22	141.58	41.47	122.32	48.88	114.92
21.80	141.99	40.70	123.09	47.97	115.82
21.32	142.47	39.80	123.99	46.90	116.89
20.75	143.04	38.74	125.06	45.65	118.14
20.08	143.71	37.49	126.30	44.18	119.61
19.30	144.50	36.02	127.77	42.45	121.34
18.37	145.42	34.30	129.50	40.42	123.37
17.29	146.50	32.27	131.52	38.03	125.76
16.01	147.78	29.89	133.90	35.23	128.56
14.51	149.28	27.09	136.70	31.93	131.86
12.75	151.04	23.80	139.99	28.06	135.74
10.68	153.11	19.94	143.85	23.50	140.29
8.25	155.54	15.40	148.39	18.15	145.64
5.39	158.40	10.06	153.73	11.86	151.93
2.01	161.60	3.74	159.87	4.41	159.20
Totals:					
$587.04	**$4326.54**	**$1095.80**	**$3817.78**	**$1291.48**	**$3622.10**

	16.50% INTEREST	ANNUAL MORTGAGE PAYMENT SCHEDULE

ANNUAL MORTGAGE PAYMENT SCHEDULE

For a mortgage of $1,000.00

MORTGAGE TERM: **15 years**
Monthly payment: **$15.04**
Annual payment: **$180.45**

Year	Balance of Loan	Principal Paid	Interest Paid	Yearly Payment
1	$983.33	$16.67	$163.78	$180.45
2	963.70	19.64	160.81	180.45
3	940.56	23.13	157.31	180.45
4	913.31	27.25	153.19	180.45
5	881.21	32.11	148.34	180.45
6	843.38	37.82	142.62	180.45
7	798.83	44.56	135.89	180.45
8	746.34	52.49	127.95	180.45
9	684.50	61.84	118.61	180.45
10	611.65	72.85	107.60	180.45
11	525.83	85.82	94.62	180.45
12	424.72	101.10	79.34	180.45
13	305.62	119.11	61.34	180.45
14	165.30	140.32	40.13	180.45
15	.00	165.30	14.94	180.24
Totals:		**$1000.00**	**$1706.47**	**$2706.47**

Multiply all figures by the number of thousands in your loan.
Net cost equals yearly payment minus tax savings.

| Federal Tax Bracket | | | | | |
| 15.0% | | 28.0% | | 33.0% | |
Tax Savings	Net Cost	Tax Savings	Net Cost	Tax Savings	Net Cost
$24.57	$155.88	$45.86	$134.59	$54.05	$126.40
24.12	156.32	45.03	135.42	53.07	127.38
23.60	156.85	44.05	136.40	51.91	128.53
22.98	157.47	42.89	137.55	50.55	129.89
22.25	158.19	41.54	138.91	48.95	131.49
21.39	159.05	39.93	140.51	47.07	133.38
20.38	160.06	38.05	142.40	44.84	135.60
19.19	161.25	35.83	144.62	42.22	138.22
17.79	162.65	33.21	147.24	39.14	141.30
16.14	164.31	30.13	150.32	35.51	144.94
14.19	166.25	26.49	153.95	31.23	149.22
11.90	168.54	22.22	158.23	26.18	154.26
9.20	171.24	17.17	163.27	20.24	160.20
6.02	174.43	11.24	169.21	13.24	167.20
2.24	178.00	4.18	176.06	4.93	175.31
Totals:					
$255.97	**$2450.50**	**$477.81**	**$2228.66**	**$563.14**	**$2143.34**

| | 16.50% INTEREST | **ANNUAL MORTGAGE PAYMENT SCHEDULE** |

For a mortgage of $1,000.00

MORTGAGE TERM: **30 years**
Monthly payment: **$13.85**
Annual payment: **$166.22**

Year	Balance of Loan	Principal Paid	Interest Paid	Yearly Payment
1	$998.69	$1.31	$164.90	$166.22
2	997.14	1.55	164.67	166.22
3	995.31	1.82	164.39	166.22
4	993.16	2.15	164.07	166.22
5	990.63	2.53	163.69	166.22
6	987.65	2.98	163.24	166.22
7	984.14	3.51	162.70	166.22
8	980.00	4.14	162.08	166.22
9	975.12	4.88	161.34	166.22
10	969.38	5.74	160.47	166.22
11	962.61	6.77	159.45	166.22
12	954.64	7.97	158.25	166.22
13	945.25	9.39	156.83	166.22
14	934.19	11.06	155.15	166.22
15	921.15	13.03	153.18	166.22
16	905.80	15.35	150.86	166.22
17	887.71	18.09	148.13	166.22
18	866.40	21.31	144.91	166.22
19	841.30	25.10	141.11	166.22
20	811.73	29.57	136.64	166.22
21	776.89	34.84	131.38	166.22
22	735.84	41.04	125.17	166.22
23	687.49	48.35	117.87	166.22
24	630.53	56.96	109.26	166.22
25	563.42	67.11	99.11	166.22
26	484.37	79.05	87.16	166.22
27	391.24	93.13	73.09	166.22
28	281.52	109.72	56.50	166.22
29	152.27	129.25	36.97	166.22
30	.00	152.27	13.76	166.03
Totals:		$1000.00	$3986.35	$4986.35

TAX-SAVINGS TABLE

16.50%
INTEREST

Multiply all figures by the number of thousands in your loan.
Net cost equals yearly payment minus tax savings.

Federal Tax Bracket					
15.0%		28.0%		33.0%	
Tax Savings	Net Cost	Tax Savings	Net Cost	Tax Savings	Net Cost
$24.74	$141.48	$46.17	$120.04	$54.42	$111.80
24.70	141.52	46.11	120.11	54.34	111.88
24.66	141.56	46.03	120.19	54.25	111.97
24.61	141.61	45.94	120.28	54.14	112.07
24.55	141.66	45.83	120.39	54.02	112.20
24.49	141.73	45.71	120.51	53.87	112.35
24.41	141.81	45.56	120.66	53.69	112.53
24.31	141.91	45.38	120.84	53.49	112.73
24.20	142.02	45.18	121.04	53.24	112.97
24.07	142.15	44.93	121.29	52.96	113.26
23.92	142.30	44.65	121.57	52.62	113.60
23.74	142.48	44.31	121.91	52.22	114.00
23.52	142.69	43.91	122.31	51.75	114.46
23.27	142.94	43.44	122.77	51.20	115.02
22.98	143.24	42.89	123.33	50.55	115.67
22.63	143.59	42.24	123.98	49.79	116.43
22.22	144.00	41.48	124.74	48.88	117.33
21.74	144.48	40.57	125.64	47.82	118.40
21.17	145.05	39.51	126.71	46.57	119.65
20.50	145.72	38.26	127.96	45.09	121.13
19.71	146.51	36.79	129.43	43.35	122.86
18.78	147.44	35.05	131.17	41.31	124.91
17.68	148.54	33.00	133.22	38.90	127.32
16.39	149.83	30.59	135.63	36.05	130.16
14.87	151.35	27.75	138.47	32.71	133.51
13.07	153.14	24.41	141.81	28.76	137.45
10.96	155.25	20.46	145.75	24.12	142.10
8.48	157.74	15.82	150.40	18.65	147.57
5.54	160.67	10.35	155.87	12.20	154.02
2.06	163.97	3.85	162.18	4.54	161.49
Totals:					
$597.95	**$4388.39**	**$1116.18**	**$3870.17**	**$1315.49**	**$3670.85**

16.75% INTEREST	ANNUAL MORTGAGE PAYMENT SCHEDULE

For a mortgage of $1,000.00

MORTGAGE TERM: **15 years**
Monthly payment: **$15.21**
Annual payment: **$182.56**

Year	Balance of Loan	Principal Paid	Interest Paid	Yearly Payment
1	$983.73	$16.27	$166.29	$182.56
2	964.52	19.21	163.34	182.56
3	941.82	22.69	159.87	182.56
4	915.02	26.80	155.76	182.56
5	883.38	31.65	150.91	182.56
6	846.00	37.38	145.18	182.56
7	801.86	44.14	138.42	182.56
8	749.73	52.13	130.43	182.56
9	688.17	61.56	121.00	182.56
10	615.46	72.70	109.85	182.56
11	529.60	85.86	96.70	182.56
12	428.20	101.40	81.16	182.56
13	308.45	119.75	62.81	182.56
14	167.02	141.43	41.13	182.56
15	.00	167.02	15.33	182.35
Totals:		**$1000.00**	**$1738.17**	**$2738.17**

TAX-SAVINGS TABLE

16.75%
INTEREST

Multiply all figures by the number of thousands in your loan.
Net cost equals yearly payment minus tax savings.

Federal Tax Bracket					
15.0%		28.0%		33.0%	
Tax Savings	Net Cost	Tax Savings	Net Cost	Tax Savings	Net Cost
$24.94	$157.62	$46.56	$136.00	$54.88	$127.68
24.50	158.06	45.74	136.82	53.90	128.66
23.98	158.58	44.76	137.80	52.76	129.80
23.36	159.19	43.61	138.95	51.40	131.16
22.64	159.92	42.25	140.30	49.80	132.76
21.78	160.78	40.65	141.91	47.91	134.65
20.76	161.80	38.76	143.80	45.68	136.88
19.56	162.99	36.52	146.04	43.04	139.52
18.15	164.41	33.88	148.68	39.93	142.63
16.48	166.08	30.76	151.80	36.25	146.31
14.50	168.05	27.07	155.48	31.91	150.65
12.17	170.38	22.72	159.83	26.78	155.78
9.42	173.14	17.59	164.97	20.73	161.83
6.17	176.39	11.52	171.04	13.57	168.98
2.30	180.05	4.29	178.06	5.06	177.29
Totals:					
$260.73	**$2477.44**	**$486.69**	**$2251.48**	**$573.60**	**$2164.57**

16.75% INTEREST	ANNUAL MORTGAGE PAYMENT SCHEDULE

For a mortgage of $1,000.00

MORTGAGE TERM: **30 years**
Monthly payment: **$14.05**
Annual payment: **$168.65**

Year	Balance of Loan	Principal Paid	Interest Paid	Yearly Payment
1	$998.76	$1.24	$167.41	$168.65
2	997.30	1.46	167.18	168.65
3	995.57	1.73	166.92	168.65
4	993.52	2.04	166.61	168.65
5	991.11	2.41	166.24	168.65
6	988.27	2.85	165.80	168.65
7	984.90	3.36	165.28	168.65
8	980.93	3.97	164.68	168.65
9	976.24	4.69	163.96	168.65
10	970.70	5.54	163.11	168.65
11	964.16	6.54	162.10	168.65
12	956.43	7.73	160.92	168.65
13	947.30	9.13	159.52	168.65
14	936.53	10.78	157.87	168.65
15	923.80	12.73	155.92	168.65
16	908.77	15.03	153.62	168.65
17	891.02	17.75	150.90	168.65
18	870.06	20.96	147.68	168.65
19	845.30	24.76	143.89	168.65
20	816.06	29.24	139.41	168.65
21	781.53	34.53	134.12	168.65
22	740.76	40.78	127.87	168.65
23	692.60	48.16	120.49	168.65
24	635.73	56.87	111.78	168.65
25	568.56	67 16	101.48	168.65
26	489.24	79.32	89.33	168.65
27	395.57	93.67	74.97	168.65
28	284.94	110.63	58.02	168.65
29	154.29	130.65	38.00	168.65
30	00	154.29	14.16	168.45
Totals:		**$1000.00**	**$4059.23**	**$5059.23**

TAX-SAVINGS TABLE

16.75%
INTEREST

Multiply all figures by the number of thousands in your loan.
Net cost equals yearly payment minus tax savings.

Federal Tax Bracket					
15.0%		28.0%		33.0%	
Tax Savings	Net Cost	Tax Savings	Net Cost	Tax Savings	Net Cost
$25.11	$143.54	$46.87	$121.77	$55.24	$113.40
25.08	143.57	46.81	121.84	55.17	113.48
25.04	143.61	46.74	121.91	55.08	113.56
24.99	143.66	46.65	122.00	54.98	113.67
24.94	143.71	46.55	122.10	54.86	113.79
24.87	143.78	46.42	122.22	54.71	113.93
24.79	143.85	46.28	122.37	54.54	114.10
24.70	143.95	46.11	122.54	54.34	114.30
24.59	144.05	45.91	122.74	54.11	114.54
24.47	144.18	45.67	122.98	53.83	114.82
24.32	144.33	45.39	123.26	53.49	115.15
24.14	144.51	45.06	123.59	53.10	115.54
23.93	144.72	44.67	123.98	52.64	116.01
23.68	144.97	44.20	124.44	52.10	116.55
23.39	145.26	43.66	124.99	51.45	117.19
23.04	145.60	43.01	125.63	50.69	117.95
22.63	146.01	42.25	126.40	49.80	118.85
22.15	146.49	41.35	127.30	48.74	119.91
21.58	147.06	40.29	128.36	47.48	121.16
20.91	147.74	39.03	129.61	46.01	122.64
20.12	148.53	37.55	131.09	44.26	124.39
19.18	149.47	35.80	132.84	42.20	126.45
18.07	150.57	33.74	134.91	39.76	128.89
16.77	151.88	31.30	137.35	36.89	131.76
15.22	153.43	28.42	140.23	33.49	135.16
13.40	155.25	25.01	143.64	29.48	139.17
11.25	157.40	20.99	147.66	24.74	143.91
8.70	159.94	16.25	152.40	19.15	149.50
5.70	162.95	10.64	158.01	12.54	156.11
2.12	166.33	3.97	164.49	4.67	163.78
Totals:					
$608.88	**$4450.35**	**$1136.58**	**$3922.65**	**$1339.55**	**$3719.68**

<table>
<tr><td>

17.00%
INTEREST

</td><td>

ANNUAL MORTGAGE PAYMENT SCHEDULE

</td></tr>
</table>

For a mortgage of $1,000.00

MORTGAGE TERM: **15 years**
Monthly payment: **$15.39**
Annual payment: **$184.68**

Year	Balance of Loan	Principal Paid	Interest Paid	Yearly Payment
1	$984.12	$15.88	$168.80	$184.68
2	965.32	18.80	165.88	184.68
3	943.06	22.26	162.42	184.68
4	916.71	26.35	158.33	184.68
5	885.52	31.20	153.48	184.68
6	848.58	36.93	147.75	184.68
7	804.86	43.72	140.96	184.68
8	753.09	51.77	132.92	184.68
9	691.81	61.28	123.40	184.68
10	619.25	72.55	112.13	184.68
11	533.36	85.90	98.78	184.68
12	431.67	101.69	82.99	184.68
13	311.27	120.39	64.29	184.68
14	168.74	142.53	42.15	184.68
15	.00	168.74	15.72	184.47
Totals:		**$1000.00**	**$1769.99**	**$2769.99**

TAX-SAVINGS TABLE

17.00% INTEREST

Multiply all figures by the number of thousands in your loan.
Net cost equals yearly payment minus tax savings.

Federal Tax Bracket					
15.0%		28.0%		33.0%	
Tax Savings	Net Cost	Tax Savings	Net Cost	Tax Savings	Net Cost
$25.32	$159.36	$47.26	$137.42	$55.70	$128.98
24.88	159.80	46.45	138.23	54.74	129.94
24.36	160.32	45.48	139.20	53.60	131.08
23.75	160.93	44.33	140.35	52.25	132.43
23.02	161.66	42.98	141.70	50.65	134.03
22.16	162.52	41.37	143.31	48.76	135.92
21.14	163.54	39.47	145.21	46.52	138.17
19.94	164.74	37.22	147.46	43.86	140.82
18.51	166.17	34.55	150.13	40.72	143.96
16.82	167.86	31.40	153.29	37.00	147.68
14.82	169.86	27.66	157.02	32.60	152.08
12.45	172.23	23.24	161.44	27.39	157.29
9.64	175.04	18.00	166.68	21.22	163.47
6.32	178.36	11.80	172.88	13.91	170.77
2.36	182.11	4.40	180.06	5.19	179.28
Totals:					
$265.50	**$2504.49**	**$495.60**	**$2274.39**	**$584.10**	**$2185.90**

	17.00% INTEREST	**ANNUAL MORTGAGE PAYMENT SCHEDULE**

For a mortgage of $1,000.00

	MORTGAGE TERM:	**30 years**
	Monthly payment:	**$14.26**
	Annual payment:	**$171.08**

Year	Balance of Loan	Principal Paid	Interest Paid	Yearly Payment
1	$998.83	$1.17	$169.91	$171.08
2	997.45	1.38	169.70	171.08
3	995.81	1.64	169.44	171.08
4	993.87	1.94	169.14	171.08
5	991.57	2.30	168.78	171.08
6	988.85	2.72	168.36	171.08
7	985.63	3.22	167.86	171.08
8	981.82	3.81	167.27	171.08
9	977.31	4.51	166.57	171.08
10	971.96	5.34	165.74	171.08
11	965.64	6.33	164.76	171.08
12	958.15	7.49	163.59	171.08
13	949.28	8.87	162.22	171.08
14	938.79	10.50	160.59	171.08
15	926.36	12.43	158.66	171.08
16	911.65	14.71	156.37	171.08
17	894.24	17.42	153.67	171.08
18	873.62	20.62	150.46	171.08
19	849.21	24.41	146.67	171.08
20	820.31	28.90	142.18	171.08
21	786.09	34.21	136.87	171.08
22	745.59	40.50	130.58	171.08
23	697.64	47.95	123.13	171.08
24	640.86	56.77	114.31	171.08
25	573.65	67.21	103.87	171.08
26	494.08	79.57	91.51	171.08
27	399.88	94.20	76.88	171.08
28	288.35	111.53	59.55	171.08
29	156.32	132.04	39.05	171.08
30	.00	156.32	14.57	170.88
Totals:		**$1000.00**	**$4132.23**	**$5132.23**

TAX-SAVINGS TABLE

17.00%
INTEREST

Multiply all figures by the number of thousands in your loan.
Net cost equals yearly payment minus tax savings.

| Federal Tax Bracket | | | | | |
| 15.0% | | 28.0% | | 33.0% | |
Tax Savings	Net Cost	Tax Savings	Net Cost	Tax Savings	Net Cost
$25.49	$145.59	$47.58	$123.51	$56.07	$115.01
25.45	145.63	47.52	123.57	56.00	115.08
25.42	145.66	47.44	123.64	55.92	115.17
25.37	145.71	47.36	123.72	55.82	115.26
25.32	145.76	47.26	123.82	55.70	115.38
25.25	145.83	47.14	123.94	55.56	115.52
25.18	145.90	47.00	124.08	55.39	115.69
25.09	145.99	46.84	124.25	55.20	115.88
24.99	146.10	46.64	124.44	54.97	116.11
24.86	146.22	46.41	124.67	54.69	116.39
24.71	146.37	46.13	124.95	54.37	116.71
24.54	146.54	45.81	125.28	53.99	117.10
24.33	146.75	45.42	125.66	53.53	117.55
24.09	146.99	44.96	126.12	52.99	118.09
23.80	147.28	44.42	126.66	52.36	118.72
23.46	147.63	43.78	127.30	51.60	119.48
23.05	148.03	43.03	128.05	50.71	120.37
22.57	148.51	42.13	128.95	49.65	121.43
22.00	149.08	41.07	130.01	48.40	122.68
21.33	149.75	39.81	131.27	46.92	124.16
20.53	150.55	38.32	132.76	45.17	125.91
19.59	151.49	36.56	134.52	43.09	127.99
18.47	152.61	34.48	136.61	40.63	130.45
17.15	153.93	32.01	139.07	37.72	133.36
15.58	155.50	29.08	142.00	34.28	136.80
13.73	157.35	25.62	145.46	30.20	140.88
11.53	159.55	21.53	149.56	25.37	145.71
8.93	162.15	16.68	154.41	19.65	151.43
5.86	165.22	10.93	160.15	12.88	158.20
2.18	168.70	4.08	166.80	4.81	166.08
Totals:					
$619.83	**$4512.40**	**$1157.02**	**$3975.21**	**$1363.64**	**$3768.60**

		ANNUAL MORTGAGE
17.25% INTEREST		**PAYMENT SCHEDULE**

For a mortgage of $1,000.00

MORTGAGE TERM: **15 years**
Monthly payment: **$15.57**
Annual payment: **$186.81**

Year	Balance of Loan	Principal Paid	Interest Paid	Yearly Payment
1	$984.50	$15.50	$171.31	$186.81
2	966.11	18.39	168.42	186.81
3	944.28	21.83	164.98	186.81
4	918.37	25.91	160.90	186.81
5	887.62	30.75	156.06	186.81
6	851.13	36.49	150.32	186.81
7	807.82	43.31	143.50	186.81
8	756.42	51.40	135.41	186.81
9	695.42	61.00	125.81	186.81
10	623.02	72.40	114.41	186.81
11	537.10	85.92	100.89	186.81
12	435.12	101.97	84.84	186.81
13	314.10	121.02	65.79	186.81
14	170.47	143.63	43.18	186.81
15	.00	170.47	16.12	186.59
Totals:		**$1000.00**	**$1801.94**	**$2801.94**

TAX-SAVINGS TABLE

17.25%
INTEREST

Multiply all figures by the number of thousands in your loan.
Net cost equals yearly payment minus tax savings.

Federal Tax Bracket					
15.0%		28.0%		33.0%	
Tax Savings	Net Cost	Tax Savings	Net Cost	Tax Savings	Net Cost
$25.70	$161.11	$47.97	$138.84	$56.53	$130.28
25.26	161.55	47.16	139.65	55.58	131.23
24.75	162.06	46.19	140.62	54.44	132.37
24.14	162.68	45.05	141.76	53.10	133.71
23.41	163.40	43.70	143.11	51.50	135.31
22.55	164.26	42.09	144.72	49.61	137.21
21.53	165.29	40.18	146.63	47.36	139.46
20.31	166.50	37.92	148.90	44.69	142.13
18.87	167.94	35.23	151.58	41.52	145.29
17.16	169.65	32.04	154.78	37.76	149.05
15.13	171.68	28.25	158.56	33.29	153.52
12.73	174.09	23.75	163.06	28.00	158.81
9.87	176.94	18.42	168.39	21.71	165.10
6.48	180.33	12.09	174.72	14.25	172.56
2.42	184.17	4.51	182.08	5.32	181.27
Totals:					
$270.29	**$2531.65**	**$504.54**	**$2297.40**	**$594.64**	**$2207.30**

17.25% INTEREST	**ANNUAL MORTGAGE PAYMENT SCHEDULE**

For a mortgage of $1,000.00

	MORTGAGE TERM:	**30 years**
	Monthly payment:	**$14.46**
	Annual payment:	**$173.52**

Year	Balance of Loan	Principal Paid	Interest Paid	Yearly Payment
1	$998.90	$1.10	$172.42	$173.52
2	997.59	1.31	172.21	173.52
3	996.04	1.55	171.96	173.52
4	994.19	1.84	171.67	173.52
5	992.00	2.19	171.33	173.52
6	989.41	2.60	170.92	173.52
7	986.33	3.08	170.44	173.52
8	982.67	3.66	169.86	173.52
9	978.33	4.34	169.18	173.52
10	973.18	5.15	168.37	173.52
11	967.06	6.11	167.40	173.52
12	959.81	7.26	166.26	173.52
13	951.19	8.61	164.91	173.52
14	940.97	10.22	163.30	173.52
15	928.84	12.13	161.39	173.52
16	914.45	14.40	159.12	173.52
17	897.36	17.08	156.43	173.52
18	877.09	20.28	153.24	173.52
19	853.02	24.06	149.45	173.52
20	824.46	28.56	144.96	173.52
21	790.57	33.90	139.62	173.52
22	750.34	40.23	133.29	173.52
23	702.60	47.74	125.78	173.52
24	645.94	56.66	116.86	173.52
25	578.69	67.25	106.27	173.52
26	498.88	79.8.	93.71	173.52.
27	404.16	94.72	78.80	173.52
28	291.75	112.41	61.11	173.52
29	158.34	133.41	40.10	173.52
30	.00	158.34	14.98	173.31
Totals:		**$1000.00**	**$4205.34**	**$5205.34**

256

TAX-SAVINGS TABLE

17.25%
INTEREST

Multiply all figures by the number of thousands in your loan.
Net cost equals yearly payment minus tax savings.

Federal Tax Bracket					
15.0%		28.0%		33.0%	
Tax Savings	Net Cost	Tax Savings	Net Cost	Tax Savings	Net Cost
$25.86	$147.66	$48.28	$125.24	$56.90	$116.62
25.83	147.69	48.22	125.30	56.83	116.69
25.79	147.72	48.15	125.37	56.75	116.77
25.75	147.77	48.07	125.45	56.65	116.87
25.70	147.82	47.97	125.55	56.54	116.98
25.64	147.88	47.86	125.66	56.40	117.11
25.57	147.95	47.72	125.80	56.24	117.27
25.48	148.04	47.56	125.96	56.05	117.46
25.38	148.14	47.37	126.15	55.83	117.69
25.26	148.26	47.14	126.38	55.56	117.96
25.11	148.41	46.87	126.65	55.24	118.27
24.94	148.58	46.55	126.96	54.87	118.65
24.74	148.78	46.17	127.34	54.42	119.10
24.49	149.02	45.72	127.79	53.89	119.63
24.21	149.31	45.19	128.33	53.26	120.26
23.87	149.65	44.55	128.96	52.51	121.01
23.47	150.05	43.80	129.72	51.62	121.90
22.99	150.53	42.91	130.61	50.57	122.95
22.42	151.10	41.85	131.67	49.32	124.20
21 74	151.77	40.59	132.93	47.84	125.68
20.94	152.57	39.09	134.42	46.08	127.44
19.99	153.52	37.32	136.20	43.99	129.53
18.87	154.65	35.22	138.30	41.51	132.01
17.53	155.99	32.72	140.80	38.56	134.96
15.94	157.58	29.76	143.76	35.07	138.45
14.06	159.46	26.24	147.28	30.92	142.59
11.82	161.70	22.06	151.45	26.00	147.51
9.17	164.35	17.11	156.41	20.16	153.35
6.02	167.50	11.23	162.29	13.23	160.28
2.25	171.07	4.19	169.12	4.94	168.37
Totals:					
$630.80	**$4574.54**	**$1177.50**	**$4027.85**	**$1387.76**	**$3817.58**

<table>
<tr><td>**17.50%**
INTEREST</td><td colspan="3">**ANNUAL MORTGAGE
PAYMENT SCHEDULE**
For a mortgage of $1,000.00</td></tr>
</table>

	MORTGAGE TERM:	**15 years**	
	Monthly payment:	**$15.75**	
	Annual payment:	**$188.95**	

Year	Balance of Loan	Principal Paid	Interest Paid	Yearly Payment
1	$984.88	$15.12	$173.82	$188.95
2	966.88	17.99	170.96	188.95
3	945.47	21.41	167.54	188.95
4	920.00	25.47	163.48	188.95
5	889.70	30.30	158.65	188.95
6	853.65	36.05	152.90	188.95
7	810.75	42.89	146.06	188.95
8	759.72	51.03	137.92	188.95
9	699.00	60.72	128.23	188.95
10	626.77	72.24	116.71	188.95
11	540.83	85.94	103.01	188.95
12	438.58	102.25	86.70	188.95
13	316.93	121.65	67.30	188.95
14	172.19	144.73	44.22	188.95
15	.00	172.19	16.53	188.72
Totals:		**$1000.00**	**$1834.01**	**$2834.01**

TAX-SAVINGS TABLE

17.50% INTEREST

Multiply all figures by the number of thousands in your loan.
Net cost equals yearly payment minus tax savings.

Federal Tax Bracket					
15.0%		28.0%		33.0%	
Tax Savings	Net Cost	Tax Savings	Net Cost	Tax Savings	Net Cost
$26.07	$162.88	$48.67	$140.28	$57.36	$131.59
25.64	163.31	47.87	141.08	56.42	132.53
25.13	163.82	46.91	142.04	55.29	133.66
24.52	164.43	45.77	143.18	53.95	135.00
23.80	165.15	44.42	144.53	52.35	136.60
22.93	166.01	42.81	146.14	50.46	138.49
21.91	167.04	40.90	148.05	48.20	140.75
20.69	168.26	38.62	150.33	45.51	143.44
19.24	169.71	35.91	153.04	42.32	146.63
17.51	171.44	32.68	156.27	38.52	150.43
15.45	173.50	28.84	160.11	33.99	154.96
13.01	175.94	24.28	164.67	28.61	160.34
10.09	178.85	18.84	170.11	22.21	166.74
6.63	182.32	12.38	176.57	14.59	174.36
2.48	186.24	4.63	184.09	5.45	183.27
Totals:					
$275.10	**$2558.91**	**$513.52**	**$2320.49**	**$605.22**	**$2228.79**

	17.50% INTEREST	ANNUAL MORTGAGE PAYMENT SCHEDULE

For a mortgage of $1,000.00

MORTGAGE TERM: **30 years**
Monthly payment: **$14.66**
Annual payment: **$175.96**

Year	Balance of Loan	Principal Paid	Interest Paid	Yearly Payment
1	$998.96	$1.04	$174.92	$175.96
2	997.72	1.24	174.72	175.96
3	996.25	1.47	174.49	175.96
4	994.50	1.75	174.21	175.96
5	992.42	2.08	173.88	175.96
6	989.94	2.48	173.48	175.96
7	986.99	2.95	173.01	175.96
8	983.48	3.51	172.45	175.96
9	979.31	4.17	171.78	175.96
10	974.34	4.97	170.99	175.96
11	968.43	5.91	170.05	175.96
12	961.40	7.03	168.93	175.96
13	953.04	8.36	167.60	175.96
14	943.09	9.95	166.01	175.96
15	931.25	11.84	164.12	175.96
16	917.16	14.08	161.87	175.96
17	900.41	16.76	159.20	175.96
18	880.47	19.94	156.02	175.96
19	856.75	23.72	152.24	175.96
20	828.53	28.22	147.74	175.96
21	794.96	33.57	142.38	175.96
22	755.01	39.94	136.01	175.96
23	707.49	47.52	128.43	175.96
24	650.95	56.54	119.42	175.96
25	583.68	67.27	108.69	175.96
26	503.64	80.03	95.93	175.96
27	408.42	95.22	80.74	175.96
28	295.14	113.29	62.67	175.96
29	160.36	134.78	41.18	175.96
30	.00	160.36	15.39	175.75
Totals:		**$1000.00**	**$4278.56**	**$5278.56**

TAX-SAVINGS TABLE

17.50%
INTEREST

Multiply all figures by the number of thousands in your loan.
Net cost equals yearly payment minus tax savings.

Federal Tax Bracket					
15.0%		28.0%		33.0%	
Tax Savings	Net Cost	Tax Savings	Net Cost	Tax Savings	Net Cost
$26.24	$149.72	$48.98	$126.98	$57.72	$118.24
26.21	149.75	48.92	127.04	57.66	118.30
26.17	149.79	48.86	127.10	57.58	118.38
26.13	149.83	48.78	127.18	57.49	118.47
26.08	149.88	48.69	127.27	57.38	118.58
26.02	149.94	48.57	127.38	57.25	118.71
25.95	150.01	48.44	127.52	57.09	118.87
25.87	150.09	48.29	127.67	56.91	119.05
25.77	150.19	48.10	127.86	56.69	119.27
25.65	150.31	47.88	128.08	56.43	119.53
25.51	150.45	47.61	128.34	56.12	119.84
25.34	150.62	47.30	128.66	55.75	120.21
25.14	150.82	46.93	129.03	55.31	120.65
24.90	151.06	46.48	129.48	54.78	121.18
24.62	151.34	45.95	130.01	54.16	121.80
24.28	151.68	45.32	130.63	53.42	122.54
23.88	152.08	44.58	131.38	52.54	123.42
23.40	152.56	43.69	132.27	51.49	124.47
22.84	153.12	42.63	133.33	50.24	125.72
22.16	153.80	41.37	134.59	48.75	127.21
21.36	154.60	39.87	136.09	46.99	128.97
20.40	155.56	38.08	137.88	44.88	131.07
19.27	156.69	35.96	140.00	42.38	133.58
17.91	158.05	33.44	142.52	39.41	136.55
16.30	159.66	30.43	145.53	35.87	140.09
14.39	161.57	26.86	149.10	31.66	144.30
12.11	163.85	22.61	153.35	26.64	149.31
9.40	166.56	17.55	158.41	20.68	155.28
6.18	169.78	11.53	164.43	13.59	162.37
2.31	173.44	4.31	171.44	5.08	170.67
Totals:					
$641.78	**$4636.78**	**$1198.00**	**$4080.56**	**$1411.92**	**$3866.64**

17.75% INTEREST	ANNUAL MORTGAGE PAYMENT SCHEDULE

For a mortgage of $1,000.00

MORTGAGE TERM: **15 years**
Monthly payment: **$15.92**
Annual payment: **$191.10**

Year	Balance of Loan	Principal Paid	Interest Paid	Yearly Payment
1	$985.24	$14.76	$176.34	$191.10
2	967.64	17.60	173.49	191.10
3	946.65	20.99	170.10	191.10
4	921.61	25.04	166.06	191.10
5	891.74	29.86	161.23	191.10
6	856.13	35.62	155.48	191.10
7	813.65	42.48	148.62	191.10
8	762.98	50.66	140.43	191.10
9	702.56	60.43	130.67	191.10
10	630.49	72.07	119.03	191.10
11	544.53	85.95	105.14	191.10
12	442.02	102.52	88.58	191.10
13	319.75	122.27	68.83	191.10
14	173.92	145.83	45.27	191.10
15	.00	173.92	16.94	190.86
Totals:		**$1000.00**	**$1866.21**	**$2866.21**

TAX-SAVINGS TABLE

17.75%
INTEREST

Multiply all figures by the number of thousands in your loan.
Net cost equals yearly payment minus tax savings.

Federal Tax Bracket					
15.0%		28.0%		33.0%	
Tax Savings	Net Cost	Tax Savings	Net Cost	Tax Savings	Net Cost
$26.45	$164.65	$49.37	$141.72	$58.19	$132.90
26.02	165.07	48.58	142.52	57.25	133.84
25.52	165.58	47.63	143.47	56.13	134.96
24.91	166.19	46.50	144.60	54.80	136.30
24.18	166.91	45.15	145.95	53.21	137.89
23.32	167.77	43.53	147.56	51.31	139.79
22.29	168.80	41.61	149.48	49.04	142.05
21.06	170.03	39.32	151.78	46.34	144.75
19.60	171.50	36.59	154.51	43.12	147.97
17.85	173.24	33.33	157.77	39.28	151.82
15.77	175.32	29.44	161.66	34.70	156.40
13.29	177.81	24.80	166.29	29.23	161.86
10.32	180.77	19.27	171.82	22.71	168.38
6.79	184.31	12.68	178.42	14.94	176.16
2.54	188.32	4.74	186.12	5.59	185.27
Totals:					
$279.93	**$2586.28**	**$522.54**	**$2343.67**	**$615.85**	**$2250.36**

ANNUAL MORTGAGE PAYMENT SCHEDULE

For a mortgage of $1,000.00

MORTGAGE TERM: **30 years**
Monthly payment: **$14.87**
Annual payment: **$178.40**

Year	Balance of Loan	Principal Paid	Interest Paid	Yearly Payment
1	$999.02	$.98	$177.42	$178.40
2	997.85	1.17	177.23	178.40
3	996.46	1.39	177.01	178.40
4	994.79	1.66	176.74	178.40
5	992.81	1.98	176.42	178.40
6	990.44	2.37	176.04	178.40
7	987.62	2.82	175.58	178.40
8	984.26	3.37	175.04	178.40
9	980.24	4.01	174.39	178.40
10	975.46	4.79	173.62	178.40
11	969.75	5.71	172.69	178.40
12	962.94	6.81	171.59	178.40
13	954.82	8.12	170.28	178.40
14	945.13	9.69	168.72	178.40
15	933.58	11.55	166.85	178.40
16	919.80	13.78	164.62	178.40
17	903.37	16.43	161.97	178.40
18	883.77	19.60	158.80	178.40
19	860.39	23.38	155.03	178.40
20	832.51	27.88	150.52	178.40
21	799.26	33.25	145.15	178.40
22	759.60	39.66	138.75	178.40
23	712.31	47.30	131.10	178.40
24	655.89	56.41	121.99	178.40
25	588.61	67.28	111.12	178.40
26	508.37	80.25	98.16	178.40
27	412.66	95.71	82.70	178.40
28	298.51	114.15	64.26	178.40
29	162.37	136.14	42.26	178.40
30	.00	162.37	15.81	178.19
Totals:		**$1000.00**	**$4351.88**	**$5351.88**

TAX-SAVINGS TABLE

17.75% INTEREST

Multiply all figures by the number of thousands in your loan.
Net cost equals yearly payment minus tax savings.

| Federal Tax Bracket | | | | | |
| 15.0% | | 28.0% | | 33.0% | |
Tax Savings	Net Cost	Tax Savings	Net Cost	Tax Savings	Net Cost
$26.61	$151.79	$49.68	$128.72	$58.55	$119.85
26.59	151.82	49.63	128.78	58.49	119.92
26.55	151.85	49.56	128.84	58.41	119.99
26.51	151.89	49.49	128.92	58.32	120.08
26.46	151.94	49.40	129.01	58.22	120.18
26.41	152.00	49.29	129.11	58.09	120.31
26.34	152.07	49.16	129.24	57.94	120.46
26.26	152.15	49.01	129.39	57.76	120.64
26.16	152.24	48.83	129.57	57.55	120.85
26.04	152.36	48.61	129.79	57.29	121.11
25.90	152.50	48.35	130.05	56.99	121.41
25.74	152.66	48.05	130.36	56.63	121.78
25.54	152.86	47.68	130.72	56.19	122.21
25.31	153.10	47.24	131.16	55.68	122.73
25.03	153.38	46.72	131.68	55.06	123.34
24.69	153.71	46.09	132.31	54.33	124.08
24.30	154.11	45.35	133.05	53.45	124.95
23.82	154.58	44.47	133.94	52.41	126.00
23.25	155.15	43.41	135.00	51.16	127.24
22.58	155.82	42.15	136.26	49.67	128.73
21.77	156.63	40.64	137.76	47.90	130.50
20.81	157.59	38.85	139.55	45.79	132.62
19.67	158.74	36.71	141.69	43.26	135.14
18.30	160.10	34.16	144.25	40.26	138.15
16.67	161.73	31.11	147.29	36.67	141.73
14.72	163.68	27.48	150.92	32.39	146.01
12.40	166.00	23.15	155.25	27.29	151.11
9.64	168.76	17.99	160.41	21.20	157.20
6.34	172.06	11.83	166.57	13.95	164.46
2.37	175.81	4.43	173.76	5.22	172.97
Totals:					
$652.78	**$4699.09**	**$1218.53**	**$4133.35**	**$1436.12**	**$3915.76**

18.00% INTEREST	**ANNUAL MORTGAGE PAYMENT SCHEDULE**

For a mortgage of $1,000.00

MORTGAGE TERM: **15 years**
Monthly payment: **$16.10**
Annual payment: **$193.25**

Year	Balance of Loan	Principal Paid	Interest Paid	Yearly Payment
1	$985.60	$14.40	$178.85	$193.25
2	968.38	17.22	176.03	193.25
3	947.80	20.59	172.67	193.25
4	923.19	24.61	168.64	193.25
5	893.76	29.43	163.82	193.25
6	858.58	35.18	158.07	193.25
7	816.51	42.07	151.19	193.25
8	766.22	50.29	142.96	193.25
9	706.08	60.13	133.12	193.25
10	634.19	71.90	121.35	193.25
11	548.23	85.96	107.29	193.25
12	445.45	102.77	90.48	193.25
13	322.57	122.88	70.37	193.25
14	175.66	146.92	46.33	193.25
15	.00	175.66	17.36	193.01
Totals:		**$1000.00**	**$1898.52**	**$2898.52**

TAX-SAVINGS TABLE

18.00%
INTEREST

Multiply all figures by the number of thousands in your loan.
Net cost equals yearly payment minus tax savings.

Federal Tax Bracket					
15.0%		28.0%		33.0%	
Tax Savings	Net Cost	Tax Savings	Net Cost	Tax Savings	Net Cost
$26.83	$166.42	$50.08	$143.17	$59.02	$134.23
26.41	166.85	49.29	143.96	58.09	135.16
25.90	167.35	48.35	144.90	56.98	136.27
25.30	167.95	47.22	146.03	55.65	137.60
24.57	168.68	45.87	147.38	54.06	139.19
23.71	169.54	44.26	148.99	52.16	141.09
22.68	170.57	42.33	150.92	49.89	143.36
21.44	171.81	40.03	153.22	47.18	146.07
19.97	173.28	37.27	155.98	43.93	149.32
18.20	175.05	33.98	159.27	40.05	153.20
16.09	177.16	30.04	163.21	35.41	157.84
13.57	179.68	25.33	167.92	29.86	163.39
10.56	182.69	19.70	173.55	23.22	170.03
6.95	186.30	12.97	180.28	15.29	177.96
2.60	190.41	4.86	188.15	5.73	187.29
Totals:					
$284.78	**$2613.74**	**$531.59**	**$2366.93**	**$626.51**	**$2272.01**

18.00% INTEREST	**ANNUAL MORTGAGE PAYMENT SCHEDULE**

For a mortgage of $1,000.00

MORTGAGE TERM: **30 years**
Monthly payment: **$15.07**
Annual payment: **$180.85**

Year	Balance of Loan	Principal Paid	Interest Paid	Yearly Payment
1	$999.08	$.92	$179.93	$180.85
2	997.97	1.10	179.75	180.85
3	996.65	1.32	179.53	180.85
4	995.07	1.58	179.27	180.85
5	993.18	1.89	178.96	180.85
6	990.93	2.26	178.59	180.85
7	988.23	2.70	178.15	180.85
8	985.00	3.23	177.62	180.85
9	981.14	3.86	176.99	180.85
10	976.53	4.61	176.24	180.85
11	971.01	5.52	175.33	180.85
12	964.42	6.59	174.26	180.85
13	956.53	7.88	172.97	180.85
14	947.10	9.43	171.42	180.85
15	935.83	11.27	169.58	180.85
16	922.36	13.48	167.37	180.85
17	906.24	16.11	164.74	180.85
18	886.98	19.26	161.59	180.85
19	863.95	23.03	157.82	180.85
20	836.41	27.54	153.31	180.85
21	803.48	32.93	147.92	180.85
22	764.12	39.37	141.48	180.85
23	717.05	47.07	133.78	180.85
24	660.78	56.27	124.58	180.85
25	593.49	67.28	113.57	180.85
26	513.05	80.44	100.41	180.85
27	416.87	96.18	84.67	180.85
28	301.88	114.99	65.86	180.85
29	164.39	137.49	43.36	180.85
30	.00	164.39	16.24	180.63
Totals:		**$1000.00**	**$4425.28**	**$5425.28**

TAX-SAVINGS TABLE

		18.00%
		INTEREST

Multiply all figures by the number of thousands in your loan.
Net cost equals yearly payment minus tax savings.

Federal Tax Bracket					
15.0%		28.0%		33.0%	
Tax Savings	Net Cost	Tax Savings	Net Cost	Tax Savings	Net Cost
$26.99	$153.86	$50.38	$130.47	$59.38	$121.47
26.96	153.89	50.33	130.52	59.32	121.53
26.93	153.92	50.27	130.58	59.24	121.61
26.89	153.96	50.20	130.65	59.16	121.69
26.84	154.01	50.11	130.74	59.06	121.79
26.79	154.06	50.01	130.84	58.94	121.91
26.72	154.13	49.88	130.97	58.79	122.06
26.64	154.21	49.73	131.12	58.62	122.23
26.55	154.30	49.56	131.29	58.41	122.44
26.44	154.41	49.35	131.50	58.16	122.69
26.30	154.55	49.09	131.76	57.86	122.99
26.14	154.71	48.79	132.06	57.50	123.35
25.94	154.91	48.43	132.42	57.08	123.77
25.71	155.14	48.00	132.85	56.57	124.28
25.44	155.41	47.48	133.37	55.96	124.89
25.11	155.74	46.86	133.99	55.23	125.62
24.71	156.14	46.13	134.72	54.36	126.49
24.24	156.61	45.24	135.61	53.32	127.53
23.67	157.18	44.19	136.66	52.08	128.77
23.00	157.85	42.93	137.92	50.59	130.26
22.19	158.66	41.42	139.43	48.82	132.04
21.22	159.63	39.62	141.23	46.69	134.16
20.07	160.78	37.46	143.39	44.15	136.70
18.69	162.16	34.88	145.97	41.11	139.74
17.04	163.82	31.80	149.05	37.48	143.37
15.06	165.79	28.11	152.74	33.13	147.72
12.70	168.15	23.71	157.14	27.94	152.91
9.88	170.97	18.44	162.41	21.73	159.12
6.50	174.35	12.14	168.71	14.31	166.54
2.44	178.19	4.55	176.08	5.36	175.27
Totals:					
$663.79	$4761.49	$1239.08	$4186.20	$1460.34	$3964.94

APPENDIX A

Combined Federal, State & Local Tax Rates

COMBINED FEDERAL, STATE AND LOCAL TAX RATES

In addition to federal income taxes, many people must pay income taxes to their resident states and municipalities. Although many of these state and local taxes are assesed on a gross basis (i.e., with no allowance for itemized deductions such as home mortgage interest expense) many allow such deductions. Where such deductions are allowed, they provide additional savings. However, the reduction in your state and local tax costs reduces the amount of your federal itemized deductions for these items. Thus, to compute your overall tax savings on your mortgage payments, it is necessary to compute your combined effective tax rate. Your combined effective tax rate combines your federal, state and local tax rates taking into account the value of deducting your state and local taxes from your federal tax expense. Once you know your combined effective tax rate, you can compute your overall tax savings from your mortgage interest and real estate taxes. Of course, if you are not subject to state and local income taxes, your combined effective tax rate is equal to your federal tax rate and you can determine your tax savings using the tables in Part II. Part II will also reflect your total tax savings where your state and local tax is assesed on a gross basis and does not permit mortgage interest deductions.

These tables present the tax rates for some states and municipalities. Tax rates vary widely from state to state and city to city, depending on income and marital status. It is beyond the scope of this book to show the rates for all fifty states. However, if your state tax rate is not shown in the table, you can easily compute your own effective tax rate, assuming full deductibility of mortgage-interest payments on state and local tax returns, and the full deductibility of state and local taxes on your federal tax return. Use the following formula employing the tax rates that apply to you:

$$\text{combined} = \text{federal} + \text{state} + \text{local} - (\text{federal} \times \text{state}) - (\text{federal} \times \text{local})$$

The subtracted terms in the above equation account for the federal deduction of state and local taxes.

Example: Computing Your Combined Effective Tax Rate

Assume you are a resident of New York City and are thus subject to a total state and local tax rate of 11.78%, comprised of New York state's maximum income tax rate of 7.875% and New York City's maximum income tax rate. You are subject to a federal tax rate of 28%. Your effective tax rate is 36.48%, computed by:

$$28\% + 7.875\% + 3.9\% - (28\% \times 7.875\%) - (28\% \times 3.9\%) = 36.48\%$$

These tables are meant as a useful tool in your search for the right mortgage. You should consult a professional tax adviser to properly evaluate your own tax situation.

TABLE OF COMBINED EFFECTIVE TAX RATES

Federal tax rate = 15%	
State or Local Tax Rate	**Effective Tax Rate**
1.00%	15.85%
1.50	16.28
2.00	16.70
2.10	16.785
2.50	17.13
3.00	17.55
3.50	17.97
4.00	18.40
4.50	18.83
5.00	19.25
5.50	19.68
6.00	20.10
6.50	20.52
7.00	20.95
7.50	21.38
7.875	21.69
8.00	21.80

Federal tax rate = 28%	
State or Local Tax Rate	**Effective Tax Rate**
1.00%	28.72%
1.50	29.08
2.00	29.44
2.10	29.51
2.50	29.80
3.00	30.16
3.50	30.52
4.00	30.88
4.50	31.24
5.00	31.60
5.50	31.96
6.00	32.32
6.50	32.68
7.00	33.04
7.50	33.40
7.875	33.67
8.00	33.76
9.30	34.70
11.78	36.48

Federal tax rate = 33%	
State or Local Tax Rate	Effective Tax Rate
1.00%	33.67%
1.50	34.01
2.00	34.34
2.10	34.407
2.50	34.68
3.00	35.01
3.50	35.35
4.00	35.68
4.50	36.02
5.00	36.35
5.50	36.69
6.00	37.02
6.50	37.36
7.00	37.69
7.50	38.03
7.875	38.28
8.00	38.36
9.30	39.23
11.78	40.89

APPENDIX B

Points Discount Tables

HOW TO USE
THE POINTS
DISCOUNT TABLES

Points are fees that lenders charge to originate a loan. They are payable over and above the monthly payments of interest and principal that you agree to make over the term of your loan. Whether they are said to be service charges or financial charges, points are always expressed in terms of a stated percentage of the original amount of the loan principal. For example, a three-point charge on a $160,000 mortgage loan will cost you 3 percent of $160,000 or $4,800.

Borrowers anxious to secure a lower nominal interest rate often agree to pay a higher amount of points. The lender is often willing to reduce the nominal interest rate over the term of the loan in exchange for a larger payment up front, in the form of points. It is important to understand, however, the effect of points on your loan transaction before you agree to pay them.

Viewed in practical terms, points are a reduction in the amount of your loan proceeds. After the loan closes, the total amount of additional cash available to you is the nominal amount of the loan less the amount of points that you must pay. This is so since you typically must fund points from resources other than the actual loan proceeds. Hence the term "points discount table"; the net payment to you is discounted by the amount of points you agree to pay.

While the loan is discounted to you, you are still obliged to repay the original amount of the loan before the discount. Your monthly payment is calculated on the gross amount of your loan, not the discounted amount. This means that the lender is, in effect, earning an interest rate that is actually higher than the nominal rate charged on your loan. To understand the actual cost of your loan, it is necessary to add the points to the interest charged over the term of your loan and to calculate the annual percentage rate, or APR, of your loan. As contrasted to the nominal interest rate charged on your loan, the APR is the true cost of your loan expressed in terms of a yearly percentage of the amount that you borrowed.

The Points Discount Tables in Appendix B reflect the annual percentage rates for loans with varying interest rates, points, and terms. The following example illustrates how the tables can be used.

Finding Your Annual Percentage Rate

Suppose you are offered a thirty-year loan with a nominal rate of 10 percent at a cost of three points. To find the annual percentage rate for the loan, scan down the interest-rate column until you arrive at the block of annual percentage rates applicable to a 10 percent nominal rate. Next, skim over to the points column until you find the row within the block that applies to three points. Then scan the three-point row until you arrive at the thirty-year column. As you can see, the annual percentage rate on a 10 percent thirty-year loan is actually 10.38 percent when three points are charged.

POINTS DISCOUNT TABLES

Points	15 Years	20 Years	25 Years	30 Years	35 Years	
5	8.86	8.70	8.61	8.55	8.51	
4	8.68	8.55	8.48	8.44	8.40	
3	8.51	8.41	8.36	8.32	8.30	**8.00%**
2	8.34	8.27	8.24	8.21	8.20	
1	8.17	8.14	8.12	8.11	8.10	
5	9.12	8.96	8.86	8.81	8.77	
4	8.94	8.81	8.74	8.69	8.66	
3	8.76	8.67	8.61	8.58	8.56	**8.25%**
2	8.59	8.53	8.49	8.47	8.45	
1	8.42	8.39	8.37	8.36	8.35	
5	9.37	9.21	9.12	9.07	9.03	
4	9.19	9.07	8.99	8.95	8.92	
3	9.02	8.92	8.87	8.83	8.81	**8.50%**
2	8.84	8.78	8.74	8.72	8.71	
1	8.67	8.64	8.62	8.61	8.60	
5	9.63	9.47	9.38	9.32	9.29	
4	9.45	9.32	9.25	9.21	9.18	
3	9.27	9.18	9.12	9.09	9.07	**8.75%**
2	9.09	9.03	9.00	8.97	8.96	
1	8.92	8.89	8.87	8.86	8.85	

POINTS DISCOUNT TABLES

	Points	15 Years	20 Years	25 Years	30 Years	35 Years
9.00%	5	9.89	9.73	9.64	9.58	9.55
	4	9.70	9.58	9.51	9.46	9.43
	3	9.52	9.43	9.38	9.34	9.32
	2	9.35	9.28	9.25	9.23	9.21
	1	9.17	9.14	9.12	9.11	9.11
9.25%	5	10.14	9.99	9.90	9.84	9.81
	4	9.96	9.83	9.76	9.72	9.69
	3	9.78	9.68	9.63	9.60	9.58
	2	9.60	9.54	9.50	9.48	9.47
	1	9.42	9.39	9.38	9.36	9.36
9.50%	5	10.40	10.24	10.16	10.10	10.07
	4	10.21	10.09	10.02	9.98	9.95
	3	10.03	9.94	9.89	9.85	9.83
	2	9.85	9.79	9.76	9.73	9.72
	1	9.67	9.64	9.63	9.62	9.61
9.75%	5	10.66	10.50	10.41	10.36	10.33
	4	10.47	10.35	10.28	10.23	10.21
	3	10.29	10.19	10.14	10.11	10.09
	2	10.10	10.04	10.01	9.99	9.97
	1	9.93	9.90	9.88	9.87	9.86

POINTS DISCOUNT TABLES

	15 Years	20 Years	25 Years	30 Years	35 Years	
Points						
5	10.91	10.76	10.67	10.62	10.59	
4	10.72	10.60	10.53	10.49	10.47	
3	10.54	10.45	10.40	10.37	10.35	**10.00%**
2	10.36	10.30	10.26	10.24	10.23	
1	10.18	10.15	10.13	10.12	10.11	
5	11.17	11.02	10.93	10.88	10.85	
4	10.98	10.86	10.79	10.75	10.72	
3	10.79	10.70	10.65	10.62	10.60	**10.25%**
2	10.61	10.55	10.52	10.50	10.48	
1	10.43	10.40	10.38	10.37	10.37	
5	11.43	11.27	11.19	11.14	11.11	
4	11.24	11.11	11.05	11.01	10.98	
3	11.05	10.96	10.91	10.88	10.86	**10.50%**
2	10.86	10.80	10.77	10.75	10.74	
1	10.68	10.65	10.63	10.62	10.62	
5	11.68	11.53	11.45	11.40	11.37	
4	11.49	11.37	11.30	11.26	11.24	
3	11.30	11.21	11.16	11.13	11.11	**10.75%**
2	11.11	11.06	11.02	11.00	10.99	
1	10.93	10.90	10.89	10.88	10.87	

POINTS DISCOUNT TABLES

	Points	15 Years	20 Years	25 Years	30 Years	35 Years
11.00%	5	11.94	11.79	11.71	11.66	11.63
	4	11.75	11.63	11.56	11.52	11.50
	3	11.56	11.47	11.42	11.39	11.37
	2	11.37	11.31	11.28	11.26	11.24
	1	11.18	11.15	11.14	11.13	11.12
11.25%	5	12.20	12.05	11.97	11.92	11.89
	4	12.00	11.88	11.82	11.78	11.76
	3	11.81	11.72	11.67	11.64	11.63
	2	11.62	11.56	11.53	11.51	11.50
	1	11.43	11.40	11.39	11.38	11.37
11.50%	5	12.46	12.31	12.23	12.18	12.15
	4	12.26	12.14	12.08	12.04	12.02
	3	12.06	11.98	11.93	11.90	11.88
	2	11.87	11.81	11.78	11.76	11.75
	1	11.69	11.66	11.64	11.63	11.63
11.75%	5	12.71	12.57	12.49	12.44	12.41
	4	12.51	12.40	12.33	12.30	12.27
	3	12.32	12.23	12.18	12.16	12.14
	2	12.13	12.07	12.04	12.02	12.01
	1	11.94	11.91	11.89	11.88	11.88

POINTS DISCOUNT TABLES

Points	15 Years	20 Years	25 Years	30 Years	35 Years	
5	12.97	12.82	12.74	12.70	12.67	
4	12.77	12.65	12.59	12.55	12.53	**12.00%**
3	12.57	12.49	12.44	12.41	12.40	
2	12.38	12.32	12.29	12.27	12.26	
1	12.19	12.16	12.14	12.13	12.13	
5	13.23	13.08	13.00	12.96	12.93	
4	13.03	12.91	12.85	12.81	12.79	**12.25%**
3	12.83	12.74	12.69	12.67	12.65	
2	12.63	12.57	12.54	12.53	12.52	
1	12.44	12.41	12.40	12.39	12.38	
5	13.49	13.34	13.26	13.22	13.19	
4	13.28	13.17	13.11	13.07	13.05	**12.50%**
3	13.08	13.00	12.95	12.92	12.91	
2	12.88	12.83	12.80	12.78	12.77	
1	12.69	12.66	12.65	12.64	12.63	
5	13.74	13.60	13.52	13.48	13.46	
4	13.54	13.42	13.36	13.33	13.31	**12.75%**
3	13.34	13.25	13.21	13.18	13.17	
2	13.14	13.08	13.05	13.03	13.02	
1	12.94	12.91	12.90	12.89	12.89	

POINTS DISCOUNT TABLES

	Points	15 Years	20 Years	25 Years	30 Years	35 Years
13.00%	5	14.00	13.86	13.78	13.74	13.72
	4	13.79	13.68	13.62	13.59	13.57
	3	13.59	13.51	13.46	13.44	13.42
	2	13.39	13.33	13.30	13.29	13.28
	1	13.19	13.17	13.15	13.14	13.14
13.25%	5	14.26	14.12	14.04	14.00	13.98
	4	14.05	13.94	13.88	13.85	13.83
	3	13.85	13.76	13.72	13.69	13.68
	2	13.64	13.59	13.56	13.54	13.53
	1	13.45	13.42	13.40	13.39	13.39
13.50%	5	14.52	14.38	14.30	14.26	14.24
	4	14.31	14.19	14.14	14.10	14.09
	3	14.10	14.02	13.97	13.95	13.94
	2	13.90	13.84	13.81	13.80	13.79
	1	13.70	13.67	13.65	13.65	13.64
13.75%	5	14.77	14.63	14.56	14.52	14.50
	4	14.56	14.45	14.39	14.36	14.35
	3	14.35	14.27	14.23	14.21	14.19
	2	14.15	14.09	14.07	14.05	14.04
	1	13.95	13.92	13.91	13.90	13.89

POINTS DISCOUNT TABLES

	15 Years	20 Years	25 Years	30 Years	35 Years	
Points						
5	15.03	14.89	14.82	14.78	14.76	
4	14.82	14.71	14.65	14.62	14.60	
3	14.61	14.53	14.48	14.46	14.45	**14.00%**
2	14.40	14.35	14.32	14.30	14.30	
1	14.20	14.17	14.16	14.15	14.15	
5	15.29	15.15	15.08	15.05	15.02	
4	15.08	14.97	14.91	14.88	14.86	
3	14.86	14.78	14.74	14.72	14.71	**14.25%**
2	14.66	14.60	14.57	14.56	14.55	
1	14.45	14.42	14.41	14.40	14.40	
5	15.55	15.41	15.34	15.31	15.29	
4	15.33	15.22	15.17	15.14	15.12	
3	15.12	15.04	15.00	14.97	14.96	**14.50%**
2	14.91	14.86	14.83	14.81	14.81	
1	14.70	14.68	14.66	14.66	14.65	
5	15.81	15.67	15.60	15.57	15.55	
4	15.59	15.48	15.43	15.40	15.38	
3	15.37	15.29	15.25	15.23	15.22	**14.75%**
2	15.16	15.11	15.08	15.07	15.06	
1	14.95	14.93	14.91	14.91	14.90	

POINTS DISCOUNT TABLES

	Points	15 Years	20 Years	25 Years	30 Years	35 Years
15.00%	5	16.07	15.93	15.86	15.83	15.81
	4	15.84	15.74	15.68	15.66	15.64
	3	15.63	15.55	15.51	15.49	15.48
	2	15.42	15.36	15.34	15.32	15.31
	1	15.21	15.18	15.17	15.16	15.16
15.25%	5	16.32	16.19	16.12	16.09	16.07
	4	16.10	16.00	15.94	15.92	15.90
	3	15.88	15.80	15.77	15.74	15.73
	2	15.67	15.62	15.59	15.58	15.57
	1	15.46	15.43	15.42	15.41	15.41
15.50%	5	16.58	16.45	16.39	16.35	16.33
	4	16.36	16.25	16.20	16.17	16.16
	3	16.14	16.06	16.02	16.00	15.99
	2	15.92	15.87	15.84	15.83	15.82
	1	15.71	15.68	15.67	15.66	15.66
15.75%	5	16.84	16.71	16.65	16.61	16.60
	4	16.61	16.51	16.46	16.43	16.42
	3	16.39	16.32	16.28	16.26	16.25
	2	16.18	16.12	16.10	16.09	16.08
	1	15.96	15.94	15.92	15.92	15.91

POINTS DISCOUNT TABLES

Points	15 Years	20 Years	25 Years	30 Years	35 Years	
5	17.10	16.97	16.91	16.88	16.86	
4	16.87	16.77	16.72	16.69	16.68	
3	16.65	16.57	16.53	16.51	16.51	**16.00%**
2	16.43	16.38	16.35	16.34	16.33	
1	16.21	16.19	16.17	16.17	16.17	
5	17.36	17.23	17.17	17.14	17.12	
4	17.13	17.03	16.98	16.95	16.94	
3	16.90	16.83	16.79	16.77	16.76	**16.25%**
2	16.68	16.63	16.61	16.59	16.59	
1	16.46	16.44	16.43	16.42	16.42	
5	17.62	17.49	17.43	17.40	17.38	
4	17.38	17.28	17.24	17.21	17.20	
3	17.16	17.08	17.05	17.03	17.02	**16.50%**
2	16.93	16.89	16.86	16.85	16.84	
1	16.72	16.69	16.68	16.67	16.67	
5	17.87	17.75	17.69	17.66	17.65	
4	17.64	17.54	17.49	17.47	17.46	
3	17.41	17.34	17.30	17.29	17.28	**16.75%**
2	17.19	17.14	17.12	17.10	17.10	
1	16.97	16.94	16.93	16.93	16.92	

POINTS DISCOUNT TABLES

	Points	15 Years	20 Years	25 Years	30 Years	35 Years
17.00%	5	18.13	18.01	17.95	17.92	17.91
	4	17.90	17.80	17.75	17.73	17.72
	3	17.67	17.59	17.56	17.54	17.53
	2	17.44	17.39	17.37	17.36	17.35
	1	17.22	17.19	17.18	17.18	17.17
17.25%	5	18.39	18.27	18.21	18.18	18.17
	4	18.16	18.06	18.01	17.99	17.98
	3	17.92	17.85	17.82	17.80	17.79
	2	17.70	17.65	17.62	17.61	17.61
	1	17.47	17.45	17.44	17.43	17.43
17.50%	5	18.65	18.53	18.47	18.45	18.43
	4	18.41	18.32	18.27	18.25	18.24
	3	18.18	18.11	18.07	18.06	18.05
	2	17.95	17.90	17.88	17.87	17.86
	1	17.72	17.70	17.69	17.68	17.68
17.75%	5	18.91	18.79	18.73	18.71	18.70
	4	18.67	18.57	18.53	18.51	18.50
	3	18.43	18.36	18.33	18.31	18.31
	2	18.20	18.15	18.13	18.12	18.12
	1	17.97	17.95	17.94	17.93	17.93

POINTS DISCOUNT TABLES

Points	15 Years	20 Years	25 Years	30 Years	35 Years	
5	19.17	19.05	19.00	18.97	18.96	
4	18.93	18.83	18.79	18.77	18.76	**18.00%**
3	18.69	18.62	18.59	18.57	18.56	
2	18.46	18.41	18.39	18.38	18.37	
1	18.23	18.20	18.19	18.19	18.18	

Costs of Closing the Purchase of a Home

COSTS OF CLOSING THE PURCHASE OF A HOME

Before you close the purchase of your home, your lender will provide you with two important statements: the Federal Truth in Lending Disclosure Statement and the Good Faith Estimate of Settlement Charges.

The Federal Truth in Lending Disclosure Statement discloses the annual percentage rate of interest (APR) applicable to the loan, the amount of interest that will be paid over the term of the loan, the amount borrowed, and the total of all monthly payments, including an estimate of taxes and insurance payments. It also discloses what the monthly payments for principal and interest will be. Borrowers are often startled to learn upon reviewing the disclosure statement that the amount they will pay in interest charges will be two or even three times the amount borrowed. Another surprising fact is that the amount financed is typically less than the nominal amount of the mortgage loan. The total amount of interest paid over the life of a 30 year, $160,000, 10.75% mortgage loan, for example, will equal more than $375,000.

The Good Faith Estimate of Settlement Charges is an estimate of the expenses you can expect to incur when you close the sale. It is important to note that mortgage-loan agreements typically prohibit a buyer from borrowing to pay the closing costs.

Points

The primary closing cost is usually points, which are a cost of obtaining the funds. As discussed in Appendix B, points paid constitute additional interest over the term of the loan.

Points are expressed as a percentage of the nominal amount borrowed, and are often called loan-origination fees or loan discount. Lenders will charge points under either or both labels. Loan-origination fees are service charges in addition to application fees (which themselves can amount to several hundred dollars) that are generally paid when the commitment to make a loan is issued. They are usually not refundable, so make sure that you will close the loan before you pay them. They are intended to cover the cost of preparing the paperwork involved in evaluating and issuing a loan and to provide the lender with additional profit.

Points are, in effect, a reduction of the amount of the loan. At closing the lender will issue its check to the seller for the full amount of the mortgage while you return a fraction of the loan principal to the lender via the points paid.

Appraisal, Inspection, and Survey

Formal appraisals of the home to be purchased are required to satisfy the lender that the property value is adequate security for its loan. The borrower must bear the expense of the appraisal. In addition to paying the fee for the appraisal report, the borrower must also pay for an inspection of the property. It is also a good idea for the borrower to obtain his or her own engineering-inspection report so that latent defects in the home and the related appliances can be discovered before you buy the home or incur significant closing costs. The borrower may also need to have the property formally surveyed to determine the legal property lines.

Credit Reports

The borrower must also pay for the cost of the lender's obtaining a credit report, so that the lender can properly evaluate the borrower's creditworthiness. Be prepared to explain any late or disputed payments in the report to the satisfaction of the lender. Since most consumer and mortgage debts are disclosed in a credit report, be sure that you have included them in your financial statement when you make your mortgage-loan application.

Prepaid Interest

It is unusual to close the purchase of a home on a date that coincides with the exact day your regular monthly mortgage payment is due. You must prepay an amount equal to the interest on the amount borrowed for the period from the closing date until the date the first monthly payment is due.

Insurance

Different types of insurance payments are due at closing. Mortgage insurance may be required if the lender feels that the mortgage loan is not as secure as it could be. This is typically the case with unconventional mortgage loans such as non-income-verification loans.

The lender usually requires a fully paid hazard-insurance policy to be in force at the date of the closing, with the lender named as a loss payee. Hazard insurance protects the lender and the borrower from total or partial destruction due to fire or other loss. A loss-payee clause requires the insurance company to pay the insurance benefit in case of loss to the lender. This protects the lender against misappropriation of the insurance benefits. The lender will, of course, refund insurance proceeds in excess of what is owed on your loan.

The amount of the policy generally does not need to equal the purchase price of the home. It is advisable to obtain an amount of insurance sufficient to pay for the reconstruction of the home in the event of a loss. Since the cost of reconstruction is generally less than the cost of purchase as current market value, and especially since the purchase price includes an amount for the land under the house, which is not ordinarily subject to destruction, it is usually economical to obtain a policy for an amount less than the purchase price or current market value. Review your policy limits regularly, since construction costs typically increase over time. Some insurance companies sell policies that have built-in inflation adjustments to protect you from unintended loss of protection.

You should also make sure that the value of your furnishings and other personal property are properly insured. Flood insurance is typically required if your home is in a flood plain or close to the shoreline. Flood insurance is obtained through the National Flood Insurance Program, which is sponsored by the federal government. If flood insurance is required, make sure that the town in which your prospective home is located is a participant in this program. If it is not, you may not easily be able to obtain the required coverage, and the lender may refuse to issue the loan.

Title insurance is also important. It insures you and the lender against loss from unrecorded claims of ownership to your prospective home. If it happens that the seller did not have a clear legal title to the home, a title-insurance policy will repay you the full amount of the purchase price. Before issuing such a policy, the insurance company will do a title search to find potential problems with the title to the home. If such problems exist and cannot be cleared, the title-insurance company will not issue the policy and the lender will not issue a mortgage loan.

Real Estate Taxes

The lender will usually insist upon acting as the disbursing agent for the real estate taxes on your home. The monthly mortgage payment is typically supplemented by an amount equal to one twelfth the expected annual real estate taxes, which is deposited in an escrow account by the lender. When the real estate taxes are due, the lender will disburse the taxes directly to the local government imposing the tax. Lenders require this arrangement to make sure taxes are paid on time. This protects their security interest against a tax foreclosure. Unpaid taxes have a higher priority in a foreclosure sale than does the mortgage-loan obligation. Insurance payments are sometimes included in the escrow arrangement.

Since monthly tax escrow payments are based upon the most recent tax rates, increases in the tax rate may create a deficit in your escrow account. Lenders may ask you to make up the deficit with a special onetime payment, but most often will spread the increase over the next year's payments. Your monthly payment can increase significantly, since you must make up the prior year's deficit as well as pay any increase in the current year.

At the closing, the lender will require you to prepay the amount that has accrued since the last tax payment. Your attorney will evaluate whether any adjustments are in order between you and the seller regarding current tax payments. If taxes are paid in advance, you will have to repay the seller for the unexpired amount of the taxes that were paid at the last payment date. If they are paid in arrears, the seller will owe you an adjustment for the taxes covering the period before your purchase.

Recording and Legal Fees

Recording fees are charged to the lender by the local government for recording the loan in the official property records. Finally, you will also pay legal fees. Since the lender usually engages an attorney to review the transaction, you will be charged a fee to cover the cost of the lender's attorney. You also must pay your own attorney. While it is sometimes possible to close the purchase of a home without an attorney, in light of the amount of money involved and the complicated nature of the transaction, it is not a good idea to act on your own behalf.

Plan Ahead

Unlike many borrowers, you now will not be surprised by the extent of closing costs you must pay out of personal funds. Since you ordinarily cannot borrow closing costs, you should plan carefully for the closing costs and factor them into the amount of your down payment and the amounts you are borrowing and spending.

ABOUT THE EDITOR

Eric Kaplan, CPA, JD, is a tax, financial, and business consultant in practice for more than twelve years. Formerly a senior tax manager with a Big 6 accounting firm based in New York City, he has served Marlboro Township, New Jersey, for several years as secretary and vice president of its planning board. Mr. Kaplan resides in Marlboro with his wife and two daughters.